W9-CZS-878

Dictionary of Networking

Third Edition

Dictionary of Networking

Third Edition

Peter Dyson

San Francisco   Paris   Düsseldorf   Soest   London

Associate Publisher: Guy Hart-Davis

Contracts and Licensing Manager: Kristine O'Callaghan

Acquisitions & Developmental Editor: Neil Edde

Editor: Pat Coleman

Project Editor: Jeremy Crawford

Technical Editor: Mark Kovach

Book Designer: Bill Gibson

Graphic Illustrators: Tony Jonick and Jerry Williams

Electronic Publishing Specialist: Bill Gibson

Project Team Leader: Lisa Reardon

Proofreaders: Susan Berge, Theresa Mori, and Catherine Morris

Companion CD: Ginger Warner

Cover Designer: Archer Design

SYBEX, Network Press, and the Network Press logo are registered trademarks of SYBEX Inc.

The CD Interface music is from GIRA Sound AURIA Music Library ©GIRA Sound 1996.

TRADEMARKS: SYBEX has attempted throughout this book to distinguish proprietary trademarks from descriptive terms by following the capitalization style used by the manufacturer.

The author and publisher have made their best efforts to prepare this book, and the content is based upon final release software whenever possible. Portions of the manuscript may be based upon pre-release versions supplied by software manufacturer(s). The author and the publisher make no representation or warranties of any kind with regard to the completeness or accuracy of the contents herein and accept no liability of any kind including but not limited to performance, merchantability, fitness for any particular purpose, or any losses or damages of any kind caused or alleged to be caused directly or indirectly from this book.

Library of Congress Card Number: 99-62864

ISBN: 0-7821-2461-5

Manufactured in the United States of America

10 9 8 7 6 5 4

Software License Agreement: Terms and Conditions

For Marianne, Jim, and Barkis. Now where's that phone?

Acknowledgments

People usually think of writing a book as being a solitary process, but in fact, nothing could be further from the truth. I had lots of help in writing this book, and this is my chance to say thanks to all the people who provided advice and technical assistance along the way.

At Sybex, thanks to Kristine O'Callaghan, Contracts and Licensing Manager; Guy Hart-Davis, Associate Publisher; Bonnie Bills and Neil Edde, Developmental Editors; Mark Kovach, Technical Editor; Jeremy Crawford, Project Editor; and Tony Jonick and Jerry Williams, Technical Illustrators. I also appreciate the hard work of the Desktop Publisher, Bill Gibson, the Project Team Leader, Lisa Reardon, and the Proofreaders, Susan Berge, Theresa Mori, and Catherine Morris. Thanks to Bill Gibson for the elegant book design. And thanks to Gary Masters who helped me hatch this project in the first place.

Many thanks to my best, favorite editor, Pat Coleman, who brought her light touch and considerable expertise to yet another manuscript. And thanks to Sonja Hertzing for helping to double-check all the cross-references.

Also, thanks to the people who reviewed the lists of terms that formed the basis of this book, particularly Tom Charlesworth, who has been heard to describe the TCP/IP specifications as "a thumping good read."

And finally, thanks to Nancy; as always, in a class by herself.

Introduction

Networks are currently one of the fastest growing and most important developments in the computer industry. Not only are more and more PCs becoming parts of networks, but networked PCs are being incorporated into larger enterprise-wide applications so that everyone in a company can access and share data.

With the expanding technology of networking comes the terminology to describe it. This *Dictionary of Networking* provides definitions for all the terms you will encounter when dealing with networks of any type.

Who Should Use This Book?

This book is designed to meet the needs of people who work with networks, communications, and mobile computing systems. Whether you are networking previously unconnected computers or downsizing from a mainframe, this book is for you. And if you are studying for one of the network certification exams, you will find this book to be an essential reference.

Network users of all levels are barraged with an almost bewildering array of terms, abbreviations, and acronyms in books, magazine and newspaper articles, advertisements, and their day-to-day conversations. Jargon is a useful shorthand, but it can easily become incomprehensible and unmanageable, even to the most seasoned network administrator.

What You'll Find in This Book

Along with clear explanations of the jargon and slang associated with networking, you'll find definitions of more than 3,000 networking technical terms, abbreviations, and acronyms. The list that follows gives you a brief overview of the topics that this book covers:

- Acronyms and abbreviations

- Active Directory

- ActiveX

- Application software

- Cables, cards, and connectors

- Certification schemes

- Chips, memory, and adapters

- Communications

- Connectivity tools, products, and equipment

- Disks and storage media

- E-mail

- Hardware

- File systems

- Industry standards

- Internet organizations

- Internet terms and abbreviations

- Intranet terms and abbreviations

- Java

- Leading hardware and software companies

- Linux, Free Software Foundation, GNU

- Microprocessors

- Microsoft Windows

- Microsoft Windows NT and NT Server

- Microsoft Windows 2000

- Mobile computing

- Networking theory and concepts

- Novell NetWare

- Novell Directory Services

- Operating systems and environments

- The OSI Reference Model

- Popular networking products

- Protocols and interfaces

- Security and network administration

- System architectures

- Trade associations

- Unix shells, tools, and utilities

- The World Wide Web

- Workstations

How This Book Is Organized

This book is organized for easy reference. Entries are arranged in letter-by-letter alphabetic order, ignoring punctuation and spaces, with terms that begin with an uppercase letter (or are all in uppercase) before those in all lowercase letters. So *Internet* comes before *internet*, and *link level* comes before *link-state routing algorithm*. Numbers and symbols are listed at the beginning of the book in ascending numeric order. If an entry begins with a letter or letters, but contains a number, it is listed alphabetically according to the letter, and then according to numerical order, so *V.42 bis* comes between *V.42* and *V.54*.

The information within each entry is always presented in the following order:

- Entry name

- Abbreviation or acronym

- Pronunciation, if it isn't obvious

- Definition, written in clear standard English

- URL pointing to further resources available on the Internet.

- Cross-references to other entries that provide additional or related information on the topic; more on the cross references in a moment.

If an entry has multiple definitions, each one is numbered to separate it from the next, and some of the entries also contain illustrations.

Extensive Cross-Referencing

The *Dictionary of Networking* is the most extensively cross-referenced dictionary of computing and networking terms available today. It contains two kinds of cross references:

- A *See* reference points to another entry that contains the information you are looking for. Thus, you can start with an abbreviation, such as *PPTP*, or with the complete term, such as *Point-to-Point Tunneling Protocol*, and be sure that you will arrive at the correct definition. You don't have to know what an abbreviation stands for to be able to look up a term. Some terms or concepts can be referred to by more than one name, such as *dialback modem* and *callback modem*; you will find both here, so you can always find your way to the appropriate definition.

- A *See also* reference points to one or more entries that contain additional information about a topic. This kind of cross-reference allows you to follow through a related set of entries, broadening your search as you move from entry to entry.

We have also added an extra element in this dictionary to help you find information, and that is the pronunciation of an acronym or abbreviation that is pronounced differently from the way it is spelled. For example, if you are reading a magazine article and come across the abbreviation *SCSI*, you can look up the abbreviation, which will point to the main entry term, *Small Computer System Interface*. But if you are discussing hard disk interfaces with a colleague and hear the term *scuzzy*, you can look that up too, and you will also find your way to the main entry, *Small Computer System Interface*.

The Appendices

This book contains four appendices to provide additional reference material:

Appendix A: Internet Resources Collects together URLs under a wide variety of headings to cut down on the amount of time you have to spend with your favorite search engine. Using this appendix, you can go straight to the right Web site every time.

Appendix B: Certification Resources Provides a guide through the complex and confusing world of computer and networking certification programs.

Appendix C: ASCII Charts Contains both the standard and the extended American Standard Code for Information Interchange charts.

Appendix D: EBCDIC Chart Contains the most widely accepted Extended Binary Coded Decimal Interchange Code chart.

A Note about the URLs in This Book

Nothing is more annoying than a dead URL, and link rot is all pervasive. (If you don't know what link rot is, go look it up.) All the URLs in this book have been individually checked by our Technical Editor; and at the time of writing, they are all active, they all work, and they all contain the information that I say they contain. But that is not to say that some of them won't have changed by the time you try them out.

The better-organized sites will simply post a link to the new site if they make substantive changes, and you can use that new link to go right to the new or reorganized site. Other sites, such as the Microsoft Web site, reorganize themselves periodically as a part of their housekeeping; the information you want is still available, but you have to look in another place to find it, or use the site's built-in search engine to find it.

Some of the sites that contain the most advanced technical information belong to the .edu domain and are usually computer science departments at the major universities. I have tried to keep the number of such sites to a minimum in this book. Although they can be extremely useful, they usually have a lifespan that closely resembles that of the average graduate student. Once the student maintaining the information graduates, the site becomes neglected and is usually removed soon after. Another dead URL.

To be consistent with current usage, I have not specified the protocol used to access each Web site; unless a different protocol is specified, you can simply assume that HTTP will work in all cases. Just add http:// to the beginning of each Web address in your browser when you access a site.

And finally, we have tried very carefully not to break a URL across a line; you should be able to type the characters you see without having to worry about whether to type that hyphen. If a URL has to break, the break is before a period (.) or after a slash (/).

About the Companion CD

The companion CD contains an electronic version of this entire book. You can use it to find entries quickly and follow cross-references without a great deal of page flipping.

And Finally...

Through more than 25 years of hands-on involvement in practical computer applications, including the management of minicomputer systems, PC-based networks, large-scale data communications systems, software development, and technical support, I have become intimately familiar with computer and networking terminology. The *Dictionary of Networking* is a direct result of that experience, and it represents a practical and down-to-earth approach to computers and computing.

Everyone who has worked on this dictionary has tried to make sure that it is as complete and accurate as possible. But if you think that we have missed a word or two that should be included in a future edition, or if you think that an entry doesn't contain enough information, please write to the following address:

Dictionary of Networking

c/o SYBEX Inc.

1151 Marina Village Parkway

Alameda, CA 94501-1044

USA

Symbols and Numbers

! *See* bang.

& *See* ampersand.

* *See* asterisk.

. *See* star-dot-star.

. *See* period and double-period directories.

.. *See* period and double-period directories.

/ *See* slash.

// *See* double-slash.

: *See* colon.

<> *See* angle brackets.

> *See* right angle bracket.

? *See* question mark.

@ *See* at symbol.

\ *See* backslash.

| *See* vertical bar.

1/4-inch cartridge *See* quarter-inch cartridge.

2B+D Common abbreviation for Basic Rate ISDN, which has two B, or bearer, channels and one D, or data, channel. *See also* 23B+D; Basic Rate ISDN.

3+ A network operating system, originally developed by 3Com, that implemented Xerox Network System (XNS) transport protocols and Microsoft MS-Net file sharing.

3Com Corporation One of the largest manufacturers of network hardware in the world, particularly known for LAN and WAN products, including remote access products, hubs, network interface cards, Gigabit Ethernet, and multimedia over networks. The company's PalmPilot handheld computer has proved to be extremely popular, with more than one million units sold to date. In 1997, 3Com merged with U.S. Robotics in a deal worth $6.6 billion.

For more information on 3Com, see www.3com.com.

4B/5B encoding A data-translation scheme used to precede signal encoding in FDDI (Fiber Distributed Data Interface) networks. In 4B/5B, each group of four bits is represented as a five-bit symbol, which is then associated with a bit pattern, which in turn is encoded using a standard method, often NRZI (non-return to zero inverted).

See also Manchester encoding.

4.4BSD Lite A version of the 4.4 Berkeley Software Distribution (BSD) Unix from which all the AT&T code has been removed in an attempt to avoid licensing conflicts. It is not possible to compile and then run 4.4BSD Lite without a preexisting system because several important utilities and other files from the operating system are missing.

The 4.4BSD Lite version has served as the basis for several other important Unix implementations, including FreeBSD and NetBSD.

1

See also Berkeley Software Distribution Unix; FreeBSD; NetBSD; Unix.

5B/6B encoding   A data-translation scheme used to precede signal encoding in 100BaseVG networks. In 5B/6B, each group of five bits is represented as a six-bit symbol, which is then associated with a bit pattern, which in turn is encoded using a standard method, often NRZI (non-return to zero inverted).

See also Manchester encoding.

9-track tape   A tape storage format that uses nine parallel tracks on 1/2-inch, reel-to-reel magnetic tape. Eight tracks are used for data, and one track is used for parity information. These tapes are often used as backup systems on minicomputer and mainframe systems; digital audio tapes (DATs) are more common on networks.

See also quarter-inch cartridge.

10/100   A term used to indicate that a device can support both Ethernet (at a data transfer rate of 10Mbps) and Fast Ethernet (at a data transfer rate of 100Mbps).

See also Ethernet.

10Base2   An implementation of the 802.3 Ethernet standard on thin Ethernet (RG-58) coaxial cable; sometimes called thinnet or cheapernet wire. The 10Base2 specification has a data-transfer rate of 10Mbps and a maximum cable-segment length of 185 meters (610.5 feet). A T-connector attaches the thin coaxial cable to the BNC connector on the Ethernet adapter.

10Base5   An implementation of the 802.3 Ethernet standard on thick Ethernet coaxial cable; sometimes called thicknet. The 10Base5 specification has a data-transfer rate of 10Mbps and a maximum cable-segment length of 500 meters (1650 feet), over a bus topology. The cable attaches to the Ethernet adapter with a vampire, or piercing, connector and a transceiver.

See also bus network.

10BaseF   An implementation of the 802.3 Ethernet standard over fiber-optic cable. This specification allows throughput of a maximum of 10Mbps and is separated into these three categories:

- **10BaseFP (fiber passive)**   Used for desktop connections

- **10BaseFL (fiber link)**   For intermediate hubs and workgroups

- **10BaseFB (fiber backbone)**   Used for central facility lines between buildings

10BaseT   An implementation of the 802.3 Ethernet standard over UTP wiring—the same wiring and RJ-45 connectors used with telephone systems. The standard is based on a star topology, with each node connected to a central wiring center and a maximum cable-segment length of 100 meters (330 feet).

See also star network.

23B+D   Common abbreviation for Primary Rate ISDN, which has 23 B, or bearer, channels and 1 D, or data, channel.

See also 2B+D; Primary Rate ISDN.

24/7   Abbreviation for round-the-clock availability, implying that the service is available 24 hours a day, 7 days a week.

56K modem standard *See* V.90.

100Base-FX A specification for Fast Ethernet over fiber-optic cable.

See also Fast Ethernet

100Base-T4 A specification for Fast Ethernet over four pairs of Category 3, 4, or 5 untwisted-pair wiring.

See also Fast Ethernet

100Base-TX A specification for Fast Ethernet over two pairs of Category 5 unshielded twisted-pair or Category 1 shielded twisted-pair cable. The 100Base-TX specification requires two pairs of wires.

See also Fast Ethernet

100VG-AnyLAN A term applied to the IEEE 802.12 standard, originally developed by Hewlett-Packard and supported by Novell, Microsoft, AT&T, and many others.

The 100VG-AnyLAN specification modifies the existing Ethernet standard to allow speeds of 10 or 100Mbps and uses the demand priority access method rather than Carrier Sense Multiple Access/Collision Detection (CSMA/CD). A speed of 100Mbps transmission is supported over Category 3 four-pair unshielded twisted-pair cabling.

See also demand priority; Fast Ethernet.

680x0 A family of 32-bit microprocessors from Motorola, used in Macintosh computers and many advanced workstations. The 680x0 is popular with programmers, because it uses a linear-addressing mode to access memory, rather than the segmented-addressing scheme used by Intel coprocessors.

Several models have been developed:

- **68000** The first microprocessor in this family, which used a 32-bit data word with a 16-bit data bus and could address 16MB of memory. It was used in the first Apple Macintosh computers as well as in Hewlett-Packard's LaserJet printers.

- **68020** A 32-bit microprocessor that runs at 16MHz, 20MHz, 25MHz, or 33MHz and is capable of addressing as much as 4GB of memory. The 68020 was used in the Macintosh II computer, but has been replaced by the 68030.

- **68030** Has a paged memory management unit built-in and, therefore, does not need external hardware to handle this function. The 68030 is used in the Macintosh II and SE computers.

- **68040** Incorporates a built-in floating-point processor and memory management unit, along with independent 4KB data and instruction caches. It can perform parallel execution by using multiple, independent instruction queues. The 68040 is used in the Macintosh Quadra line of computers.

See also PowerPC.

802.x A set of communications standards defining the physical and electrical connections in LANs, originally defined by the Institute of Electrical and Electronics Engineers (IEEE).

A number followed by an uppercase letter indicates a stand-alone standard; a number followed by a lowercase letter indicates either a supplement to a standard or a part of a multiple-number standard.

Many of the IEEE standards have also been adopted by the International Organization for Standardization (ISO), whose standards are accepted all over the world; IEEE standards 802.1 to 802.11 are now also known as ISO 8802.1 to 8802.11. You will see both designations in networking books and magazines; it will take a while for everyone to get used to these numbers.

See also IEEE standards.

802.1 An IEEE standard that specifies the media-access-control level for bridges linking 802.3, 802.4, and 802.5 networks. It includes a spanning-tree algorithm for Ethernet media-access-control layer bridges and the heterogeneous LAN management specification for Ethernet and token-ring hubs.

See also IEEE standards.

802.2 An IEEE standard that specifies the logical link sublayer of the data-link layer in the OSI protocol stack. The data-link layer in the OSI protocol stack is divided into the logical link layer and the media-access-control layer. The logical link layer provides framing, addressing, and error-control functions.

See also IEEE standards.

802.3 An IEEE standard for CSMA/CD (Carrier Sense Multiple Access/Collision Detection) LANs, including both baseband and broadband networks. The baseband version is based on the Ethernet network, originally developed by Xerox Corporation.

The 802.3 standard includes the following:

- **10Base2** An implementation of the Ethernet standard on thin Ethernet cable, with a data-transfer rate of 10Mbps and a maximum cable-segment length of 185 meters (600 feet).

- **10Base5** An 802.3 Ethernet standard on thick Ethernet cable, with a 10Mbps data-transfer rate and a cable-segment length of a maximum of 500 meters (1650 feet), over a bus topology.

- **10BaseT** Establishes a standard for Ethernet over UTP wiring, the same wiring and RJ-45 connectors used with telephone systems. The standard is based on a star topology. Each node is connected to a wiring center, with a cable-length limitation of 100 meters (330 feet).

- **1Base5** A 1Mbps network standard with twisted-pair cable based on AT&T's StarLAN.

- **10Broad36** Defines a long-distance Ethernet with a 10Mbps data-transfer rate and a maximum cable-segment length of 3600 meters (11,880 feet).

- **10BaseF** Explicitly specifies fiber-optic cable in three settings; 10Base-FP (fiber passive) for desktops, 10Base-FL (fiber link) for intermediate hubs and workgroups, and 10Base-FB (fiber backbone) for central facility lines between buildings.

- **100BaseVG** A 100Mbps Ethernet network developed by Hewlett-Packard and AT&T Microelectrics.

- **100BaseT** A 100Mbps Ethernet developed by Grand Junction Networks.

See also 100VG-AnyLAN; Ethernet; Fast Ethernet; Gigabit Ethernet; IEEE standards.

802.4 An IEEE standard for bus topology networks that use token passing to control access and network traffic, running at 10Mbps a second. Token-bus networks are sometimes used in manufacturing settings, but they are not often found in office networks.

See also ARCnet; IEEE standards; Technical and Office Protocol.

802.5 An IEEE standard that defines ring networks using token passing to control access and network traffic, running at 4 or 16Mbps. It is used by IBM's Token Ring network over STP, UTP, or fiber-optic cabling. Also known as ANSI 802.1-1985.

See also IEEE standards.

802.6 An IEEE standard for metropolitan-area networks (MANs). It describes a DQDB (Distributed Queue Dual Bus) used for transmitting voice, video, and data over two parallel fiber-optic cables, with signaling rates in excess of 100Mbps per second.

See also IEEE standards; Switched Multimegabit Data Services.

802.7 An IEEE Technical Advisory Group (TAG) report on broadband networks carrying voice, data, and video traffic.

See also IEEE standards.

802.8 An IEEE Technical Advisory Group (TAG) report on the use of fiber optics as alternatives to copper-based cable in LANs.

See also IEEE standards.

802.9 An IEEE advisory committee on integrated data, voice, and video networking.

The specification has been called IVD (Integrated Voice and Data), but is now more commonly referred to as Iso-Ethernet.

See also IEEE standards; Iso-Ethernet.

802.10 An IEEE Technical Advisory Group (TAG) working on the definition of a standard security model for use over a variety of network types that incorporates authentication and encryption methods.

See also IEEE standards.

802.11 A proposed IEEE standard that will define wireless LANs, including spread-spectrum radio, narrowband radio, infrared transmission, and transmission over power lines.

See also IEEE standards.

802.12 An IEEE working group defining the 100Mbps Ethernet 100VG-AnyLAN originally developed by Hewlett-Packard and several other vendors.

See also 100VG-AnyLAN; IEEE standards.

802.14 An IEEE working group defining standards for data transmission over traditional cable TV networks using cable modems.

See also IEEE standards.

1394 An IEEE standard for a digital plug-and-play bus, originally conceived by Apple Computer in 1986. The 1394 standard supports a maximum of 63 nodes per bus and a maximum of 1023 buses.

Three speeds for device connections are available:

- 100Mbps

- 200Mbps

- 400Mbps

All devices are hot pluggable, and both self-powered and bus-powered devices can be attached to the same bus. Also known as FireWire, 1394 uses six-pair shielded twisted-pair cable and is intended for high-end applications such as digitized video.

See also Universal Serial Bus.

3270   A general description for the family of products from IBM that includes terminals, printers, and terminal cluster controllers. These products all communicate with a mainframe computer using the SNA (Systems Network Architecture) protocol.

80286   Also called the 286. A 16-bit microprocessor from Intel, first released in February 1982, used by IBM in the IBM PC/AT computer in 1984. Since then, it has been used in many other IBM-compatible computers.

The 80286 uses a 16-bit data word and a 16-bit data bus, with 24 bits to address memory. It has two modes:

- Real mode effectively limits performance to that of an 8086 microprocessor and can address 1MB of memory.

- Protected mode prevents an application from stopping the operating system be-cause of an error and can address 16MB of memory.

80386   Also called the 386DX and the 386. A full 32-bit microprocessor introduced by Intel in October 1985 and used in many IBM and IBM-compatible comput-ers. The 80386 has a 32-bit data word, can transfer information 32 bits at a time over the data bus, and can use 32 bits in address-ing memory. It has the following modes:

- Real mode effectively limits performance to that of an 8086 microprocessor and can address 1MB of memory.

- Protected mode prevents an application from stopping the operating system be-cause of an error, and it can address 4GB of memory.

- Virtual 8086 mode allows the operating system to divide the 80386 into several virtual 8086 microprocessors, all running with their own 1MB of space, and all run-ning a separate program.

80486   Also called the 486 or i486. A 32-bit microprocessor introduced by Intel in April 1989. The 80486 adds several notable features to the 80386, including an on-board cache, a built-in floating-point pro-cessor, and a memory management unit (MMU), as well as advanced provisions for multiprocessing and a pipelined execution scheme.

A

A+ Certification A certification program from the CompTIA (Computer Technology Industry Association) designed to measure competence in basic computer repair and aimed at the computer technician. Certification requires passing two tests: a core exam to test general knowledge of PCs, including configuration, installation and upgrading, diagnosis, repair, maintenance, customer interaction, and safety, and at least one specialty exam that tests operating system knowledge.

A+B signaling A type of in-band signaling used in T1 transmission; 1 bit from each of the 24 subchannels in every sixth frame is used to carry dialing and other control information. A+B signaling reduces the T1 bandwidth from 1.544Mbps to 1.536 Mbps.

See also T1.

a-b box A switching box that allows two or more computers to share a peripheral device such as a printer. It can be switched manually or through software.

A/UX A version of the Unix operating system that runs on the Macintosh. A/UX is based on the System V release 2 of Unix and includes a number of Apple features, such as support for the Macintosh Toolbox. This support allows applications running under A/UX to use the familiar Macintosh user interface. You need a Macintosh II with a Motorola 68020 or higher microprocessor and at least 4MB of memory to use A/UX.

See also Unix.

AASE *See* Associate Accredited Systems Engineer.

ABCP *See* Associate Business Continuity Professional.

abend Contraction of *abnormal end.* A message issued by an operating system when it detects a serious problem, such as a hardware failure or major software damage.

ABI *See* Application Binary Interface.

ABR *See* Available Bit Rate.

ABUI *See* Association of Banyan Users International.

accelerator board An add-in, printed circuit board that replaces the main processor with a higher-performance processor. Using an accelerator board can reduce upgrading costs substantially, because you don't need to replace the monitor, case, keyboard, and so on. However, the main processor is not the only component that affects the overall performance of your system. Other factors, such as disk-access time and video speed, contribute to a system's performance.

See also graphics accelerator board.

access To use, write to, or read from a file, or to log in to a computer system or network.

AccessBuilder Remote access software from 3Com Corporation that lets you access network resources over a dial-up connection from a remote location.

access control list Abbreviated ACL. A list or table containing information about the users, processes, and objects that can access a specific file or object. ACLs are usually attached to file-system directories, and they specify access permissions such as read, write, execute, delete, and so on.

ACLs are implemented in Novell NetWare, Microsoft Windows 2000, and Unix:

- In Novell Directory Services, ACLs are associated with every object in the NDS tree, storing the list of rights for each trustee that can access the object.

- In the Unix Network File System, ACLs include the name of the user or group, along with the rights granted to that user or group.

- In Windows 2000, everything is an object, and every object has an associated ACL.

See also Active Directory; authentication; NDS tree; Novell Directory Services; rights; security.

access method The set of rules that determines which node in a network has access to the transmission media at any moment.

Attempts at simultaneous access are either managed by a collision detection mecha-

nism such as CSMA/CD or prevented by use of a token-passing method.

access protocol The set of rules that workstations use to avoid collisions when sending information over shared network media. Also known as the media access control protocol.

access rights *See* rights.

access server A computer that provides access for remote users who dial in to the system and access network resources as though their computers were directly attached to the network.

See also communications/modem server; mobile computing.

access time The period of time that elapses between a request for information from disk or memory and the arrival of that information at the requesting device.

Memory-access time refers to the time it takes to transfer a character between memory and the processor. Disk-access time refers to the time it takes to place the read/write heads over the requested data. RAM may have an access time of 80 nanoseconds or less, while hard-disk access time could be 10 milliseconds or less.

access token In Microsoft Windows 2000, an object that contains the Security Identifier of a running process; the access token is a combination of the Security Identifiers for a user account and the group accounts that the user belongs to, along with additional information about the user.

See also authentication.

account   On LANs or multiuser operating systems, an account is set up for each user. Accounts are usually kept for administrative or security reasons. For communications and online services, accounts identify a subscriber for billing purposes.

See also user account.

accounting   The process of tracking the resources on a network. The network administrator can charge for files accessed, connect time, disk space used for file storage, and service requests by assigning account balances to users. The users can then draw from their account balances as they use network services.

account lockout   In Microsoft Windows 2000 and other operating systems, a count of the number of invalid logon attempts allowed before a user is locked out.

See also authentication; user account.

account policy   On networks and multiuser operating systems, the set of rules that defines whether a new user is permitted access to the system and whether an existing user is granted additional rights or expanded access to other system resources. Account policy also specifies the minimum length of passwords, the frequency with which passwords must be changed, and whether users can recycle old passwords and use them again.

Accredited Systems Engineer   Abbreviated ASE. A certification from Compaq designed to evaluate and recognize expertise in installing and administering Compaq workstations and servers running both Mi-

crosoft Windows 2000 and Novell NetWare network operating systems.

See also Associate Accredited Systems Engineer.

Acer Group   One of the top five PC makers in the world, with factories in Malaysia, the Netherlands, the Philippines, Taiwan, and the United States. The Acer Group bought Texas Instrument's notebook computer business in 1997 and has formed business alliances with companies, including 3Com and Hitachi, for the development of advanced digital consumer products such as PC-ready televisions and DVD systems.

For more information on the Acer Group, see www.acer.com.tw.

ACF   *See* Advanced Communications Function.

ACK   *See* acknowledgment.

acknowledgment   Abbreviated ACK. In communications, ACK is a control code, ASCII 06, sent by the receiving computer to indicate that the data has been received without error and that the next part of the transmission may be sent.

See also NAK.

ACL   *See* access control list.

ACONSOLE   A Novell NetWare 3.*x* workstation utility that controls a modem attached to the workstation. ACONSOLE is used to establish an asynchronous remote console connection to a server. The RS232 NetWare Loadable Module (NLM) must be loaded on the server to which you want to

A

connect. In NetWare 4.*x*, use RCONSOLE to perform this function.

acoustic coupler   A modem that includes a pair of rubber cups that fit over the mouthpiece and earpiece of a standard telephone handset (to prevent external noise from being picked up). An acoustic coupler allows you to connect your computer to a telephone system that does not have the standard RJ-11 connections used with conventional modems.

ACPI   *See* Advanced Configuration and Power Interface.

across-the-wire migration   A method of migrating file-server data, trustee rights, and other information to a Novell NetWare server using the NetWare Migration utility. You can also use across-the-wire migration to upgrade from LAN Manager, LAN Server, and earlier versions of NetWare; a similar process known as BMIGRATE allows users to migrate from Banyan VINES.

ACS   *See* Advanced Communications Service.

ACTE   *See* Ascend Certified Technical Expert.

Active Directory   In Microsoft Windows 2000, a system for large-scale network management that views the network as a hierarchy of objects. Active Directory does the following:

- Provides a hierarchy for the management of all network objects, including users, servers, services, file shares, Web pages, printers, and so on.

- Divides administration and security into subdomains, domains, and trees of domains.

- Scales to 10 million users per domain.

- Implements MIT's Kerberos authentication system based on private key encryption and also supports public key encryption for authentication of clients and business partners.

- Emulates Windows NT 4.*x* directory services for backward compatibility.

- Uses DNS rather than WINS, and requires all user and host names to be in DNS form.

- Uses LDAP rather than a proprietary protocol so that non-Microsoft applications can query the name database.

- Interoperates with Novell NetWare Directory Services.

See also forest; Kerberos; Lightweight Directory Access Protocol; NetWare Directory Services; Microsoft Windows 2000; tree.

active hub   A device that amplifies transmission signals in a network, allowing signals to be sent over a much greater distance than is possible with a passive hub.

An active hub may have ports for coaxial, twisted-pair, or fiber-optic cable connections, as well as LEDs to show that each port is operating correctly.

See also repeater.

Active Monitor   The first station to be started on a Token Ring network. The Active Monitor is responsible for passing and maintaining the token and detects error conditions. The Active Monitor's performance

A

is constantly monitored by the Standby Monitor

See also Standby Monitor.

Active Server Pages   Abbreviated ASP. In Microsoft Internet Information Server, a script interpreter and execution environment that supports VBScript and JavaScript and is compatible with other scripting languages such as Perl, REXX, Tcl, and Python through add-ins from third-party developers.

ASP allows you to combine HTML, scripts, and ActiveX components on the same Web server; all the code runs on the server and presents the results of this dynamic process to the client browser as a standard HTML page.

See also JavaScript; Perl; Tcl; VBScript.

active termination   A technique used to terminate a SCSI. Active termination reduces electrical interference in a long string of SCSI devices.

See also forced perfect termination; passive termination.

ActiveX   The latest development of Microsoft's COM, the foundation that supported OLE. By adding network capabilities (and so creating DCOM, or Distributed COM) and by reducing the scope of OLE to create ActiveX, Microsoft has created a comprehensive set of component-based Internet- and intranet-oriented applications.

In an attempt to promote ActiveX as a standard, in 1996 Microsoft turned over control of ActiveX to the Open Group to manage future developments.

See also ActiveX control; Distributed Component Object Model; Java.

ActiveX control   The basic building block of Microsoft's ActiveX specification. An ActiveX control is a software module that cannot run by itself, but requires an ActiveX container such as a Web browser, a word processor, or a spreadsheet. Each control delivers a specific function such as database access, user-interface elements, or file access and can communicate with another ActiveX control, an ActiveX container, or the underlying Windows operating system.

Unlike Java applets, which for security reasons run in a sandbox designed to protect the file system from unauthorized access, ActiveX can directly access files. To provide a measure of security, ActiveX controls are packaged with digital certificates that prove the origin of the control.

See also ActiveX; certificate; Java; Java applet; Java Virtual Machine; sandbox.

Adaptec, Inc.   A leading manufacturer of high-performance networking and connectivity products, including SCSI adapters, RAID products, Fast Ethernet adapters, ATM network interface cards, and server management software. In 1998, Adaptec acquired Ridge Technologies, a manufacturer of RAID and other storage solutions for Microsoft Windows 2000.

For more information on Adaptec, see www.adaptec.com.

adapter   A printed circuit board that plugs into a computer's expansion bus to provide added capabilities.

Common adapters include video adapters, joy-stick controllers, and I/O adapters, as well as other devices, such as internal modems, CD-ROMs, and network interface cards. One adapter can often support several different devices. Some of today's PC designs incorporate many of the functions previously performed by these individual adapters on the motherboard.

adaptive equalization   *See* adaptive speed leveling.

adaptive routing   A mechanism that allows a network to reroute messages dynamically, using the best available path, if a portion of the network fails.

See also alternative route.

adaptive speed leveling   A modem technology that allows a modem to respond to changing line conditions by changing its data rate. As line quality improves, the modem attempts to increase the data rate; as line quality declines, the modem compensates by lowering the data rate. Also known as adaptive equalization.

ADCCP   *See* Advanced Data Communications Control Procedures.

address   1. The precise location in memory or on disk where a piece of information is stored. Each byte in memory and each sector on a disk has its own unique address.

2. The unique identifier for a specific node on a network. An address may be a physical address specified by switches or jumpers on the network interface card hardware, or it can be a logical address established by the network operating system.

3. To reference or manage a storage location.

4. In Unix, an IP address as specified in the /etc/hosts file.

5. Information used by a network or the Internet to specify a specific location in the form username@hostname; username is your user name, logon name, or account name or number, and hostname is the name of the Internet Service Provider (ISP) or computer system you use. The hostname may consist of several parts, each separated from the next by a period.

See also address bus; Domain Name Service; e-mail address; Internet Service Provider; IP address; memory address.

address bus   The electronic channel, usually from 20 to 64 lines wide, used to transmit the signals that specify locations in memory.

The number of lines in the address bus determines the number of memory locations that the processor can access, because each line carries one bit of the address. A 20-line address bus (used in early Intel 8086/8088 processors) can access 1MB of memory, a 24-line address bus can access 16MB, and a 32-line address bus can access more than 4GB. A 64-line address bus (used in the DEC Alpha APX) can access 16EB.

address classes   In a 32-bit IP address, which is shown in the accompanying illustration, the number of bits used to identify the network and the host vary according to the network class of the address, as follows:

- Class A is used only for very large networks. The high-order bit in a Class A network is always zero, leaving 7 bits available to define 127 networks. The remaining 24 bits of the address allow each Class A network to hold as many as 16,777,216 hosts. Examples of Class A networks include General Electric, IBM, Hewlett-Packard, Apple Computer, Xerox, Digital Equipment Corporation, and MIT. All the Class A networks are in use, and no more are available.

- Class B is used for medium-sized networks. The 2 high-order bits are always 10, and the remaining bits are used to define 16,384 networks, each with as many as 65,535 hosts attached. Examples of

Class B networks include Microsoft and Exxon. All Class B networks are in use, and no more are available.

- Class C is for smaller networks. The 3 high-order bits are always 110, and the remaining bits are used to define 2,097,152 networks, but each network can have a maximum of only 254 hosts. Class C networks are still available.

- Class D is a special multicast address and cannot be used for networks. The 4 high-order bits are always 1110, and the remaining 28 bits allow for more than 268 million possible addresses.

- Class E is reserved for experimental purposes. The first four bits in the address are always 1111.

See also Classless Inter-Domain Routing; IP address; subnet mask.

IP ADDRESS STRUCTURE

Class	Bit Allocation		

Class		Bit Allocation
A	0	Network (7 bits) / Host (24 bits)
B	10	Network (14 bits) / Host (16 bits)
C	110	Network (21 bits) / Host (8 bits)
D	1110	Multicast Addresses (28 bits)
E	1111	Experimental (28 bits)
Loopback	01111111	Unused

addressing space   The amount of RAM available to the operating system running on a server.

address mask   *See* subnet mask.

Address Resolution Protocol   Abbreviated ARP. A protocol within TCP/IP (Transmission Control Protocol/Internet Protocol) and AppleTalk networks that allows a host to find the physical address of a node on the same network when it knows only the target's logical or IP address.

Under ARP, a network interface card contains a table (known as the address resolution cache) that maps logical addresses to the hardware addresses of nodes on the network. When a node needs to send a packet, it first checks the address resolution cache to see if the physical address information is already present. If so, that address is used, and network traffic is reduced; otherwise, a normal ARP request is made to determine the address.

See also IP address.

adjacency   A term describing the relationship formed between certain neighboring routers for the purpose of swapping routing information. Adjacency is based on the use of a common network segment.

administrative alerts   In Windows 2000, informational messages sent to specific accounts, groups, or computers to announce security events, impending shutdown due to loss of server power, performance problems, and printer errors.

When a server generates an administrative alert, the appropriate message is sent to a predefined list of users and computers.

See also Alerter service.

administrative distance   A term used by Cisco Systems, Inc., to express the integrity of a routing-information source. Administrative distance is expressed as a value in the range 0 through 255; the higher the value, the lower the quality of the routing information.

Administrator account   In Microsoft Windows 2000, a special account with the maximum authority and permissions that can assign any permission to any user or group.

The Administrator account cannot be deleted, but it can be renamed, which is probably a good security policy.

See also permissions.

ADMIN object   A NetWare Directory Services User object, created during the installation of NetWare, that has special privileges, including the supervisory rights to create and manage other objects.

ADMIN has Supervisor rights and can, therefore, manage the NetWare Directory Services tree and add or delete Directory objects.

ADSL   *See* Asymmetric Digital Subscriber Line.

Advanced Communications Function   Abbreviated ACF. A set of program packages from IBM that allows computer resources to be shared over communications links using the concepts of SAA (Systems Application Architecture).

For example, ACF/TCAM (Advanced Communications Functions/Telecommunications Access Method) and ACF/VTAM (Advanced Communications Functions/Virtual Telecommunications Access Method) allow the interconnection of two or more domains into one multiple-domain network.

Advanced Communications Service

Abbreviated ACS. A large data-communications network established by AT&T.

Advanced Configuration and Power Interface

Abbreviated ACPI. An interface specification developed by Intel, Microsoft, and Toshiba for controlling power use on the PC and all other devices attached to the system. A BIOS-level hardware specification, ACPI depends on specific hardware that allows the operating system to direct power management and system configuration.

See also Advanced Power Management.

Advanced Data Communications Control Procedures

Abbreviated ADCCP. A bit-oriented, link-layer, ANSI-standard communications protocol.

See also High-level Data Link Control.

Advanced Interactive Executive

Abbreviated AIX. A version of Unix from IBM that runs on its RS/6000 workstations and on minicomputers and mainframes.

Although AIX is based on Unix System V Release 3, it contains many of the features available in System V Release 4, is

POSIX-compliant, and meets the Trusted Computer Base (TCB) Level C2 security.

One of the major enhancements of AIX is Visual Systems Management (VSM), a graphical interface into the older Systems Management Interface Tool (SMIT). VSM contains four main elements: Print Manager, Device Manager, Storage Manager, and Users and Groups Manager.

Advanced Micro Devices, Inc.

Abbreviated AMD. The fifth largest manufacturer of integrated circuits, flash memory, and microprocessors, specializing in clones of Intel's popular PC chips, including the AMD386, AMD486, AMDK5, and the AMDK6.

For more information about AMD, see www.amd.com.

See also Cyrix; Intel Corporation; Pentium; Pentium II; Pentium III.

Advanced Mobile Phone Service

Abbreviated AMPS. Currently the cellular telephone standard in the United States; an analog, cellular communications system developed by AT&T. AMPS uses frequency-division multiplexing (FDM) and operates in the 825 to 890MHz range.

See also Cellular Digital Packet Data.

Advanced Peer-to-Peer Internetworking

An SNA routing scheme proposed by Cisco Systems and eventually abandoned.

Advanced Peer-to-Peer Networking

Abbreviated APPN. IBM's SNA (Systems Network Architecture) protocol, based on APPC (Advanced Program-to-Program

Communications). APPN allows nodes on the network to interact without a mainframe host computer and implements dynamic network directories and dynamic routing in an SNA network.

APPN can run over a variety of network media, including Ethernet, token ring, FDDI, ISDN, X.25, SDLC, and higher-speed links such as B-ISDN or ATM.

See also Asynchronous Transfer Mode; Customer Information Control System; Systems Network Architecture.

Advanced Power Management Abbreviated APM. An API specification from Microsoft and Intel intended to monitor and extend battery life on a laptop computer by shutting down certain system components after a period of inactivity.

See also Advanced Configuration and Power Interface.

Advanced Program-to-Program Communications Abbreviated APPC. A set of protocols developed by IBM as a part of its SNA (Systems Network Architecture), designed to allow applications running on PCs and mid-range hosts to exchange data easily and directly with mainframes. APPC can be used over an SNA, Ethernet, X.25, or Token Ring network and is an open, published communications protocol.

APPC/PC is a PC-based version of APPC used over a Token Ring network.

advanced run-length limited encoding Abbreviated ARLL. A technique used to store information on a hard disk that increases the capacity of run-length limited (RLL) storage by more than 25 percent and increases the data-transfer rate to 9Mbps.

See also RLL encoding.

Advanced Technology Attachment Abbreviated ATA. The ANSI X3T10 standard for the disk-drive interface usually known as Integrated Drive Electronics (IDE).

See also Integrated Drive Electronics.

advertising The process by which services on a network inform other devices on the network of their availability. Novell NetWare uses the Service Advertising Protocol (SAP) for this purpose.

AFP *See* AppleTalk Filing Protocol.

AFS *See* Andrews File System.

aftermarket The market for related hardware, software, and peripheral devices created by the sale of a large number of computers of a specific type.

agent **1.** A program that performs a task in the background and informs the user when the task reaches a certain milestone or is complete.

2. A program that searches through archives looking for information specified by the user. A good example is a spider that searches Usenet articles. Sometimes called an intelligent agent.

3. In SNMP (Simple Network Management Protocol), a program that monitors network traffic.

4. In client-server applications, a program that mediates between the client and the server.

Aggregate Route-Based IP Switching   Abbreviated ARIS. A scheme from IBM used to establish switched paths through networks that act as virtual circuits, transmitting data packets through the network without the need to make routing decisions at every step. ARIS uses tagging techniques to add information to the data packets that can be used to guide the packets through the virtual circuits based on information already established by protocols such as Open Shortest Path First (OSPF) and Border Gateway Protocol (BGP).

AIX   *See* Advanced Interactive Executive.

Alerter service   A Microsoft Windows 2000 service that warns a predefined list of users and computers of an administrative alert. The Alerter service is used by the Server service and requires the Messenger service.

See also administrative alerts; Messenger service; service.

Alias object   In Novell NetWare, a leaf object that references the original location of an object in the directory. Using Alias objects, one object can appear in several containers at the same time, allowing users to locate and use the object quickly and easily.

See also leaf object.

alphanumeric   Consisting of letters, numbers, and sometimes special control characters, spaces, and other punctuation characters.

See also American Standard Code for Information Interchange; Extended Binary Coded Decimal Interchange Code; Unicode.

alpha testing   The first stage in testing a new hardware or software product, usually performed by the in-house developers or programmers.

See also beta testing.

alternative route   A secondary communications path to a specific destination. An alternative route is used when the primary path is not available.

See also adaptive routing.

alt newsgroups   A set of Usenet newsgroups containing articles on controversial subjects often considered outside the mainstream. Alt is an abbreviation for alternative.

These newsgroups were originally created to avoid the rigorous process required to create an ordinary newsgroup. Some alt newsgroups contain valuable discussions on subjects ranging from agriculture to wolves, others contains sexually explicit material, and others are just for fun. Not all ISPs and online services give access to the complete set of alt newsgroups.

See also mailing list; moderated newsgroup; newsgroup; unmoderated newsgroup.

AMD   *See* Advanced Micro Devices, Inc.

American National Standards Institute   Abbreviated ANSI. A nonprofit organization of more than 1000 business and industry groups, founded in 1918, devoted to the development of voluntary standards.

A

ANSI represents the United States in the International Organization for Standardization (ISO) and is affiliated with CCITT. ANSI committees have developed many important standards, including the following:

- ANSI X3J11: Standard for the C programming language, including language semantics, syntax, execution environment, and the definition of the library and header files.

- ANSI X3J16: Standard for the C++ programming language.

- ANSI X3J3: Definition of the Fortran programming language compiler.

- ANSI X3.131-1986: Definition of the SCSI standard. The X3T9.2 standard contains the extensions for SCSI-2.

- ANSI X3T9.5: The working group for the FDDI definition.

American Standard Code for Information Interchange   Abbreviated ASCII, pronounced "as-kee." A standard coding scheme that assigns numeric values to letters, numbers, punctuation characters, and control characters to achieve compatibility among different computers and peripheral devices. In ASCII, each character is represented by a unique integer value in the range 0 through 255. See Appendix C.

See also ASCII extended character set; ASCII file; ASCII standard character set; double-byte character set; Extended Binary Coded Decimal Interchange Code; Unicode.

American Wire Gauge   Abbreviated AWG. A measurement system that specifies copper wire by thickness; as thickness

increases, the AWG number decreases. Some common conductor gauges are:

- RS-232-C: 22 or 24 AWG
- Thick Ethernet: 12 AWG
- Thin Ethernet: 20 AWG

See also cabling standards; EIA/TIA 586; Type 1–9 cable.

America Online, Inc.   Abbreviated AOL. The world's largest online service, headquartered in Vienna, Virginia, with more than 15 million subscribers. AOL provides a gateway to the Internet, as well as its own news, sports, e-mail, chat rooms, and other fee-based services. In 1997, AOL bought CompuServe, and in 1998, Netscape Communications.

For more information about America Online, see www.aol.com.

ampersand (&)   **1.** In Unix, a command suffix used to indicate that the preceding command should be run in the background.

2. In Unix, a root user command used to start a daemon that is to keep running after logout.

3. In HTML, a special character entry in a document.

See also daemon; HyperText Markup Language.

AMPS   *See* Advanced Mobile Phone Service.

analog   Describes any device that represents changing values by a continuously variable physical property, such as a voltage in a circuit. Analog often refers to transmission methods developed to transmit voice signals rather than high-speed digital signals.

Andrews File System   Abbreviated AFS. A protocol developed at Carnegie Mellon University; used to share remote files across systems using TCP/IP.

AFS has certain advantages over NFS in that it only allows users to access files linked to AFS rather than giving access to all files, it has a built-in cache that helps to reduce the demands made on the system, and system administrators can allocate disk space on the fly as required.

See also Distributed File System; Network File System; Transmission Control Protocol/Internet Protocol.

angle brackets   The less-than (<) and greater-than (>) symbols used to identify a tag in an HTML document.

Also used to identify the return address in an e-mail message header.

See also HyperText Markup Language; tag.

ANI   *See* automatic number identification.

anonymous FTP   A method used to access an Internet computer that does not require you to have an account on the target computer system. Simply log on to the Internet computer with the user name *anonymous,* and use your e-mail address as your password. This access method was originally provided as a courtesy so that system administrators could see who had logged on to their systems, but now it is often required

to gain access to an Internet computer that has FTP service.

You cannot use anonymous FTP with every computer on the Internet, only with those systems set up to offer the service. The system administrator decides which files and directories will be open to public access, and the rest of the system is considered off limits and cannot be accessed by anonymous FTP users. Some sites only allow you to download files; as a security precaution, you are not allowed to upload files.

See also File Transfer Protocol; Telnet.

anonymous posting   In a Usenet newsgroup, a public message posted via an anonymous server in order to conceal the identity of the original sender.

anonymous remailer   *See* anonymous server.

anonymous server   A special Usenet service that removes from a Usenet post all header information that could identify the original sender and then forwards the message to its final destination. If you use an anonymous server, be sure to remove your signature from the end of the message; not all anonymous servers look for and then strip a signature. Also known as an anonymous remailer.

ANSI   *See* American National Standards Institute.

answer mode   A function that allows a modem to answer an incoming call, detect the protocol being used by the calling modem, and synchronize with that protocol.

See also auto-answer; auto-dial.

antivirus program   A program that detects or eliminates a computer virus. Some antivirus programs can detect suspicious activity on your computer as it happens; others must be run periodically as part of your normal housekeeping activities.

An antivirus program locates and identifies a virus by looking for characteristic patterns or suspicious activity in the system, such as unexpected disk access or .EXE files changing in some unusual way. It recognizes the virus by comparing information from the system against a database of known viruses, which is kept on disk.

Be sure you test an antivirus program carefully on your network before you employ it everywhere; some programs impose an enormous overhead on normal network operations.

See also file-infecting virus; macro virus; multipart virus; polymorphic virus; stealth virus; Trojan Horse; vaccine; virus.

AnyNet   A family of gateway products from IBM used to integrate SNA, TCP/IP, and NetBIOS networks with products running on IBM's AIX/6000, OS/2, and OS/400 and with Microsoft Windows.

AOL   *See* America Online, Inc.

Apache HTTP Server   A freeware Web server, supported by the Unix community, in use on almost half of the Web sites on the Internet. So called because the original university-lab software was patched with new features and fixes until it became known as "a patchy server."

Apache dominates the Web because of its low cost, excellent performance, good scalability, and great flexibility. Don't expect easy graphical configuration programs and hypertext help; you'll get the command line and the man pages instead, so it certainly helps to have staff with Unix experience.

Apache Server is available as part of the Red Hat Software Linux distribution, which also provides developers with full support for CGI, Perl, Tcl, a C or C++ compiler, an Apache server API, and a SQL database.

For more information on Apache Server, see The Apache Group Web site at www.apache.org.

See also Linux; Red Hat Software.

API   *See* application programming interface.

APM   *See* Advanced Power Management.

app   *See* application.

APPC   *See* Advanced Program-to-Program Communications.

APPI   *See* Advanced Peer-to-Peer Internetworking.

Apple Computer, Inc.   Manufacturer of the successful Macintosh and Quadra series of computers based on Motorola chips. The company was founded by Steve Wozniak and Steve Jobs in a garage on April 1, 1976.

In 1993, Apple entered the consumer electronics marketplace with a personal digital assistant known as Newton, combining fax, electronic mail, and other functions into a unit small enough to fit into a pocket.

In 1994, Apple launched a new series of computers called the Power Macintosh (or Power Mac), based on the PowerPC, capable of running either the Macintosh operating system or Windows programs under software emulation.

Apple always kept the architecture of the Mac proprietary, a move that has cost the company considerable market share; nevertheless, Apple has always had a strong following among musicians and graphical designers.

In 1997, Steve Jobs rejoined Apple and, after realigning Apple's product line, led the development and launch of the popular and capable Internet-ready iMac computer.

For more information on Apple Computer, Inc., see www.apple.com.

Apple Desktop Bus   A serial communications link that connects low-speed input devices, such as a mouse or a keyboard, to the computer on the Macintosh SE, II, IIx, IIcx, and SE/30.

Light pens, trackballs, and drawing tablets may also be connected via the Apple Desktop Bus. Most Apple Desktop Bus devices allow one device to be daisy-chained to the next, up to a maximum of 16 devices.

Apple Macintosh   *See* Macintosh.

AppleShare   Network software from Apple Computer that requires a dedicated Macintosh computer acting as a centralized server and includes both server and workstation software. AppleShare uses the AppleTalk Filing Protocol (AFP).

AppleTalk   An Apple Macintosh network protocol, based on the OSI Reference Model, which gives every Macintosh networking capabilities. AppleTalk can run under several network operating systems, including Apple Computer's AppleShare, Novell NetWare for the Macintosh, and TOPS from Sun Microsystems.

AppleTalk includes specifications for the data-link layer as LocalTalk, EtherTalk, FDDI-Talk, or TokenTalk, and the network layer as Datagram Delivery Protocol. The transport layer contains four protocols:

- Routing Table Maintenance Protocol (RTMP)
- AppleTalk Echo Protocol (AEP)
- AppleTalk Transaction Protocol (ATP)
- Name Binding Protocol (NBP)

The session layer includes

- AppleTalk Data Stream Protocol (ADSP)
- AppleTalk Session Protocol (ASP)
- Printer Access Protocol (PAP)
- Zone Information Protocol (ZIP)

The presentation layer adds the AppleTalk Filing Protocol (AFP) for access to remote files on shared disks.

AppleTalk Filing Protocol   Abbreviated AFP. AFP is located in the presentation and application layers of the AppleTalk protocol stack. AFP lets users access remote files as though they were local, as well as providing security features that can restrict user access to certain files.

APPLETALK PROTOCOL STACK

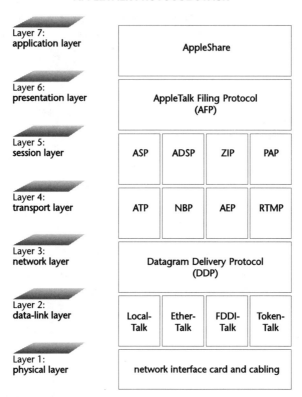

Layer 7:
application layer — AppleShare

Layer 6:
presentation layer — AppleTalk Filing Protocol (AFP)

Layer 5:
session layer — ASP | ADSP | ZIP | PAP

Layer 4:
transport layer — ATP | NBP | AEP | RTMP

Layer 3:
network layer — Datagram Delivery Protocol (DDP)

Layer 2:
data-link layer — Local-Talk | Ether-Talk | FDDI-Talk | Token-Talk

Layer 1:
physical layer — network interface card and cabling

application Abbreviated app, or if the application is a small one, it is referred to as an applet. A computer program designed to perform a specific task, such as accounting, scientific analysis, word processing, or desktop publishing.

In general, applications can be distinguished from system software, system utilities, and computer language compilers, and they can be categorized as either stand-alone or network applications. Stand-alone applications run from the hard disk in an independent computer, so only one user at a time can access the application. Network applications run on networked computers and can be shared by many users. Advanced applications such as groupware and e-mail allow communications between network users.

See also application metering; client/server architecture; LAN-aware.

Application Binary Interface Abbreviated ABI. A specification that aims to ensure binary compatibility between applications running on the same family of processors or CPUs using Unix System V Release 4.

Applications developed using ABI can run on hardware from different manufacturers without being recompiled; any system calls needed for specific hardware are maintained in libraries.

The specification was originally developed by AT&T and Sun Microsystems and includes a test and verification suite used to determine if a system complies with the standard.

See also application programming interface.

application layer The seventh, or highest, layer in the OSI Reference Model for computer-to-computer communications. This layer uses services provided by the lower layers but is completely insulated from the details of the network hardware. It describes how applications interact with the network operating system, including database management, electronic mail, and terminal emulation programs.

See also OSI Reference Model.

application-level filter A category of firewall that provides a high degree of security but at the cost of lower speed and greater complexity. Typical application-level filters can provide proxy services for applications and protocols such as Telnet, FTP, HTTP, and SMTP.

See also firewall; packet-level filter; stateless filter.

application metering The process of counting the number of executions of the copies of an application in use on the network at any given time and ensuring that the number does not exceed preset limits.

Application metering is usually performed by a network management application running on the file server. Most application metering software will allow only a certain number of copies (usually that number specified in the application software license) of an application to run at any one time and will send a message to any users who try to exceed this limit.

See also concurrent license.

Application object In Novell Directory Services (NDS), a leaf object that represents a network application in a NetWare Directory tree.

See also Computer object; container object; leaf object; Novell Directory Services.

application programming interface Abbreviated API. The complete set of all operating system functions that an application can use to perform such tasks as managing files and displaying information.

An API provides a standard way to write an application, and it also describes how the application should use the functions it provides. Using an API is quicker and easier than developing functions from scratch and helps to ensure some level of consistency among all the applications developed for a specific operating system.

In operating systems that support a graphical user interface, the API also defines functions to support windows, icons, drop-down menus, and other components of the interface. In network operating systems, an API defines a standard method that applications can use to take advantage of all the network features.

application server   A special-purpose file server that is optimized for a specific task, such as communications or a database application, and that uses higher-end hardware than a typical file server.

See also superserver.

application-specific integrated circuit   Abbreviated ASIC. A computer chip developed for a specific purpose, designed by incorporating standard cells from a library rather than created from scratch. Also known as gate arrays, ASICs are found in all sorts of appliances, including modems, security systems, digital cameras, and even microwave ovens and automobiles.

APPN   *See* Advanced Peer-to-Peer Networking.

arbitration   The set of rules used to manage competing demands for a computer resource, such as memory or peripheral devices, made by multiple processes or users.

See also contention.

Archie   A system used on the Internet to locate files available by anonymous FTP. Once a week, special programs connect to all the known anonymous FTP sites on the Internet and collect a complete listing of all the publicly available files. This listing of files is kept in an Internet Archive Database, and when you ask Archie to look for a file, it searches this database rather than the whole Internet; you then use anonymous FTP to retrieve the file.

See also anonymous FTP.

architecture   1. The overall design and construction of all or part of a computer, particularly the processor hardware and the size and ordering sequence of its bytes.

2. The overall design of software, including interfaces to other software, the operating system, and to the network.

See also client/server architecture; closed architecture; complex instruction set computing; open architecture; reduced instruction set computing.

archive   1. To transfer files to some form of long-term storage, such as magnetic tape or large-capacity disk, when the files are no longer needed regularly but must be maintained for periodic reference.

2. On the Internet, a site containing a collection of files available via anonymous FTP.

3. A compressed file.

archive file   A single file that contains one or more files or directories that may have been compressed to save space. Archives are often used as a way to transport large numbers of related files across the Internet.

An archive file created under Unix may have the filename extension .TAR (for tape archive), .GZ (for gzip), or .Z (for compress or pack). Those created in Windows may have the filename extension .ZIP from the PKZIP or WinZip programs. Archive files created on a Macintosh will have the filename extension .SAE or .SIT from the StuffIt program.

An Internet host that provides access to large numbers of archive files is known as an archive site.

ARCNet   Acronym for Attached Resources Computing Network. A network available from the Datapoint Corporation and other vendors that can connect a wide variety of PCs and workstations (up to a maximum of 255) on coaxial, twisted-pair, or fiber-optic cable. ARCnet uses a proprietary token-passing access method at speeds of 2.5Mbps. ARCNet Plus is Datapoint's proprietary product that runs at 20Mbps.

ARCNet was popular for smaller networks, because it is relatively easy to set up and to operate and also because the components are inexpensive and widely available. These days, however, it is showing its age and is no longer sold by the major vendors.

See also Token Ring network.

ARIS   *See* Aggregate Route-Based IP Switching.

ARLL   *See* advanced run-length limited encoding.

ARP   *See* Address Resolution Protocol.

ARPAnet   Acronym for Advanced Research Projects Agency Network. A research network funded by the Defense Advanced Research Projects Agency (DARPA) to link universities and government research agencies, originally built by BBN, Inc., in 1969. It was the backbone for the now huge Internet. TCP/IP protocols were pioneered on ARPAnet. In 1983, the military communications portion was split off into the MILnet.

article   An e-mail message posted to one of the Usenet newsgroups, accessible by anyone with a newsreader and a connection to the Internet. Also called a post.

See also newsreader.

AS/400   A series of mid-range minicomputers from IBM, first introduced in 1988, that replaces the System/36 and System/38 series of computers. The AS/400 can serve in a wide variety of network configurations: as a host or an intermediate node to other AS/400 and System/3*x* computers, as a remote system to System/370-controlled networks, or as a network server to a group of PCs.

Ascend Certified Technical Expert

Abbreviated ACTE. A certification scheme from Ascend Communications, Inc., aimed at technical professionals with experience in installing, configuring, and troubleshooting Ascend remote-access products. Two written exams, the Networking and Telecommunications exam, and the Remote Access exam, are followed by a hands-on lab test administered at Ascend's headquarters in Alameda, CA.

Ascend Communications, Inc.   A leading provider of solutions for telecommunications carriers, ISPs, and corporate customers, Ascend manufactures products for remote access, for wide area networking, and for linking telephone switches, network connections, and videoconferencing facilities to phone company networks.

Ascend recently acquired Cascade Communications, establishing the company as one of the largest suppliers of frame-relay and

ATM equipment. In 1999, Ascend was bought by Lucent Technologies.

For more information on Ascend, see www.ascend.com.

ASCII   *See* American Standard Code for Information Interchange.

ASCII extended character set   The second group of characters, from 128 through 255, in the ASCII character set. The extended ASCII character set is assigned variable sets of characters by computer hardware manufacturers and software developers, and it is not necessarily compatible between different computers. The IBM extended character set used in the PC (see Appendix C) includes mathematics symbols and characters from the PC line-drawing set.

See also American Standard Code for Information Interchange; ASCII file; ASCII standard character set; double-byte character set; Extended Binary Coded Decimal Interchange Code; Unicode.

ASCII file   A file that contains only text characters from the ASCII character set. An ASCII file can include letters, numbers, and punctuation symbols, but does not contain any hidden text-formatting codes. Also known as a text file or an ASCII text file.

See also American Standard Code for Information Interchange; ASCII extended character set; ASCII standard character set; binary file.

ASCII standard character set   A character set that consists of the first 128 (from 0 through 127) ASCII characters. The values 0 through 31 are used for nonprinting control codes (see Appendix C), and the range 32 through 127 is used to represent the letters of the alphabet and common punctuation symbols. The entire set from 0 through 127 is referred to as the standard ASCII character set. All computers that use ASCII can understand the standard ASCII character set.

See also American Standard Code for Information Interchange; ASCII file; ASCII extended character set; double-byte character set; Extended Binary Coded Decimal Interchange Code; Unicode.

ASCII text file   *See* ASCII file.

ASE   *See* Accredited Systems Engineer.

ASIC   *See* application-specific integrated circuit.

ASP   *See* Active Server Pages.

assembly language   A low-level programming language in which each program statement must correspond to a single machine language instruction that the processor can execute.

Assembly languages are specific to a given microprocessor and, as such, are not portable; programs written for one type of processor must be rewritten before they can be used on another type of processor.

You use assembly language for two reasons:

- To wring as much performance out of the processor as possible

• To gain access to specific characteristics of the hardware that might not be possible from a higher-level language

See also compiler; interpreter; machine language; microcode

Associate Business Continuity Professional

Abbreviated ABCP. A certification from Disaster Recovery Institute International (DRII) that covers basic information on business continuity planning and disaster recovery.

See also Certified Business Continuity Professional; Master Business Continuity Professional.

Associated Accredited Systems Engineer

Abbreviated AASE. A certification from Compaq designed to evaluate and recognize basic knowledge of PC architecture and operations. An AASE may choose to specialize in Microsoft Windows 2000 or Novell NetWare operation.

See also Accredited Systems Engineer.

Association of Banyan Users International

Abbreviated ABUI. The Banyan user group, with 1700 members worldwide, concerned with all hardware and software related to the Banyan system, including Banyan VINES.

See also Banyan VINES.

asterisk In several operating systems, you can use the asterisk (*) as a wildcard character to represent one or more unknown characters in a filename or filename extension.

See also question mark; star-dot-star.

AST Research One of the world's top ten computer manufacturers, AST Research makes desktop, laptop, notebook, and hand-held computers, as well as monitors, graphics cards, and memory products. A subsidiary of Samsung Electronics Company Limited.

For more information on AST Research, see www.ast.com.

asymmetrical multiprocessing A multiprocessing design in which the programmer matches a specific task to a certain processor when writing the program.

This design makes for a much less flexible system than SMP (symmetrical multiprocessing) and may result in one processor being overworked while another stands idle. SMP allocates tasks to processors as the program starts up, on the basis of current system load and available resources. Needless to say, asymmetrical multiprocessing systems are easier to design, code, and test than symmetrical multiprocessing systems.

Asymmetric Digital Subscriber Line

Abbreviated ADSL. A high-speed data transmission technology originally developed by Bellcore and now standardized by ANSI as T1.413. ADSL delivers high bandwidth over existing twisted-pair copper telephone lines. Also called Asymmetric Digital Subscriber Loop.

ADSL supports speeds in the range of 1.5 to 9Mbps in the downstream direction (from the network to the subscriber) and supports upstream speeds in the range of 16 Kbps to 640 Kbps; hence, the term *asymmetric*.

See also Digital Subscriber Line; High-Bit-Rate Digital Subscriber Line; Rate-Adaptive

A

Digital Subscriber Line; Single-Line Digital Subscriber Line; Very-High-Bit-Rate Digital Subscriber Line.

Assymetric Digital Subscriber Loop
See Assymetric Digital Subscriber Line.

asynchronous communications *See* asynchronous transmission.

asynchronous communications server A LAN server that allows a network user to dial out of the network into the public switched telephone system or to access leased lines for asynchronous communications. Asynchronous communications servers may also be called dial-in/dial-out servers or modem servers.

Asynchronous Transfer Mode Abbreviated ATM. A method used for transmitting voice, video, and data over high-speed LANs and WANs. ATM uses continuous bursts of fixed-length packets called cells to transmit data. The basic packet consists of 53 bytes, 5 of which are used for control functions and 48 for data.

ATM is a connection-oriented protocol, and two kinds of connections are possible:

- Permanent virtual circuits (PVCs), in which connections are created manually

- Switched virtual circuits (SVCs), in which connections are made automatically

Speeds of up to 2.488Gbps have been achieved in testing. ATM will find wide acceptance in the LAN and WAN arenas as a solution to integrating disparate networks over large geographical distances. Also known as cell relay.

See also permanent virtual circuit; switched virtual circuit.

asynchronous transmission A method of data transmission that uses start bits and stop bits to coordinate the flow of data so that the time intervals between individual characters do not need to be equal. Parity also may be used to check the accuracy of the data received.

See also communications parameters; data bits; synchronous transmission.

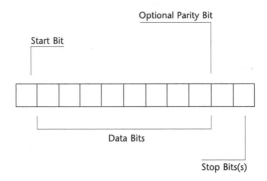

ASYNCHRONOUS TRANSMISSION

Optional Parity Bit

Start Bit

Data Bits

Stop Bits(s)

ATA   *See* Advanced Technology Attachment.

AT command set   A set of standard instructions used to activate features on a modem. Originally developed by Hayes Microcomputer Products, the AT command set is now used by almost all modem manufacturers.

See also modem.

ATM   *See* Asynchronous Transfer Mode.

at symbol   The separating character (@) between account name and domain name in an Internet e-mail address.

See also bang path.

AT&T   The parent company of Bell Laboratories, the original developers of Unix. For many years Bell Labs was one of the two major development centers for Unix (the other being the Computer Systems Research Group at the University of California at Berkeley), but in 1990, AT&T formed Unix Systems Laboratories, or USL, to continue the development of Unix. In 1993, USL was sold to Novell, and in 1995, Novell sold the rights to SCO (Santa Cruz Operation).

See also Baby Bells; Regional Bell Operating Companies.

attach   To establish a connection between a workstation and a network file server; particularly, to access additional servers after logging on to one server.

attachment   *See* enclosure.

Attachment Unit Interface   Abbreviated AUI. A 15-pin socket used by some Ethernet devices. AUI connections adapt between two different cabling types and work with a wide range of wiring schemes. Also known as a DIX (for Digital, Intel, Xerox) connector.

attack   An attempt to circumvent the security measures in place on a network either to gain unauthorized access to the system or to force a denial of service.

See also brute-force attack; dictionary attack; social engineering.

attenuation   The decrease in power of a signal with increasing distance. Attenuation is measured in decibels, and it increases as the power of the signal decreases. The best cables (those exhibiting the least attenuation) are fiber-optic lines, and the worst cables are unshielded, untwisted-pair lines, such as the silver, flat-satin cables used in short-run telephone and modem lines.

In a LAN, attenuation can become a problem when cable lengths exceed the stated network specification; however, the useful length of a cable may be extended by the use of a repeater.

attribute   **1.** A file attribute is a technique for describing access to and properties of files and directories within a file system. You may see the term *attribute* used interchangeably with the term *property*.

2. A screen attribute controls a character's background and foreground colors, as well as other characteristics, such as underlining, reverse video, and blinking or animation.

A

3. In operating systems, a characteristic that indicates whether a file is a read-only file, a hidden file, or a system file or has changed in some way since it was last backed up.

4. In markup languages such as HTML and SGML, a name-value pair within a tagged element that modifies certain characteristics of that element.

5. In a database record, the name or structure of a field.

See also tag.

AUDITCON   A Novell NetWare and IntranetWare workstation utility that creates a log file to allow an independent auditor to verify that network transactions are accurate and that confidential information is secure. When auditing is enabled, an auditor can track when files or directories are created, deleted, modified, salvaged, moved, or renamed. Changes to security rights can also be tracked.

audit trail   An automatic feature of certain programs or operating systems that creates a running record of all transactions. An audit trail allows you to track a piece of data from the moment it enters the system to the moment it leaves and to determine the origin of any changes to that data.

auditing   The process of scrutinizing network security-related events and transactions to ensure that they are accurate, particularly reviewing attempts to create, access, and delete files and directories and reviewing security violations. Records of these events are usually stored in a security log file, which can only be examined by users with special permissions.

AUI   *See* Attachment Unit Interface.

authentication   In a network operating system or multiuser system, the process that validates a user's logon information.

Authentication may involve comparing the user name and password to a list of authorized users. If a match is found, the user can log on and access the system in accordance with the rights or permissions assigned to his or her user account.

See also authorization; Kerberos; password; user; user account.

authoring   The process of preparing a multimedia presentation or a Web page. This involves not only writing the text of the presentation or Web page, but also the production of the slides, sound, video, and graphical components.

authorization   The provision of rights or permissions based on identity. Authorization and authentication go hand in hand in networking; your access to services is based on your identity, and the authentication processes confirm that you are who you say you are.

See also authentication.

auto-answer   A feature of a modem that allows it to answer incoming calls automatically.

See also answer mode; dialback modem.

auto-dial   A feature of a modem that allows it to open a telephone line and start a call. To auto-dial, the modem sends a series of pulses or tones that represent a stored telephone number.

See also callback modem.

AUTOEXEC.BAT   A contraction of Automatically Executed Batch. A special MS-DOS batch file, located in the root directory of the startup disk, that runs automatically every time you start or restart your computer. The commands contained in AUTOEXEC.BAT are executed one by one, just as if you typed them at the system prompt. An AUTOEXEC.BAT file can be used to load hardware device drivers, set the system prompt, change the default drive to the first network drive, and log the user in to the file server.

In OS/2, you can select any batch file to be used as AUTOEXEC.BAT for a specific MS-DOS session, so you can tailor specific environments for separate MS-DOS sessions, each using a different AUTOEXEC.BAT file.

See also AUTOEXEC.NCF; boot; bootstrap; CONFIG.SYS.

AUTOEXEC.NCF   A Novell NetWare batch file usually located on the NetWare partition of the server's hard disk, used to set the NetWare operating system configuration. AUTOEXEC.NCF loads the LAN drivers, the NLMs, and the settings for the network interface boards and then binds the protocols to the installed drivers.

Automatic Client Upgrade   A mechanism used to upgrade Novell client software during the logon process by executing four separate programs called by the logon

script. Automatic Client Upgrade can be very useful when all client workstations use standard configurations.

automatic forwarding   A feature of many e-mail programs that automatically retransmits incoming messages to another e-mail address.

automatic number identification   Abbreviated ANI. A method of passing a caller's telephone number over the network to the recipient so that the caller can be identified. ANI is often associated with ISDN and is sometimes known as caller ID.

automatic rollback   In a Novell NetWare network, a feature of the Transaction Tracking System (TTS) that abandons the current transaction and returns a database to its original condition if the network fails in the middle of a transaction. Automatic rollback prevents the database from being corrupted by information from incomplete transactions.

See also backing out.

AutoPlay   A feature of Microsoft Windows that automatically executes an application from a CD-ROM or automatically plays an audio CD when the disk is inserted into the CD-ROM drive.

Available Bit Rate   A Type 3 or Type 4 Asynchronous Transfer Mode Adaption Layer (AAL) service designed for non–time-critical applications such as LAN emulation and LAN internetworking.

See also Constant Bit Rate; Unspecified Bit Rate; Variable Bit Rate.

A

avatar **1.** In Unix, another name for the superuser account; an alternative to the name root. **2.** A visual representation of a user in a shared virtual-reality environment.

AWG *See* American Wire Gauge.

B

Baan Advanced Certification Abbreviated BAC. A certification from Baan available in four specialties covering the Baan IV suite of products: Enterprise Logistics, Enterprise Finance, Enterprise Tools, and Enterprise Modeler.

See also Baan Basic Certification.

Baan Basic Certification Abbreviated BBC. A certification from Baan designed to evaluate basic proficiency with the Baan IV suite of products; a prerequisite qualification to taking the Baan Advanced Certification exams.

See also Baan Advanced Certification.

Baan Company A leading provider of enterprise and inter-enterprise business software used for managing finance, manufacturing, inventory, distribution, transportation, and administrative functions for large companies.

For more information on Baan, see www2.baan.com.

Baby Bells A slang term for the 22 Regional Bell Operating Companies (RBOC), formed when AT&T was broken up in 1984.

See also Bell Labs.

BAC *See* Baan Advanced Certification.

backbone That portion of the network that manages the bulk of the traffic. The backbone may connect several locations or buildings, and other, smaller networks may be attached to it. The backbone often uses a higher-speed protocol than the individual LAN segments.

back-end processor A secondary processor that performs one specialized task very effectively, freeing the main processor for other, more important work.

back-end system The server part of a client/server system that runs on one or more file servers and provides services to the front-end applications running on networked workstations. The back-end system accepts query requests sent from a front-end application, processes those requests, and returns the results to the workstation.

Back-end systems may be PC-based servers, superservers, midrange systems, or mainframes.

See also client/server architecture.

33

BACKBONE

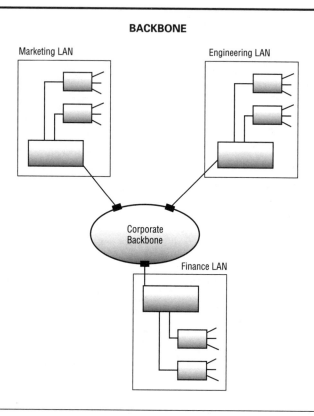

background **1.** On a computer screen, the color on which characters are displayed; for example, white characters may appear on a blue background.

2. In an operating system, a process that runs in the background generally runs at a lower level of priority than a foreground task and does not accept input from the user. Only multitasking operating systems support true background and foreground processing, but some applications can mimic it. For example, many word processors can print a document while still accepting input from the keyboard. In older systems, a process spends its entire existence in either the background or the foreground; in newer systems, you can change the processing environment and move foreground programs into the background, and vice versa.

See also ampersand; foreground; multitasking.

background authentication The process used to give a workstation access to a particular server. For example, in Novell

NetWare, password authentication uses a public key encryption scheme to protect password information before it is transmitted over the network. All this activity takes place in the background, and all the user has to do is enter his or her password.

background noise   Any unwanted signal that enters a line, channel, or circuit; for example, electrical interference on a telephone circuit.

See also noise.

backing out   The process of abandoning the current transaction and returning a database to its original condition if the network fails during the transaction. This process prevents the database from being corrupted by information from the incomplete transaction.

See also automatic rollback; Transaction Tracking System.

backlink   In Novell Directory Services, an attribute used by a directory to indicate the external references to a property.

backslash   **1.** In MS-DOS, OS/2, and other operating systems, you must use the backslash character (\) to separate directory or subdirectory names in a path statement or when changing to another directory.

2. A shorthand name for the root directory.

Sometimes called the reverse slash or backslant.

See also slash.

backup   An up-to-date copy of all your files. You make a backup for several reasons:

- Insurance against possible hard-disk or file-server failure. Hard disks often fail completely, taking all your work with them. If this failure occurs, you can reload your files and directories from the backup copy. A backup is your insurance against disk failure affecting the thousands or possibly tens of thousands of files you might have on your file server.

- Protection against accidental deletion of files or directories. Again, if you mistakenly delete a file or directory, you can retrieve a copy from your last backup.

- Protection against the new version of software you are about to install not working to your expectations; make a backup before installing new software.

- As an archive at the end of a project, when a person leaves your company, or at the end of a financial period such as year-end close.

Your decision when or how often to make a backup depends on how frequently important data on your system changes. If you rely on certain files always being available on your system, it is crucial that you make regular, consistent backups. Here are some backup tips:

- Keep multiple copies; redundancy should be a part of your backup plan.

- Test your backups to make sure they are what you think they are before you bring

B

the server into service, and make sure you can reload the information you need.

- Store your backups in a secure off-site location; do not leave them right next to the computer (if the computer is damaged by an accident, the backup may be damaged as well).

- Replace your backup media on a regular basis.

- Consider making incremental backups of critical data at more frequent intervals.

It all comes down to one very simple rule: back up all the files that you cannot afford to lose. Do it now.

See also archive; differential backup; disk duplexing; disk mirroring; full backup; incremental backup.

backup domain controller In Microsoft Windows NT, a server containing accurate replications of the security and user databases.

The backup domain controller receives a copy of the domain's directory database, containing all the account and security information for the domain, from the primary domain controller. This copy is periodically synchronized with the original master database. A domain can contain several backup domain controllers.

See also domain controller; primary domain controller.

backup program An application that you use to make archive or backup copies of important data files.

Most operating systems offer commands for making backups, but many are limited

in capability. The most cost-effective backup programs are from third-party vendors.

See also disk duplexing; disk mirroring; full backup; incremental backup; tape cartridge; tape drive.

backward compatibility Full compatibility with earlier versions of the same application or computer system.

Backward Error Correction Abbreviated BEC. An error-correction method in which an error can be detected by the recipient, which immediately requests a retransmission of the affected data.

See also error detection and correction.

BACP *See* Bandwidth Allocation Control Protocol.

bad sector An area on a hard disk or floppy disk that cannot be used to store data because of a manufacturing defect or accidental damage.

The operating system will find, mark, and isolate bad sectors. Almost all hard disks have some bad sectors, often listed in the bad track table. Usually, bad sectors are a result of the manufacturing process and not a concern; the operating system will mark them as bad, and you will never even know they are there.

bad track table A list of the defective areas on a hard disk, usually determined during final testing of the disk at the factory. Some disk-preparation programs ask you to enter information from this list to reduce the time that a low-level format takes to prepare the disk for use by the operating system.

balun   A contraction of *balanced unbalanced*. A small device used to connect a balanced line (such as a twisted-pair cable) to an unbalanced line (such as a coaxial cable). The balun matches impedances between the two media.

bandwidth   **1.** In communications, the difference between the highest and lowest frequencies available for transmission in any given range.

2. In networking, the transmission capacity of a computer or a communications channel, stated in megabits per second (Mbps). For example, FDDI (Fiber Distributed Data Interface) has a bandwidth of 100Mbps. To relate this to a real-world example, a complete page of text, in English, is approximately 16,000 bits.

Bandwidth Allocation Control Protocol   Abbreviated BACP. A proposed Internet protocol designed to manage a combination of dial-up links, usually over ISDN connections.

BACP provides bandwidth on demand and can combine two or more circuits into a single circuit with a higher data rate.

See also bandwidth on demand.

bandwidth on demand   A technique that allows the user to add additional bandwidth as the application requires it.

Most network traffic does not flow in steady and easily predictable streams, but in short bursts, separated by longer periods of inactivity. This pattern makes it difficult to predict peak loads. Bandwidth on demand is useful for applications such as backups and videoconferencing and allows the user to pay for only the amount of bandwidth used.

See also virtual data network.

bandwidth reservation   A technique used to reserve channel capacity for special time-sensitive transmissions such as videoconferencing and real-time audio transmissions.

bandwidth throttling   A feature in some Web server software that allows the system administrator to control or alter the proportions of bandwidth available to the services that the server provides.

bang   A name given in the Unix and Internet worlds to the exclamation point (!) character; also known as *pling* in the United Kingdom.

See also bang path.

bang path   An old-style uucp e-mail address that uses exclamation points to separate the sequence of computer names needed to get to the addressee.

Bang paths list addresses—general to specific—from left to right, which is the reverse of the sequence used by other addressing schemes.

See also at symbol; domain name; e-mail address; uucp.

Banyan Systems, Inc.   A leading provider of enterprise network products, including the Banyan VINES network operating system, products based on the Banyan StreetTalk Directory, and Beyond-Mail messaging technologies.

B

For more information on Banyan, see www.banyan.com.

Banyan VINES   A network operating system from Banyan Systems. VINES (a contraction of Virtual Networking Software) is based on a special version of the Unix System V operating system.

The following illustration shows the internal organization of VINES. The Unix layer is hidden from view by VINES and is not available for other applications. VINES provides all server functions, including those of a communications/modem server, and offers many options for connecting to minicomputers, mainframes, and other network file servers. VINES automatically manages protocol binding and translations required between the network interface cards for routing to different LAN segments. A complete set of network management tools is also available.

Workstations can run MS-DOS, Microsoft Windows, Unix, or OS/2, and they can store native-form files on the server. Macintosh computers can also attach to the network. VINES offers special support for very large LANs and WANs with multiple file servers. VINES also allows PCs that support multiple processors to use multiprocessing to divide the file-server processing load.

See also Enterprise Network Services; StreetTalk.

base 10 radix   *See* decimal.

base64   An encoding scheme used by MIME-compliant mail systems to convert binary files into a text format that can be processed and sent as e-mail.
See also binary file; Multipurpose Internet Mail Extension.

baseband modem   *See* line driver.

baseband network   A technique for transmitting signals as direct-current pulses rather than as modulated signals. The entire bandwidth of the transmission medium is used by a single digital signal, so computers in a baseband network can transmit only when the channel is not busy. However, the network can use techniques such as multiplexing to allow channel sharing.

A baseband network can operate over relatively short distances (up to 2 miles if network traffic is light) at speeds from 50Kbps to 100Mbps. Ethernet, AppleTalk, and most PC local-area networks (LANs) use baseband techniques.

See also bandwidth; broadband network; frequency-division multiplexing; statistical multiplexing; time-division multiplexing.

baseline   The process of determining and documenting network throughput and other performance information when the network is operating under what is considered a normal load. Measured performance characteristics might include error-rate and data-transfer information, along with information about the most active users and their applications.

Basic Rate ISDN

BANYAN VINES

Layer 7: application layer	VINES File Service	VINES Applications Services
Layer 6: presentation layer	VINES Remote Procedure Calls (RPC)	Servers Message Block (SMB)
Layer 5: session layer	Socket Interface	
Layer 4: transport layer	VINES Interprocess Communications Protocol (VICP) / VINES Sequenced Packet Protocol (VSPP)	Transmission Control Protocol (TCP) / User Datagram Protocol (UDP)
Layer 3: network layer	VINES Internet Protocol (VIP) / Internet Protocol (IP)	X.25
Layer 2: data-link layer	Network Driver Interface Specification (NDIS)	X.25 HDLC
Layer 1: physical layer	network interface card and cabling	

B

Bash   In Unix, a popular command interpreter. Bash, the Bourne-Again Shell, was first released in 1989 by Brian Fox and Chet Ramey, as part of the Free Software Foundation GNU Project.

Bash provides features found in the other Unix shells, particularly the Bourne shell, the C shell, and the Korn shell, and includes Bourne shell syntax, redirection and quoting, C-shell command-line editing and tilde expansion, job control, and command history. Bash also includes built-in commands and variables, as well as aliases from the Korn shell.

See also Bourne shell; C shell; Korn shell; Linux; Unix shell.

Basic Rate ISDN   Abbreviated BRI. An ISDN service that offers two 64Kbps B channels used for data transfer and one 16Kbps D channel used for signaling and control information.

Each B channel can carry a single digital voice call or can be used as a data channel; the B channels can also be combined into a single 128Kbps data channel.

See also 23B+D; 2B+D; Primary Rate ISDN.

39

BASIC RATE ISDN

64Kbps B channel (voice/data)

64Kbps B channel (voice/data)

15Kbps D channel (signaling)

bastion host   A computer system that acts as the main connection to the Internet for users of a LAN. A bastion host is usually configured in such a way as to minimize the risk of intruders gaining access to the main LAN. It gets its name from the fortified projections on the outer walls of medieval European castles.

See also firewall; proxy server.

batch file   An ASCII file that contains operating system commands and other commands supported by the batch processor. Batch files are used to automate repetitive tasks. The commands in the file are executed one line at a time, just as if you had typed them at the system prompt.

baud   A measurement of data-transmission speed. Originally used in measuring the speed of telegraph equipment, it now usually refers to the data-transmission speed of a modem or other serial device.

See also baud rate.

baud rate   In communications equipment, a measurement of the number of state changes (from 0 to 1 or vice versa) per sec-

ond on an asynchronous communications channel.

Baud rate is often assumed to correspond to the number of bits transmitted per second, but baud rate and bits per second (bps) are not always the same. In high-speed digital communications systems, one state change can be made to represent more than one data bit.

See also baud; bits per second.

Bay Networks Certified Expert   A certification from Bay Networks, Inc., designed to recognize technical expertise in constructing enterprise-wide networking solutions. Currently, this certification is available in Router, Hub, and Network Management technologies.

Bay Networks Certified Specialist   A certification from Bay Networks, Inc., designed to evaluate a basic level of technical expertise in one or more Bay Networks product areas. Currently, this certification is available in Router, Hub, Network Management, Remote Access, and Switching technologies.

B

Bay Networks, Inc. A leading manufacturer of networking products such as hubs, routers, and switches, now venturing into the areas of network management and virtual private networks. In 1998, the company announced a merger with Northern Telecom.

For more information on Bay Networks, see www.baynetworks.com.

BBC *See* Baan Basic Certification.

BBS *See* bulletin board system.

bcc *See* blind carbon copy.

BCD *See* binary coded decimal.

beaconing In a token-ring network, the process of informing other nodes that token passing has been suspended because of a severe error condition, such as a broken cable. Communication cannot resume until the condition is resolved.

BEC *See* Backward Error Correction.

Bell communications standards A set of data-transmission standards developed by AT&T in the 1980s that rapidly became the de facto standard for modem manufacturers. Although several of these standards are still widely used in the United States, the CCITT V series definitions are now generally accepted as the defining standards for modem use, data compression, and associated hardware.

Bell Labs The research arm of AT&T and the birthplace of the Unix operating system and the C programming language in the 1970s.

See also Berkeley Software Distribution Unix; Computer Systems Research Group.

benchmark A specific standard against which some aspect of computer performance can be compared.

A benchmark is a test that attempts to quantify hardware, software, or system performance—usually in terms of speed, reliability, or accuracy. One of the major problems in determining performance is deciding which of the many benchmarks available actually reflects the way you intend to use the system.

See also benchmark program.

benchmark program A program that attempts to provide a consistent measurement of system performance. Here are some examples:

- Dhrystone, which measures microprocessor and memory performance

- Whetstone, which measures speed of arithmetic operations

- Khornerstone, which measures overall system performance, including disk-drive access speed, memory access speed, and processor performance

The Systems Performance Evaluation Cooperative (SPEC) developed a set of ten tests to measure performance in actual application environments. The results of these tests are known as SPECmarks.

BER *See* bit error rate; error rate.

Berkeley Software Distribution Unix
Abbreviated BSD Unix, and also known as
Berkeley Unix. BSD Unix was developed at
the University of California at Berkeley by
researchers working in the Computer Systems Research Group (CSRG) from the
1970s to 1993 when the group finally
closed its doors. BSD added many significant advanced features to Unix, including
the C shell, the vi editor, TCP/IP networking additions, and virtual memory.

Because the CSRG was an academic group
producing state-of-the-art software with no
support obligations, BSD Unix was not supported in the normal way; bug fixes were
sometimes made available, but it was a hit-
and-miss process at best. For this reason,
BSD Unix appealed to the research community and scientific users rather than to commercial users who tended to use Unix from
AT&T.

BSD Unix 4.1 through to the last release,
version 4.4, and the related commercial
products, including those from Sun Microsystems, DEC, and Mt Xinu, are still
popular and in use in universities and commercial institutions all over the world.

See also FreeBSD; Linux; NetBSD; Unix.

Berkeley Unix   *See* Berkeley Software
Distribution Unix.

beta site   A location where beta testing is
performed before a hardware or software
product is formally released for commercial
distribution.

See also beta software; beta testing.

beta software   Software that has been
released to a cross-section of typical users

for testing before the commercial release of
the package.

See also beta testing.

beta testing   The process of field testing
new hardware or software products before
the product's commercial or formal release.
Beta testing is usually done by a cross-section of users, not just programmers. The
purpose of beta testing is to expose the new
product to as many real-life operating conditions as possible.

If the beta tests indicate a higher-than-
expected number of bugs, the developer
usually fixes the problems and sends the
product out again for another round of beta
testing. Preliminary versions of the product
documentation are also circulated for review during the beta testing.

See also alpha testing.

BGP   *See* Border Gateway Protocol.

Big Blue   A nickname for International
Business Machine Corporation (IBM),
which uses blue as its corporate color.

big endian   A computer architecture in
which the most significant byte has the lowest address and so is stored big end first.

Many processors, including those from
Motorola and Sun, certain RISC processors, the PDP-11, and the IBM 3270 series
are all big endian. The term comes from
Jonathan Swift's *Gulliver's Travels,* in
which wars were fought over whether
boiled eggs should be opened at the big end
or the little end.

See also holy wars; little endian.

binaries   A slang term for a group of binary files.

binary   Any scheme that uses two different states, components, conditions, or conclusions.

In mathematics, the binary or base-2 numbering system uses combinations of the digits 0 and 1 to represent all values. The more familiar decimal system has a base of 10 (0–9).

Unlike computers, people find binary numbers that consist of long strings of zeros and ones difficult to read, so most programmers use hexadecimal (base-16) or octal (base-8) numbers instead.

Binary also refers to an executable file containing a program.

binary coded decimal   Abbreviated BCD. A simple system for converting decimal numbers into binary form, in which each decimal digit is converted into binary and then stored as a single character.

binary file   A file consisting of binary information. Usually, a binary file is a program or data file in machine-readable form rather than in human-readable ASCII text. You can convert a binary file into a text-based form so that you can transmit it over the Internet.

See also base64; Multipurpose Internet Mail Extension.

binary license   A license granted to a user by a software developer, entitling the user to run a specific software package under well-defined circumstances, using the binary files provided by the developer.

A binary license does not entitle the user to a copy of the source code for the package, although a certain level of configuration can be done, and the user does not have the right to modify the software in any way beyond this simple configuration.

See also open source software; source license.

BIND   **1.** A Novell NetWare server utility used to bind a protocol to a network interface card or device driver.

2. Abbreviation for Berkeley Internet Name Domain, a BSD client/server program that manages host and IP addresses by matching the host name with the IP dotted decimal address.

See also Domain Name Service; dotted decimal.

bindery   A database maintained by older Novell NetWare network operating systems. The bindery contains information about users, servers, and other important network configuration details in a flat database. The bindery is crucial to NetWare's operation and is constantly consulted by the operating system.

In NetWare 4.*x* and later systems, the bindery is replaced by NetWare Directory Services (NDS).

See also NetWare Directory Services.

bindery emulation   A NetWare 4.*x* and later feature that allows bindery-based utilities to work with NetWare Directory Services (NDS) on the same network. Bindery

B

emulation applies only to leaf objects within the Organizational container object.

See also container object; leaf object; NetWare Directory Services.

Bindery object   A leaf object that represents an object placed in the Directory tree by an upgrade utility, but that cannot be further identified by NetWare Directory Services (NDS). The Bindery object is available for the purposes of backward compatibility with older, bindery-based utilities and applications.

See also leaf object; NetWare Directory Services.

bindery services   *See* bindery emulation.

binding   The process of establishing communications between the protocol device driver and the network interface card driver.

BIOS   Acronym for basic input/output system, pronounced "bye-os." In the PC, the BIOS is a set of instructions that tests the hardware when the computer is first turned on, starts to load the operating system, and lets the computer's hardware and operating system communicate with applications and peripheral devices, such as hard disks, printers, and video adapters. These instructions are stored in ROM as a permanent part of the computer.

As new hardware is developed, new BIOS routines must be created to service those devices. For example, BIOS support has been added for power management and for ever-larger hard disks. If you are experiencing problems accessing such devices after add-ing them to an existing system, your computer's BIOS may be out of date. Contact your computer supplier for information about BIOS updates.

bis   A term describing a secondary CCITT (Consultative Committee for International Telephony and Telegraphy) recommendation that is an alternative or extension to the primary recommendation. For example, the CCITT V.42 standard refers to error correction, and the V.42 bis standard refers to data compression.

See also ter.

B-ISDN   *See* Broadband Integrated Services Digital Network.

bisynchronous communications   A protocol used extensively in mainframe computer networks. With bisynchronous communications, both the sending and receiving devices must be synchronized before data transmission begins.

Data is collected into a package known as a *frame*. Each frame contains leading and trailing characters that allow the computers to synchronize their clocks. The structure of a bisynchronous communications frame is shown in the accompanying illustration. The STX and ETX control characters mark the beginning and end of the message. BCC is a set of characters used to verify the accuracy of the transmission.

A more modern form of this kind of protocol is SDLC (Synchronous Data Link Control), which is used in IBM's proprietary networking scheme, SNA.

See also asynchronous transmission; Synchronous Data Link Control.

BISYNCHRONOUS COMMUNICATIONS

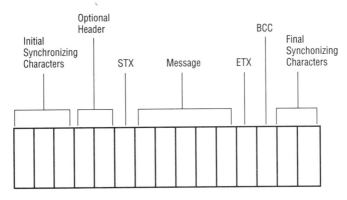

bit Contraction of binary digit. A bit is the basic unit of information in the binary numbering system, representing either 0 (off) or 1 (on). Bits can be grouped to form larger storage units; the most common grouping is the 7- or 8-bit byte.

See also octet.

bit error rate Abbreviated BRI. The number of erroneous bits in a data transmission or in a data transfer, such as from CD-ROM to memory.

bit-oriented protocol A communications protocol in which data is transmitted as a stream of bits rather than as a stream of bytes.

A bit-oriented protocol uses specific sequences of bits as control codes, unlike a byte-oriented protocol, which uses reserved characters. HDLC (High-level Data Link Control) and IBM's SDLC (Synchronous Data Link Control) are both bit-oriented protocols.

See also byte-oriented protocol.

bit rate The rate at which bits are transmitted over a communications channel, described in terms of bits per second (bps).

See also baud rate.

bits per inch Abbreviated bpi. The number of bits that a tape or tape cartridge can store per inch of length.

bits per second Abbreviated bps. The number of binary digits, or bits, transmitted every second during a data-transfer procedure. Bits per second is a measurement of the speed of operation of equipment, such as a computer's data bus or a modem that connects a computer to a communications circuit.

bit stuffing A technique used to ensure that a specific bit pattern never occurs in the data transmitted over a communications channel. Additional bits are added at the transmitting end and removed at the receiving end of the channel as the data is processed.

blackout A total loss of commercial electric power. To avoid loss of computer data due to a blackout, use a battery-backed UPS (uninterruptible power supply).

See also brownout; power conditioning.

blind carbon copy Abbreviated bcc. A list of recipients of an e-mail message whose names do not appear in the normal message header, so the original recipient of the message does not know that copies have been forwarded to other locations. Sometimes called blind courtesy copy.

block In communications, a unit of transmitted information that includes header codes (such as addresses), data, and error-checking codes.

See also checksum; error; error detection and correction.

blocks Sections of a tape or disk that are read or written at the same time; units of storage that are transferred as single units.

block size The largest contiguous amount of disk space allocated by the file system. Files larger than the file system's block size may be broken into smaller fragments when they are stored, with sections of the file being stored in different locations across the disk. This is known as *fragmentation* and, in some cases when

taken to an extreme, can severely limit system performance.

The file system's block size is often different from the hard disk's physical block size.

See also fragmentation.

block suballocation A mechanism used in Novell NetWare that allows files to share the same block space by dividing each 8K hard-disk block into smaller 512-byte segments. Files needing extra space can use these smaller segments rather than wasting a whole new disk block, making for more efficient disk-space use.

blue screen of death Abbreviated BSOD. An affectionate name for the screen displayed when Microsoft Windows encounters an error so serious that the operating system cannot continue to run. Windows may also display information about the failure and may perform a memory dump and an automatic system restart.

BNC connector A small connector with a half-turn locking shell for coaxial cable, used with thin Ethernet and RG-62 cabling. The accompanying illustration shows both male and female connectors.

BNCE *See* Bay Networks Certified Expert.

BNCS *See* Bay Networks Certified Specialist.

bookmark 1. In the Microsoft Windows NT Performance Monitor, a feature that allows you to mark a point of interest in a log file and then return to that same point in the file at a later time.

2. An option available in a Web browser that lets you mark a Web page so that you can identify and return to a favorite site quickly and easily without having to retype the URL or even remember how you got there.

Boolean   Any variable that can have a logical value of true or false. Named after George Boole, the developer of a branch of algebra based on the values of true and false, Boolean works with logical rather than numeric relationships.

Boolean operators include AND (logical conjunction), OR (logical inclusion), XOR (exclusive or), and NOT (logical negation) and are sometimes described as logical operators.

Many popular Internet search engines allow Boolean searches.

See also search engine.

boot   To load an operating system into memory, usually from a hard disk, although occasionally from a floppy disk. Booting is generally an automatic procedure that begins when you turn on or reset your computer. A set of instructions contained in ROM begins executing. The instructions run a series of power-on self tests (POSTs) to check that devices such as hard disks are in working order, locate and load the operating system, and finally pass control over to that operating system.

Boot may be derived from the expression "pulling yourself up by your own bootstraps" and is sometimes called bootstrap.

See also BIOS; cold boot; warm boot.

bootable disk   Any disk capable of loading and starting the operating system. Bootable floppy disks are becoming less common because operating systems are growing larger. In some cases, all the files needed to start the operating system will not fit on even the largest-capacity floppy disk, which makes it impossible to boot from a floppy disk.

B

BNC CONNECTOR

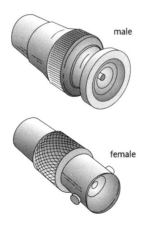

male

female

BOOTCONF.SYS   A Novell NetWare configuration file that specifies how a diskless workstation boots the operating system from the file server. If the file server contains several remote boot image files, BOOTCONF.SYS determines which one will be loaded onto the workstation.

See also diskless workstation.

BOOTP   *See* Bootstrap Protocol.

boot ROM   A type of ROM that allows a workstation to communicate with the network file server and to read an image file containing an operating system program. In this way, a workstation without a local disk can boot the operating system from the file server.

See also diskless workstation.

boot sector virus   A virus that infects the master boot record of a computer by overwriting the original boot code with infected boot code. This kind of virus is usually spread to a hard disk from an infected floppy disk being used as a boot disk.

See also antivirus program; file-infecting virus; macro virus; multipart virus; polymorphic virus; stealth virus; Trojan Horse; vaccine; virus.

bootstrap   *See* boot.

Bootstrap Protocol   Abbreviated BOOTP. An Internet protocol that provides network configuration information to a diskless workstation.

When the workstation first boots, it sends out a BOOTP message on the network. This message is received by the server, which obtains the appropriate configuration information and returns that information to the workstation. This information includes the workstation's IP address, the IP address of the server, the host name of the server, and the IP address of a default router.

See also Dynamic Host Configuration Protocol.

border   A security perimeter formed by logical boundaries that can only be crossed at specifically defined locations known as border gateways.

See also border gateway.

border gateway   A router that connects a private LAN to the Internet. A border gateway is a security checkpoint used to force all network traffic, either inbound or outbound, through a single point of control.

See also border; firewall; Novell Border-Manager; router.

Border Gateway Protocol   Abbreviated BGP. A routing protocol designed to replace EGP (External Gateway Protocol) and interconnect organizational networks. BGP, unlike EGP, evaluates each of the possible routes for the best one.

Borland International, Inc.   *See* Inprise Corporation.

bot   *See* robot.

bounce   The return of an e-mail message to its original sender due to an error in delivery. You may have made a simple spelling mistake in the e-mail address, the recipient's computer system may be down, or the recipient may no longer subscribe to or have an account on the system. A returned e-mail message will usually contain a description of why the message bounced.

Bourne shell In Unix, a popular command interpreter with a built-in programming language.

The Bourne shell, developed by Dr. Steven Bourne of Bell Labs, is the oldest Unix shell still in popular use and features a built-in command set for writing shell scripts, background execution of commands, input and output redirection, job control, and a set of shell variables to allow environment customization.

See also Bash; C shell; Korn shell; Linux; Unix shell.

bpi *See* bits per inch.

bps *See* bits per second.

brain damaged An expression used to describe any poorly designed program or piece of hardware that does not include those features most users would consider essential. The implication is that the designer should have known better than to leave those features out of the product.

breach A loss of network security as a result of a successful attack.

See also brute-force attack; dictionary attack; social engineering.

breakout box A small device that can be connected into a multicore cable for testing the signals in a transmission. Small LEDs in the breakout box indicate when a signal is transmitted over one of the lines. Switches or short jumper cables can be used to reroute these signals to other pins as required for troubleshooting.

See also sniffer.

BRI *See* Basic Rate ISDN.

bridge A hardware device used to connect LANs so that they can exchange data. Bridges can work with networks that use different wiring or network protocols, joining two or more LAN segments to form what appears to be a single network.

A bridge operates at the data-link layer of the OSI Reference Model for computer-to-computer communications. It manages the flow of traffic between the two LANs by reading the address of every packet of data that it receives.

See also brouter; gateway; OSI Reference Model; router.

BrightWorks A package of network management utilities from McAfee Associates that includes hardware and software inventory, application metering, remote control of clients, virus detection, and a help-desk utility.

B

BRIDGE

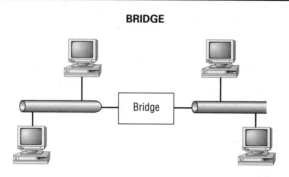

Broadband Integrated Services Digital Network Abbreviated B-ISDN. A high-speed communications standard for WANs that handles high-bandwidth applications, such as video, voice, data, and graphics.

SMDS (Switched Multimegabit Data Services) and ATM (Asynchronous Transfer Mode) are two BISDN services that can provide a huge bandwidth.

See also Asynchronous Transfer Mode; SONET; Switched Multimegabit Data Services.

broadband network A technique for transmitting a large amount of information, including voice, data, and video, over long distances using the same communications channel. Sometimes called wideband transmission, it is based on the same technology used by cable television.

The transmission capacity is divided into several distinct channels that can be used concurrently by different networks, normally by frequency-division multiplexing (FDM). The individual channels are protected from each other by guard channels of unused frequencies. A broadband network can operate at speeds of up to 20Mbps.

See also baseband network; multiplexer.

BROADBAND INTEGRATED SERVICES DIGITAL NETWORK

B

BROADBAND NETWORK

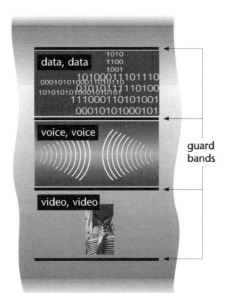

data, data
1010
1100
1001
00010101000110101110
101010101000101
01010111110100
111000110101001
00010101000101

voice, voice

guard
bands

video, video

---

broadcast   To send a message to all users currently logged in to the network.

See also multicast.

broadcast storm   Congestion on a network that occurs when a large number of frames are transmitted by many workstations in response to a transmission from one workstation.

broker   A Novell Distributed Print Services (NDPS) service providing management services for network printers, including event notification and storage of printer resources such as device drivers.

brouter   A networking device that combines the attributes of a bridge and a router. A brouter can route one or more specific protocols, such as TCP/IP, and bridge all others, for example, and can operate at either the data-link layer or the network layer of the OSI Reference Model.

See also gateway.

brownout   A short period of low voltage, often the result of an unusually heavy demand for power, that may cause your computer to crash. If your area experiences frequent brownouts, consider using a

UPS (uninterruptible power supply) as a battery backup system.

browse list   A list of computers and services available on a network.

browser   **1.** An application program used to explore Internet resources. A browser lets you wander from Web site to Web site without concern for the technical details of the links between them or the specific methods used to access them and presents the information—text, graphics, sound, or video—as a document on the screen.

2. A small application used to scan a database or a list of files.

3. In Windows NT networking, a mechanism used as a name service.

See also Web browser; World Wide Web.

brute-force attack   A technique employed by intruders that checks every password in a password file against every possible password generated sequentially. A brute-force attack is very clumsy, is usually considered the last resort in an attack, takes a long time to run, and is easily detected by even the most modest security precautions. Also called a keyspace attack.

See also denial of service attack; dictionary attack; social engineering; Trojan Horse.

BSD Unix   *See* Berkeley Software Distribution Unix.

BSOD   *See* blue screen of death.

buffer   An area of memory set aside for temporary storage of data. Often, the data remains in the buffer until some external event finishes. A buffer can compensate for the differences in transmission or processing speed between two devices or between a computer and a peripheral device, such as a printer.

Buffers are implemented in a variety of ways, including first-in-first-out (FIFO) used for pipes and last-in-last-out used for stacks and circular buffers such as event logs.

See also pipe.

buffered repeater   Any device that amplifies and retransmits a signal so that it can travel greater distances. A buffered repeater can also control the flow of information to prevent collisions.

See also repeater.

bug   A logical or programming error in hardware or software that causes a malfunction of some sort. If the problem is in software, it can be fixed by changes to the program. If the fault is in hardware, new circuits must be designed and constructed. Some bugs are fatal and may cause a program to stop responding or cause data loss, others are just annoying, and many are not even noticeable. The term apparently originates from the days of the first electromechanical computers, when a problem was traced to a moth caught between two contacts inside the machinery.

See also bug fix.

bug fix   A release of hardware or software that corrects known bugs but does not contain new features. Such releases are usually designated by an increase in the decimal portion of the revision number; for example, the revision level may advance from 2.0 to 2.01 or 2.1, rather than from 2.0 to 3.0.

built-in groups   The default groups provided with some operating systems that define a collection of rights and permissions for members. Using built-in groups is an easy way of providing access to commonly used network resources.

bulletin board system   Abbreviated BBS. A computer system equipped with one or more modems, serving as a message-passing system or centralized information source, usually for a particular special interest group. Bulletin board systems were often established by software vendors and by PC user groups in the past, but have been replaced in recent times by Web sites.

bundled software   Programs combined into a single package sold for a single price. Sales aimed at a specific target, such as the medical profession, usually bundle hardware with application-specific software suited to that profession.

See also unbundled software.

burned-in address   The hardware address on a network interface card (NIC). This address is assigned by the manufacturer of the interface card, which ensures that every card has a unique address.

See also hardware address.

burst mode   A method of data transmission in which information is collected and then sent in one single high-speed transmission, rather than one packet or character at a time.

Systems that use multiplexers to serve several channels often use burst mode to service each channel in turn. Much LAN traffic can be considered burst mode transmission: long periods of inactivity punctuated by short bursts of intense activity. In Novell NetWare, burst mode is known as packet burst.

bus   An electronic pathway along which signals are sent from one part of a computer to another. A PC contains several buses, each used for a different purpose:

- The address bus allocates memory addresses.
- The data bus carries data between the processor and memory.
- The control bus carries signals from the control unit.

See also architecture; Extended Industry Standard Architecture; Industry Standard Architecture; local bus; Microchannel Architecture; Peripheral Component Interconnect local bus.

bus mastering   A technique that allows certain advanced bus architectures to delegate control of data transfers between the CPU and associated peripheral devices to an add-in board. This technique gives network interface cards (NICs) greater system bus access and higher data-transfer speeds.

In the PC, bus mastering is supported by all the common architectures except for the older Industry Standard Architecture.

See also Extended Industry Standard Architecture; Industry Standard Architecture; local bus; MicroChannel Architecture; Peripheral Component Interconnect local bus.

bus network   In networking, a topology that allows all network nodes to receive the same message through the network cable at the same time.

See also ring network; star network; token-ring network.

byte   Contraction of binary digit eight. A group of bits. In computer storage terms, a byte usually holds a single character, such as a number, letter, or symbol. A byte usually contains 8 bits, but on some older systems, a byte may only have 7 bits or may have as many as 11.

Because bytes represent a very small amount of storage, they are usually grouped into kilobytes (1,024 bytes), megabytes (1,048,576 bytes), and gigabytes (1,073,741,824 bytes) for convenience when describing hard-disk capacity or computer memory size.

See also octet.

bytecode   An intermediate form of computer code produced by Java and other programming languages.

Most language compilers create code that is ready to run on a specific kind of processor. Java creates the bytecode in an abstract, processor-independent form, which requires further processing before it can actually execute on a computer. When a byte-code file is downloaded into your computer from a Web page, it provides 70 to 80 percent of the data needed to run the Java applet; the other 20 to 30 percent is provided by the Java run-time environment, which tells the applet how to perform on the target computer system.

See also Java; Java applet; just-in-time compiler; sandbox.

byte-oriented protocol   A communications protocol in which data is transmitted as a series of bytes, or characters. In order to distinguish the data from the control information, the protocol uses control characters that have a special meaning for the transmitting and receiving stations. Most of the common asynchronous communications protocols used in conjunction with modems are byte-oriented protocols.

See also bit-oriented protocol.

BUS NETWORK

C

C2 One of a series of seven levels of computer security defined by the National Security Agency.

C2-level security requires that users are logged in and tracked during their session, that all resources have owners, that objects such as files be protected from processes that might damage them, that events can be audited, and that the system has adequate protection against intrusion.

C2 security applies to a stand-alone system, so in theory a networked computer cannot be C2-compliant; following the guidelines can certainly help you to set up a more secure system.

CA *See* certificate authority.

cable modem A modem that sends and receives signals through a coaxial cable connected to a cable-television system, rather than through conventional telephone lines.

Cable modems, with speeds of up to 500Kbps, are faster than current conventional modems, but are subject to performance changes as system load increases. Theoretical data rates are much higher than those achieved with conventional modems; downstream rates of up to 36Mbps are possible, with 3Mbps to 10Mbps likely, and upstream rates up to 10Mbps.

Cabletron Systems A leading producer of Internet and intranet hardware and management solutions, Cabletron is also moving into Gigabit Ethernet and data, voice, and video systems.

For more information about Cabletron, see `www.cabletron.com`.

cabling standards National cabling standards, concerned with the performance of cables and connectors under conditions of actual use, are specified by the National Electric Code, American National Standards Institute, and Underwriters Laboratories. Other standards have been specified by the Electronics Industry Association/Telecommunications Industries Association (EIA/TIA). Standards include:

- ANSI/EIA/TIA-568-1991 Commercial Building Telecommunications Wiring.

- EIA/TIA TSB-36 Additional Cable Specifications for UTP Cables. 1991.

- EIA/TIA TSB-40 Telecommunications Systems Bulletin—Additional Transmission Specifications for UTP Connecting Hardware. 1992.

- ANSI/EIA/TIA-568A 1995 revises the original 568 document and adds material from TSB-36 and TSB-40.

- ANSI/EIA/TIA-569-1990 Commercial Building Standard for Telecommunications Pathways and Spaces.

- ANSI/EIA/TIA-570-1991 Residential and Light Commercial Telecommunications Wiring Standard.

- ANSI/EIA/TIA-606-1993 Administration Standard for the Telecommunications Infrastructure of Commercial Buildings.

- ANSI/EIA/TIA-607-1994 Commercial Building Grounding and Bonding Requirements for Telecommunications.

Local codes and standards may impose additional requirements.

Underwriters Laboratories (UL) tests cable and other devices to determine the conditions under which the device will function safely. Two important tests for cable performance are:

- UL-910, which tests smoke emission and flame spread for plenum cable

- UL-1666, which tests smoke emission and flame spread for riser cable

cache   Pronounced "cash." A special area of memory, managed by a cache controller, that improves performance by storing the contents of frequently accessed memory locations and their addresses.

A memory cache and a disk cache are not the same. A memory cache is implemented in hardware and speeds up access to memory. A disk cache is software that improves hard-disk performance.

When the processor references a memory address, the cache checks to see if it holds that address. If it does, the information is passed directly to the processor, so RAM access is not necessary. A cache can speed up operations in a computer whose RAM access is slow compared with its processor speed, because cache memory is always faster than normal RAM.

There are several types of caches:

- **Direct-mapped cache**   A location in the cache corresponds to several specific locations in memory, so when the processor calls for certain data, the cache can locate it quickly. However, since several blocks in RAM correspond to that same location in the cache, the cache may spend its time refreshing itself and calling main memory.

- **Fully associative cache**   Information from RAM may be placed in any free blocks in the cache so that the most recently accessed data is usually present; however, the search to find that information may be slow because the cache has to index the data in order to find it.

- **Set-associative cache**   Information from RAM is kept in sets, and these sets may have multiple locations, each holding a block of data; each block may be in any of the sets, but it will only be in one location within that set. Search time is shortened, and frequently used data are less likely to be overwritten. A set-associative cache may use two, four, or eight sets.

See also disk cache; wait state; write-back cache; write-through cache.

cache buffer   A Novell NetWare implementation of a disk cache used to speed server disk accesses, thereby allowing workstations to access data more quickly. Reading data from cache memory is much faster than reading data from the hard disk.

NetWare uses cache buffers for a variety of purposes:

- For use by NetWare Loadable Modules (NLMs), such as LAN drivers, database servers, communications servers, and print servers

- To cache each volume's FAT
- To cache files currently in use
- To build a hash table of directory information

See also disk cache.

cache buffer pool   In Novell NetWare, the amount of memory available for use after the SERVER.EXE file has been loaded into memory. Memory in the pool can be used for a variety of purposes, including caching the file allocation tables for each volume and creating a hash table of directory information.

See also hash table.

cache controller   Pronounced "cash controller." A special-purpose processor whose sole task is to manage cache memory. On newer processors, such as the Intel Pentium II, cache management is integrated directly into the processor.

See also cache.

cache memory   Pronounced "cash memory." A relatively small section of very fast memory (often static RAM) reserved for the temporary storage of the data or instructions likely to be needed next by the processor.

Cache memory integrated directly onto the microprocessor is called primary cache or L1 cache, and cache memory located in an external circuit is known as secondary cache or L2 cache.

See also cache.

caddy   The flat plastic container used to load a compact disc into certain CD-ROM disk drives. Most current CD-ROM drives do not require a caddy.

CAE   *See* Common Application Environment.

CAI   *See* Computer Associates International.

Caldera, Inc.   A software company in Provo, Utah, that repackages one of the most popular versions of Linux under the name of OpenLinux.

For more information on Caldera, see www.caldera.com.

callback modem   Also known as a dial-back modem. A special modem that does not answer an incoming call, but instead requires the caller to enter a code and hang up so that the modem can return the call. As long as the entered code matches a previously authorized number, the modem dials the number. Callback modems are useful in installations for which communications lines must be available for remote users but data must be protected from intruders.

caller ID   *See* automatic number identification.

call packet   A block of data that carries addressing information, as well as any other information needed to establish an X.25 switched virtual circuit.

campus network   A network that connects LANs from multiple departments inside a single building or set of buildings. Campus networks are LANs because they

C

do not include WAN services, even though they may extend for several miles.

canonical   The usual standard Unix way of doing something. This term has a more precise meaning in mathematics, in which rules dictate the way that formulas are written, but in Unix, it tends to mean "according to ancient or religious law."

See also holy wars.

Canon, Inc.   One of the world's leading suppliers of imaging products, electronic equipment, computer printers, fax machines, and scanners.

For more information on Canon, see www.canon.com.

CAPI   *See* Cryptography API.

card   A printed circuit board or adapter that you plug into a computer to add support for a specific piece of hardware.

See also expansion board; expansion bus.

card services   Part of the software support needed for PCMCIA hardware devices in a portable computer. Card services control the use of system interrupts, memory, and power management.

When an application wants to access a PCMCIA card, it always goes through the card services software and never communicates directly with the underlying hardware. For example, if you use a PCMCIA modem, it is the card services, not the applications program, that establishes which communications port and which interrupts and I/O addresses are in use.

See also device driver; PC Memory Card International Association; socket services.

carriage return   A control character (ASCII 13) that signals the print head or display cursor to return to the first position of the current line.

See also line feed.

carrier   An analog signal of fixed amplitude and frequency that is combined with a data-carrying signal to produce an output signal suitable for transmitting data.

See also carrier signal.

carrier detect   Abbreviated CD. An electrical signal sent from a modem to the attached computer to indicate that the modem is online.

See also Data Carrier Detect; RS-232-C.

Carrier Sense Multiple Access/ Collision Detection   Abbreviated CSMA/CD. A baseband protocol with a built-in collision-detection technique. Each node on the network listens first and transmits only when the line is free. If two nodes transmit at exactly the same time and a collision occurs, both nodes stop transmitting. Then, to avoid a subsequent collision, each node waits for a different random length of time before attempting to transmit again. Ethernet and 802.3 LANs use CSMA/CD access methods.

See also collision; demand priority; Fast Ethernet; token passing.

carrier signal   A signal of chosen frequency generated to carry data; often used for long-distance transmissions. A carrier signal does not convey any information until the data is added to the signal by modulation and then decoded on the receiving end by demodulation.

cascaded star A network topology in which multiple hubs or data centers are connected in a succession of levels, which permits many more connections than a single level.

Castanet A collection of software-update tools from Marimba, Inc. that operate over the Internet. Based on Java technology, Castanet can automatically deliver software updates not only for Java programs, but also for those written in C, C++, and Visual Basic, and because only the updated content is downloaded, performance is optimized.

For more information on Castanet, see www.marimba.com.

See also server push.

Category 1–5 The Electronics Industry Association/Telecommunications Industry Association (EIA/TIA) 586 cabling standards, sometimes abbreviated CAT 1-5, as follows:

- **Category 1** For unshielded twisted-pair (UTP) telephone cable. This cable may be used for voice, but is not suitable for data transmissions.
- **Category 2** For UTP cable use at speeds up to 4Mbps. Category 2 cable is similar to IBM Cabling System Type 3 cable.
- **Category 3** For UTP cable use at speeds up to 10Mbps. Category 3 cable is the minimum requirement for 10BaseT and is

required for Token Ring. This cable has four pairs of conductors and three twists per foot.

- **Category 4** For the lowest acceptable grade of UTP cable for use with 16Mbps Token Ring.
- **Category 5** For 100-ohm, four-wire twisted-pair copper cable for use at speeds up to 100Mbps with Ethernet or ATM (Asynchronous Transfer Mode). This cable is low-capacitance and shows low crosstalk when installed according to specifications.

See also cabling standards; Type 1–9 cable.

CAU *See* Controlled Access Unit.

CAV *See* constant angular velocity.

CBCP *See* Certified Business Continuity Professional.

CBE *See* Certified Banyan Engineer.

CBR *See* Constant Bit Rate.

CBS *See* Certified Banyan Specialist.

CCDA *See* Cisco Certified Design Associate.

CCDP *See* Cisco Certified Design Professional.

CCIE *See* Cisco Certified Internetworking Expert.

CCITT *See* Consultative Committee for International Telephony and Telegraphy.

CASCADED STAR

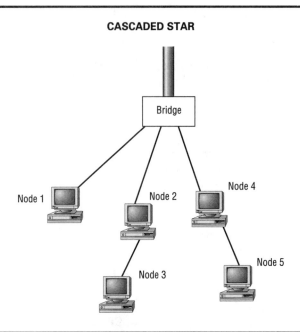

Bridge

Node 1
Node 2
Node 4
Node 3
Node 5

CCITT Groups 1–4   A set of four standards for facsimile transmissions. Groups 1 and 2, which are no longer used, define analog facsimile transmissions. Groups 3 and 4 describe digital systems, as follows:

- **CCITT Group 3**   Specifies a 9600bps modem to transmit standard images of 203 dpi horizontally by 98 dpi vertically in standard mode, and 203 dpi by 198 dpi in fine mode.

- **CCITT Group 4**   Supports images up to 400 dpi for high-speed transmission over a digital data network (for example, ISDN), rather than over a dial-up telephone line.

- CCITT is now known as the International Telecommunication Union.

See also International Telecommunication Union.

CCITT V Series   A set of recommended standards for data communications, including transmission speeds and operational modes, issued by CCITT, now known as the International Telecommunication Union.

Each standard is assigned a number, although not in chronological order. Higher numbers do not always indicate a newer standard. A second or revised version is indicated by *bis*, and *ter* indicates a third version.

See also International Telecommunication Union.

CCITT X Series   A set of recommended standards issued by CCITT to standardize protocols and equipment used in public and private computer networks. The standards include transmission speeds, interfaces to and between networks, and operation of user hardware. CCITT is now known as the International Telecommunication Union.

See also International Telecommunication Union.

CCNA   *See* Cisco Certified Network Associate.

CCNP   *See* Cisco Certified Network Professional.

CCP   *See* Certified Computing Professional.

CD   *See* carrier detect.

CDA   *See* Certified Database Administrator.

CDDI   *See* Copper Distributed Data Interface.

CDE   *See* Common Desktop Environment.

CD-I   *See* Compact Disc-Interactive.

CDIA   *See* Certified Document Imaging Architect.

CDMA   *See* Code Division Multiple Access.

CDPD   *See* Cellular Digital Packet Data.

CD-R   *See* CD-Recordable.

CD-Recordable   Abbreviated CD-R. Using CD-R, you can write to the disc only once; after that, the disc can only be read from and not written to.

From a functional point of view, a CD-R and a CD-ROM are identical; you can read CD-R discs using almost any CD-ROM drive, although the processes that create the discs are slightly different. Low-cost CD-R drives are available from several manufacturers, including Kao, Kodak, Mitsui, Phillips, Ricoh, Sony, TDK, 3M, and Verbatim.

See also CD ReWritable; digital video disc; Magneto-optical storage; WORM.

CD ReWritable   Abbreviated CD-RW. A CD format that can be written to and erased as many as 1000 times.

From a functional point of view, a CD-RW and a CD-ROM are identical, but not all CD-ROM drives can read CD-RW discs. Low-cost CD-RW drives are available from several manufacturers, including Kodak, Mitsui, Phillips, and Sony.

See also CD-Recordable; digital video disc; Magneto-optical storage; WORM.

CD-ROM   *See* Compact Disc—Read-Only Memory.

CD-ROM disk drive   A disk device that uses compact disc technology for information storage. Many CD-ROM disk drives also have headphone jacks, external speaker jacks, and a volume control.

CD-ROM disk drives designed for computer use are more expensive than audio CD players, because CD-ROM disk drives are manufactured to much higher tolerances. If a CD player misreads a small

C

amount of data, the human ear probably will not detect the difference; if a CD-ROM disk drive misreads a few bytes of a program, the program will not run.

The two most popular CD-ROM drive interface cards are SCSI and ATAPI (AT Attachment Packet Interface). ATAPI is part of the Enhanced IDE specification introduced by Western Digital in 1994 and lets you plug an IDE CD-ROM directly into an IDE controller on the system's motherboard. Other CD-ROM drives may use the computer's parallel port or a PCMCIA connection.

See also Compact Disc—Read-Only Memory.

CD-ROM Extended Architecture Abbreviated CD-ROM/XA. An extension to the CD-ROM format, developed by Microsoft, Phillips, and Sony, that allows for the storage of audio and visual information on compact disc so that you can play the audio at the same time you view the visual data.

CD-ROM/XA is compatible with the High Sierra specification, also known as ISO standard 9660.

CD-ROM/XA *See* CD-ROM Extended Architecture.

CD-RW *See* CD ReWritable.

cell Any fixed-length data packet. For example, Asynchronous Transfer Mode (ATM) uses 53-byte cells, consisting of 48 bytes of data and 5 bytes of header information.

Cell Loss Priority Abbreviated CLP. In an Asynchronous Transfer Mode (ATM) cell, a field contained in the 5-byte cell

header that defines how to drop a cell if network congestion occurs. The value holds priority values, with 0 indicating a cell with the highest priority.

See also Header Error Control; Payload Type Identifier; Virtual Channel Identifier; Virtual Path Identifier.

cell relay A form of packet transmission used in Broadcast Integrated Services Digital Network (B-ISDN) networks that uses a fixed-length, 53-byte cell over a packet-switched network. Also known as Asynchronous Transfer Mode (ATM).

cell switching A term that describes how a cellular telephone system switches from one cell to the next as the signal strength fades. The switch takes about 300 milliseconds to complete and is not noticeable by the user.

Cellular Digital Packet Data Abbreviated CDPD. A method used in cellular communications and wireless modems for sending data more efficiently by using any idle cellular channel. Capacity becomes available for data transmissions when a voice call is terminated or when a call is switched from cell to cell.

CDPD uses voice channels, but can switch to a new frequency if a voice transmission begins in the cell currently in use.

central processing unit Abbreviated CPU. The computing and control part of the computer. The CPU in a mainframe computer may be contained on many printed circuit boards. In a minicomputer, the CPU may be contained on several boards.

The CPU in a PC is usually contained in a single, extremely powerful microprocessor.

Centrex Acronym formed from Central Exchange. Services provided to a company by the local telephone company. All the switching takes place at the telephone company's central office rather than at the customer site, so Centrex services are easy to expand.

Centronics parallel interface A standard 36-pin interface used to connect a PC to a peripheral device, such as a printer; originally developed by the printer manufacturer Centronics, Inc. The standard defines eight parallel data lines, plus additional lines for status and control information.

See also parallel port.

CERN *See* Conseil Européen pour la Researche Nucléaire.

CERT *See* Computer Emergency Response Team.

certificate An encrypted digital signature used for authentication to prove that you are who you claim to be, either as an individual, the provider of a service, the vendor of a product, or a corporation, or to guarantee that an e-mail message is actually from the person you think it is from and that it has not been altered in any way during transmission.

See also authentication; certificate authority; Secure Sockets Layer.

certificate authority Abbreviated CA. A trusted organization that validates and issues certificates; often called a "trusted authority."

Certified Application Developer for Developer/2000 A certification from Oracle consisting of a set of exams covering Structured Query Language, the creation of procedures using Oracle Procedure Builder, using Developer/2000, and managing the user interface.

Certified Banyan Engineer Abbreviated CBE. A premium certification from Banyan designed to evaluate technical knowledge of the Banyan VINES network operating system. A candidate must complete two required courses and pass two exams.

Certified Banyan Specialist Abbreviated CBS. A basic certification from Banyan designed to evaluate technical knowledge of the Banyan VINES network operating system. A candidate must complete one required course and pass three exams. An additional certification concentrates on the integration of Banyan's StreetTalk onto Microsoft Windows 2000 servers; to complete this certification, you must first become a Microsoft Certified Professional.

Certified Business Continuity Professional Abbreviated CBCP. A certification from Disaster Recovery Institute International (DRII) that covers intermediate information on business continuity planning and disaster recovery and associated work experience and board certification.

See also Associate Business Continuity Professional; Master Business Continuity Professional.

C

Certified Computing Professional

Abbreviated CCP. A certification from the Institute for Certification of Computing Professionals designed for experienced professionals with more than four years experience in a wide variety of computing and related tasks.

Certified Database Administrator

1. Abbreviated CDA. A certification from Oracle that covers knowledge of Structured Query Language, administration of Oracle products, along with backup and recovery, and system performance tuning.

2. Abbreviated CDA. A certification from Sybase that covers designing, building, and supporting Sybase SQL Server databases.

See also Certified Performance and Tuning Specialist.

Certified Document Imaging Architect

Abbreviated CDIA. A certification from the Computer Technology Industry Association (CompTIA) that assesses skills in document management, including scanning and storing documents in digital form and using optical character recognition software.

Certified Information System Auditor

Abbreviated CISA. A certification from the Information Systems Audit and Control Association (ISACA) that covers ethics, security, system organization and management, and system development, acquisition, and maintenance.

Certified Information Systems Security Professional

Abbreviated CISSP. A certification from the International Information System Security Certification Consortium $(ISC)^2$ designed for system security experts with at least three years of practical experience. The exam covers access control systems, operations security, cryptography, applications and systems planning, business continuity and disaster planning, telecommunications and network security, ethics, and the law.

Certified Java Developer

Abbreviated CJD. An advanced certification from Sun Microsystems designed to evaluate Java programming language skills.

See also Certified Java Programmer.

Certified Java Programmer

Abbreviated CJP. A certification from Sun Microsystems designed to evaluate Java programming language skills.

See also Certified Java Developer.

Certified Lotus Professional

Abbreviated CLP. A certification from Lotus designed to evaluate a wide range of skills and knowledge of Lotus products. Several certifications are available, including CLP: Application Developer, CLP: Principal Application Developer, CLP: System Administrator, CLP: Principal System Administrator, CLP: cc:Mail System Administrator.

See also Certified Lotus Specialist.

Certified Lotus Specialist

Abbreviated CLS. A certification from Lotus designed to evaluate knowledge of a single Lotus product. Options include certification in Lotus Domino, Lotus 1-2-3, Lotus Notes, and cc:Mail.

See also Certified Lotus Professional.

Certified Network Professional Abbreviated CNP. A certification from the Network Professional Association (NPA) that involves meeting requirements in the areas of client operating systems, networking hardware, network operating systems, communications protocols, and network topologies. Two years of relevant work experience and two vendor-based certifications are required to complete the program.

Certified Novell Administrator Abbreviated CNA. A Novell certification program for network administrators responsible for the day-to-day operation of a network. Within the CNA program, a candidate can specialize in one or more Novell products, including IntranetWare, NetWare, or GroupWise.

See also Certified Novell Engineer; Master Certified Novell Engineer.

Certified Novell Engineer Abbreviated CNE. A Novell certification program for technical professionals concerned with network system design, implementation, and maintenance. Within the CNE program, a candidate can specialize in one or more Novell products, including IntranetWare, NetWare, or GroupWise.

See also Certified Novell Administrator; Master Certified Novell Engineer.

Certified Novell Engineer Professional Association Abbreviated CNEPA. An association of Certified Novell Engineers (CNEs) that provides benefits, such as workshops demonstrating how to configure and troubleshoot Novell products, as well as admission to network-related events and complementary subscriptions.

See also Certified Novell Engineer.

Certified Novell Instructor Abbreviated CNI. A Novell certification program for trainers who want to teach Novell courses. Once certified, by passing the appropriate exam at the instructor level, a CNI can teach any instructor-led Novell course, including those for Certified Novell Administrator (CNA), Certified Novell Engineer (CNE), and Master CNE (MCNE).

See also Master Certified Novell Instructor.

Certified Performance and Tuning Specialist Abbreviated CPTS. A certification from Sybase that tests for proficiency across a wide range of database administration, tuning, and performance concepts.

See also Certified Database Administrator.

Certified PowerBuilder Developer Associate Abbreviated CPDA. A certification from Sybase designed for experienced PowerBuilder developers that tests knowledge in the areas of client/server architecture, object-oriented programming, relational databases, and Structured Query Language.

See also Certified PowerBuilder Developer Professional.

Certified PowerBuilder Developer Professional Abbreviated CPDP. A certification from Sybase designed for experienced PowerBuilder developers that requires hands-on experience building PowerBuilder applications as well as a demonstration of good development practices.

C

See also Certified PowerBuilder Developer Associate.

Certified Solutions Expert Abbreviated CSE. A pair of Internet certifications from IBM. CSE: Net.Commerce is aimed at the developers of Internet store fronts and other financial transactions over the Internet. CSE: Firewall is a security-related certification.

Certified Unicenter Engineer Abbreviated CUE. A certification from Computer Associates designed to evaluate expertise in the Unicenter TNG product line.

CGI *See* Common Gateway Interface.

Challenge-Handshake Authentication Protocol Abbreviated CHAP. A method of authentication that you can use when connecting to an ISP that allows you to log on automatically.

See also Password Authentication Protocol.

challenge-response authentication A method of authentication used by Microsoft Windows 2000 and other operating systems.

When a user contacts a server, the server responds with a challenge, upon which the user then performs a cryptographic operation and returns the result to the server. The server then performs the same operation, and if the two results are the same, the user is considered authentic.

See also clear text authentication.

channel **1.** In communications, any connecting path that carries information from a sending device to a receiving device. A

channel may refer to a physical medium (for example, a coaxial cable) or to a specific frequency within a larger channel.

2. In Internet Relay Chat (IRC), a named forum where you can chat in real time with other users; also known as a chat room.

channelization The process of dividing the bandwidth of a communications circuit into smaller increments.

See also T1.

channelized T1 *See* T1.

Channel Service Unit Abbreviated CSU. A device that functions as a certified safe electrical circuit, acting as a buffer between the customer's equipment and a public carrier's WAN.

A CSU prevents faulty CPE (customer-premises equipment), such as DSUs (data service units), from affecting a public carrier's transmission systems and ensures that all signals placed on the line are appropriately timed and formed. All CSU designs must be approved and certified by the FCC.

See also Data Service Unit.

CHAP *See* Challenge-Handshake Authentication Protocol.

character A symbol that corresponds to a key on the keyboard. A character can be a letter, a number, punctuation, or a special symbol and is usually stored as a single byte. A collection of related characters is known as a *character set*, and the most common character set on PC systems is the American Standard Code for Information Interchange (ASCII). Some larger IBM systems still use Extended Binary Coded Decimal Interchange

Code (EBCDIC). In an attempt to rationalize the many international character sets in use these days, some systems use more than one byte to store a character.

See also American Standard Code for Information Interchange; Extended Binary Coded Decimal Interchange Code; Unicode.

character-based interface   An operating system or application that uses text characters rather than graphical techniques for the user interface.

See also command line; graphical user interface.

character code   A code that represents one specific alphanumeric or control character in a set of characters.

See also American Standard Code for Information Interchange; Extended Binary Coded Decimal Interchange Code; Unicode.

character mode   A mode in which the computer displays characters on the screen using the built-in character set, but does not show any graphics characters or a mouse pointer. Also known as text mode.

character set   A standard group of letters, numbers, punctuation marks, special symbols, and control characters used by a computer.

See also American Standard Code for Information Interchange; Extended Binary Coded Decimal Interchange Code; Unicode.

characters per second   Abbreviated cps. The number of characters, or bytes, transmitted every second during a data transfer. A measurement of the speed of operation of equipment, such as serial printers and terminals.

character string   Any group of alphanumeric characters treated as a single unit. Also known as a string.

cheapernet wire   *See* thin Ethernet.

checkpointing   The process of moving transactions from the transaction log to their permanent disk location.

checksum   A method of providing information for error detection, usually calculated by summing a set of values.

The checksum is usually appended to the end of the data that it is calculated from so that they can be compared. For example, Xmodem, a popular file-transfer protocol, uses a 1-byte checksum calculated by adding all the ASCII values for all 128 data bytes and ignoring any numeric overflow. The checksum is added to the end of the Xmodem data packet. This type of checksum does not always detect all errors. In later versions of the Xmodem protocol, cyclical redundancy check (CRC) is used instead for more rigorous error control.

See also cyclical redundancy check; error detection and correction.

chip   A slang expression for integrated circuit.

See also integrated circuit.

choke packet   A packet used for flow control. A node that notices congestion on the network generates a choke packet and sends it toward the source of the congestion, which is then required to reduce its sending rate.

CHRP   *See* Common Hardware Reference Platform.

CICS   *See* Customer Information Control System.

CIDR   *See* Classless Inter-Domain Routing.

CIFS   *See* Common Internet File System.

circuit   1. A communications channel or path between two devices capable of carrying electrical current.

2. A set of components connected to perform a specific task.

circuit switching   A temporary communications connection established as required between the sending and receiving nodes. Circuit switching is often used in modem communications over dial-up telephone lines. It is also used in some privately maintained communications networks.

See also message switching; packet switching; virtual circuit.

Cirrus Logic, Inc.   A leading manufacturer of integrated circuits, particularly semiconductor wafers, Cirrus Logic has also moved into the areas of 56K modem chip sets and sound-card chip sets.

For more information on Cirrus Logic, see www.cirrus.com.

CIS   *See* CompuServe.

CISA   *See* Certified Information System Auditor.

CISC   *See* complex instruction set computing.

Cisco Certified Design Associate   Abbreviated CCDA. A certification from Cisco designed to evaluate knowledge of relatively simple networks.

See also Cisco Certified Design Professional.

Cisco Certified Design Professional   Abbreviated CCDP. A certification from Cisco designed to evaluate knowledge of complex networks based on Cisco LAN and WAN routers and LAN switches.

See also Cisco Certified Design Associate.

Cisco Certified Internetworking Expert   Abbreviated CCIE. An advanced certification from Cisco offered in three areas: CCIE-Routing and Switching, CCIE-Internet Service Provider (ISP) Dial, and CCIE-WAN Switching.

Cisco Certified Network Associate   Abbreviated CCNA. A certification from Cisco designed to evaluate network support knowledge.

See also Cisco Certified Network Professional.

Cisco Certified Network Professional   Abbreviated CCNP. An advanced certification from Cisco designed to evaluate network support knowledge.

See also Cisco Certified Network Associate.

Cisco Systems, Inc. The world's leading manufacturer of routers and internetworking hardware and software products. More than 80 percent of the backbone routers currently in use on the Internet were made by Cisco, and its Internetwork Operating System (IOS) is quickly becoming an industry standard that other vendors are incorporating into their own products.

For more information on Cisco, see www.cisco.com.

Ciscoworks A set of management applications from Cisco Systems, Inc., designed for use with Cisco routers.

CISSP *See* Certified Information Systems Security Professional.

CIX *See* Commercial Internet Exchange.

CJD *See* Certified Java Developer.

CJP *See* Certified Java Programmer.

cladding The transparent material, usually glass, that surrounds the core of an optical fiber. Cladding has a lower refractive index than the core and so prevents the light signal from spreading out due to modal dispersion, by reflecting the signal back into the central core. This helps to maintain the signal strength over long distances.

See also dispersion.

Class A certification An FCC certification for computer equipment, including mainframe computers and minicomputers destined for industrial, commercial, or office use, rather than for personal use at home. The Class A commercial certification is less restrictive than the Class B

certification for residential use, because it assumes that most residential areas are more than 30 feet from any commercial computer equipment.

See also Class B certification.

Class A network In the IP addressing scheme, a very large network. The high-order bit in a Class A network is always zero, leaving 7 bits available to define 127 networks. The remaining 24 bits of the address allow each Class A network to hold as many as 16,777,216 hosts. Examples of Class A networks include General Electric, IBM, Hewlett-Packard, Apple Computer, Xerox, Digital Equipment Corporation, and MIT. All the Class A networks are in use, and no more are available.

See also address classes; IP address.

Class B certification An FCC certification for computer equipment, including PCs, laptops, and portables destined for use in the home rather than in a commercial setting. Class B levels of radio frequency interference (RFI) must be low enough so that they do not interfere with radio or television reception when there is more than one wall and 30 feet separating the computer from the receiver. Class B certification is more restrictive than the commercial Class A certification.

See also Class A certification.

Class B network In the IP addressing scheme, a medium-sized network. The 2 high-order bits are always 10, and the remaining bits are used to define 16,384 networks, each with as many as 65,535 hosts attached. Examples of Class B networks include Microsoft and Exxon. All Class B networks are in use, and no more are available.

See also address classes; IP address.

Class C network   In the IP addressing scheme, a smaller network. The 3 high-order bits are always 110, and the remaining bits are used to define 2,097,152 networks, but each network can have a maximum of only 254 hosts. Class C networks are still available.

See also address classes; IP address.

Class D network   In the IP addressing scheme, a special multicast address that cannot be used for networks. The 4 high-order bits are always 1110, and the remaining 28 bits allow access to more than 268 million possible addresses.

See also address classes; IP address.

Class E network   In the IP addressing scheme, a special address reserved for experimental purposes. The first 4 bits in the address are always 1111.

See also address classes; IP address.

classes   In Novell Directory Services, an object can be defined as an instance of an object class. Classes include User, Group, Printer, Print Server, Computer, and so on.

Classless Inter-Domain Routing   Abbreviated CIDR, pronounced "cider." An interim solution to the problem that the Internet is running out of addresses.

Blocks of Class C addresses are assigned to a site based on the number of addresses that site requires, to prevent wasted addresses.

Also, the Class C address space is divided into four major areas—Europe, North America, Central and South America, and Asia and the Pacific—and each zone is assigned 32 million addresses.

CIDR networks are often described as "slash x" networks; the x represents the number of bits in the IP address range controlled by the granting authority. For example, a Class C network in CIDR terms becomes a slash 24 network.

See also address classes; IP address.

cleartext   Text that has not been encrypted in any way and that can be intercepted and read easily while in transit; usually applied to an unencrypted password.

See also plaintext.

clear text authentication   An authentication method that encodes user name and password information according to a freely available 64-bit encoding utility.

See also challenge-response authentication; encryption.

Clear to Send   Abbreviated CTS. A hardware signal defined by the RS-232-C standard that indicates that the transmission can proceed.

See also RS-232-C; Request to Send.

CLEC   *See* Competitive Local Exchange Carrier.

client   A device or application that uses the services provided by a server.

A client may be a PC or a workstation on a network using services provided from the network file server, or it may be that part of an application program that runs on the workstation supported by additional software running on the server.

One of the most familiar clients is the Web browser.

See also client/server architecture; DOS client; Macintosh client; OS/2 client; Unix client; Windows client.

client application   In OLE, the application that starts a server application to manipulate linked or embedded information.

client pull   A mechanism used on the Internet whereby a client application, usually a Web browser, initiates a request for services from a Web site.

See also server push.

Client Services for NetWare   A software package included with Microsoft Windows 2000 that connects a Windows 2000 client to a Novell NetWare file server.

client/server architecture   A computing architecture that distributes processing between clients and servers on the network.

In the past, traditional computing has relied on a hierarchical architecture based on non-programmable dumb terminals connected to a mainframe computer. In this scheme, the database was on the same computer that was running the application. A client/server approach replaces this structure by dividing the application into two separate parts: a front-end client and a back-end server, usually referred to as a *client* and a *server*.

The client component provides the user with the power to run the data-entry part of the application, and this part of the client is usually optimized for user interaction with the system.

The server component, which can be either local or remote, provides the data management, administration, and system security features and manages information sharing with the rest of the network.

In other words, clients request information from the servers, and the servers store data and programs and provide network services to clients.

Client/server architecture can sustain several levels of organizational complexity, including the following:

- Stand-alone (non-networked) client applications, such as local word processors

- Applications that run on the client but request data from the server, such as spreadsheets

- Programs that use server capabilities to share information among network users, such as electronic mail systems

- Programs in which the physical search of records takes place on the server, while a much smaller program running on the client handles all user-interface functions, such as database applications

Client/server computing lightens the processing load for the client PCs, but increases the load on the server. For this reason, server computers tend to have larger and faster hard-disk drives and much more memory installed than conventional file servers. The server may also be a minicomputer or a mainframe computer.

Typically, a client/server approach reduces network traffic, because relatively small

C

amounts of data are moved over the network. This is in sharp contrast to the typical network, in which entire files are constantly being transmitted between the workstation and the file server.

Database applications were some of the first to embrace the client/server concept, particularly those using Structured Query Language (SQL). SQL has grown into an industry standard database language; it is relatively easy to implement, it is robust and powerful, and it is easy for users to learn.

See also network computer; thin client.

Clipper chip   A low-cost encryption device backed by the U.S. federal government.

The chip would allow businesses to transmit encoded messages, but at the same time, allow certain government agencies to intercept and decode the messages if criminal activities were suspected. Needless to say, this proposal has generated a lot of intense discussion, particularly from civil rights groups concerned with an individual's right to privacy and other ethical issues; other potential users want access to the best available encryption systems, not just those put forward by the government.

CLNP   *See* Connectionless Network Protocol.

clock   An electronic circuit that generates regularly spaced timing pulses at speeds up to millions of cycles per second. These pulses are used to synchronize the flow of information through the computer's internal communications channels.

See also clock speed.

clock-multiplying   A mechanism used by some Intel processors that allows the chip to process data and instructions internally at a speed different from that used by the rest of the system.

clock speed   The internal speed of a computer or processor, normally expressed in megahertz (MHz). Also known as clock rate.

The faster the clock speed, the faster the computer will perform a specific operation (assuming the other components in the system, such as disk drives, can keep up with the increased speed).

The Intel 8088 processor used in the original IBM PC had a clock speed of 4.77MHz—painfully slow when compared with speeds used by current processors, which can run at clock speeds of several hundred MHz.

clone   Hardware that is identical in function to an original.

For example, an IBM clone is a PC that uses an Intel (or similar) microprocessor and functions in the same way as the IBM PC standard. A Macintosh clone functions in the same way as a computer manufactured by Apple Computer, Inc.

Although most clones do perform as intended, small internal differences can cause problems in some cases. It can be difficult to ensure consistency of components and level of operation when using a number of clones purchased over a long period of time.

See also Advanced Micro Devices, Inc.; Cyrix.

closed architecture   A design that does not allow for easy, user-supplied additions. This term is often used to describe some of the early Macintosh computers, which did not allow easy expansion of the system with add-in cards. Closed architecture can also refer to a computer design whose specifications are not published or generally available, making it impossible for third-party companies to provide products that work with the computer.

See also open architecture.

CLP *See* Cell Loss Priority; Certified Lotus Professional.

CLS *See* Certified Lotus Specialist.

CLTP *See* Connectionless Transport Protocol.

cluster controller An IBM or IBM-compatible device located between a group of 3270 terminals and the mainframe computer. The cluster controller communicates between the computer and the terminals using SDLC (Synchronous Data Link Control) or a bisynchronous communications protocol.

clustering A fault-tolerant technology designed to keep server availability at a very high level.

Clustering groups servers and other network resources into a single system; if one of the servers in the cluster fails, the other servers can take over the workload. Clustering software also adds a load-balancing feature to make sure that processing is distributed in such as way as to optimize system throughput.

CLV *See* constant linear velocity.

CMIP *See* Common Management Information Protocol.

CMIS *See* Common Management Information Services.

CMOS *See* Complementary Metal-Oxide Semiconductor.

CNA *See* Certified Novell Administrator.

CNE *See* Certified Novell Engineer.

CNEPA *See* Certified Novell Engineer Professional Association.

CNI *See* Certified Novell Instructor.

CNP *See* Certified Network Professional.

coax *See* coaxial cable.

coaxial cable Abbreviated coax, pronounced "co-ax." A high-capacity cable used in networking that contains a solid inner copper conductor surrounded by plastic insulation, and an outer braided copper or foil shield.

Coaxial cable is used for broadband and baseband communications networks (and for cable television), because the cable is usually free from external interference and permits high transmission rates over long distances.

See also fiber-optic cable; RG-58; RG-59; RG-62; thick Ethernet; thin Ethernet.

C

COAXIAL CABLE

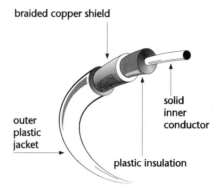

braided copper shield

outer plastic jacket

solid inner conductor

plastic insulation

codec **1.** Acronym for coder/decoder, pronounced "coe-deck." A device that converts analog signals (such as voice or video) into a digital bit stream suitable for transmission and then converts those digital signals back into analog signals at the receiving end.

2. Acronym for compression/decompression, pronounced "coe-deck." An overall term to describe the hardware and software used in processing animation, digital video, and stereo-quality audio.

See also lossless compression; lossy compression.

Code Division Multiple Access Abbreviated CDMA, also known as spread spectrum. A digital cellular standard approved by the Telecommunications Industry Association (TIA) in 1993 and known as IS-95.

CDMA combines both data and voice into a single wireless network and can provide users with digital voice services, voice mail, text messaging, and caller ID. CDMA also increases system capacity up to 10 times that of analog systems.

See also Advanced Mobile Phone Service; Cellular Digital Packet Data; wireless communications.

cold boot The computer startup process that begins when you turn on power to the computer. You are doing a cold boot when you first turn on your computer. A cold boot might also be necessary if a program or the operating system crashes and freezes entirely. If your keyboard is operational, a warm boot may suffice.

See also boot; warm boot.

collaboration software A set of network-based applications that let users share information quickly and easily.

See also whiteboard.

collision   In networking or communications, an attempt by two nodes to send a message on the same channel at exactly the same moment.

See also Carrier Sense Multiple Access/Collision Detection; token-ring network.

colon   The symbol used after the protocol name in a URL.

See also Uniform Resource Locator.

COM   *See* Common Object Model; Component Object Model.

COM 1–4   *See* COM port.

command interpreter   *See* command processor.

command line   Any interface between the user and the command processor that allows you to enter commands from the keyboard for execution by the operating system.

See also graphical user interface; shell; text mode.

command-line argument   A parameter that alters the default mode of a command. In many operating systems, a command-line argument is one or more letters or numbers preceded by the / (slash) character. In Unix, a command-line argument may be called an option or a flag and is usually a single character preceded by a hyphen (as in -r). With some commands, you can group several switches. Sometimes called a command-line switch.

See also command line.

command processor   The part of the operating system that displays the command prompt on the screen, interprets and executes all the commands and filenames that you enter, and displays error messages when appropriate. Also called the command interpreter. The command processor also contains the system environment.

command prompt   A symbol (character or group of characters) on the screen that lets you know that the operating system is available and ready to receive input.

Commercial Internet Exchange   Abbreviated CIX, pronounced "kicks." A connection point between ISPs.

A location where top-tier ISPs maintain the routers used to route packets between their respective network segments.

Common Application Environment   Abbreviated CAE. A set of standards, developed by X/Open for application development, including standards for the operating system, compilers, software development tools, data management, networking, and the graphical user interface.

common carrier   A communications company, such as AT&T or MCI, that provides data and voice telecommunication services to the general public.

See also Postal Telephone and Telegraph.

Common Desktop Environment   Abbreviated CDE. A set of specifications developed by the Common Open Software Environment (COSE) that defines an API for a common Unix graphical user interface. The specifications cover the interoperability of applications across different

C

hardware platforms, multimedia and networking operations, as well as object-oriented technology and system administration issues.

Common Gateway Interface Abbreviated CGI. A standard way that programs can interface with Web servers and allow them to run applications such as search engines and to access databases and other back-end applications.

CGI defines the field specifics and control tags to be placed in an HTML document, the environment variables where the Web server places information for use by scripts, and the flow of information between client Web browser, the server, and the Web server scripts. CGI is platform-independent.

See also HyperText Markup Language; script; Web server.

Common Internet File System Abbreviated CIFS. A file system supported by Microsoft, DEC, Data General, SCO, and others, which allows users and organizations to run file systems over the Internet.

CIFS is an extension to Microsoft's Server Message Blocks (SMB) file-sharing protocol and allows users to share files over the Internet in the same way that they share files using networking services on Windows clients.

See also WebNFS.

Common Hardware Reference Platform Abbreviated CHRP. An open hardware architecture, based on the Power-PC and originally defined by IBM, that ensures compatibility between systems made by different manufacturers.

Common Management Information Protocol Abbreviated CMIP. The Open Systems Interconnection (OSI) management information protocol for network monitoring and control information, designated ISO 9596.

CMIP includes fault management, configuration management, performance management, and security and accounting management. It is not widely available.

See also Common Management Information Services; Simple Network Management Protocol.

Common Management Information Services Abbreviated CMIS. The Open Systems Interconnect (OSI) standard functions for network monitoring and control.

See also Common Management Information Protocol.

Common name In Novell Directory Services, every object has a name that is unique within its context in the directory structure. This name is known as the Common name when it refers to users, nodes, or servers.

See also Distinguished Name.

Common Object Model Abbreviated COM. A specification from Microsoft and DEC to provide cross-platform interoperability across non-Windows platforms.

COM was developed to allow networks using Microsoft's OLE technology to communicate with networks using DEC's Object-Broker technology.

Common Object Request Broker Architecture Abbreviated CORBA. A standard from the Object Management Group (OMG), whose members include Sun Microsystems, Hewlett-Packard, DEC, and IBM, that enables communications between distributed object-oriented applications, regardless of the language they are written in and the hardware platform on which they run.

CORBA uses Object Request Brokers to set up communications between objects and to invoke methods on behalf of these objects.

CORBA competes with Microsoft's Distributed Component Object Model (DCOM) and ActiveX technology.

See also Distributed Component Object Model.

Common Open Software Environment Abbreviated COSE, pronounced "cosy." An industry group consisting of almost 100 members, organized to develop a standard graphical user interface for Unix, known as the Common Desktop Environment, or CDE. Original members included Sun Microsystems, Hewlett-Packard, IBM, SCO, and the UNIX Systems Group.

Common Programming Interface for Communications Abbreviated CPI-C. A cross-platform API from IBM that interfaces to the Advanced Program-to-Program Communications (APPC) environment.

CPI-C is designed to support a common environment for application execution across several IBM operating systems, including MVS, VS, OS/400, and OS/2-based systems.

See also Advanced Peer-to-Peer Networking; Advanced Program-to-Program Communications; Advanced Interactive Executive; Multiple Virtual Storage.

communications/modem server In a network, a server equipped with a bank of modems, which can be shared by users for outgoing calls.

See also access server.

communications parameters Any of several settings required to allow computers to communicate successfully. In asynchronous transmissions, commonly used in modem communications, the settings for baud rate, number of data bits, number of stop bits, and parity parameters must all be correct.

communications protocol 1. A standard way of communicating between computers or between computers and terminals. Communications protocols vary in complexity, ranging from Xmodem, a simple file-transfer protocol used to transfer files from one PC to another, to the seven-layer OSI Reference Model used as the theoretical basis for many large, complex computer networks.

2. A hardware interface standard, such as RS-232-C.

communications satellite A satellite in geostationary orbit, acting as a microwave relay station. The satellite receives signals

C

from a groundstation, amplifies them, and retransmits them on a different frequency to another groundstation.

See also downlink; propagation delay; uplink.

compact disc   Abbreviated CD. A nonmagnetic, polished, optical disc used to store large amounts of digital information. A CD can store approximately 650MB of information, equivalent to more than 1700 low-density floppy disks. This storage capacity translates into approximately 300,000 pages of text or 72 minutes of music, all on a single 4.72-inch disc.

Digital information is stored on the compact disc as a series of microscopic pits and smooth areas that have different reflective properties. A beam of laser light shines on the disc so that the reflections can be detected and converted into digital data.

See also CD-Recordable; CD ReWritable; CD-ROM Extended Architecture; Compact Disc-Interactive; Compact Disc—Read-Only Memory; digital video disc.

Compact Disc-Interactive   Abbreviated CD-I. A hardware and software standard disc format for data, text, audio, still video images, and animated graphics. The standard also defines methods of encoding and decoding compressed data, as well as displaying data.

See also compact disc; Compact Disc—Read-Only Memory.

Compact Disc—Read-Only Memory
Abbreviated CD-ROM. A high-capacity, optical storage device that uses the same technology used to make ordinary music discs to store large amounts of information. A single 4.72-inch disc can hold up to 650MB.

CD-ROMs are important components of multimedia applications. They are also used to store encyclopedias, dictionaries, and other large reference works, as well as libraries of fonts and clip art for desktop publishing. CD-ROMs have replaced floppy disks as the distribution mechanism for software packages, including network operating systems and large applications; you can load the whole package from a single compact disc, and you can load an operating system from a set of discs.

A CD-ROM uses the constant linear velocity data encoding scheme to store information in a single, spiral track, divided into many equal-length segments. To read data, the CD-ROM disk drive must increase the rotational speed as the read head gets closer to the center of the disk and must decrease as the head moves back out.

See also CD-Recordable; Compact Disc-Interactive; constant angular velocity; High Sierra specification.

Compaq Computer Corporation   One of the world's largest computer manufacturers, Compaq recently acquired the Digital Equipment Corporation (DEC), which boosted the company into the top three along with IBM and Hewlett-Packard.

By acquiring DEC, Compaq gained a world-wide service and support structure, as well as access to DEC's highly regarded hardware and software products.

Compaq also shook up the computer industry when it introduced the first PC that cost less than $1,000.

For more information about Compaq, see www.compaq.com.

compatibility The extent to which a given piece of hardware or software conforms to an accepted standard, regardless of the original manufacturer.

In hardware, compatibility is often expressed in terms of widely accepted models—this designation implies that the device will perform in the same way as the standard device.

In software, compatibility is usually described as the ability to read data file formats created by another vendor's software or the ability to work together and share data.

See also plug-compatible.

Competitive Local Exchange Carrier Abbreviated CLEC. A term coined from the Telecommunications Act of 1996 to describe the deregulated, competitive phone companies that will be able to offer local exchange service as well as long distance and international services, Internet access, and cable and video on-demand services.

See also Incumbent Local Exchange Carrier; Local Exchange Carrier.

compiler A program that converts a set of program language source code statements into a machine-readable form suitable for execution by a computer.

Most compilers do much more than this, however; they translate the entire program into machine language, while at the same time, they check your source code syntax for errors and then post error messages or warnings as appropriate.

See also just-in-time compiler.

Complementary Metal-Oxide Semiconductor Abbreviated CMOS, pronounced "See-moss." A type of integrated circuit used in processors and for memory. Because CMOS devices operate at very high speeds and use little power, they generate little heat. In the PC, battery-backed CMOS memory is used to store operating parameters, such as the hard disk type, when the computer is switched off.

complex instruction set computing Abbreviated CISC, pronounced "sisk." A processor that can recognize and execute more than 100 different assembly-language, or low-level, instructions. CISC processors can be powerful, but the instructions take a high number of clock cycles to execute.

This complexity is in contrast to the simplicity of reduced instruction set computing (RISC) processors, in which the number of available instructions has been cut to a minimum. RISC processors are common in workstations and can be designed to run up to 70 percent faster than CISC processors.

See also assembly language; reduced instruction set computing.

Component Object Model Abbreviated COM. A specification from Microsoft that defines how objects interact in the Windows environment.

COM components can be written in any programming language and can be added to or removed from a program without

C

requiring recompilation. COM is the foundation of the Object Linking and Embedding (OLE) and ActiveX specifications.

See also ActiveX; Common Object Request Broker Architecture; Distributed Component Object Model.

COM port In MS-DOS and Microsoft Windows, the device name used to denote a serial communications port. In versions of MS-DOS after 3.3, four COM ports are supported: COM1, COM2, COM3, and COM4. Earlier versions support only COM1 and COM2.

compound document A document file that consists of information created by two or more applications, for example, a database document embedded within a word-processing document.

Object Linking and Embedding (OLE) can link and embed documents and can be used to start the appropriate application program.

See also Object Linking and Embedding.

compressed file A file that has been processed by a special utility so that it occupies as little hard-disk space as possible. When the file is needed, the same program decompresses the file back into its original form so that it can be read by the computer.

Popular compression techniques include schemes that replace commonly occurring sequences of characters by tokens that take up less space. Some utilities use Huffman coding to shrink a file, and others use adaptive Lempel-Ziv coding.

See also data compression; file compression; PKZip; WinZip; ZIP file.

CompuServe Abbreviated CIS. A major provider of online services including e-mail, file downloading, forums on a variety of topics, chat rooms, and Internet access, as well as commercial services offered to a large number of business users. In 1998, CompuServe was bought by America Online.

For more information on CompuServe, see www.compuserve.com.

computation bound A condition in which the speed of operation of the processor actually limits the speed of program execution. The processor is limited by the number of arithmetic operations it can perform.

See also input/output bound.

computer account In Microsoft Windows 2000, an object in the Security Accounts Manager that describes a specific computer within a network domain. A computer account is added for each node added to the domain.

Computer Associates International Abbreviated CAI. A leading supplier of enterprise applications and services to the corporate world, including defense contractors and Fortune 500 companies.

CAI's rapid expansion in recent years has been due to an aggressive acquisitions policy that has led to the incorporation of Legent and Cheyenne Software and to a joint venture with Fujitsu that created the object-oriented database Jasmine.

CAI currently enjoys success with Unicenter TNG, a collection of applications and tools used to manage enterprise computing.

For more information on CAI, see www.cai.com.

Computer Emergency Response Team   Abbreviated CERT. Founded in 1988 at Carnegie-Mellon University, CERT works with the Internet community to increase awareness of security issues; it conducts research into improving existing systems and provides 24-hour technical assistance service for responding to security incidents.

computer name   **1.** In Microsoft Windows NT, a name of up to 15 uppercase letters that identifies a specific computer to the other computers on the network. The computer name is created during installation and must be unique within the workgroup or domain; you can change the computer name using the Network applet in Control Panel.
2. In NetBIOS, a name of up to 15 characters that uniquely identifies a workstation to computers and users. Once a computer is named, NetBIOS can establish sessions between computers and use those links to exchange data between systems. These exchanges can be either NetBIOS requests or Server Message Block (SMB) data. Network applications use NetBIOS names to locate resources, although the Windows Sockets API is now more commonly used.

See also NetBIOS; WinSock.

Computer object   In NetWare Directory Services, a leaf object representing a computer on the network. The Computer object's properties can contain information such as the computer's physical serial number and

the name of the person to whom the computer is currently assigned.

See also leaf object; Novell Directory Services.

Computer Systems Research Group   Abbreviated CSRG. The University of California, Berkeley, group responsible for the development of the Berkeley Software Distribution (BSD).

CSRG was home to some remarkable programmers over the years and introduced into Unix many of the fundamental features we take for granted. The last BSD release, 4.4BSD, was made during 1993, and the group was disbanded shortly afterward.

concentrator   A repeater or hub that joins communications channels from several network nodes. Concentrators are not just simple wire-concentration centers, but also provide bridging, routing, and other management functions.

concurrent   When two or more programs (processes) have access to the processor at the same time and must share the system resources, they are said to be "running concurrently." Because a computer can perform operations so quickly, the processes seem to be occurring at the same time, although actually they are not.

See also multiprocessing; task; task switching; thread.

concurrent license   A software license that allows more than one person at a company to share an application over a network, providing that, at any given time, only one person is using it.

Different versions of concurrent licensing allow a fixed number of people in an office to share one copy of an application and allow the application to be used on both desktop and portable PCs, rather than run only from the file server.

See also application metering.

CONFIG.SYS   In MS-DOS and OS/2, a special text file containing settings that control the way the operating system works.

In MS-DOS, the CONFIG.SYS file may contain 10 to 20 lines of entries. In OS/2, it is likely to contain between 70 and 100 lines of configuration information. CONFIG.SYS must be in the root directory of the default boot disk, normally drive C, and is read once as the system starts running.

configuration   The process of establishing your own preferred setup for an application, expansion board, computer system, or network. Most current software can establish a configuration for you automatically, although you may need to adjust that configuration to get the best results.

See also Desktop Management Interface; Plug and Play.

configuration file   A file, created by an application or an operating system, containing configuration information specific to your own computing environment. Application configuration files may have a filename extension of CFG or SET; Windows configuration files use the INI filename extension.

If you accidentally erase an application's configuration file, the program will return to using its default settings. Although the program will continue to function, its configuration settings may not be suitable for your system.

See also AUTOEXEC.BAT; CONFIG.SYS; NET.CFG.

configuration management   A term covering a wide range of network administration tasks, often performed by the network administrator, including:

• Maintaining a hardware database containing details of routers, bridges, and connections so that changes in the network can be made quickly in the event of a failure

• Adding and removing workstations and users to the network as needed

• Adding and configuring new servers and cabling systems as the network expands

See also Desktop Management Interface.

congestion   An excessive amount of traffic on the network, causing messages to be blocked for long periods of time and adversely affecting network performance.

You may see a very slow response from a server, or you may see an error message telling you that no ports are available at the present time for the service or host you are requesting.

See also Ethernet meltdown.

connectionless   A protocol in which the source and destination addresses are included inside each packet so that a direct connection between sender and receiver or an established session between nodes is not required for communications. In a connectionless service, data packets may not reach their destination in the same order in which they were sent. UDP is a connectionless transport service.

See also connection-oriented; User Datagram Protocol.

Connectionless Network Protocol

Abbreviated CLNP. An Open Systems Interconnect (OSI) protocol that provides the OSI Connectionless Network Service for the delivery of data. It uses datagrams that include addressing information to route network messages. CLNP is used for LANs rather than WANs. CLNP is the OSI equivalent of IP (Internet Protocol).

See also Connection-Oriented Network Service.

Connectionless Transport Protocol

Abbreviated CLTP. An Open Systems Interconnect (OSI) protocol that provides end-to-end transport data addressing and error correction, but does not guarantee delivery or provide any flow control. CLTP is the OSI equivalent of UDP.

See also Connection-Oriented Network Service; User Datagram Protocol.

connection number   A number assigned to a workstation that attaches to a server; it may be a different number each time the workstation attaches. Connection numbers are also assigned to print servers, as well as

other applications and processes that use the server connections.

connection-oriented   A term used to describe a communications model that goes through three well-defined stages: establishing the connection, transferring the data, and releasing the connection. Analogous to a voice telephone call. In a connection-oriented service, data packets always reach their destination in the same order in which they were sent. TCP is a connection-oriented transport service.

See also connectionless; Transmission Control Protocol.

Connection-Oriented Network Service   Abbreviated CONS. A data transmission service in which data is only transmitted once a connection has been established. Asynchronous Transfer Mode (ATM) is a connection-oriented service.

See also Connectionless Network Protocol; Connectionless Transport Protocol.

connection speed   The speed of a data communications circuit. Some circuits are symmetrical and can maintain the same speed in both directions; others are asymmetrical and use a faster speed in one direction, usually the downstream side. Table C.1 compares the connection speeds available for several technologies.

See also Asymmetric Digital Subscriber Line; cable modem; High-Bit-Rate Digital Subscriber Line; Integrated Services Digital Network; modem; Single-Line Digital Subscriber Line; Very-High-Bit-Rate Digital Subscriber Line.

C

TABLE C.1 CONNECTION SPEEDS

Technology	Speed	Distance Limitation
Conventional modem	56Kbps downstream, up to 33.6Kbps upstream	None
ISDN	Up to 128Kbps symmetric	18,000 ft
Cable modem	Up to 30Mbps downstream, to 10Mbps upstream	30 mi
ADSL	1.5 to 8Mbps downstream, to 1.544Mbps upstream	18,000 ft
SDSL	1.544 to 2.048Mbps symmetric	10,000 ft
HDSL	1.544 to 2.048Mbps symmetric (over 3 phone lines)	15,000 ft
VDSL	13 to 52Mbps downstream, 1.5 to 2.3Mbps upstream	4,500 ft

connectivity The degree to which any given computer or application can cooperate with other network components purchased from other vendors, in a network environment in which resources are shared.

connect time The period of time during which a user is logged on to the network.

ConnectView An application with a graphical user interface used to manage NetWare Connect and Novell Internet Access Server (NIAS) communication servers.

CONS *See* Connection-Oriented Network Service.

cons *See* console.

Conseil Européen pour la Researche Nucléaire Abbreviated CERN. The European Laboratory for Particle Physics located in Geneva, Switzerland, where Tim Berners-Lee and associates created the communications protocols that led to the World Wide Web.

For more information on CERN, see www.cern.ch.

console Sometimes abbreviated cons. The monitor and keyboard from which the server or host computer activity can be monitored.

Certain operating system commands and utilities must be executed from the console device; they will not operate from a workstation. In some systems, the console is a virtual device that can be invoked from any workstation by a network administrator with the appropriate rights and privileges.

constant angular velocity Abbreviated CAV. An unchanging speed of rotation. Hard disks use a CAV encoding scheme. The constant rate of rotation means that sectors on the disk are at the maximum density along the inside track of the disk. As the read/write heads move outward, the sectors must spread out to cover the increased track circumference, and therefore the data-transfer rate falls off.

See also constant linear velocity.

Constant Bit Rate Abbreviated CBR. A type of Asynchronous Transfer Mode (ATM) service reserved for voice or video or other data that must be transmitted at a constant rate and are intolerant of data loss.

See also Asynchronous Transfer Mode; Available Bit Rate; Unspecified Bit Rate; Variable Bit Rate.

constant linear velocity Abbreviated CLV. A changing speed of rotation. CD-ROM disk drives use a CLV encoding scheme to make sure that the data density remains constant. Information on a compact disc is stored in a single, spiral track, divided into many equal-length segments. To read the data, the CD-ROM disk drive must increase the rotational speed as the read head gets closer to the center of the disc and decrease as the head moves back out.

See also constant angular velocity.

Consultative Committee for International Telephony and Telegraphy Abbreviated CCITT. An organization based in Geneva that develops worldwide data communications standards. Three main sets of standards have been established:

- CCITT Groups 1–4 standards apply to facsimile transmissions.

- CCITT V series of standards apply to modems and error detection and correction methods.

- CCITT X series standards apply to LANs.

Recommendations are published every four years. In 1993, after a reorganization, the name was changed to International Telecommunication Union (ITU), and even though ITU now creates recommendations and standards, you will still hear the CCITT standards mentioned.

See also International Telecommunication Union.

container One of the Java programming language classes that can contain graphical user interface components. Components in a container usually appear within the boundaries of that container. For example, the classes `Dialog`, `Frame`, and `Window` are all containers.

See also Java.

container administrator In Novell Directory Services, an administrator who is granted rights to a container object and all the objects that the container holds. A container administrator can be exclusive, indicating that no other administrator is allowed access to that container.

See also container object; leaf object.

container object   In Novell Directory Services, an object that can contain other objects and that is used to represent a logical or physical organizational element within a company, such as a department or a division. The Tree, Country, Organization, and Organizational Unit objects are all container objects.

See also container administrator; Country object; leaf object; Organization object; Organizational Unit object; Tree object.

container security equivalence   *See* implied security equivalence.

contention   The competition between transmitting nodes for access to communications lines or network resources. The first device to gain access to a channel takes control of the channel. In the event of a collision, when two nodes attempt to transmit at the same time, some arbitration scheme must be invoked.

See also Carrier Sense Multiple Access/ Collision Detection; token passing.

context   In Novell Directory Services, an object's location within the Directory tree. The context is the full path to the container object in which the object is placed. If an object is moved from one container to another, it has changed contexts.

See also container object; leaf object.

context switching   Switching from one program to another without ending the first program. Context switching allows you to operate several programs at the same time; but it differs from true multitasking in that when you are using one program, all the other programs loaded onto your system must halt.

control character   A nonprinting character with a special meaning.

Control characters, such as Carriage Return, Line Feed, Bell, or Escape, perform a specific operation on a terminal, printer, or communications line. They are grouped together as the first 32 characters in the ASCII character set; see Appendix C for details.

You can type a control character from the keyboard by pressing and holding the Ctrl key while you simultaneously press another key. For example, if you press and hold the Ctrl key and then press C, you generate Ctrl+C, also known as Break. Control character sequences are often used inside application programs as menu command shortcuts.

See also American Standard Code for Information Interchange; Extended Binary Coded Decimal Interchange Code; Unicode.

control code   A sequence of one or more characters used for hardware control; also known as setup strings or escape sequences. Control codes are used with printers, modems, and displays. Printer control codes often begin with an escape character, followed by one or more characters that the printer interprets as commands it must perform rather than as text it must print.

Controlled Access Unit   Abbreviated CAU. An intelligent Multistation Access Unit (MAU) or multiport wiring hub for a token-ring network that allows ports to be switched on and off.

controllerless modem   A modem that shifts all the protocol management, error detection and correction, and data compression onto software running on the system's CPU. This allows the modem manufacturer to make a much cheaper modem that does not require the memory or processing power of a traditional modem. Also known as a soft modem.

control set   That portion of the Microsoft Windows Registry that contains information required to boot the operating system and restore the last known good configuration.

conventional memory   The amount of memory accessible by MS-DOS in PCs using an Intel processor operating in real mode; normally the first 640KB.

The designers of the original IBM PC made 640KB available to the operating system and applications and reserved the remaining space for internal system use, the BIOS, and video buffers. Although 640KB may not seem like much memory space now, it was ten times the amount of memory available in other leading personal computers available at the time. Since then, applications have increased in size to the point that 640KB is inadequate.

See also expanded memory; extended memory; high memory area; memory management; protected mode.

convergence   The synchronization process that a network must go through immediately after a routing change takes place on the network. Convergence time is the time required to update all the routers on the network with routing information changes.

See also routing table.

cookie   **1.** A block of data sent from a server to a client in response to a request by the client.

2. On the World Wide Web, a block of data stored by the server on the system running the browser or client software, which can be retrieved by the server during a future session. A cookie contains information that can identify the user for administrative reasons or to prepare a custom Web page.

cooperative multitasking   A form of multitasking in which all running applications must work together to share system resources.

The operating system supports cooperative multitasking by maintaining a list of the active applications and the order in which they execute. When control is transferred to an application, the other applications cannot run until that application returns control back to the operating system once again.

A cooperative multitasking system differs from a preemptive multitasking system, in which the operating system executes each application in turn for a specific period of time (depending on priority) before switching to the next application, regardless of whether the applications themselves return control to the operating system.

See also context switching; time-slice multitasking.

C

Copper Distributed Data Interface

Abbreviated CDDI. A version of the FDDI standard designed to run on shielded and unshielded twisted-pair cable rather than on fiber-optic cable. CDDI is capable of 100Mbps data transfer rates.

See also Fiber Distributed Data Interface.

coprocessor A secondary processor used to speed up operations by taking over a specific part of the main processor's work. The most common type of coprocessor is the math, or floating-point, coprocessor, which is designed to manage arithmetic calculations many times faster than does the main processor.

copy left The copyright or General Public License of the Free Software Foundation (FSF), which states that any of the software developed using free software from the FSF must be distributed to others without charge.

See also open source software.

CORBA *See* Common Object Request Broker Architecture.

COSE *See* Common Open Software Environment.

Country object In Novell Directory Services, a container object placed directly under the Root object in the Directory tree that defines the country for a specific part of your network. Country object names are defined by the International Organization for Standardization (ISO) and follow a standard naming convention. You must specify the Country object if you want to connect to external networks using X.500 directory services.

CPDA *See* Certified PowerBuilder Developer Associate.

CPDP *See* Certified PowerBuilder Developer Professional.

CPE *See* customer-premises equipment.

CPI-C *See* Common Programming Interface for Communications.

cps *See* characters per second.

CPTS *See* Certified Performance and Tuning Specialist.

CPU *See* central processing unit.

cracker An unauthorized person who breaks into a computer system planning to do harm or damage or with criminal intent. The popular press often portrays crackers as people with exceptional talent for eluding detection, and some of them are, but most of them use a set of well-worn tricks to exploit common security weaknesses in the systems they target.

See also attack; hacker; intruder.

crash An unexpected program halt, sometimes due to a hardware failure but most often due to a software error, from which there is no recovery. You usually need to reboot the computer to recover after a crash.

See also blue screen of death.

CRC *See* cyclical redundancy check.

critical error An error in a program that forces the program to stop until the user corrects the error condition. Examples of this kind of error are attempts to write to a floppy disk when there is no disk in the drive or to print to a printer that has run out of paper.

crosstalk   In communications, any interference from a physically adjacent channel that corrupts the signal and causes transmission errors.

See also far-end crosstalk; near-end crosstalk.

Cryptography API   Abbreviated CAPI. An API first introduced in Microsoft Windows NT 4 that provides encryption and decryption functions for application developers.

CSE   *See* Certified Solutions Expert.

C shell   In Unix, a popular command interpreter; pronounced "sea shell."

Developed at the University of California at Berkeley as part of the BSD development as an alternative to the Bourne shell. In addition to the features found in the Bourne shell, the C shell adds integer arithmetic, a history mechanism that can recall past commands in whole or in part, aliasing of frequently used commands, job control, and a built-in set of operators based on the C programming language used for writing shell scripts.

See also Bash; Bourne shell; Korn shell; Linux; Unix shell.

CSMA/CD   *See* Carrier Sense Multiple Access/Collision Detection.

CSRG   *See* Computer Systems Research Group.

CSU   *See* Channel Service Unit.

Ctrl+Alt+Del   A three-key combination used to reset the machine and reload the operating system. By pressing Ctrl+Alt+Del, you initiate a warm boot, which restarts the computer without going through the power-on self tests (POSTs) normally run when the computer goes through a cold boot.

In Windows 98 and 2000, the sequence opens a dialog box from which you can either end a task or shut down the computer. Sometimes called the three-finger salute.

See also warm boot.

Ctrl+Break   *See* Ctrl+C.

Ctrl+C   **1.** A key combination recognized by Unix, MS-DOS, and other operating systems as a user-initiated interruption. Pressing Ctrl+C stops a batch file, macro, or command (for example, a directory listing, a search, or a sort).

2. A keyboard shortcut recognized by many programs as the instruction to copy the selected item.

Ctrl key   A key on the keyboard that, when pressed at the same time as another key, generates a nonprinting control character.

On some keyboards, this key is labeled Control rather than Ctrl, but it produces the same function.

CTS   *See* Clear to Send.

CUE   *See* Certified Unicenter Engineer.

C

current directory In many operating systems, the directory that will be searched first for any file you request, and the directory in which any new files will be stored (unless you specifically designate another directory). The current directory is not the same as the default directory, which is the directory that an application uses unless you specify another.

See also dot; dot dot; period and double-period directories.

current drive In many operating systems, the disk drive that is being used for reading and writing files. The current drive is not the same as the default drive, which is the drive that an application uses unless you specify another.

See also drive mapping.

cursor A special character displayed on a monitor to indicate where the next character will appear when it is typed. In text or character mode, the cursor is usually a blinking rectangle or underline. In a graphical user interface, the mouse cursor can take many shapes, depending on the current operation and its screen location.

cursor-movement keys The keys on the keyboard that move the cursor; also called cursor-control keys. These keys include the four labeled with arrows and the Home, Pg Up, End, and Pg Dn keys.

On full-size keyboards, cursor-movement keys are often found on the numeric keypad; laptops and notebooks often have separate cursor-movement keys.

CU-SeeMe A popular videoconferencing and videophone product that works over the Internet.

CU-SeeMe was originally developed at Cornell University and is available free for the PC and the Macintosh. An enhanced commercial version that adds an electronic chalkboard is available from White Pine Software. The software is designed for personal use and for use in instruction and in business communications.

See also White Pine Software.

Customer Information Control System Abbreviated CICS. An IBM-mainframe client/server program that manages transaction processing in IBM's VM and MVS operating systems and that is scalable to thousands of users. It also provides password security, transaction logging for backup and recovery, and an activity log that can be used to analyze session performance, as well as facilities for creating, using, and maintaining databases.

customer-premises equipment Abbreviated CPE. Communications equipment, either leased or owned, used at a customer site.

cut through A technique used by some Ethernet hardware to speed up packet forwarding. Only the first few bytes of the packet are examined before it is forwarded or filtered. This process is much faster than looking at the whole packet, but it does allow some bad packets to be forwarded.

See also store-and-forward.

cut-through switching A type of switching used on a Token Ring network in which data is forwarded as soon as the first 20 or 30 bytes in a data frame have been read.

After the header information has been read, the connection is established between input and output ports, and the transmission begins immediately. Sometimes known as on-the-fly switching.

See also store-and-forward.

cyclical redundancy check   Abbreviated CRC. A complex calculation method used to check the accuracy of a digital transmission over a communications link or to ensure the integrity of a file stored on a hard disk.

The sending computer uses one of several formulas to calculate a value from the information contained in the data, and this value is appended to the message block before it is sent. The receiving computer performs the same calculation on the same data and compares this number with the received CRC. If the two CRCs do not match, indicating a transmission error, the receiving computer asks the sending computer to retransmit the data.

This procedure is known as a redundancy check because each transmission includes extra or redundant error-checking values as well as the data itself.

As a security check, a CRC may be used to compare the current size of an executable file against the original size to determine if the file has been tampered with or changed in some way.

See also checksum; Kermit; Xmodem; Ymodem; Zmodem.

Cyrix   A designer of microprocessors, including clones of popular Intel chips such as the 6x86MX and the MII (pronounced M-two). Cyrix was bought by National Semiconductor in 1998.

For more information about Cyrix, see www.cyrix.com.

See also Advanced Micro Devices, Inc.; Pentium; Pentium II; Pentium III.

C

D

DACL *See* Discretionary Access Control List.

daemon Pronounced "dee-mon." A background program that runs unattended and is usually invisible to the user, providing important system services.

Daemons manage all sorts of tasks, including e-mail, networking, and Internet services. Some daemons are triggered automatically by events to perform their work; others operate at timed intervals. Because daemons spend so much of their time idle, waiting for something to happen, they do not consume large amounts of system resources.

DAP *See* Directory Access Protocol.

DAS *See* dual-attached station.

DAT *See* digital audio tape.

data Information in a form suitable for processing by a computer, such as the digital representation of text, numbers, graphic images, or sounds. Strictly speaking, data is the plural of the Latin word *datum*, meaning an item of information; but the term is commonly used in both plural and singular constructions.

database A collection of related objects, including tables, forms, reports, queries, and scripts, created and organized by a database management system (DBMS). A database can contain information of almost any type, such as a list of magazine subscribers,

personal data on the space shuttle astronauts, or a collection of graphical images and video clips.

See also database management system; database model; table.

database management system Abbreviated DBMS. Software that controls the data in a database, including overall organization, storage, retrieval, security, and data integrity. A DBMS can also format reports for printed output and can import and export data from other applications using standard file formats. A data-manipulation language is usually provided to support database queries.

See also database; database model; query language.

database model The method used by a database management system (DBMS) to organize the structure of the database. The most common database model is the relational database.

See also relational database.

database server Any database application that follows the client/server architecture model, which divides the application into two parts: a front-end running on the user's workstation and a back-end running on a server or host computer. The front-end interacts with the user and collects and displays the data. The back-end performs all the computer-intensive tasks, including data analysis, storage, and manipulation.

Database Specialist: Informix Dynamic Server A certification from Informix designed for computer professionals who implement and manage Informix Dynamic Server databases. The associated exams cover relational database design, Structured Query Language (SQL), and management and optimization of Informix Dynamic Server databases.

See also Informix-4GL Certified Professional; system administration.

data bits In asynchronous transmissions, the bits that actually make up the data. Usually, seven or eight data bits are grouped together. Each group of data bits in a transmission is preceded by a start bit and followed by an optional parity bit as well as one or more stop bits.

See also communications parameters; parity; start bit; stop bit(s).

Data Carrier Detect Abbreviated DCD. A hardware signal defined by the RS-232-C standard that indicates that the device, usually a modem, is online and ready for transmission.

data communication The transfer of information from one computer to another over a communications link. The transfer can be occasional, continuous, or a combination of both.

data communications equipment Abbreviated DCE. In communications, any device that connects a computer or terminal

to a communications channel or public network; usually a modem.

See also data terminal equipment.

data compression Any method of encoding data so that it occupies less space than it did in its original form, thus allowing that data to be stored, backed up, retrieved, or transmitted more efficiently.

Data compression is used in fax and many other forms of data transmission, CD-ROM publishing, still-image and video-image manipulation, and database management systems.

See also Huffman coding; Joint Photographic Experts Group; lossless compression; lossy compression; Moving Pictures Experts Group.

data connector (Type 1) A connector for use with Type 1 cable, designed by IBM for use in Token Ring network wiring centers.

data-encoding scheme The method used by a hard-disk controller to store information onto a hard disk or a floppy disk. Common encoding schemes include the run-length limited (RLL) and advanced run-length limited (ARLL) methods.

See also advanced run-length limited encoding; RLL encoding.

Data Encryption Standard Abbreviated DES. A standard method of encrypting and decrypting data, developed by the U.S. National Bureau of Standards. DES works by a combination of transposition and substitution. It is used by the federal government and most banks and money-transfer

D

systems to protect all sensitive computer information.

See also encryption; Pretty Good Privacy.

data file   A file that contains information—text, graphics, or numbers—rather than executable program code.

datagram   A message unit that contains source and destination address information, as well as the data itself, which is routed through a packet-switching network.

The data held in the datagram is often referred to as the payload, and the addressing information is usually contained in the header. Because the destination address is contained in all datagrams, they do not have to arrive in consecutive order. Datagrams are commonly used in connectionless transmission systems. IP (Internet Protocol) and IPX (Internetwork Packet Exchange) are both datagram services.

See also frame; data packet.

Datagram Delivery Protocol   Abbreviated DDP. A routing protocol developed by Apple Computer as a part of its AppleTalk network.

data-link layer   The second of seven layers of the OSI Reference Model for computer-to-computer communications. The data-link layer validates the integrity of the flow of data from one node to another by synchronizing blocks of data and controlling the flow of data.

The Institute of Electrical and Electronic Engineers (IEEE) has divided the data-link layer into two other layers—the logical link

control (LLC) layer sits above the media access control (MAC) layer.

See also OSI Reference Model.

Data Link Switching   Abbreviated DLSw. A standard for encapsulating or tunneling IBM Systems Network Architecture (SNA) and NetBIOS applications across IP networks.

See also Advanced Peer-to-Peer Networking; Systems Network Architecture.

data mining   The process of displaying historical commercial data in a multidimensional form so that previously hidden relationships are exposed through the use of advanced statistical tools, making them easier to group and summarize.

See also data warehousing; online analytical processing; online transaction processing.

data packet   One unit of information transmitted as a discrete entity from one node on the network to another. More specifically, a packet is a transmission unit of a fixed maximum length that contains a header with the destination address, a set of data, and error control information.

See also frame.

data processing   Abbreviated DP. Also called electronic data processing (EDP). A term used to describe work done by minicomputers and mainframe computers in a data center or business environment.

data protection   Techniques used by network operating systems to ensure the integrity of data on the network, including protecting data against surface defects developing on the disk and storing redundant copies of important system data, such as file indices and file allocation tables (FATs). Disk duplexing, disk mirroring, a well thought out backup scheme, and RAID techniques all provide different levels of data protection.

See also diskless workstation; disk striping; disk striping with parity; fault tolerance; Hot Fix; intruder; redundant array of inexpensive disks; virus.

Data Service Unit   Abbreviated DSU. A device that connects DTE (data terminal equipment) to digital communications lines. A DSU formats the data for transmission on the public carrier WANs and ensures that the carrier's requirements for data formats are met.

See also Channel Service Unit.

Data Set Ready   Abbreviated DSR. A hardware signal defined by the RS-232-C standard to indicate that the device is ready to operate.

See also Clear to Send.

data terminal equipment   Abbreviated DTE. In communications, any device, such as a terminal or a computer, connected to a communications device, channel, or public network.

See also data communications equipment.

Data Terminal Ready   Abbreviated DTR. A hardware signal defined by the RS-232-C standard sent from a computer to a modem to indicate that the computer is ready to receive a transmission.

data-transfer rate   **1.** The speed at which a disk drive can transfer information from the drive to the processor, usually measured in megabits or megabytes per second.

2. The rate of information exchange between two systems. For example, an Ethernet LAN may achieve 10Mbps, and a Fiber Distributed Data Interface (FDDI) system may reach 100Mbps.

See also connection speed.

data warehousing   A method of storing very large amounts of data, usually historical transaction processing data, for later analysis and reporting.

The data warehouse is accessed by software capable of extracting trends from the raw data and creating comparative reports.

See also data mining.

dB   *See* decibel.

DB connector   Any of several types of cable connectors used for parallel or serial cables. The number following the letters DB (for data bus) indicates the number of pins that the connector usually has; a DB-25 connector can have a maximum of 25 pins, and a DB-9 connector can have as many as 9. In practice, not all the pins (and not all the lines in the cable) may be present in the larger connectors. If your situation demands that all the lines be present, make sure you buy the right cable. Common DB connectors include the following:

- DB-9   Defined by the RS-449 standard as well as the ISO (International Organization for Standardization).

D

• **DB-25**   A standard connector used with RS-232-C wiring, with 25 pins (13 on the top row and 12 on the bottom).

• **DB-37**   Defined as the RS-449 primary channel connector.

DB-15, DB-19, and DB-50 connectors are also available. The accompanying illustration shows a male and female DB-25 connector.

DBCS   *See* double-byte character set.

DBMS   *See* database management system.

DC-2000   A quarter-inch tape minicartridge used in some tape backup systems. DC-2000 has a capacity of up to 250MB when some form of data compression is used.

See also quarter-inch cartridge.

DCD   *See* Data Carrier Detect.

DCE   *See* data communications equipment.

DCE   *See* Distributed Computing Environment.

D channel   The channel in ISDN that is used for control signals and customer data. In the Base Rate ISDN (BRI), the D channel operates at 16Kbps; in the Primary Rate ISDN (PRI), it operates at 64Kbps.

DCOM   *See* Distributed Component Object Model.

DDCMP   *See* Digital Data Communications Message Protocol.

DDD   *See* direct distance dialing.

DDE   *See* Dynamic Data Exchange.

DDP   *See* Datagram Delivery Protocol.

deadlock   An error condition or stalemate that occurs when two programs or devices are each waiting for a signal from the other before they can continue.

DEC   *See* Digital Equipment Corporation.

DB CONNECTOR

female

male

DEC Alpha Also called the DEC Alpha AXP or the DECchip 21264. A 64-bit, RISC (reduced instruction set computing) microprocessor from Digital Equipment Corporation (DEC), first introduced in 1992.

The Alpha is a superscalar, superpipelined design, which allows the processor to execute more than one instruction per clock cycle; it can execute as many as six instructions per clock cycle and can sustain four instructions per clock cycle.

It has data and instruction caches, a floating-point processor, 64-bit registers, 64-bit data and address buses, and a 128-bit data path between the processor and memory. The internal architecture is symmetrical multiprocessing (SMP) compliant, meaning that it can be used in multiprocessing configurations. The chip is available in several models with operating frequencies in the 300 to 700MHz range; a 1GHz model is expected by the year 2000.

decapsulation A process used in networking in which the receiving system looks at the header of an arriving message to determine if the message contains data. If the message does contain data, the header is removed and the data decoded.

See also encapsulation.

decibel Abbreviated dB. One-tenth of a bel, a unit of measurement common in electronics that quantifies the loudness or strength of a signal. A decibel is a relative measurement derived by comparing a measured level against a known reference.

decimal The base-10 numbering system that uses the familiar numbers 0–9; also known as the base 10 radix or the decimal radix.

See also binary; hexadecimal.

decimal radix *See* decimal.

DECnet A series of communications and networking products from Digital Equipment Corporation (DEC). DECnet is compatible with Ethernet, as well as with WANs using baseband and broadband private and public communications channels. DECnet is built into the VAX VMS operating system.

See also Digital Network Architecture.

decode 1. To decompress a video file after receipt so that you can view it. Most decoding is done by the client browser.

2. To convert coded data back into its original form, usually as readable text.

See also codec; decryption; encode; uuencode.

decryption The process of converting encrypted data back into its original form.

See also encryption.

dedicated circuit *See* dedicated line; direct connection.

dedicated line A communications circuit used for one specific purpose and not used by or shared between other users. You need only dial a dedicated line to restore service after an unscheduled interruption. Also known as a dedicated circuit.

See also leased line.

D

dedicated server   A computer on the network that functions only as a server performing specific networking tasks, such as storing files, printing, or managing external communications.

Dedicated Token Ring   An IEEE 802.5r Token Ring specification that allows for full-duplex connections at a speed of up to 32Mbps. By enabling full-duplex communications, the token-passing mechanism is not used, and communications can take place between a device and a switch at any time.

See also 802.x; token-ring network.

default   A standard setting, used until an alternative is chosen. The default server is the first server that you log on to. The default drive is the drive that a workstation is currently using.

A default is usually a relatively safe course of action to try first; many programs provide defaults you can use until you know enough about the program to specify your own settings.

default directory   A standard directory or set of directories used by the operating system or by an application.

Some operating systems create several default directories when the file system is created. For example, Novell NetWare creates the following directories when the SYS volume is created:

- SYS:SYSTEM, for the NetWare operating system files

- SYS:PUBLIC, for utility and user programs

- SYS:LOGIN, for programs allowing users to log in to the server

- SYS:MAIL, a directory used by NetWare-compatible electronic-mail applications

default server   In Novell NetWare, the server that responds to the Get Nearest Server request made as a user starts the logon process. Novell Directory Services has replaced the need for the default server destination with the default context.

See also Context.

defense in depth   A term borrowed from the military used to describe defensive measures that reinforce each other, hiding the defenders activities from view and allowing the defender to respond to an attack quickly and effectively.

In the network world, defense in depth describes an approach to network security that uses several forms of defense against an intruder and that does not rely on one single defensive mechanism.

defragmentation   The process of reorganizing and rewriting files so that they occupy one large area on a hard disk rather than several smaller areas.

When a file on a hard disk is updated, it may be written into different areas all over the disk. This outcome is particularly likely when the hard disk is continuously updated over a long period of time. This file fragmentation can lead to significant delays in loading files, but its effect can be reversed by defragmentation.

See also disk optimizer.

defragmenter   Any utility that rewrites all the parts of a fragmented file into contiguous areas on a hard disk. A defragmenter (such as the Microsoft Windows 98 utility Disk Defragmenter) can restore performance lost because of file fragmentation.

See also defragmentation; disk optimizer.

delay   In communications, a pause in activity, representing the time during which transmission-related resources are unavailable for relaying a message.

See also propagation delay.

delay distortion   The distortion of a signal caused by the relative difference in speed of the various components of that signal; in particular, the distortion of the high-frequency component. Also called envelope delay.

delete   To remove a file from a disk or to remove an item from a file. Files can be deleted using operating system commands or directly from within an application.

When a file is deleted from a disk, the file is not physically removed; although it is hidden, it is still there on the disk until it is overwritten. In certain circumstances it is possible to undelete or recover the original information with utilities designed for that purpose. If you find you have deleted an important file by accident, do not write any other files to that disk so that you do not overwrite the deleted file. Some network operating systems use a delete inhibit attribute to prevent accidental deletions; other operating systems rely on a read-only attribute.

delimiter   **1.** Any special character that separates individual items in a data set or file. For example, in a comma-delimited

file, the comma is placed between each data value as the delimiter.

2. In a token-ring network, a delimiter is a bit pattern that defines the limits of a frame or token on the network.

Dell Computer Corporation   One of the world's top five PC manufacturers. Dell pioneered direct sales of the PC using a configure-it-yourself Web site.

Best known for PC and laptop sales, Dell is also pursuing the server market and has recently expanded into the enterprise storage market with the PowerVault line of SCSI-based storage subsystems, tape backup systems, and scalable disk subsystems.

For more information on Dell, see www.dell.com.

demand paging   A common form of virtual memory management in which pages of information are read into memory from disk only when required by the program.

See also swapping.

demand priority   A technique used in 100VG-AnyLAN to arbitrate access to the network and avoid collisions. Demand priority replaces CSMA/CD, which is used in slower Ethernet networks.

Demand priority can also prioritize specific network traffic such as video and other time-critical data, giving it a higher precedence; if multiple requests are received, the highest priority is always serviced first.

See also Fast Ethernet.

demodulation   In communications, the process of retrieving the data from a

D

99

modulated carrier signal; the reverse of modulation.

See also modem.

denial of service attack   An attack by an intruder that prevents a computer system from providing a service.

A denial-of-service attack will typically involve opening and dropping a large number of TCP/IP connections very quickly so that the target system spends all its time dealing with the connection overhead to the point that it cannot respond to valid user requests. Other attacks may exploit known software security holes to crash servers.

A denial-of-service attack is much easier to execute than an attempt at unauthorized access, because the denial-of-service attack never actually requires access to the system.

See also brute-force attack; dictionary attack; mail bombing; social engineering; Trojan Horse.

departmental LAN   A local-area network used by a relatively small group of people working on common tasks; it provides shared local resources, such as printers, data, and applications.

DES   *See* Data Encryption Standard.

descendant key   In Microsoft Windows, all the subkeys that appear when you expand a key in the Windows Registry.

See also key; Registry.

DeskSet   A collection of graphical desktop applications bundled with Sun Microsystem's Solaris.

DeskSet includes a file manager with options for copying, moving, renaming, and deleting files, a terminal emulator, text editor, calculator, clock, and calendar, as well as special programs and utilities.

See also Solaris.

desktop management   The process of managing desktop workstation hardware and software components automatically, often from a central location.

See also total cost of ownership; Zero Administration for Windows.

Desktop Management Interface   Abbreviated DMI. A standard API for identifying desktop workstation hardware components automatically, without intervention from the user.

At a minimum, DMI identifies the manufacturer, component name, version, serial number (if appropriate), and installation time and date of any component installed in a networked workstation. This information is designed to help network administrators resolve configuration problems quickly and easily and to indicate when and where system upgrades should be applied. PCs, Macintosh computers, and Unix systems are all covered by DMI.

DMI is backed by Digital Equipment Corporation (DEC), IBM, Intel, Microsoft, Novell, Sun, and more than 300 other vendors.

See also Plug and Play; total cost of ownership; Web-based Enterprise Management; Wired for Management; Zero Administration for Windows.

desktop video   The combination of video capture hardware and application software that controls the display of video or television pictures on a desktop PC.

Desktop video is becoming increasingly important with the sharp increase in videoconferencing applications now available.

destination address   The address portion of a packet or datagram that identifies the intended recipient station.

See also source address.

destination host   A computer system on the network that is the final destination for a file transfer or for an e-mail message.

device   A general term used to describe any computer peripheral or hardware element that can send or receive data.

Some examples are modems, printers, serial ports, disk drives, routers, bridges, and concentrators. Some devices require special software, or device drivers, to control or manage them; others have built-in intelligence.

In Unix and certain other operating systems, all peripherals are treated as though they were files. When Unix writes information to your terminal, it is actually writing to a special file that represents your terminal.

See also device driver.

device dependence   The requirement that a specific hardware component be present for a program to work. Device-dependent software is often difficult to move or port to another computer because of its reliance on specific hardware.

See also device independence.

device driver   A small program that allows a computer to communicate with and control a device. Each operating system contains a standard set of device drivers for the keyboard, the monitor, and so on. When you add specialized peripheral devices, such as a CD-ROM disk drive or a network interface card, you must install the appropriate device driver so that the operating system knows how to manage the device.

See also Plug and Play.

D

device independence   The ability to produce similar results in a variety of environments, without requiring the presence of specific hardware.

The Java programming language and the PostScript page-description language are examples of device independence. Java runs on a wide range of computers, from the PC to a Cray; PostScript is used by many printer manufacturers.

See also device dependence.

device name   The name used by the operating system to identify a computer-system component. For example, COM1 is the Windows device name for the first serial port on the PC.

device number   A unique number assigned to a device so that it can operate on the network. Devices are identified by three numbers:

- A physical address set by jumpers on the adapter board

- A device code determined by the physical address

• A logical address determined by the order in which the drivers are loaded and by the physical address of the adapter

See also Ethernet address; hardware address.

DFS *See* Distributed File System.

DHCP *See* Dynamic Host Configuration Protocol.

diagnostic program A program that tests computer hardware and peripheral devices for correct operation. Some faults, known as hard faults, are relatively easy to find, and the diagnostic program will diagnose them correctly every time. Other faults, called soft faults, can be difficult to find, because they occur under specific circumstances rather than every time the memory location is tested.

Most computers run a simple set of system checks when the computer is first turned on. The PC tests are stored in ROM and are known as power-on self tests (POSTs). If a POST detects an error condition, the computer stops and displays an error message on the screen.

dialback modem *See* callback modem.

dial-in/dial-out server *See* asynchronous communications server.

Dialogic Corp A major manufacturer of high-performance telephony products, including those used in voice, data, fax, speech synthesis, ISDN networking, and call center management applications.

For more information on Dialogic, see www.dialogic.com.

dialup line A nondedicated communication line in which a connection is established by dialing the destination code and then broken when the call is complete.

See also dedicated line; leased line.

Dial-Up Networking Software provided with Microsoft's Windows products that allows the clients to dial out and establish Point-to-Point Protocol (PPP) connections.

dictionary attack An attack by an intruder that checks passwords in a password file against a list of words likely to be used as passwords. Some versions of this attack check the entire language lexicon.

See also brute-force attack; denial of service attack; mail bombing; social engineering; Trojan Horse.

differential backup A backup of a hard disk that includes only the information that has changed since the last complete backup.

A differential backup assumes that a full backup already exists and that in the event of an accident, this complete backup will be restored before the differential backup is reloaded.

differential SCSI A Small Computer System Interface (SCSI) bus wiring scheme that uses two wires for each signal on the bus. One wire carries the signal, while the other carries its inverse. Differential SCSI minimizes the effects of external interference and so allows longer SCSI cable lengths to be used.

See also single-ended SCSI; Small Computer System Interface.

digest   A collection of Internet mailing list posts collected together and sent out as a single large message rather than as a number of smaller messages. Using a digest is a good way to cut down on the number of noncritical e-mail messages you receive.

See also LISTSERV; listserver; mailing list.

digital   Describes any device that represents values in the form of binary digits or bits.

See also analog.

digital audio tape   Abbreviated DAT. A method of recording information in digital form on a small audio tape cassette, originally developed by Sony and Hewlett-Packard. The most common format is a 4-millimeter, helical-scan drive, which can hold more than 3GB of information. DATs can be used as backup media; however, like all tape devices, they are relatively slow.

Digital Data Communications Message Protocol   Abbreviated DDCMP. A byte-oriented, link-layer synchronous protocol from Digital Equipment Corporation (DEC), used as the primary data-link component of DECnet.

Digital Equipment Corporation   Abbreviated DEC. A major manufacturer of minicomputers and mainframe computers, founded in 1957, long recognized for its high-quality computer systems. DEC's most popular product line, the VAX series, ranges from small desktop systems to large mainframes suitable for scientific and commercial processing. DEC was bought by Compaq Computer Corporation in 1998.

For more information on DEC, see www.digital.com.

See also DEC Alpha.

Digital Network Architecture   Abbreviated DNA. The framework within which Digital Equipment Corporation (DEC) designs and develops all its communications products.

digital service   *See* digital signal.

digital signal   Abbreviated DS; also known as digital service. There are several levels of common carrier digital transmission service:

- **DS-0**   64Kbps.
- **DS-1**   1.544Mbps (T1).
- **DS-1C**   Two DS-1 channels are multiplexed into a single DS-1C 3.152Mbps channel.
- **DS-2**   Two DS-1C channels are multiplexed into one DS-2 6.312Mbps (T2) channel.
- **DS-3**   Seven DS-2 channels are multiplexed into a single 44.736Mbps (T3) channel.
- **DS-4**   Six DS-3 channels are multiplexed into one 274.176Mbps (T4) DS-4 channel.

The higher-capacity channels are constructed by multiplexing the lower-bandwidth channels together, with some additional framing and administrative overhead.

DS-0 is also referred to as fractional T1, because it bridges the gap between 56-Kbps direct dial service (DDS) and a full T1 implementation.

DIGITAL SIGNAL

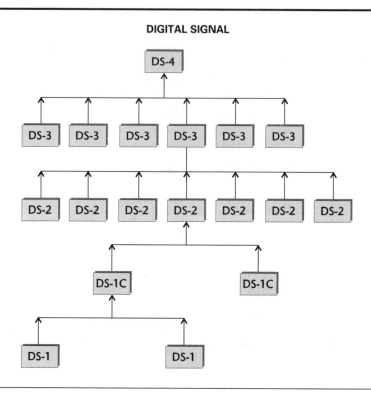

Digital Signal Processing Abbreviated DSP. An integrated circuit used in high-speed data manipulation. You will find DSP chips integrated into sound cards, modems, and video-conferencing hardware for use in communications, image manipulation, and other data-acquisition applications.

See also codec; desktop video.

digital signature An electronic signature that cannot be forged. A digital signature confirms that the document or e-mail in question originated from the individual or company whose name appears on the document and that the document has not been altered or tampered with in any way since it was signed.

See also certificate.

Digital Subscriber Line Abbreviated DSL. A high-speed data transmission technology originally developed by Bellcore that delivers high bandwidth over existing twisted-pair copper telephone lines.

There are several DSL services, providing data rates from 16Kbps to 52Mbps. The services can be symmetrical, with the same data rate in both upstream and downstream directions, or asymmetrical, with the downstream capacity greater than the upstream capacity. Asymmetric services are particularly suitable for Internet users, because more information is downloaded than is uploaded.

As DSL data rates increase, the distance over which the service is provided decreases; certain users who are located too far from the telephone company's central office may not be able to obtain the higher speeds or, in some cases, may not be able to receive the service at all.

See also Asymmetric Digital Subscriber Line; High-Bit-Rate Digital Subscriber Line; Rate-Adaptive Digital Subscriber Line; Single-Line Digital Subscriber Line; Very-High-Bit-Rate Digital Subscriber Line.

digital versatile disc   *See* digital video disc.

digital video disc   Abbreviated DVD; sometimes called digital versatile disc. A compact disc format. A standard single-layer single-sided disc can currently store 4.7GB of information; a two-layer standard increases this to 8.5GB, and eventually double-sided discs are expected to store 17GB per disc. DVD drives can also read conventional compact discs.

digital video disc-erasable   Abbreviated DVD-E. An extension to the digital video disc format to allow multiple re-recordings.

See also digital video disc-recordable.

digital video disc-recordable   Abbreviated DVD-R. An extension to the digital video disc format to allow one-time recording.

See also digital video disc-erasable.

digital video disc-ROM   Abbreviated DVD-ROM. A computer-readable form of digital video disc with either 4.7 or 8.5GB of storage per side.

dimmed command   In a graphical user interface, a command that is not currently available. Also known as a grayed command, because it is often displayed in light gray rather than the usual black. For example, a command to perform a network action will be dimmed until you log on to the network.

DIN connector   A connector that meets the specification of the German national standards body, Deutsche Industrie Norm (DIN).

Several models of Macintosh computers use 8-pin DIN connectors as the serial port connector. On many IBM-compatible computers, a 5-pin DIN connector connects the keyboard to the system unit.

DIP   *See* dual in-line package.

DIP switch   A small switch used to select the operating mode of a device, mounted as a dual in-line package. DIP switches can be either sliding or rocker switches, and they are often grouped for convenience. They are used in printed circuit boards, dot-matrix printers, modems, and many other peripheral devices.

D

DIP SWITCH

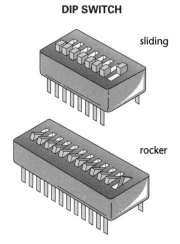

sliding

rocker

direct access *See* random access.

direct connection A communications circuit used for one specific purpose and not used by or shared with other users. Also known as a dedicated circuit or a direct line. An ISDN qualifies as a direct connection.

See also Integrated Services Digital Network.

direct distance dialing Abbreviated DDD. Use of the normal long-distance telephone system without the need for the intervention of an operator.

direct distance dial network *See* public network.

direct line *See* direct connection.

direct manipulation In a graphical user interface, the process of working with objects using a mouse or other pointing device, rather than using menu selections to manipulate the objects. Using drag-and-drop to print a file or using the mouse to adjust the size of a window are both examples of direct manipulation.

direct memory access Abbreviated DMA. A method of transferring information directly from a mass-storage device, such as a hard disk, into memory without the information passing through the processor. Because the processor is not involved in the transfer, DMA is usually fast.

Directory 1. In Novell Directory Services (NDS), the Directory database contains and organizes all the NDS objects.

2. In the Microsoft Active Directory structure, a Directory contains information about users, groups of users, computers, and so on.

See also Active Directory; Directory object; Directory Schema; directory tree; Novell Directory Services.

directory In a hierarchical file system, a convenient way of organizing and grouping files and other directories on a disk. Sometimes called a folder. The beginning directory is known as the root directory, from which all other directories must branch. Directories inside another directory are called subdirectories.

Depending on the operating system, you can list the files in a directory in a variety of ways: by name, by creation date and time, by file size, or by icon if you use a graphical user interface.

See also current directory; default directory; directory services; file allocation table; parent directory; period and double-period directories.

Directory Access Protocol Abbreviated DAP. A mail standard used to access white page directories containing names, addresses, e-mail addresses, and telephone numbers. Because of its complexity, DAP has been largely replaced by Lightweight Directory Access Protocol (LDAP).

See also Lightweight Directory Access Protocol.

directory caching A feature of Novell NetWare that copies the file allocation table (FAT) and the directory entry table into the network server's memory. When file requests are made, information is retrieved from the cache rather than from the hard disk, thus speeding the retrieval

process significantly. As the directory cache fills up, the least-used directory entries are eliminated from the cache.

directory hashing A feature of Novell NetWare that indexes file locations on disk, thus speeding file retrieval.

Directory Map object In Novell Directory Services (NDS), a leaf object that refers to a directory on a volume. The Directory Map object allows a drive to be mapped to an application or to a login script without requiring the actual path and volume where the application is physically located. This is done so that login scripts don't have to be rewritten when a drive path changes; you can simply change the Directory Map object.

See also Novell Directory Services.

Directory object In Novell Directory Services (NDS), a set of properties stored in the Directory database. A Directory object can represent a physical or a logical network resource, but it does not actually contain the resource.

See also Directory; Novell Directory Services.

directory path *See* path.

Directory replica In Novell NetWare, a copy of the NetWare Directory partition that allows the NetWare Directory Database to be stored on several servers on the network without having to duplicate the entire database on each server. Directory replicas remove a single point of failure from the network and thereby increase fault tolerance.

See also NetWare Directory Database.

D

directory replication A process that copies a master set of directories from a server, called an export server, to other specified servers or workstations, known as import computers. This process simplifies the task of maintaining and synchronizing identical sets of directories and files, because only one master copy of the data is maintained. A file is replicated when it is added to an exported directory, as well as when changes are made to the file.

Directory Schema In Novell Directory Services (NDS), a set of rules that defines how information can be stored in the Directory database. The Schema contains four major definitions:

- **Attribute information** Describes the kinds of information that can be associated with an object.

- **Inheritance** Defines which objects can inherit the rights and properties of other objects.

- **Naming** Determines the structure of the Directory tree.

- **Subordination** Specifies the location of objects in the Directory tree.

See also Novell Directory Services.

Directory services In the Microsoft Active Directory structure, a directory as well as the services it provides, such as security and replication.

See also Active Directory.

directory services A listing of all users and resources on a network, designed to help clients locate network users and services. Some examples are the OSI's X.500, Novell

Directory Services (NDS), Microsoft's Active Directory, and Banyan's StreetTalk.

See also domain directory services; global directory services.

directory structure duplication A technique that maintains duplicate copies of the file allocation table (FAT) and directory entry table in separate areas of a hard disk. If the first copy is damaged or destroyed, the second copy is immediately available for use.

See also directory verification.

directory tree A method of representing the hierarchical structure of the directories, subdirectories, and files on a disk. The term is often used in graphical user interfaces. In object-oriented systems, this structure may also represent a group of objects, as in Novell Directory Services (NDS).

directory verification A process that performs a consistency check on duplicate sets of file allocation tables (FATs) and directory entry tables to verify that they are identical. The verification occurs every time the server is started.

See also directory structure duplication.

disable To turn a function off or prevent something from happening. In a graphical user interface, disabled menu commands are often shown in gray to indicate that they are not available.

See also dimmed command; enable.

disaster recovery The process used to restore services after a major interruption in computing or in communications. Large events such as earthquakes or fires can interrupt networked computing activities, but so can more mundane events such as hard-disk failure or a construction worker accidentally cutting through a power or telephone line. The whole point to disaster recovery is to plan for it before anything happens and then follow the plan when restoring services.

See also backup; disk duplexing; disk mirroring; redundant array of inexpensive disks.

Discretionary Access Control List   Abbreviated DACL. In Microsoft Windows NT, a list of user and group accounts that have permission to access an object's services. The DACL has as many Access Control Entries as there are user or group accounts with access to the object.

disk cache   Pronounced "disk cash." An area of computer memory where data is temporarily stored on its way to or from a disk. When an application asks for information from the hard disk, the cache program first checks to see if that data is already in the cache memory. If it is, the disk cache program loads the information from the cache memory rather than from the hard disk. If the information is not in memory, the cache program reads the data from the disk, copies it into the cache memory for future reference, and then passes the data to the requesting application. This process is shown in the accompanying illustration.

A disk cache program can significantly speed most disk operations. Some network operating systems also cache other often accessed and important information, such as directories and the file allocation table (FAT).

See also directory caching.

D

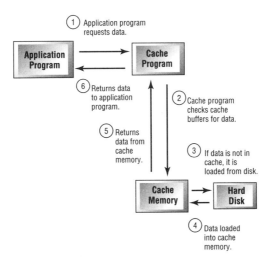

DISK CACHE

1. Application program requests data.

Application Program → Cache Program

6. Returns data to application program.

2. Cache program checks cache buffers for data.

5. Returns data from cache memory.

3. If data is not in cache, it is loaded from disk.

Cache Memory → Hard Disk

4. Data loaded into cache memory.

disk controller   The electronic circuitry that controls and manages the operation of floppy disks and hard disks.

A single disk controller may manage more than one hard disk. Many disk controllers also manage floppy disks and compatible tape drives. In the Macintosh, the disk controller is built into the system. In the PC, the disk controller may be a printed circuit board inserted into the expansion bus, or it may be part of the hard disk drive itself.

disk coprocessor board   *See* host bus adapter.

disk drive   A peripheral storage device that reads and writes magnetic or optical disks. When more than one disk drive is installed on a computer, the operating system assigns each drive (or logical drive) a unique name.

Several types of disk drives are in common use: floppy disk drives, hard disk drives, compact disc drives, digital video disc drives, Zip drives, and magneto-optical disc drives.

disk duplexing   A fault-tolerant technique that writes the same information simultaneously onto two hard disks.

Each hard disk uses a different disk controller to provide greater redundancy. If one disk or disk controller fails, information from the other system can be used to continue operations. Disk duplexing is offered by most major network operating systems. It is designed to protect the system against a single disk failure, not multiple disk failures. Disk duplexing is no substitute for a well-planned series of disk backups.

See also data protection; disk mirroring; redundant array of inexpensive disks.

diskless workstation   A networked computer that does not have any local disk storage capability. The computer boots and loads all its programs from the network file server. Diskless workstations are particularly valuable when sensitive information is processed; information cannot be copied from the file server onto a local disk, because the workstation does not have one.

See also dumb terminal; network computer; thin client.

disk mirroring   A fault-tolerant technique that writes the same information simultaneously onto two hard disks or two hard-disk partitions, using the same disk controller. If one disk or partition fails, information from the other can be used to continue operations. Disk mirroring is offered by most major network operating systems. It is designed to protect the system against a single disk failure, not multiple disk failures. Disk mirroring is no substitute for a well-planned series of disk backups.

See also data protection; disk duplexing; redundant array of inexpensive disks.

disk optimizer   A utility that rearranges files and directories on a disk for optimum performance. By reducing or eliminating file fragmentation (storage in pieces in different locations on the hard disk), a disk optimizer can restore the original level of performance of your disk system. Also, it is usually easier to undelete, or recover, an unfragmented file than a fragmented one.

Many disk optimizers will not only rewrite files as contiguous files, but will also place specific unchanging files in particular locations on the disk, optimize directories, and even place specific applications on the disk so that they load more quickly.

See also defragmentation.

disk striping   The technique of combining a set of disk partitions located on different hard disks into a single volume, creating a virtual "stripe" across the partitions that the operating system recognizes as a single drive. Disk striping can occur at the bit level or at the sector level and allows multiple concurrent disk accesses that can improve performance considerably.

See also disk striping with parity; redundant array of inexpensive disks; stripe set.

disk striping with parity   The addition of parity information across a disk stripe so that if a single disk partition fails, the data on that disk can be re-created from the information stored across the remaining partitions in the disk stripe.

See also disk striping; redundant array of inexpensive disks; stripe set.

dispersion   The degree of scattering that takes place as a beam of light travels along a fiber-optic cable.

See also cladding.

D

DISK STRIPING

file

byte 1   byte 4   byte 7   disk 1

byte 2   byte 5   byte 8   disk 2

byte 3   byte 6   byte 9   disk 3

distance vector algorithm A family of routing algorithms that calculate the best-path route to use for data transmission from information present in adjacent nodes on the network. Routing information is broadcast periodically rather than only when a change occurs, which makes the method bandwidth intensive. For this reason, distance vector algorithm is best used in relatively small networks with few inter-router connections.

Distinguished Name In Novell Directory Services (NDS), the full name of an object, including the object's Common name and its context. Sometimes called the Full Distinguished Name.

See also Common name; Context; Relative Distinguished Name.

Distributed Component Object Model Abbreviated DCOM. A specification from Microsoft that enables communications between distributed objects.

DCOM extends the Component Object Model (COM) so that clients can communicate directly with other processes on different computers on a LAN or on the Internet.

See also ActiveX; Component Object Model.

distributed computing *See* distributed processing.

Distributed Computing Environment Abbreviated DCE. The Open Software Foundation's (OSF) architecture for developing application software for use on different networks.

DCE hides the differences between products, technologies, and standards, providing independence from the operating system and underlying network. No particular communications protocol is specified, so the network can run on IP (Internet Protocol), IPX (Internetwork Packet Exchange), or SNA (Systems Network Architecture).

distributed database A database managed as a single system even though it includes many clients and many servers at both local and remote sites. A distributed database requires that data redundancy is managed and controlled.

Distributed File System **1.** Abbreviated DFS. A specification from Microsoft designed to make it easier to access files and directories on a network. To a user, the files on the network all appear in a single hierarchical tree, rather than on separate computers, making it easy to find a specific file.

2. Abbreviated DFS. A version of the Andrews File System included with the Open Group's Distributed Computing Environment (DCE).

See also Andrews File System; Network File System; Remote File System.

distributed file system Any file system in which files and programs are located on more than one computer or server. Users can access files and applications as though they were stored on a single local system.

Distributed System Object Model Abbreviated DSOM. IBM's extension to System Object Model (SOM) that allows objects to communicate in a distributed processing environment.

distributed processing   A computer system in which processing is performed by several separate computers linked by a communications network.

The term often refers to any computer system supported by a network, but more properly refers to a system in which each computer is chosen to handle a specific workload and the network supports the system as a whole. Each computer contributes to the completion of a common task by completing one or more subtasks independently of its peers and then reporting the results from these subtasks. All this is totally transparent to the users; all they see are the results of the process.

See also client/server architecture.

distribution medium   The type of data-storage device used to distribute original software or software updates.

Tapes used to be the favorite distribution medium, but compact discs are rapidly gaining popularity.

DIX connector   *See* Attachment Unit Interface.

DLL   *See* Dynamic Link Library.

DLSw   *See* Data Link Switching.

DMA   *See* direct memory access.

DMI   *See* Desktop Management Interface.

DNA   *See* Digital Network Architecture.

DNS   *See* Domain Name Service.

DNS alias   A host name that the Domain Name Service (DNS) server knows points to another host. Computers always have one real name, but they can also have several aliases. A DNS alias is sometimes called a CNAME or a canonical name.

See also Domain Name Service.

DNS name server   A server containing information that is part of the Domain Name Service (DNS) distributed database, which makes computer names available to client programs querying for name resolution on the Internet.

See also Domain Name Service.

docking station   A hardware system into which a portable computer fits so that it can be used as a full-fledged desktop computer.

Docking stations vary from simple port replicators that allow you access to parallel and serial ports and a mouse to complete systems that give you access to network connections, CD-ROMs, and even a tape backup system or PCMCIA ports. The portable computer and docking station are designed as two parts of the same system; you cannot swap computers and docking stations from different manufacturers or even from different models.

See also port replicator.

document database   A carefully organized collection of related documents; for example, a set of technical support bulletins.

document instance   In Standard Generalized Markup Language (SGML), the text component of a document as distinct from the structure of the document.

See also document type definition; Standard Generalized Markup Language.

document management   The cataloging, storage, and retrieval of documents in a networked environment. In this context, a document may be text, scanned graphics, a spreadsheet, a form, a Web page, or any other unique file.

Each file is tagged with information that includes the name of the original author, document description, creation date, and the name of the application used to create the document.

See also groupware; Lotus Notes; workflow software.

document root   On a Web server, a directory that contains the files, images, and data you want to present to all users who access the server with a browser.

document type definition   Abbreviated DTD. In Standard Generalized Markup Language (SGML), the structural component of a document as distinct from the actual data or content of the document.

See also document instance; Standard Generalized Markup Language.

documentation   The instructions, tutorials, specifications, troubleshooting advice, and reference guides that accompany a computer program or a piece of hardware. Documentation can be in printed or online format. Early system documentation was often written by programmers and engineers and was usually filled with technical jargon. Today's documentation is generally better written and easier to understand.

domain   A description of a single computer, a whole department, or a complete site, used for naming and administrative purposes.

Top-level domains must be registered to receive mail from outside the organization; local domains have meaning only inside their own enterprise. Depending on the context, the term can have several slightly different meanings:

- On the Internet, a domain is part of the Domain Name Service (DNS).

- In Novell NetWare, a domain is a special area of memory where a new NetWare Loadable Module (NLM) can be tested without the risk of corrupting the operating system memory.

- In IBM's Systems Network Architecture (SNA), a domain represents all the terminals and other network resources controlled by a single processor or processor group.

- In Microsoft Windows NT, a group of computers, users, and network peripherals managed with a single set of account descriptions and security policies. A user can log on to the local computer and be authenticated to access just that one system, or a user can log on to a domain and be authenticated to access other servers within that domain.

- In Lotus Notes, a domain is one or more Notes servers that share the same Public Name and Address Book database. This database contains information about the users within the domain, including their e-mail addresses and other information.

See also domain name.

domain component   In the Microsoft Active Directory structure, a portion of a domain name. For example, in `computer.sybex.com`, each element of the name—`computer`, `sybex`, and `com`–is a domain component.

See also Active Directory.

domain controller   In Microsoft Windows NT, a server that stores and shares domain information, including the central database of users, passwords, and permissions.

A domain controller can be a primary domain controller, which stores the master copy of the domain information, or a backup domain controller, which uses a replicated version of this data to verify user logons and rights.

domain directory services   Directory services that consist of one or more linked servers. Each domain within a network must be managed and administered separately. Windows NT Server and IBM's LAN Server both use domain directory services.

See also global directory services.

domain name   In the Domain Name Service (DNS), an easy-to-remember name that identifies a specific Internet host, as opposed to the hard-to-remember numeric IP address.

See also bang path.

Domain Name Service   Abbreviated DNS, sometimes referred to as Domain Naming System. A distributed addressing system that resolves the domain name into

the numeric IP address. DNS lets you use the Internet without having to remember long lists of cryptic numbers.

The most common high-level domains on the Internet include:

`.com`   A commercial organization

`.edu`   An educational establishment such as a university

`.gov`   A branch of the U.S. government

`.int`   An international treaty organization

`.mil`   A branch of the U.S. military

`.net`   A network provider

`.org`   A nonprofit organization

Most countries also have unique domains named after their international abbreviation—for example, `.uk` for the United Kingdom and `.ca` for Canada.

See also IP address; name resolution.

DOS   Acronym for Disk Operating System. An operating system originally developed by Microsoft for the IBM PC.

DOS existed in two similar versions: MS-DOS, developed and marketed by Microsoft for use with IBM-compatible computers, and PC-DOS, supported and sold by IBM for use on computers manufactured by IBM.

See also MS-DOS.

DOS client   A workstation that boots MS-DOS and gains access to the network using either a NetWare shell or the NetWare DOS Requester software.

D

DOS prompt *See* MS-DOS prompt.

dot   A synonym for the name of the current directory, usually invisible as its name begins with a period.

In Unix, a file whose name begins with a dot usually contains configuration information; you can customize your environment by creating the appropriate dot file in the current directory or in your home directory.

See also current directory; dot dot; period and double-period directories.

dot dot   A synonym for the name of the parent directory to the current directory, usually invisible as its name begins with a period.

See also current directory; dot; period and double-period directories.

dotted decimal   A method of representing an IP address as four decimal numbers separated by dots, or periods; for example, 194.65.87.3.

See also IP address.

double-byte character set   Abbreviated DBCS. A method that uses two bytes to hold the definition of the character rather than the single byte used by the American Standard Code for Information Interchange (ASCII) or the Extended Binary Coded Decimal Interchange Code (EBCDIC).

By utilizing two bytes instead one, the many international character sets in use these days can be managed much more easily.

See also ASCII standard character set; ASCII extended character set; Unicode.

double-slash   Notation used with a colon to separate the communications protocol from the host computer name in a Uniform Resource Locator (URL) as in http://www.sybex.com.

See also Uniform Resource Locator.

downlink   The transmission of information from a satellite to an earth station.

See also uplink.

download   **1.** In communications, to transfer a file or files from one computer to another over a network or using a modem.

2. To send information, such as font information or a PostScript file, from a computer to a printer.

downsizing   The redesign of mainframe-based business applications to applications capable of running on smaller, less-expensive systems, often PC LANs. Client/server architecture is the model most often implemented during downsizing.

When applications are moved from large computer systems to PCs, security, integrity, and overall control may be compromised, and development and training costs can be high. However, a collection of appropriately configured PCs, networked together, can provide more than ten times the power for the same cost as a mainframe computer supporting remote terminals.

A more accurate term might be *rightsizing*, to match the application requirements of the corporation to the capabilities of the hardware and software systems available.

See also outsourcing.

downtime   The amount of time during which a computer system is not available to users, because of a hardware or software failure.

downward compatibility   *See* backward compatibility.

DP   *See* data processing.

drag-and-drop   In a graphical user interface, to move a selected object onto another object with the mouse to initiate a process. For example, if you drag a document icon and drop it onto a word processor's icon, the program will run, and the document will be opened. To print a file, you can drag the file to the printer icon using the mouse and then release the mouse button. You can also use drag-and-drop to copy a file from one disk to another or to move a marked block of text to a new location inside a word-processed document.

DRAM   *See* dynamic RAM.

drive array   The group of hard disk drives used in one of the RAID (redundant array of inexpensive disks) configurations.

See also redundant array of inexpensive disks.

drive letter   A designation used to specify a PC disk drive. For example, the first floppy disk drive is usually referred to as drive A, and the first hard disk drive is usually referred to as drive C.

drive mapping   The technique of assigning a drive letter to represent a complete directory path statement. Novell NetWare supports four types of drive mapping:

- **Local drive mapping**   Maps drives to local hard disk and floppy disk drives

- **Network drive mapping**   Maps drives to volumes and directories on the network

- **Network search drive mapping**   Maps drives to directories that should be searched if an application or file is not found in the current directory

- **Directory map object**   Maps drives to directories that contain frequently used files, such as applications, without having to specify the actual physical location of the file

See also Directory Map object.

driver   Jargon for device driver.
See also device driver.

drop   1. The location in a multidrop line where a tap is inserted to allow the connection of a new device.

2. To lose part of a signal, usually unintentionally, as in dropping bits.

drop cable   The cable used in thick Ethernet to connect a network device to a Multistation Access Unit (MAU). The maximum cable length is 50 meters (165 feet). Sometimes called a transceiver cable.

DS   *See* digital signal.

DSL   *See* Digital Subscriber Line.

DSOM   *See* Distributed System Object Model.

D

DSP   *See* Digital Signal Processing.

DSR   *See* Data Set Ready.

DSU   *See* Data Service Unit.

DTD   *See* document type definition.

DTE   *See* data terminal equipment.

DTR   *See* Data Terminal Ready; Dedicated Token Ring.

dual-attached station   Abbreviated DAS. In the Fiber Distributed Data Interface (FDDI), a device attached to both of the dual, counter-rotating rings. Concentrators, bridges, and routers often use DAS connections to provide fault tolerance. In contrast, a single attached station (SAS) connects to only one ring.

dual-homed host   A network server configured with two network interface cards, each connected to a different network. Dual-homed hosts are often used with firewalls to increase network security.

See also firewall; proxy server.

dual homing   In Fiber Distributed Data Interface (FDDI), a method of cabling concentrators and stations in a tree configuration, providing an alternative route to the FDDI network should the primary connection fail.

dual in-line package   Abbreviated DIP. A standard housing constructed of hard plastic commonly used to hold an integrated circuit. The circuit's leads are connected to two parallel rows of pins designed to fit

snugly into a socket; these pins may also be soldered directly to a printed circuit board.

See also DIP switch.

dumb terminal   A combination of keyboard and screen that has no local computing power, used to input information to a large, remote computer, often a minicomputer or a mainframe. The remote computer provides all the processing power for the system.

See also diskless workstation; intelligent terminal; network computer; thin client.

duplex   In asynchronous transmissions, the ability to transmit and receive on the same channel at the same time; also referred to as full duplex. Half-duplex channels can transmit only or receive only.

See also communications parameters.

DVD   *See* digital video disc.

DVD-E   *See* digital video disc-erasable.

DVD-R   *See* digital video disc-recordable.

DVD-ROM   *See* digital video disc-ROM.

dynamic adaptive routing   *See* dynamic routing.

dynamic bandwidth allocation   A method of bandwidth allocation that subdivides the available bandwidth between multiple applications almost instantaneously, to provide each application with just the amount of bandwidth that it currently needs.

Dynamic Data Exchange Abbreviated DDE. A technique used for application-to-application communications, available in several operating systems, including Microsoft Windows, Macintosh, and OS/2. When two or more programs that support DDE are running at the same time, they can exchange data and commands, by means of conversations. A DDE conversation is a two-way connection between two applications, used to transmit data by each program alternately.

DDE is used for low-level communications that do not need user intervention. For example, a communications program might feed stock market information into a spreadsheet program, where that data can be displayed in a meaningful way and recalculated automatically as it changes.

DDE has largely been superseded by Object Linking and Embedding (OLE).

See also Object Linking and Embedding.

Dynamic Host Configuration Protocol Abbreviated DHCP. A system based on network interface card addresses that is used to allocate IP addresses and other configuration information automatically for networked systems. DHCP is an update of the Bootstrap Protocol.

See also Bootstrap Protocol; hardware address; IP address; Transmission Control Protocol/Internet Protocol.

Dynamic Link Library Abbreviated DLL. A program module that contains executable code and data that can be used by applications, or even by other DLLs, in performing a specific task.

DLLs are used extensively throughout the family of Microsoft Windows products. DLLs may have filename extensions of .DLL, .DRV, or .FON.

The DLL is linked into the application only when the program runs, and it is unloaded again when no longer needed. If two DLL applications are running at the same time and both perform a particular function, only one copy of the code for that function is loaded, for more efficient use of limited memory. Another benefit of using dynamic linking is that the .EXE files are not as large as they would be, because frequently used routines can be put into a DLL rather than repeated in each .EXE file that uses them. A smaller .EXE file means saved disk space and faster program loading.

dynamic RAM Abbreviated DRAM, pronounced "dee-ram." A common type of computer memory that uses capacitors and transistors storing electrical charges to represent memory states. These capacitors lose their electrical charge, so they need to be refreshed every millisecond, during which time they cannot be read by the processor.

DRAM chips are small, simple, cheap, easy to make, and hold approximately four times as much information as a static RAM (SRAM) chip of similar complexity. However, they are slower than SRAM.

dynamic routing A routing technique that allows the route that a message takes to change, as the message is in transit through the network, in response to changing network conditions. Conditions forcing a route change might include unusually heavy traffic on a particular section of the network or a cable failure. Also known as dynamic adaptive routing.

DynaText   A form of electronic document and viewer used in Novell NetWare for online manuals. You can use DynaText directly from the CD, or you can install it on the server or on a workstation. Replaces Electrotext.

E

E   *See* exa-.

E1   A point-to-point, dedicated, 2.048Mbps communications circuit capable of supporting thirty-two 64Kbps channels used as 30 voice channels, 1 control channel, and 1 synchronization and framing channel. The European equivalent of North America's T1.

E1 circuits carry more channels than the 24 channels used in T1 systems, and repeaters are required every 6000 feet when copper wire is used.

E2   A European point-to-point, dedicated, 8.848Mbps communications circuit equivalent to four E1 circuits. E2 is the European equivalent of North America's T2 and is rarely used.

E3   A European point-to-point, dedicated, 34.368Mbps communications circuit equivalent to 16 E1 circuits. The European equivalent of North America's T3.

E4   A European point-to-point, dedicated, 139.26Mbps communications circuit equivalent to 4 E3 or 64 E1 circuits.

E5   A European point-to-point, dedicated, 565.148Mbps communications circuit equivalent to 4 E4 or 256 E1 circuits.

eavesdropping   The process of gathering information about a target network by listening in on transmitted data.

EB   *See* exabyte.

EBCDIC   *See* Extended Binary Coded Decimal Interchange Code.

echo   **1.** A transmitted signal that is reflected back to the sender strongly enough so that it can be distinguished from the original signal; often encountered on long-distance telephone lines and satellite links.

2. A form of repetition, used as a mechanism in testing network nodes, in which each receiving station on the network echoes a message back to the main server or host computer.

echo cancellation   A mechanism used to control echoes on communications links such as satellite links.

The modem checks for a delayed duplication of the original signal and adds a reversed version of this transmission to the channel on which it receives information. This process effectively removes the echo without affecting the incoming signal.

ECNE   *See* Master Certified Novell Engineer.

EDI   *See* electronic data interchange.

EDO RAM   Abbreviation for extended data out RAM. A type of RAM that keeps data available to the processor while the next memory access is being initialized, thus speeding overall access times. EDO RAM is significantly faster than conventional dynamic RAM.

EDP   *See* data processing.

E

EEMS *See* Enhanced Expanded Memory Specification.

effective rights In Novell Directory Services (NDS), any rights an object can use to look at or change a specific directory, file, or other object.

Effective rights are recalculated every time an object attempts such an operation and are controlled by the Inherited Rights Filter, the trustee assignment, and the specified security restrictions. Effective rights are of two types:

- Object rights determine what a user can do with an object.

- Property rights control a user's access to that object.

See also Inherited Rights Filter; Novell Directory Services; rights; trustee assignments.

EFS *See* Encrypted File System.

EGP *See* External Gateway Protocol.

EIA *See* Electronic Industries Association.

EIA/TIA 586 A standard, jointly defined by the Electronic Industries Association and the Telecommunications Industry Association (EIA/TIA), for telecommunications wiring used in commercial buildings.

The standard is designed to do the following:

- Specify a generic wiring system for all commercial buildings

- Define media types, as well as connections and terminations

- Provide a basis for interoperation between competing products and services in wiring, design, installation, and management

- Allow for the wiring of a building before the definition of the products that will use that wiring, and allow for elegant future expansion

EIA/TIA 586 applies to all unshielded twisted-pair wiring that works with Ethernet, Token Ring, ISDN, and other networking systems.

See also cabling standards; Category 1–5.

EIDE *See* Enhanced IDE.

EISA *See* Extended Industry Standard Architecture.

electromagnetic interference Abbreviated EMI. Any electromagnetic radiation released by an electronic device that disrupts the operation or performance of another device.

EMI is produced by many sources commonly found in an office environment, including fluorescent lights, photocopiers, and motors such as those used in elevators. EMI is also produced by natural atmospheric or solar activity.

See also Class A certification; Class B certification; Federal Communications Commission; radio frequency interference.

electronic commerce   The buying and selling of goods and services over the Internet. Electronic commerce may also involve business-to-business transactions in the exchange of purchase orders, invoices, and other electronic documents.

electronic data interchange   Abbreviated EDI. A method of electronically exchanging business documents, including bills of materials, purchase orders, and invoices.

Customers and suppliers can establish an EDI network by means of Open Systems Interconnect (OSI) standards or by using proprietary products. Widely accepted standards include ANSI X.12, ISO 9735, and CCITT X.435.

electronic data processing   *See* data processing.

Electronic Industries Association   Abbreviated EIA. A trade association representing American manufacturers in standards organizations. The EIA has published and formalized several important standards, including RS-232-C, RS-422, RS-423, RS-449, RS-485, and RS-530. Standards having to do with communications are produced jointly with the Telecommunications Industry Association.

For more information on the EIA, see www.eia.org.

See also EIA/TIA 586.

electronic mail   The use of a network to transmit text messages, memos, and reports; usually referred to as e-mail. Users can send a message to one or more individuals, to a predefined group, or to all users on the system. When you receive a message, you can read, print, forward, answer, or delete it.

An e-mail system may be implemented on a peer-to-peer network, a client/server architecture, a mainframe computer, or on a dial-up service, such as America Online. E-mail is by far the most popular Internet application, with well over 80 percent of Internet users taking advantage of the service.

E-mail has several advantages over conventional mail systems, including:

- E-mail is fast—very fast when compared with conventional mail.

- If something exists on your computer as a file—text, graphical images, even program files and video segments—you can usually send it as e-mail.

- E-mail is very extensive. You can now send e-mail to well over half the countries in the world.

The problems associated with e-mail are similar to those associated with online communications in general, such as security, privacy (always assume that your e-mail is not private), and the legal status of documents exchanged via e-mail.

See also mailbox; Multipurpose Internet Mail Extension; voice mail.

element   A unit of structure in HyperText Markup Language (HTML), such as a title or a list. Some elements have start and stop tags; others have only a single tag. Certain elements can be nested within other elements.

See also HyperText Markup Language; tag.

E

elevator seeking A technique that allows the server hard disk head to access files in the direction that the head is already traveling across the disk, rather than in the order in which they were requested. This feature allows the drive heads to operate continuously and thus improves disk performance and minimizes disk-head seek times.

ELF *See* extremely low-frequency emission.

emacs A popular Unix editor, written by Richard Stallman, founder of the Free Software Foundation.

The name *emacs* is a contraction of "editing macros," but it is much more than a simple text editor and includes extensions for all sorts of common tasks, ranging from compiling and debugging programs to reading and sending e-mail. You can even extend emacs yourself as the editing commands are written in the Lisp programming language.

See also Free Software Foundation; vi.

e-mail *See* electronic mail.

e-mail address The addressing information required for an e-mail message to reach the correct recipient.

See also bang path; Internet address; mailbox.

EMI *See* electromagnetic interference.

EMM *See* expanded memory manager.

emoticon A collection of text characters often used in e-mail and posts to newsgroups to signify emotions.

An emoticon can be as simple as including <g> or <grin> in your text, an indication that the writer is joking, and as complex as some of the smiley faces, which are all designed to be read sideways, such as the wink ;-) or the frown :-(.

See also Internet abbreviations.

EMS *See* Expanded Memory Specification.

emulator A device built to work exactly like another device—hardware, software, or a combination of both.

For example, a terminal emulation program lets a PC pretend to be a terminal attached to a mainframe computer or to an online service by providing the control codes that the remote system expects to receive. In printers, some brands emulate popular models such as Hewlett-Packard's LaserJet line.

enable To turn a function on or allow something to happen. When a function is enabled, it is available for use. In a graphical user interface, enabled menu commands are often shown in black type.

See also disable.

Encapsulated PostScript Abbreviated EPS. The file format of the PostScript page-description language.

The EPS standard is device independent, so images can easily be transferred between applications, and they can be sized and output to different printers without any loss of image quality or distortion.

The EPS file contains the PostScript commands needed to recreate the image, but the image itself cannot be displayed on a monitor unless the file also contains an optional preview image stored in TIFF or PICT format.

You can print an EPS file only on a PostScript-compatible laser printer, and the printer itself determines the final printing resolution. A laser printer might be capable of 600 dpi, whereas a Linotronic printer is capable of 2450 dpi.

encapsulation   The process of inserting the frame header and data from a higher-level protocol into the data frame of a lower-level protocol.

See also tunneling.

enclosure   A term for a file—text, fax, binary, or image—sent as a part of an e-mail message. Sometimes called an attachment.

See also Multipurpose Internet Mail Extension.

encode   1. To compress a video file using a codec so that the file can be transmitted in the shortest possible time.

2. To convert a binary file into a form suitable for data transmission.

See also codec; decode; decryption; uuencode.

Encrypted File System   In Microsoft Windows 2000, a feature that lets mobile users, who are concerned with the security of their files in the case of unauthorized

access to their computers, encrypt designated files and directories using a public key encryption scheme.

encryption   The process of encoding information in an attempt to make it secure from unauthorized access, particularly during transmission. The reverse of this process is known as decryption.

Two main encryption schemes are in common use:

* **Private (Symmetrical) Key**   An encryption algorithm based on a private encryption key known to both the sender and the recipient of the information. The encrypted message is unreadable and can be transmitted over nonsecure systems.

* **Public (Asymmetrical) Key**   An encryption scheme based on using the two halves of a long bit sequence as encryption keys. Either half of the bit sequence can be used to encrypt the data, but the other half is required to decrypt the data.

See also Data Encryption Standard; Pretty Good Privacy; ROT-13.

encryption key   A unique and secret number used to encrypt data to protect it from unauthorized access.

end-of-file   Abbreviated EOF. A special code placed after the last byte in a file that indicates to the operating system that no more data follows.

An end-of-file code is needed because disk space is assigned to a file in blocks, and the file may not always terminate at the end of

E

a block. In the ASCII system, an EOF is represented by the decimal value 26 or by the Ctrl+Z control character.

end node A networked node such as a PC that can only send and receive information for its own use; it cannot route or forward information to another node.

end-of-text Abbreviated ETX. A character used in computer communications to indicate the end of a text file.

In the ASCII system, an ETX is represented by the decimal value 3 or by the Ctrl+C control character. A different symbol, end-of-transmission (EOT, ASCII 4, or Ctrl+D) is used to indicate the end of a complete transmission.

end-of-transmission Abbreviated EOT. A character used in computer communications to indicate the end of a transmission. In the ASCII system, an EOT is represented by the decimal value 4 or by the Ctrl+D control character.

end user Often refers to people who use an application to produce their own results on their own computer or workstation.

During the mainframe computer era, end users were people who received output from the computer and used that output in their work. They rarely, if ever, actually saw the computer, much less learned to use it themselves. Today, end users often write macros to automate complex or repetitive tasks and sometimes write procedures using command languages.

Enhanced Expanded Memory Specification Abbreviated EEMS. A revised version of the original Lotus-Intel-Microsoft Expanded Memory Specification (LIM EMS) that lets MS-DOS applications use more than 640KB memory space.

See also Expanded Memory Specification.

Enhanced IDE An extension to the Integrated Drive Electronics (IDE) interface standard, which supports hard disks as large as 8.4GB (IDE supports hard disks of up to 528MB) and transfer rates of up to 13.3MBps (IDE allows rates of up to 3.3MBps).

See also Integrated Drive Electronics; Small Computer System Interface.

Enhanced Small Device Interface Abbreviated ESDI. A popular hard disk, floppy disk, and tape drive interface standard, capable of a data-transfer rate of 10 to 20Mbps. ESDI is most often used with large hard disks.

See also Integrated Drive Electronics; Small Computer System Interface.

ENS *See* Enterprise Network Services.

Enter key Also known as the Return key, short for carriage return. The key that indicates the end of a command or the end of user input from the keyboard.

enterprise A term used to encompass an entire business group, organization, or corporation, including all local, remote, and satellite offices.

Enterprise CNE   *See* Master Certified Novell Engineer.

enterprise network   A network that connects every computer in every location of a business group, organization, or corporation and runs the company's mission-critical applications.

In many cases, an enterprise network includes several types of computers running several different operating systems.

Enterprise Network Services   Abbreviated ENS. A software product based on Banyan Systems' StreetTalk Directory Service for VINES that brings global directory service features to other networks. ENS includes StreetTalk Directory Assistance, the Banyan Security Service, and Banyan Network Management.

Specific versions of ENS are available for Novell NetWare, SCO Unix, and HP-UX so that servers running those operating systems can interoperate and share management in a network with VINES servers.

See also Banyan VINES.

Enterprise Systems Connection   Abbreviated ESCON. A set of products and services from IBM that provide direct channel-to-channel connections between ES/9000 mainframes and peripheral devices over 10 to 17MBps fiber-optic links.

envelope delay   *See* delay distortion.

environment   **1.** The complete set of hardware and software resources made available to any user of a system.

2. The operating system that a program needs in order to execute. For example, a

program may be said to be running in the Unix environment.

EOF   *See* end-of-file.

EOT   *See* end-of-transmission.

EPS   *See* Encapsulated PostScript.

equalization   The process of balancing a circuit by reducing frequency and phase distortion so that it passes all expected frequencies with equal efficiency.

error   The difference between the expected and the actual.

In computing, the way that the operating system reports unexpected, unusual, impossible, or illegal events is by displaying an error number or error message. Errors range from trivial, such as an attempt to write a file to a disk drive that does not contain a disk, to fatal, such as when a serious operating system bug renders the system useless.

In communications, errors are often caused by line noise and signal distortion. Parity or cyclical redundancy check (CRC) information is often added as overhead to the data stream, and techniques such as error detection and correction are employed to detect and correct as many errors as possible.

See also attenuation; crosstalk; error handling; error message; error rate; parity error.

error detection and correction   A mechanism used to determine whether transmission errors have occurred and, if so, to correct those errors.

E

Some programs or transmission protocols simply request a retransmission of the affected block of data if an error is detected. More complex protocols attempt to both detect and determine at the receiving end what the correct transmission should have been.

See also checksum; cyclical redundancy check; forward error correction; Hamming code; parity.

error handling The way that a program copes with errors or exceptions that occur as the program is running.

Good error handling manages unexpected events or wrongly entered data gracefully, usually by opening a dialog box to prompt the user to take the appropriate action or to enter the correct information. Badly written programs may simply stop running when the wrong data is entered or when an unanticipated disk error occurs.

error message A message from the program or the operating system that contains information about a condition that requires some human intervention to solve.

Error messages can indicate relatively trivial problems, such as a disk drive that does not contain a disk, as well as fatal problems, such as when a serious operating system bug renders the system useless and requires a system reboot.

error rate In communications, the ratio between the number of bits received incorrectly and the total number of bits in the transmission, also known as bit error rate (BER).

Some methods for determining error rate use larger or logical units, such as blocks, packets, or frames. In these cases, the measurement of error rate is expressed in terms of the number of units found to be in error out of the total number of units transmitted.

escape code *See* escape sequence.

Escape key The key on the keyboard labeled Esc. The Escape key generates an escape code, ASCII 27. In most applications, pressing the Escape key cancels the current command or operation.

escape sequence A sequence of characters, beginning with Escape (ASCII 27) and followed by one or more other characters, that performs a specific function. Sometimes called an escape code.

Escape sequences are often used to control printers or monitors, which treat them as commands and act upon them rather than processing them as characters to print or display.

ESCON *See* Enterprise Systems Connection.

ESDI *See* Enhanced Small Device Interface.

Ethernet A popular network protocol and cabling scheme with a transfer rate of 10Mbps, originally developed at Xerox in 1970 by Dr. Robert Metcalf. Ethernet uses a bus topology, and network nodes are connected by either thick or thin coaxial cable, fiber-optic cable, or twisted-pair cable.

Ethernet uses CSMA/CD (Carrier Sense Multiple Access/Collision Detection) to prevent network failures or collisions when two devices try to access the network at exactly the same time.

The original DIX (Digital Equipment, Intel, Xerox), or Blue Book, standard has evolved into the slightly more complex IEEE 802.3 standard and the ISO's 8802.3 specification.

The advantages of Ethernet include:

- It's easy to install at a moderate cost.

- Technology is available from many sources and is very well known.

- It offers a variety of cabling options.

- It works very well in networks with only occasional heavy traffic.

And the disadvantages include:

- Heavy traffic can slow down the network.

- A break in the main cable can bring down large parts of the network.

- Troubleshooting a bus topology can prove difficult.

See also 10/100; 100VG-AnyLAN; 10Base2; 10Base5; 10BaseF; 10BaseT; demand priority; Fast Ethernet; Gigabit Ethernet.

Ethernet address   The address assigned to a network interface card by the original manufacturer or by the network administrator if the card is configurable.

This address identifies the local device address to the rest of the network and allows messages to reach the correct destination. Also known as the media access control (MAC) or hardware address.

Ethernet meltdown   An event that causes saturation on an Ethernet-based system, often the result of illegal or misdirected packets. An Ethernet meltdown usually lasts for only a short period of time.

Ethernet packet   A variable-length unit in which information is transmitted on an Ethernet network.

An Ethernet packet consists of a synchronization preamble, a destination address, a source address, a field that contains a type code indicator, a data field that can vary from 46 to 1500 bytes, and a cyclical redundancy check (CRC) that provides a statistically derived value used to confirm the accuracy of the data.

EtherTalk   An implementation of the Ethernet LAN developed for Apple computers, designed to work with the Apple-Share network operating system.

EtherTalk operates over coaxial cable at the Ethernet transfer rate of 10Mbps, much faster than the 230.4Kbps rate available with AppleTalk. Each networked Macintosh computer must be supplied with a special EtherTalk network interface card.

ETX   *See* end-of-text.

Eudora   A popular and widely used e-mail application originally developed by Steve Dorner at the University of Illinois and now available from Qualcomm, Inc.

European Laboratory for Particle Physics   *See* Conseil Européen pour la Researche Nucléaire.

E

ETHERNET PACKET

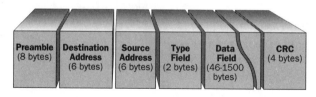

| Preamble (8 bytes) | Destination Address (6 bytes) | Source Address (6 bytes) | Type Field (2 bytes) | Data Field (46-1500 bytes) | CRC (4 bytes) |

even parity   *See* parity.

Event Log service   A Microsoft Windows 2000 service that logs important application, security, and system events into the event log.

exa-   Abbreviated E. A prefix meaning one quintillion, or 10^{18}. In computing, the prefix means 1,152,921,504,606,846,976, or the power of 2 closest to one quintillion (2^{60}).

exabyte   Abbreviated EB. 1 quintillion bytes, or 1,152,921,504,606,846,976 bytes.

exclusive container administrator   In Novell NetWare, a special type of container administrator who is given the rights to a container and all the objects within that container. The Inherited Rights Filter prevents other administrators from having rights in the container.

See also container administrator; Inherited Rights Filter.

executable file   Any file that can be executed by the operating system. Some executable files contain compiler binary instructions, and others are text files containing commands or shell scripts.

execute   **1.** To run a program, command, or script.

2. One of the permissions assigned to a file or directory; you can only execute a file when the execute permission is enabled.

execute permission   An access permission on a file or directory that gives you permission to execute the file or to access the contents of the directory.

expandability   The ability of a system to accommodate expansion. In hardware, this may include the addition of more memory, more or larger disk drives, and new adapters. In software, expandability may include the ability of a network to add users, nodes, or connections to other networks.

expanded memory   An MS-DOS mechanism by which applications can access more than the 640KB of memory normally available to them. The architecture of the early Intel processors restricted the original IBM PC to accessing 1MB of memory, 640KB of which was available for applications; the remaining 384KB was reserved for system use, the BIOS, and the video system. At that time, 640KB was more than ten times the amount of memory available in other personal computers. However, as both applications and MS-DOS grew, they began to run out of room.

The Expanded Memory Specification LIM 4.0 let programs running on the Intel family of processors access as much as 32MB of expanded memory. The expanded memory manager (EMM) creates a block of addresses into which data (held in memory above the 1MB limit) is swapped in and out as needed by the program. In other words, a 64KB segment of addressable memory creates a small window through which segments of expanded memory can be seen, but only one segment at a time.

expanded memory manager Abbreviated EMM. A device driver that supports the software portion of the Expanded Memory Specification (EMS) in an IBM-compatible computer.

Expanded Memory Specification Abbreviated EMS. The original version of the Lotus-Intel-Microsoft Expanded Memory Specification (LIM EMS), which let MS-DOS applications use more than 640KB of memory space.

These days Microsoft Windows running in protected mode on 80386 and later processors is free of this limitation.

expansion board A printed circuit board that plugs into a computer's expansion bus to provide added capabilities. Also called an adapter.

Common expansion boards include video adapters, joy-stick controllers, and input/output (I/O) adapters, as well as other devices, such as internal modems, CD-ROMs, and network interface cards (NICs). One expansion board can often support several different devices. Some current PC designs incorporate many of the functions previously performed by these individual adapters on the motherboard.

expansion bus An extension of the main computer bus that includes expansion slots for use by compatible adapters, such as memory boards, video adapters, hard-disk controllers, and SCSI (Small Computer System Interface) interface cards.

expansion slot One of the connectors on the expansion bus that gives an adapter access to the system bus. You can install as many additional adapters as there are expansion slots inside your computer.

For portable computers, an expansion slot is often supplied by a PCMCIA connection designed to accept a PC Card.

expansion unit An external housing available with certain portable computers designed to contain additional expansion slots and maintain a connection to the main expansion bus in the computer's system unit.

See also port replicator.

explicit rights In Novell Directory Services (NDS), any rights granted directly to a user for a directory or other NDS object. Explicit rights always override inherited rights.

See also inherited rights.

E

explicit security equivalence　In Novell Directory Services (NDS), a technique used to give one trustee the same rights as another trustee. Explicit security equivalence can be assigned with group membership, an Organizational Role, or the trustee's Security Equal To property.

See also implied security equivalence; security equivalence.

extended ASCII character set　*See* ASCII extended character set.

Extended Binary Coded Decimal Interchange Code　Abbreviated EBCDIC; pronounced "eb-se-dic." EBCDIC is the character set commonly used on large IBM mainframe computers, most IBM minicomputers, and computers from many other manufacturers.

It is an 8-bit code, allowing 256 different characters (see Appendix D). Unlike ASCII, the placement of the letters of the alphabet in EBCDIC is discontinuous. Also, there is no direct character-to-character match when converting from EBCDIC to ASCII; some characters exist in one set but not in the other.

See also American Standard Code for Information Interchange; double-byte character set; ISO 10646; Unicode.

Extended Industry Standard Architecture　Abbreviated EISA, pronounced "ee-sah." A PC bus standard that extends the traditional AT-bus to 32 bits and allows more than one processor to share the bus.

EISA was developed by the so-called Gang of Nine (AST Research, Compaq Computer Corporation, Epson, Hewlett-Packard, NEC, Olivetti, Tandy, Wyse Technology, and Zenith Data Systems) in reply to IBM's introduction of its proprietary MCA (Microchannel Architecture). EISA maintains compatibility with the earlier ISA (Industry Standard Architecture), and it also provides for additional features introduced by IBM in the MCA standard. EISA accepts ISA expansion cards and so, unlike MCA, is compatible with earlier systems. EISA has been eclipsed by Peripheral Control Interconnect-based systems.

See also local bus; PCI local bus; PC Memory Card International Association.

extended LAN　A term used to describe a network that consists of a series of LANs connected by bridges.

extended memory　Memory beyond 1MB on computers using the Intel 80286 and later processors, not configured for expanded memory.

PCs based on the early Intel processors could access only 1MB of memory, of which 640KB was available for applications, and the remaining 384KB was reserved for MS-DOS, the BIOS, and video settings.

Later processors can access more memory, but it was the 80386 with its ability to address 4GB of memory that really made extended memory usable. Also, Microsoft Windows and other operating systems running on Intel processors using the protected mode of the 80386 and later processors can access all the available system memory in the same way.

extended memory manager   A device driver that supports the software portion of the Extended Memory Specification in an IBM-compatible computer.

Extended Memory Specification   Abbreviated XMS. A standard developed by Microsoft, Intel, Lotus, and AST Research that became the preferred way of accessing extended memory in the PC. MS-DOS includes the extended memory device driver HIMEM.SYS, and this command or an equivalent must be present in CONFIG.SYS to allow you to access extended memory.

Extensible Markup Language   Abbreviated XML. A technology, based on Standard Generalized Markup Language (SGML), that allows the data on a HyperText Markup Language (HTML) page to be described in terms of the information it represents.

See also document type definition; HyperText Markup Language.

external command   A command that is a separate program, and not built in to the operating system. FORMAT, BACKUP, and FDISK are examples of external commands.

See also internal command.

External Gateway Protocol   Abbreviated EGP. A routing protocol used to exchange network availability information among organizational networks. EGP indicates whether a given network is reachable,

but it does not evaluate that information or make routing or priority decisions.

See also Border Gateway Protocol.

external modem   A stand-alone modem, separate from the computer and connected to it by a serial cable. LEDs on the front of the chassis indicate the current modem status. An external modem can be used with different computers at different times and also with different types of computers.

external reference   In Novell NetWare, a pointer to a NetWare Directory Services (NDS) object that is not located on the current server.

extranet   Originally coined as a term to describe any network in which part of the network was protected behind a firewall and part of the network was accessible from the Internet.

In current usage, an extranet describes a technology that allows different corporate intranets to communicate for the purposes of electronic commerce and collaboration. Those parts of an extranet outside the firewall contain their own set of security safeguards, allowing only limited access for specific purposes.

See also intranet.

extremely low-frequency emission
Abbreviated ELF. Radiation emitted by a computer monitor and other common electrical appliances.

ELF emissions fall into the range of 5 to 2000 hertz and decline with the square of the distance from the source. Emissions are not constant around a monitor; they are

E

higher from the sides and rear and weakest from the front of the screen. Low-emission models are available, and laptop computers with an LCD display do not emit any ELF fields.

See also electromagnetic interference; radio frequency interference; very low-frequency emission.

F

facsimile *See* fax.

fading In both electrical and wireless systems, a decrease in a signal's strength. Fading may be due to physical obstructions of the transmitter or receiver, to distance from the source of the transmission, or to some form of external interference from other signals or from atmospheric conditions.

fail-safe system Any computer system that is designed to keep operating, without losing data, when part of the system seriously malfunctions or fails completely.

fail-soft system Any computer system that is designed to fail gracefully, with the minimum amount of data or program destruction, when part of the system malfunctions. Fail-soft systems close down nonessential functions and operate at a reduced capacity until the problem is resolved.

fake root A subdirectory that functions as the root directory.

Fake roots can be useful with network applications that must be installed in the root directory. You can install the application in a subdirectory and then map a fake root on the file server to the subdirectory containing the application. Many Web servers use a fake root.

fall back A technique used by modems to adjust their data rate in response to changing line conditions.

FAQ *See* frequently asked questions.

far-end crosstalk Abbreviated FEXT. Interference that occurs when signals on one twisted-pair are coupled with another pair as they arrive at the far end of a multipair cable system.

FEXT becomes a problem on short loops supporting high-bandwidth services such as Very-High-Bit-Rate Digital Subscriber Line (VDSL) because of the high carrier frequencies used.

See also crosstalk; near-end crosstalk.

Fast Ethernet A term applied to the IEEE 802.3 Higher Speed Ethernet Study Group proposals, which were originally developed by Grand Junction Networks, 3Com, SynOptics, Intel, and others. Also known as 100BaseT.

Fast Ethernet modifies the existing Ethernet standard to allow speeds of 10Mbps or 100Mbps or both and uses the CSMA/CD access method.

The official standard defines three physical-layer specifications for different cabling types:

- 100BaseTX for two-pair Category 5 unshielded twisted-pair

- 100BaseT4 for four-pair Category 3, 4, or 5 unshielded twisted-pair

- 100BaseFX for fiber-optic cable

See also 100VG-AnyLAN; demand priority.

Fast IP A technology from 3Com Corporation that gives certain types of network

135

traffic, such as real-time video, a higher priority than other, less urgent network traffic such as e-mail messages.

3Com achieves this using what it calls policy management. A workstation requests a certain level of priority, tags the data accordingly, and begins the transmission. When the transmission is complete, the workstation indicates that to the network, and previously reserved resources are freed up for use.

See also IP over ATM; IP switching; quality of service.

Fast IR   A 4Mbps extension to the Serial Infrared Data Link Standard that provides wireless data transmission between IrDA-compliant devices.

See also Infrared Data Association.

Fast SCSI   A version of the SCSI-2 interface that can transfer data 8 bits at a time at data rates of up to 10MBps. The Fast SCSI connector has 50 pins.

See also Fast/Wide SCSI; SCSI-2; Small Computer System Interface; Ultra SCSI; Ultra Wide SCSI; Wide SCSI.

Fast/Wide SCSI   A version of the SCSI-2 interface that can transfer data 16 bits at a time at data rates of up to 20MBps. The Fast/Wide SCSI connector has 50 pins.

See also Fast SCSI; SCSI-2; Small Computer System Interface; Ultra SCSI; Ultra Wide SCSI; Wide SCSI.

FAT   *See* file allocation table.

FAT16   In Microsoft Windows, a file allocation table that uses a 16-bit cluster addressing scheme which restricts the maximum hard-disk size to 2.6GB. Also, FAT16 is inefficient in disk-space utilization as the default cluster size can be as large as 32KB.

See also FAT32; file allocation table.

FAT32   In Microsoft Windows 95 (release 2) and later versions of Windows, a file allocation table that uses a 32-bit cluster addressing scheme to support hard disks larger than 2.6GB, as well as a default cluster size of as small as 4KB. FAT32 can support hard disks of up to 2 terabytes in size.

See also FAT16; file allocation table.

fatal error   An operating system or application program error from which there is no recovery without reloading the program or rebooting the operating system.

fault management   One of the five basic types of network management defined by the International Organization for Standardization (ISO) and CCITT. Fault management is used in detecting, isolating, and correcting faults on the network.

fault tolerance   A design method that ensures continued system operation in the event of individual failures by providing redundant elements.

At the component level, the design includes redundant chips and circuits and the capability to bypass faults automatically. At the computer-system level, any elements that are likely to fail, such as processors and large disk drives, are replicated.

Fault-tolerant operations often require backup or UPS (uninterruptible power supply) systems in the event of a main power failure. In some cases, the entire computer system is duplicated in a remote location to protect against vandalism, acts of war, or natural disaster.

See also clustering; data protection; disk duplexing; disk mirroring; redundant array of inexpensive disks; System Fault Tolerance.

fax Short for facsimile. The electronic transmission of copies of documents for reproduction at a remote location. The term *fax* can be used as a verb for the process and as a noun for the machine that does the work and also for the item that is actually transmitted.

The sending fax machine scans a paper image and converts the image into a form suitable for transmission over a telephone line. The receiving fax machine decodes and prints a copy of the original image. Each fax machine includes a scanner, modem, and printer.

Originally, facsimile machines were rotating drums (CCITT Groups 1 and 2); then came modems (CCITT Group 3), and eventually they will be completely digital (CCITT Group 4).

See also CCITT Groups 1–4; fax modem.

fax board *See* fax modem.

fax modem An adapter that fits into a PC expansion slot providing many of the capabilities of a full-sized fax machine, but at a fraction of the cost. Some external modems also have fax capabilities.

The advantages of a fax modem include ease of use and convenience; the main disadvantage is that the material you want to fax must be present in digital form in the computer. Unless you have access to a scanner, you cannot fax handwritten notes, line art, or certain kinds of graphics. Most faxes sent directly from a PC using a fax modem are text files.

fax server A dedicated server that provides fax sending and receiving services to users on the network.

FCC *See* Federal Communications Commission.

FCC certification Approval by the FCC (Federal Communications Commission) that a specific computer model meets its standards for radio frequency interference (RFI) emissions. There are two levels of certification:

- Class A certification, which is for computers used in commercial settings, such as mainframes and minicomputers

- The more stringent Class B certification, which is for computers used in the home and in home offices, such as PCs, laptops, and portables

See also extremely low-frequency emission; radio frequency interference; very low-frequency emission.

FDDI *See* Fiber Distributed Data Interface.

FDDI-II A variation of the Fiber Distributed Data Interface standard. The FDDI-II version is designed for networks transmitting real-time full-motion video (or other

F

137

information that cannot tolerate any delays) and requires that all nodes on the network use FDDI-II; otherwise, the network automatically reverts to FDDI.

FDDI-II divides the bandwidth into 16 dedicated circuits operating at from 6.144Mbps to a maximum of 99.072Mbps. Each of these channels can be further subdivided for a total of 96 separate 64Kbps circuits.

FDDI-II is not widely used because it is incompatible with FDDI and because Fast Ethernet and Asynchronous Transfer Mode (ATM) both provide better solutions.

FDM   *See* frequency-division multiplexing.

FDX   *See* full-duplex.

Federal Communications Commission   Abbreviated FCC. A U.S. government regulatory body for radio, television, all interstate telecommunications services, and all international services that originate inside the United States. All computer equipment must be certified by the FCC before it can be offered for sale in the United States. The certification ensures that the equipment meets the legal limits for conductive and radio frequency interference, which could otherwise interfere with commercial broadcasts.

For more information on the FCC, see www.fcc.gov.

See also FCC certification.

female connector   Any cable connector with receptacles designed to receive the pins on the male connector.

See also male connector.

FEXT   *See* far-end crosstalk.

FF   *See* form feed.

Fiber Distributed Data Interface   Abbreviated FDDI. The ANSI X3T9.5 specification for fiber-optic networks transmitting at a speed of up to 100Mbps over a dual, counter rotating, token-ring topology.

FDDI's 100Mbps speed is close to the internal speed of most computers, which makes it a good choice to serve as a super backbone for linking two or more LANs or as a fiber-optic bus connecting high-performance engineering workstations. FDDI is suited to systems that require the transfer of large amounts of information, such as medical imaging, three-dimensional seismic processing, and oil reservoir simulation. The FDDI-II version of the standard is designed for networks transmitting real-time full-motion video (or other information that cannot tolerate any delays) and requires that all nodes on the network use FDDI-II; otherwise, the network automatically reverts to FDDI.

A FDDI network using multimode fiber-optic cable can include as many as 500 stations up to 2 kilometers (1.25 miles) apart; with single-mode fiber, run length increases up to 60 kilometers (37.2 miles) between stations. This type of network can also run over shielded and unshielded twisted-pair cabling (when it is known as CDDI, or Copper Distributed Data Interface) for shorter distances.

See also FDDI-II.

FEMALE CONNECTOR

FIBER DISTRIBUTED DATA INTERFACE

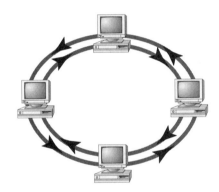

F

fiber-optic cable   A transmission technology that sends pulses of light along specially manufactured optical fibers.

Each fiber consists of a core, thinner than a human hair, surrounded by a sheath with a much lower refractive index. Light signals introduced at one end of the cable are conducted along the cable as the signals are reflected from the sheath.

Fiber-optic cable is lighter and smaller than traditional copper cable, is immune to electrical interference, offers better security, and has better signal-transmitting qualities. However, it is more expensive than traditional cables and is more difficult to repair. Fiber-optic cable is often used for high-speed backbones, but as prices drop, we may even see fiber-optic cable running to the desktop.

See also multimode fiber; single-mode fiber.

FIBER-OPTIC CABLE

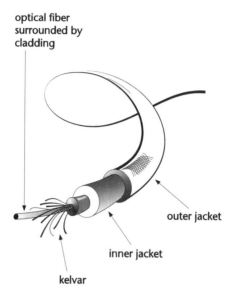

optical fiber
surrounded by
cladding

outer jacket

inner jacket

kelvar

Fibre Channel An interconnection standard designed to connect peripherals, mass storage systems, archiving and imaging systems, and engineering workstations.

Fibre Channel provides bandwidth from 100Mbps to 800Mbps over a variety of cable types, including multimode fiber, coaxial cable, and shielded twisted-pair.

The Fibre Channel Interconnect Standard was developed by the American National Standards Institute (ANSI) X3T9 committee.

file A named collection of information that appears to the user as a single entity and is stored on disk.

A file can contain a program or part of a program, just data, or a user-created document. Files may actually be fragmented or stored in many different places across the disk. The operating system manages the task of locating all the pieces when a request is made to read the file.

file allocation table Abbreviated FAT, pronounced "fat." A table, maintained by the operating systems, that lists all the blocks of disk space available on a disk.

The FAT includes the location of each block, as well as whether it is in use, available for use, or damaged in some way and therefore unavailable. Because files are not necessarily stored in consecutive blocks on a disk, the FAT also keeps track of which pieces belong to which file.

See also FAT16; FAT32; file fragmentation.

file compression   A technique that shrinks program or data files so that they occupy less disk space. The file must then be extracted or decompressed before use. Some types of files, such as word processor documents, can be compressed by 50 percent or more. Recompressing an already compressed file usually makes the file slightly larger because of the compression overhead.

File compression can be automatic and performed by the operating system, or it can be manual and performed by a file-compression program.

See also file-compression program.

file-compression program   An application that compresses files so that they take up less space on the disk. Some file-compression programs are individual, stand-alone applications; others are built into the operating system.

Individual file-compression programs can compress one or more files at a time. The utilities PKZIP and WinZip (for Microsoft Windows) and StuffIt (for the Macintosh) operate that way. When compression is built into the operating system, it usually compresses all the files on a specific disk, disk partition, or volume.

Many of the stand-alone file-compression programs, such as PKZIP, LHArc, and StuffIt, are available as shareware, and many popular utility packages, such as the

Norton Utilities from Symantec, also contain file-compression programs.

file-conversion program   An application that converts a file from one format to another without altering the contents of the file.

The conversion may be between the formats of two applications that use the same operating system (such as between two different Microsoft Windows word processors) or between the formats of applications from different operating systems. Applications are also available that convert a graphical image from one file format to another.

Many of the applications that change a Macintosh file into a PC-compatible file, or vice versa, consist of two programs running simultaneously on two physically connected computers. MacLink Plus from Data Viz and LapLink Mac from Traveling Software are two examples of this type of file-conversion program.

file format   A file structure that defines the way information is stored in the file and how the file appears on the screen or on the printer.

The simplest file format is a plain ASCII file. Some of the more complex formats are DCA (Document Content Architecture) and RTF (Rich Text Format), which include control information for use by a printer; TIFF (Tagged Image File Format) and EPS (Encapsulated PostScript), which hold graphics information; and DBF (Xbase database file) and DB (Paradox file), which are database formats. Word processing programs, such as Microsoft Word, also create files in special formats.

F

file fragmentation   Storage of files in pieces scattered on a disk. As files grow on a hard disk, they can be divided into several small pieces. By fragmenting files, the operating system makes reasonable use of the disk space available. The problem with file fragmentation is that the disk heads must move to different locations on the disk to read or write to a fragmented file. This process takes more time than reading the file as a single piece. To speed up file operations, you can use a disk optimizer or defragmenter.

See also FAT16; FAT32; defragmenter.

file indexing   A technique used in Novell NetWare to speed up accesses to large files by indexing file allocation table (FAT) entries.

file-infecting virus   Any virus that infects files on disk, usually executable files with filename extensions of .COM, .EXE, and .OVL. An unexpected change in the file size may indicate an infection. In certain cases, the original program is replaced with a new file containing an infected program.

See also antivirus program; boot sector virus; infection; macro virus; multipart virus; polymorphic virus; stealth virus; Trojan Horse; vaccine; virus.

file locking   *See* file and record locking.

filename   The name of a file on a disk used so that both you and the operating system can find the file again. Every file in a directory must have a unique name, but files in different directories can share the same name.

In MS-DOS, file and directory names have two parts. They can have up to eight characters in the name and up to three characters in the optional filename extension, separated from the name by a period. Many applications take over the extension part of the filename, using specific groups of characters to designate a particular file type.

In the Macintosh operating system, filenames can be up to 32 characters and can contain any character except a colon (:), which is used to separate elements of a path name.

Microsoft Windows allows 255-character filenames including spaces, but the name cannot include any of the following characters: \ / : * ? " < > |.

filename extension   In the MS-DOS file allocation table (FAT) file system, an optional three-character suffix added to the end of a filename and separated from the name by a period.

file permissions   A set of permissions associated with a file (or a directory) that specifies who can access the file and in what way. There are three basic permissions:

- Read permission lets you read files.

- Write permission lets you write (or overwrite) files.

- Execute permission lets you execute files.

Additional file permissions vary according to the operating system in use and the security system in place. For example, Novell NetWare has the following file permissions: Access Control, Create, Erase, File Scan, Modify, Read, Supervisor, and Write. Microsoft Windows 2000 has Add and Read,

Change Permissions, Delete, Full Control, No Access, and Take Ownership.

See also rights.

File and Print Services for NetWare

An add-on product for Microsoft Windows 2000 that allows Novell NetWare clients to access Windows servers as though they were NetWare servers.

FILER

A Novell NetWare workstation utility used to manage the NetWare file system. Almost any task related to the file system can be performed using FILER. Administrators can view information about files, directories, and volumes; modify and view attributes, rights, and trustee assignments for files and directories; search for files and directories; copy files; and recover and purge deleted files. In NetWare 3.*x*, these last two functions are found in the SALVAGE and PURGE commands.

file and record locking

A method of controlling file access in a multiuser environment, where there is always a possibility that two users will attempt to update the same file at the same time but with different information. The first user to access the file locks out all the other users, preventing them from opening the file. After the file is updated and closed again, the next user can gain access.

File locking is a simple way to prevent simultaneous updates, but it can seriously degrade system performance if many users attempt to access the same files time after time. To prevent this slowdown, many database management systems use record locking instead. Record locking limits access to individual records within the database file.

file recovery

The process of recovering deleted or damaged files from a disk. A file can be deleted accidentally or can become inaccessible when part of the file's control information is lost. In many operating systems, a deleted file still exists on disk until the space it occupies is overwritten with something else or until the file is purged.

See also undelete.

file server

A networked computer used to store files for access by other client computers on the network.

On larger networks, the file server runs a special network operating system. On smaller installations, the file server may run a PC operating system supplemented by peer-to-peer networking software.

See also client; server.

file sharing

The sharing of files over a network or between several applications running on the same workstation.

Shared files can be read, reviewed, and updated by more than one individual. Access to the file or files is often regulated by password protection, account or security clearance, or file locking to prevent simultaneous changes by multiple users.

See also file and record locking.

filespec

A contraction of *file specification*, commonly used to denote the complete drive letter, path name, directory name, and filename needed to access a specific file.

file system

In an operating system, the structure by which files are organized, stored, and named.

Some file systems are built-in components of the operating system; others are installable. For example, OS/2, Unix, and Microsoft Windows are all capable of supporting several different file systems at the same time. Other, installable file systems provide support for specific devices such as CD-ROM or DVD.

File Transfer Access and Management Abbreviated FTAM. The Open Systems Interconnect (OSI) protocol for transferring and remotely accessing files on different makes and models of computers that are also using FTAM.

file-transfer program An application used to move a file from a computer of one type to a computer of another type. The file format itself may also be changed during this transfer.

Many of the applications that change a Macintosh file into a PC-compatible file, or vice versa, consist of two programs running simultaneously on two physically connected computers. MacLink Plus from Data Viz and LapLink Mac from Traveling Software are two file-transfer programs that also offer a wide variety of popular file-format conversions.

See also file-conversion program; File Transfer Protocol; Kermit; Xmodem; Ymodem; Zmodem.

File Transfer Protocol Abbreviated FTP. The TCP/IP Internet protocol used when transferring single or multiple files from one computer system to another.

FTP uses a client/server model, in which a small client program runs on your computer and accesses a larger FTP server running on an Internet host. FTP provides all the tools needed to look at directories and files, change to other directories, and transfer text and binary files from one system to another.

See also anonymous FTP; ftp; Telnet.

FILTCFG A Novell NetWare 4.*x* NetWare Loadable Module (NLM) that allows you to set up and configure filters for Internetwork Packet eXchange (IPX), TCP/IP, and AppleTalk protocols. Filters help to control the type and amount of information sent to and received by a router, to limit traffic to certain segments of the network, and to provide security.

filtering 1. The mechanism that prevents certain source and destination addresses from crossing a bridge or router onto another part of the network.

2. The process of automatically selecting specific frequencies and discarding others.

finger A utility found on many Internet systems that displays information about a specific user, including full name, logon time, and location. Originated in the Unix world.

The finger utility may also display the contents of the user's .plan or .profile file, and there are those who exploit this in novel ways to display such varied information as instructions for using a university's Coke-vending machine, posting sports scores, and listing earthquake activity.

FIRE PHASERS A Novell NetWare login script command that makes a noise using the workstation's speaker.

The sound is supposed to resemble the phasers on the USS *Enterprise*. With fire phasers, you can have the computer emit up to nine sounds or blasts.

firewall   A barrier established in hardware or in software, or sometimes in both, that monitors and controls the flow of traffic between two networks, usually a private LAN and the Internet.

A firewall provides a single point of entry where security can be concentrated. It allows access to the Internet from within the organization and provides tightly controlled access from the Internet to resources on the organization's internal network.

See also application-level filter; dual-homed host; Intrusion Detection System; packet-level filter; proxy server; stateless filter.

FireWire   *See* 1394.

firmware   Any software stored in a form of read-only memory (ROM), erasable programmable read-only memory (EPROM), or electrically erasable programmable read-only memory (EEPROM) that maintains its contents when power is removed.

flame   A deliberately insulting e-mail message or post to a Usenet newsgroup, often containing a personal attack on the writer of an earlier post.

See also flame bait; flame war.

flame bait   An insulting or outrageous e-mail post to a Usenet newsgroup specifically

designed to provoke other users into flaming the originator.

See also flame; flame war.

flame war   In a Usenet newsgroup, a prolonged series of flames, which may have begun as a creative exchange of views but which quickly descended into personal attacks and crude name-calling.

See also flame bait.

flash memory   A special form of ROM that can be erased at signal levels commonly found inside the PC.

This ability allows the contents to be reprogrammed without removing the chips from the computer. Also, once flash memory has been programmed, you can remove the expansion board it is mounted on and plug it into another computer without loss of the new information.

See also PC Card.

flavor   A slang expression meaning type or kind, as in "Unix comes in a variety of flavors."

floating-point processor   A special-purpose, secondary processor designed to perform floating-point calculations much faster than the main processor.

Many processors, such as the Intel 80386, had matched companion floating-point processors. However, the current trend in processor design is to integrate the floating-point unit into the main processor, as in the Intel Pentium.

F

flooding A denial of service attack in which a huge number of nuisance connection attempts are made in order to consume all the available processing time.

See also brute-force attack; denial of service attack; dictionary attack; social engineering; Trojan Horse.

flow control **1.** In communications, control of the rate at which information is exchanged between two computers over a transmission channel. Flow control is needed when one of the devices cannot receive the information at the same rate as it can be sent, usually because some processing is required on the receiving end before the next transmission unit can be accepted. Flow control can be implemented either in hardware or in software.

2. In networking, control of the flow of data throughout the network, ensuring that network segments are not congested. A router controls data flow by routing around any trouble spots.

See also handshaking.

followup A reply to a post in a Usenet newsgroup or to an e-mail message. A followup post may quote the original post so that other readers are reminded of the discussion so far, and this quoted part of the post is usually indicated by greater than symbols (>). If you do quote from a previous post, only quote the minimum amount to get your point across; never quote the whole message as this is considered a waste of time and resources.

See also thread.

footprint The amount of desktop space or floor space occupied by a computer, printer, or monitor.

forced perfect termination A technique used to terminate a Small Computer System Interface (SCSI). Forced perfect termination actively monitors the bus to ensure that no signal reflection occurs.

See also active termination; passive termination.

foreground In an operating system, a process that runs in the foreground is running at a higher level of priority than is a background task.

Only multitasking operating systems support true foreground and background processing; however, some application programs can mimic it. For example, many word processors will print a document while still accepting input from the keyboard.

See also background.

forest In Microsoft Windows 2000, a collection of Active Directory trees that do not share a contiguous namespace, but do share a common schema and global catalog.

For example, if `acme.com` and `widget.com` were linked via a trust relationship but shared a common schema and global catalog, they would be considered a forest; in other words, a forest is a group of trees that trust each other.

See also Active Directory; Global Catalog; schema; tree.

formatting   The process of initializing a new, blank floppy disk or hard disk so that it can be used to store information.

form feed   Abbreviated FF. A printer command that advances the paper in the printer to the top of the next page. The Form Feed button on the printer also performs this same function. An application can also issue the command. In the ASCII character set, a form feed has the decimal value of 12.

forward error correction   A technique used to control errors that insert extra or redundant bits into the data stream. The receiving device uses the redundant bits to detect and, if possible, correct the errors in the data.

See also error detection and correction.

forwarding   The process of passing data on to an intermediate or final destination. Forwarding takes place in network bridges, routers, and gateways.

four-wire circuit   A transmission system in which two half-duplex circuits, consisting of two wires each, are combined to create one full-duplex circuit.

fps   *See* frames per second.

FQDN   *See* fully qualified domain name.

fractional T1   One portion of a T1 circuit. A T1 circuit has a capacity of 1.544Mbps, the equivalent of twenty-four 64Kbps channels. Customers can lease as many of these 64Kbps channels as they need; they are not required to lease the entire 1.544Mbps circuit.

fragmentation   *See* file fragmentation.

frame   **1.** A block of data suitable for transmission as a single unit; also referred to as a packet or a block. Some media can support multiple frame formats.

2. In digital video, one screen of information, including both text and graphics.

See also frames per second.

frame relay   A CCITT standard for a packet-switching protocol, running at speeds of up to 2Mbps, that also provides for bandwidth on demand. Frame relay is less robust than X.25 but provides better efficiency and higher throughput.

Frame relay is available from many companies, including AT&T, CompuServe, Sprint, WilTel, and the Bell companies.

See also Asynchronous Transfer Mode.

frames per second   Abbreviated fps. The number of video frames displayed each second. Although 24fps is considered the slowest frame rate that provides convincing motion to the human eye, most Internet video runs at between 5 and 15fps. To maintain a 15fps rate, you need a fast Pentium-based system with a 56Kbps modem.

framing   The process of dividing data for transmission into groups of bits and adding a header as well as a checksum to form a frame. In asynchronous communications, framing is the process of inserting start bits and stop bits before and after the data to be transmitted.

FreeBSD   A free implementation of Unix for the Intel family of processors, derived from the 4.4BSD Lite releases.

F

The distribution is free, but there may be a small charge to cover the distribution media and packaging. FreeBSD also includes XFree86, a port of the X Window system to the Intel processors.

Most of FreeBSD is covered by a license that allows redistribution as long as the code acknowledges the copyright of the Regents of the University of California and the FreeBSD Project. Those parts of Free-BSD that include GNU software are covered separately by the Free Software Foundation license.

See also copy left; Free Software Foundation; freeware; GNU; Linux; open source software.

free memory Any area of memory not currently in use. Often refers to the memory space remaining for applications to use after the operating system and the system device drivers have been loaded.

Free Software Foundation Abbreviated FSF. An organization founded by Richard Stallman that develops the freely available GNU software.

The FSF philosophy is that all software should be free for everyone to use and that source code should always accompany the software. The theory being, that if you make a modification or fix an error, the change can be sent out to all the other users, saving time and preventing duplication of effort.

Also, any software developed under the FSF General Public License (GPL) must also be covered by the same terms of the GPL; in other words, you cannot use the free soft-

ware to develop a commercial product for sale.

For more information on the Free Software Foundation, see `www.gnu.org/fsf`.

See also copy left; FreeBSD; freeware; GNU; open source software.

freeware A form of software distribution in which the author retains copyright to the software, but makes the program available to others at no cost. The program cannot be resold by a third party for profit.

See also copy left; Free Software Foundation; GNU; open source software.

frequency-division multiplexing Abbreviated FDM. A method of sharing a transmission channel by dividing the bandwidth into several parallel paths, defined and separated by guard bands of different frequencies designed to minimize interference. All signals are carried simultaneously.

FDM is used in analog transmissions, such as in communications over a telephone line.

See also inverse multiplexing; statistical multiplexing; time-division multiplexing; wavelength division multiplexing.

frequently asked questions Abbreviated FAQ, pronounced "fack." A document that contains answers to questions that new users often ask when they first subscribe to a newsgroup or first access a Web site.

The FAQ contains answers to common questions that the seasoned users have grown tired of answering. New users should look for and read the FAQ before posting their question, just in case the FAQ contains the answer.

fried   A slang expression for burned-out hardware, especially hardware that has suffered from a power surge. Also applied to people, as in "My brain is fried; I haven't slept since last weekend."

front-end application   An application running on a networked workstation that works in conjunction with a back-end system running on the server. Examples are e-mail and database programs.

See also client/server architecture.

front-end processor   A specialized processor that manipulates data before passing it on to the main processor.

In large computer-to-computer communications systems, a front-end processor is often used to manage all aspects of communications, leaving the main computer free to handle the data processing.

See also back-end processor.

Frye Utilities   A package of network management utilities from Frye Computer Systems that includes hardware and software inventory, NetWare server monitoring, traffic monitoring, application metering, and software distribution.

FSF   *See* Free Software Foundation.

FTAM   *See* File Transfer Access and Management.

FTP   *See* File Transfer Protocol.

ftp   A command used to transfer files to and from remote computers using the File Transfer Protocol. You can use ftp to log on to an Internet computer and transfer text and binary files.

When you use ftp, you start a client program on your computer that connects to a server program on the Internet computer. The commands that you give to ftp are translated into instructions that the server program executes for you.

The original ftp program started life as a Unix utility, but versions are now available for all popular operating systems; ftp is also built into all the major Web browsers.

See also anonymous ftp; File Transfer Protocol.

full backup   A backup that includes all files on a hard disk or set of hard disks. A network administrator must decide how often to perform a full backup, balancing the need for security against the time taken for the backup.

See also differential backup; incremental backup.

full-duplex   Abbreviated FDX. The capability for simultaneous transmission in two directions so that devices can be sending and receiving data at the same time.

See also four-wire circuit; half-duplex.

full-page display   Any monitor capable of displaying a whole page of text. Full-page displays are useful for graphical art and desktop publishing applications, as well as medical applications.

F

fully qualified domain name A host name with the appropriate domain name appended. For example, on a host with the host name wallaby and the Domain Name Service (DNS) domain name my-company.com, the fully qualified domain name becomes wallaby.my-company.com.

See also Domain Name Service.

function keys The set of programmable keys on the keyboard that can perform special tasks assigned by the current application.

Most keyboards have 10 or 12 function keys (F1 to F10 or F1 to F12), some of which are used by an application as shortcut keys. For example, many programs use F1 to gain access to the Help system. In some programs, the use of function keys is so complex that special plastic key overlays are provided as guides for users.

G

G   Abbreviation for giga-, meaning 1 billion, or 10^9.

See also gigabyte.

Gartner Group, Inc.   An independent research organization for the computer hardware, software, communications, and related industries.

Gartner Group first developed the concept of total cost of ownership (TCO) and now provides TCO software tools since the acquisition of Interpose. Gartner Group also owns Datapro Information Services and the market analysis company Dataquest.

For more information on Gartner Group, see www.gartner.com.

See also total cost of ownership.

gate array   *See* application-specific integrated circuit.

gateway   A shared connection between a LAN and a larger system, such as a mainframe computer or a large packet-switching network, whose communications protocols are different. Usually slower than a bridge or router, a gateway is a combination of hardware and software with its own processor and memory used to perform protocol conversions.

See also bridge; brouter; router.

Gateway, Inc.   A leading direct-marketer of PCs, servers, and related peripherals, originally known as Gateway 2000. Also an ISP offering Internet access through gateway.net.

For more information on Gateway, Inc., see www.gateway.com.

gateway server   A communications server that provides access between networks that use different access protocols.

Gateway Services for NetWare   A Microsoft Windows NT Server service that allows an NT server to act as a gateway to a NetWare network. NT clients can access a NetWare server using the same methods used to access an NT server.

gauge   A measurement of the physical size of a cable. Under the American Wire Gauge (AWG) standards, higher numbers indicate thinner cable.

See also cabling standards.

GB   *See* gigabyte.

Gb   *See* gigabit.

Gbit   *See* gigabit.

GDS   *See* Global Directory Service.

gender changer   A special intermediary connector for use with two cables that both have only male connectors or only female connectors.

GENDER CHANGER

male to male

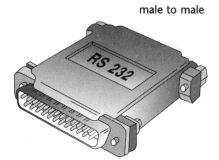

geostationary   Also known as geosyn-chronous. The type of orbit required to keep a communications satellite in a fixed position relative to the earth.

The satellite's angular rate and direction of rotation are matched to those of the earth, and the satellite orbits the earth every 24 hours at about 36,000 kilometers (22,350 miles). Three satellites in geostationary or-bit can cover 95 percent of the earth's sur-face (the remaining 5 percent is above the Arctic Circle).

geosynchronous   *See* geostationary.

GIF   *See* Graphics Interchange Format.

giga-   A prefix meaning 1 billion, or 10^9. *See also* gigabyte.

gigabit   Abbreviated Gbit and Gb. Usu-ally 1,073,824 binary digits or bits of data. Sometimes used as equivalent to one bil-lion bits.

See also kilobit; megabit.

Gigabit Ethernet   A 1Gbps (1,000Mbps) extension of the IEEE 802.3 Ethernet stan-dard, known as 1000Base-X.

This standard has been developed by the IEEE 802.3z Task Group and a number of interested companies collectively known as the Gigabit Ethernet Alliance. Gigabit Ethernet runs over multimode fiber-optic cable and is intended for use as a backbone and a way to connect high-speed routers, switches, and hubs.

See also Ethernet; Fast Ethernet.

gigabyte   Abbreviated GB. Strictly speaking, one billion bytes; however, in computing, in which bytes are most often counted in powers of 2, a gigabyte becomes 2^{30}, or 1,073,741,824 bytes.

global account   In Microsoft Windows NT Server, a user or group account defined on a primary domain controller that can be used from all the computers in the domain.

Global Catalog   In Microsoft Active Directory, the storage of selected properties for all the objects in the Active Directory.

The Global Catalog allows users in an organization with multiple sites to locate resources quickly, without having to cross WAN links. In this way, users can examine a local source to find the location of a network resource.

See also Active Directory; forest; tree.

Global Directory Service   Abbreviated GDS. An implementation of the X.500 directory service for managing remote users and addresses.

See also X.500.

global directory services   Directory services that view the entire network as a single entity. A global directory system allows the network administrator to define all network resources—users, printers, and servers—at one time.

Banyan's StreetTalk and Novell's NetWare Directory Services (NDS) are examples of global directory services.

See also domain directory services.

global group   In Microsoft Windows NT Server, user accounts granted server and workstation rights in their own and other domains whose security systems allow access. Global groups are a means of providing rights and permissions to resources inside and outside the domain to a group of users within a single domain.

See also local group.

global login   A mechanism that permits users to log on to the network, rather than repeatedly logging on to individual servers. A global logon can provide access to all network resources.

global network   An international network that spans all departments, offices, and subsidiaries of the corporation.

Global networks bring their own set of problems, including those of different time zones, languages, established standards, and PTT (Postal Telephone and Telegraph) companies.

GNU   Pronounced "ga-noo." A Free Software Foundation (FSF) project devoted to developing a complete, freely available Unix system that contains no AT&T code. The name GNU is a recursive acronym for "GNU's not Unix!"

Many of the tools and utilities developed for this project have been released and are very popular with users of 4.4BSD, FreeBSD, and Linux.

For more information on GNU, see `www.gnu.org`.

See also 4.4BSD Lite; FreeBSD; Hurd; Linux; open source software.

Gopher   A client/server application that presents Internet text resources as a series of menus, shielding the user from the underlying mechanical details of IP addresses and different access methods.

Gopher menus may contain documents you can view or download, searches you can perform, or additional menu selections. When you choose one of these items, Gopher does whatever is necessary to obtain

153

the resource you requested, either by downloading a document or by jumping to the selected Gopher server and presenting its top-level menu.

Gopher clients are available for most popular operating systems, including the Macintosh, MS-DOS, Windows, and Unix.

See also Gopherspace; World Wide Web.

Gopherspace   A collective term used to describe all the Internet resources accessible using Gopher. Gopher is so good at hiding the mechanical details of the Internet that this term was coined to represent all the resources reachable using Gopher.

GOSIP   Acronym formed from Government Open System Interconnection Profile. A suite of standards intended for use in government projects and based on the Open Systems Interconnect (OSI) reference model. Some measure of GOSIP compliance is required for government networking purchases. GOSIPs exist in many countries, including the United States, Canada, France, Germany, Australia, and the United Kingdom.

grace login   Allows a user to finish logging on using an expired password without changing it. You can set the number of grace logons a user is allowed.

graphical user interface   Abbreviated GUI, pronounced "gooey." A graphics-based user interface that allows users to select files, programs, and commands by pointing to pictorial representations on the screen rather than by typing long, complex commands from a command prompt.

Applications execute in windows, using a consistent set of drop-down menus, dialog boxes, and other graphical elements, such as scroll bars and icons. This consistency among interface elements is a major benefit for the user, because as soon as you learn how to use the interface in one program, you can use it in all other programs running in the same environment.

The use of graphical elements in a user interface was pioneered at Xerox Corporation's Palo Alto Research Center (PARC) in the early 1970s. Unfortunately, at that time the hardware needed to support such a user interface was well beyond the reach of most users. In 1979, Steve Jobs of Apple Computer visited PARC and recognized the importance of the user-interface work being done; this visit led to the development of the interface for the ill-fated Apple Lisa computer, and eventually to the Apple Macintosh series of computers. Since then, GUIs have been developed for most computing environments.

graphics accelerator board   A specialized expansion board containing a graphics coprocessor as well as all the other circuitry found on a video adapter. Sometimes called a video accelerator board.

Transferring most of the graphics processing tasks from the main processor to the graphics accelerator board improves system performance considerably, particularly for Microsoft Windows users.

graphics coprocessor   A fixed-function graphics chip, designed to speed up the processing and display of high-resolution images. Popular coprocessors include S3

Inc's 86C911 and Weitek's W5086 and W5186.

Graphics Interchange Format   Abbreviated GIF; pronounced "gif." A graphics file format, originating on CompuServe, that results in relatively small graphics files. An image may contain as many as 256 colors, including a transparent color, and a lossless compression method reduces the size of the file. A graphic in this format can be used as an inline image on a Web page. A revision of this format, known as GIF89a, adds animation features, transparent backgrounds, and image interleaving.

See also lossless compression; Joint Photographic Experts Group.

graphics mode   A video adapter mode in which everything displayed on the screen is created pixel by pixel. Text mode, by contrast, uses ready-made characters from a built-in character set.

grayed command   *See* dimmed command.

group   A collection of network users who all have the same level of security and can all be managed collectively.

group account   An account containing other member accounts. All the rights and permissions accorded to the group are also granted to the group members, making group accounts a convenient way to pro-

vide a common set of capabilities to collections of user accounts.

group identifiers   Security identifiers containing the set of permissions granted to the group. If a user account is part of a group, the group identifier is appended to that user's security identifier, granting the user all the permissions granted to that group.

See also security identifier.

Group object   In Novell NetWare Directory Services (NDS), an object that contains a list of user object names.

See also leaf object; NetWare Directory Services.

groupware   Network software designed for use by a group of people all working on the same project or who need access to the same data.

See also Lotus Notes; workflow software; workgroup.

guard band   A small-frequency band used to separate multiple bands in a broadband transmission and prevent interference between the communications channels.

GUI   *See* graphical user interface.

guru   An operating system expert with a reputation for being helpful to other, less knowledgeable users.

H

H.323 A videoconferencing standard developed by the International Telecommunication Union (ITU) that defines videoconferencing from the desktop over LANs, intranets, and the Internet.

H.323 specifies techniques for compressing and transmitting real-time voice, video, and data between a pair of videoconferencing workstations. It also describes signaling protocols for managing audio and video streams, as well as procedures for breaking data into packets and synchronizing transmissions across communications channels.

See also Real-time Transport Protocol; T.120.

hack Originally, an expedient, although short-term, solution to a programming problem. This solution often bypassed some of the more traditional software-development processes. Now the word *hack* is often used to describe a well-crafted piece of work that produces just what is needed; it does not imply malicious intent to break into other people's systems for gain.

See also hacker; kluge.

hacker In the programming community, where the term originated, this term describes a person who pursues knowledge of computer systems for its own sake—someone willing to "hack through" the steps of putting together a working program.

More recently, in popular culture at large, the term has come to mean a person who breaks into other people's computers with malicious intent (what programmers call a "cracker"). Many countries now treat convicted crackers in the same way that they treat conventional breaking-and-entering criminals.

See also intruder.

HAL *See* Hardware Abstraction Layer.

half-duplex Abbreviated HDX. In asynchronous transmissions, the ability to transmit on the same channel in two directions, but only in one direction at a time.

See also communications parameters; duplex; full-duplex.

Hamming code A forward-error correction technique used to detect and correct single-bit errors during transmission.

The Hamming code adds three verification bits to the end of each four bits of data. The receiving device performs a similar process to ensure that the four data bits were received correctly and to detect any missing bits.

See also error detection and correction.

hand-held computer A portable computer that is small enough to be held in one hand, such as the enormously popular PalmPilot from 3Com Corporation.

handshaking   The exchange of control codes or particular characters to maintain and coordinate data flow between two devices so that data is only transmitted when the receiving device is ready to accept the data.

Handshaking can be implemented in either hardware or software, and it occurs between a variety of devices. For example, the data flow might be from one computer to another computer or from a computer to a peripheral device, such as a modem or a printer.

See also flow control; XON/XOFF.

hang   1. When a program waits for an event that never occurs, as in "the program hangs waiting for a character from the keyboard."

2. A slang expression used when attaching a new piece of hardware to a system, usually an external device attached by one or more cables, as in "I'm going to hang a new tape drive on the server this afternoon."

See also deadlock.

hard-coded   A description of software written in a way that does not allow for flexibility or future expansion. For example, when program variables are placed directly in the code rather than supplied as input from the user, the entire program must be recompiled to change the value, an obvious waste of resources.

See also hard-wired.

hard disk   The part of a hard disk drive that stores data, rather than the mechanism for reading and writing to it. Sometimes called a platter.

hard-disk controller   An expansion board that contains the necessary circuitry to control and coordinate a hard disk drive.

Many hard-disk controllers can manage more than one hard disk, as well as floppy disks and tape drives. On some PCs, the hard-disk controller is built into the motherboard, and in the case of an Integrated Drive Electronics hard disk, the controlling circuitry is mounted on the drive itself, eliminating the need for a separate controller.

hard disk drive   A storage device that uses a set of rotating, magnetically coated disks called platters to store data or programs. In everyday use, the terms *hard disk, hard disk drive,* and *hard drive* are used interchangeably, because the disk and the drive mechanism are a single unit.

A typical hard-disk platter rotates at several thousand revolutions per minute, and the read/write heads float on a cushion of air from 10 to 25 millionths of an inch thick so that the heads never come into contact with the recording surface. The whole unit is hermetically sealed to prevent airborne contaminants from entering and interfering with these close tolerances.

Hard disks range in storage capacity from a few tens of megabytes to several terabytes. The more storage space on the disk, the more important your backup strategy becomes. Hard disks are reliable, but they do

H

fail, and usually at the most inconvenient moment.

See also high-capacity storage system; mini-hard disk; redundant array of inexpensive disks; single large expensive disk.

hard-disk interface   A standard way of accessing the data stored on a hard disk. Several hard-disk interface standards have evolved over time, including the ST506 Interface, the Enhanced Small Device Interface (ESDI), the Integrated Drive Electronics Interface (IDE), and the SCSI (Small Computer System Interface).

See also PC Memory Card International Association.

hard-disk type   A number stored in a personal computer's CMOS random access memory area that defines certain hard-disk characteristics, such as the number of read/ write heads and the number of cylinders on the disk. This number is not directly accessible from the operating system. Some PCs require a special configuration program to access the hard-disk type; others permit access via the computer's built-in ROM BIOS setup program.

hard reset   A system reset made by pressing the computer's Reset button or by turning the power off and then on again. A hard reset is used only when the system has crashed so badly that pressing Ctrl+Alt+Del to reboot does not work.

See also hang; deadlock.

hardware   All the physical electronic components of a computer system, including peripheral devices, printed-circuit

boards, displays, and printers. If you can stub your toe on it, it must be hardware.

See also firmware; liveware; software.

Hardware Abstraction Layer   Abbreviated HAL. The lowest level of the Microsoft Windows NT operating system, which is specifically tailored to the type of hardware used in the server. If the hardware changes, changes also have to be made to the HAL.

hardware address   The address assigned to a network interface card (NIC) by the original manufacturer or by the network administrator if the interface card is configurable.

This address identifies the local device address to the rest of the network and allows messages to find the correct destination. Also known as the physical address, media access control (MAC) address, or Ethernet address.

Hardware Compatibility List   Abbreviated HCL. A list of all the hardware devices supported by Microsoft Windows NT and Windows 2000. Items on this list have actually been tested and verified to work properly with Windows.

hardware dependent   The requirement that a specific hardware component be present for a program to work. Hardware-dependent software is often difficult to move or port to another computer.

See also hardware independent.

hardware independent   The ability to produce similar results in a wide variety of environments, without requiring the presence of specific hardware. The Java programming language and the PostScript page-description language are both examples of hardware independence. Java runs on a wide range of computers, from the PC to a mainframe; PostScript is used by many printer manufacturers.

See also hardware dependent.

hardware interrupt   An interrupt or request for service generated by a hardware device, such as a keystroke or a tick from the clock. Because the processor may receive several such signals simultaneously, hardware interrupts are usually assigned a priority level and processed according to that priority.

See also interrupt request; software interrupt.

hard-wired   Describes a system designed in a way that does not allow for flexibility or future expansion. May also refer to a device that is connected directly to the network, such as a printer.

See also hard-coded.

hash function   A function that maps a data item to a numeric value by use of a transformation. A hash function can convert a number that has meaning to a user, such as a key or other identifier, into a value for the location of that data in a structure such as a table.

See also hashing; hash table.

hashing   The process of creating or recreating a hash table by recalculating the search index code assigned to each piece of data in the table.

See also hash function; hash table.

hash table   A method of representing data so that it can be found again very quickly.

A hash table assigns a special index code to each piece of data, and specially designed software uses this code to locate the data, rather than repeating what might be a very lengthy search each time the data is requested.

See also hash function; hashing.

Hayes-compatible modem   Any modem that recognizes the commands in the industry-standard AT command set, originally defined by Hayes Microcomputer Products, Inc.

HBA   *See* host bus adapter.

H-channel   A set of ISDN Primary Rate Interface (PRI) services with predefined speeds, designed to carry videoconferencing data streams.

H-channel services are created from multiple 64Kbps B channels. Three service levels are commonly available:

- H0 operating at 384Kbps
- H11 operating at 1,536Kbps
- H12 operating at 1,920Kbps

See also Integrated Services Digital Network; Primary Rate ISDN.

HCL   *See* Hardware Compatibility List.

HCSS   *See* high-capacity storage system.

HDLC   *See* High-level Data Link Control.

H

HDSL   *See* High-Bit-Rate Digital Sub-scriber Line.

HDX   *See* half-duplex.

header   Information placed at the beginning of a file, a data transmission, or an archive.

In an e-mail message, the header contains information about the message, including sender and recipient information, and information about the route the message took as it was being delivered.

In a data transmission, the header may contain source and destination address information, as well as other control data.

In an archive, the header is a block that contains information describing the contents of the archive.

Header Error Control   In an Asynchronous Transfer Mode (ATM) cell header, an 8-bit field used for detecting errors and correcting single-bit errors.

See also Asynchronous Transfer Mode.

headless server   A server computer with no monitor attached.

heartbeat   An Ethernet signal quality test function. This signal proves that a component is working and can detect collisions. Also known as signal quality error (SQE).

HEC   *See* Header Error Control.

helper   A program launched or used by a Web browser to process a file type that the browser cannot handle. Sometimes called a plug-in.

A helper may view an image, play a sound file, or expand a compressed file. A helper

that deals with video, graphics, or animation is called a viewer; a helper that deals with sound files is called a player.

See also player; viewer; Web browser.

hertz   Abbreviated Hz. A unit of frequency measurement; 1 hertz equals one cycle per second.

See also megahertz.

heterogeneous network   A network that consists of workstations, servers, network interface cards, operating systems, and applications from many vendors, all working together as a single unit. The network may also use different media and different protocols over different network links.

See also enterprise network; homogeneous network.

Hewlett-Packard Company   Abbreviated HP. A major manufacturer of hand-held calculators, personal computers, servers, minicomputers, mainframes, scientific and medical equipment, test and measurement equipment, laser and ink jet printers, plotters, and software.

Founded by William Hewlett and David Packard in 1939 in a garage, the company is now headquartered in Palo Alto, California. HP has a widely diversified product line of more than 10,000 items, and it has a well-earned reputation for building rugged and reliable equipment.

For more information on Hewlett-Packard, see www.hp.com.

hex   *See* hexadecimal.

hexadecimal   Abbreviated hex. The base-16 numbering system that uses the digits 0 through 9, followed by the letters A through F, which are equivalent to the decimal numbers 10 through 15.

Hex is a convenient way to represent the binary numbers that computers use internally because it fits neatly into the 8-bit byte. All the 16 hex digits 0 through F can be represented in 4 bits, and 2 hex digits (1 digit for each set of 4 bits) can be stored in a single byte. This means that 1 byte can contain any one of 256 different hex numbers, from 0 through FF.

See also binary; decimal.

HFS   *See* Hierarchical File System.

hidden file   In many operating systems, any file that has the hidden attribute set, which indicates to the operating system that information about the file should not appear in normal directory listings. There may also be further restrictions on a hidden file, and users may not be able to delete, copy, or display the contents of such a file.

Hierarchical File System   Abbreviated HFS. A tree-structured file system used on the Macintosh; designed for use with hard disks.

Hierarchical Storage Management   Abbreviated HSM. A combination of several types of file-storage systems, managed by intelligent software.

In HSM, data is moved from one type of storage to another depending on how frequently the data is accessed. Active data is held on hard disks, less frequently used data is held in near-line storage such as an opti-

cal disk system, and data used only infrequently is stored in a tape backup.

See also archive; high-capacity storage system; jukebox.

High-Bit-Rate Digital Subscriber Line   Abbreviated HDSL. A high-speed data transmission technology originally developed by Bellcore that delivers high bandwidth over existing twisted-pair copper telephone lines.

HDSL is the most common Digital Subscriber Line (DSL) service and provides T1 data rates of 1.544Mbps over lines of up to 3.6 kilometers, or 12,000 feet, in length. HDSL is symmetric, providing the same data rate in each direction.

The service is not intended for residential purposes, but is used in the telephone company's own private data networks, Internet servers, and interexchange connections.

See also Asymmetric Digital Subscriber Line; Digital Subscriber Line; Rate-Adaptive Digital Subscriber Line; Single-Line Digital Subscriber Line; Very-High-Bit-Rate Digital Subscriber Line.

high-capacity storage system   Abbreviated HCSS. A data-storage system that extends the storage capacity of a Novell NetWare server by integrating an optical-disk library, or jukebox, into the NetWare file system.

Network users and applications can access files and directories on the jukebox with the same NetWare commands and function calls used to access files from a hard disk. The most frequently used HCSS files may be cached temporarily on the server hard

H

disk to speed up access times. HCSS can also access a magnetic tape system.

See also archive.

high-end   An expensive, full-featured product from the top of a company's product list.

See also low-end.

High-level Data Link Control   Abbreviated HDLC. An international protocol defined by the ISO (International Organization for Standardization), included in CCITT X.25 packet-switching networks. HDLC is a bit-oriented, synchronous protocol that provides error correction at the data-link layer. In HDLC, messages are transmitted in variable-length units known as frames.

See also Synchronous Data Link Control.

high-level language   Any machine-independent programming language that uses English-like syntax in which each statement corresponds to many assembly language instructions. High-level languages free programmers from dealing with the underlying machine architecture and allow them to concentrate on the logic of the problem at hand.

See also low-level language.

high memory area   Abbreviated HMA. In a computer running MS-DOS, the first 64KB of extended memory above the 1MB limit of 8086 and 8088 addresses.

Programs that conform to the Extended Memory Specification (EMS) can use this memory as an extension of conventional memory. However, only one program can use or control HMA at a time. If MS-DOS is loaded into the HMA, approximately 50KB more conventional memory becomes available for use by applications.

See also expanded memory; extended memory; memory management.

High-Performance File System   Abbreviated HPFS. A file system available in OS/2 and Microsoft Windows NT that supports the following:

- Long, mixed-case filenames of up to 255 characters

- As much as 64KB of extended attributes per file

- Faster disk access with an advanced disk cache for caching files and directory information

- Highly contiguous file allocation that eliminates file fragmentation

- Hard disks of up to 64GB in size

MS-DOS does not recognize the HPFS file structure, it cannot be used on a floppy disk, and it is not supported in Windows NT 4 or later.

HIGH-LEVEL DATA LINK CONTROL FRAME

flag	address	control	data	frame check sequence	flag

High-Performance Parallel Interface

Abbreviated HPPI. A parallel interface standard from the American National Standards Institute (ANSI) known as X3T9.3, originally developed as an interface between supercomputers and fast peripherals such as disk arrays and frame buffers.

Recently, HPPI has been extended for use in networked computers and high-end workstations. It provides a data rate of 800Mbps over 32-pair twisted-pair copper wire, known as single HPPI, and 1,600Mbps over 64 pairs, known as double HPPI. Connection length is limited to 25 meters (82 feet).

High-Performance Routing

Abbreviated HPR. An internetworking protocol from IBM, intended as an upgrade to its Advanced Peer-to-Peer Networking (APPN) package. HPR provides internetworking capabilities similar to those of TCP/IP.

See also Advanced Peer-to-Peer Networking; Data Link Switching.

High Sierra specification

A specification for CD-ROM data that served as the basis for the ISO (International Organization for Standardization) 9660 standard. It is called High Sierra because it was defined at a meeting held near Lake Tahoe in November 1985.

High Speed Serial Interface

Abbreviated HSSI. A serial data communications interface optimized for speeds of up to 52Mbps. Often used for connecting an Asynchronous Transfer Mode (ATM) switch to a T3 Data Service Unit.

See also Asynchronous Transfer Mode; Data Service Unit; T3.

hijacking   An attack on a computer system in which an established TCP/IP session is redirected in mid-session to an unauthorized host system.

See also spoofing.

hit   On the World Wide Web, a request from a browser for a file on the server. A hit on a Web page occurs whenever any file is accessed, whether it is a text document, a graphic, a script, or an audio or video clip. If you access three files on a Web page, you generate three hits, so a hit is a poor measure of the number of people visiting a Web site, as it simply reflects the number of file requests made.

hive   A major logical division within the Microsoft Windows Registry. The Registry is divided into several hives:

- HKEY_CLASSES_ROOT contains information about file associations.

- HKEY_CURENT_USER contains information about the currently logged on user.

- HKEY_LOCAL_MACHINE contains information about the computer running Windows, including details of applications, device drivers, and hardware.

- HKEY_USERS contains information about each active user with a user profile.

- HKEY_CURRENT_CONFIG contains details about the current system configuration.

- HKEY_DYN_DATA contains information about plug-and-play devices on the system.

H

You can view and edit the Registry using the regedit.exe program.

See also key; sub-key.

HMA *See* high memory area.

holy wars A fundamentally unresolvable computer-related argument, in which the participants spend most of their time trying to establish often wildly personal choices as carefully thought out and deeply considered technical evaluations. Topics might include any version of Unix versus any other version of Unix, the C programming language versus C++ (or any other programming language), big endian systems versus little endian systems, and so on.

home directory In Unix, a directory that contains the files for a specific user. The name of your home directory is kept in the password file, and when you log in, your current directory is always set to be your home directory.

home page On the World Wide Web, an initial starting page. A home page may be prepared by an individual or by a corporation and is a convenient jumping-off point to other Web pages or Internet resources.

See also portal.

homogeneous network A network that consists of one type of workstation, server, network interface card, and operating system, with a limited number of applications, all purchased from a single vendor. All nodes use the same protocol and the same control procedures.

See also enterprise network; heterogeneous network.

hooked vector An intercepted interrupt vector that now points to a replacement interrupt service routine (ISR) rather than to the original service routine.

hop A single link between two computer systems that an e-mail message must cross on its way to its destination. A message may have to pass over many hops to reach its ultimate destination; if it must pass between five computers, it is said to have taken four hops to reach its destination.

See also hop count.

hop count In routing, the number of links that must be crossed to get from any given source node to any given destination node. Hop count is often used as a metric for evaluating a route for a least-cost routing algorithm.

horizontal application Any application software that is broad in scope and not designed for use in one specific industry or setting. Word-processing software falls into this category, but software specifically designed to manage a medical practice does not.

See also vertical application.

host The central or controlling computer in a networked or distributed processing environment which provides services that other computers or terminals can access via the network.

host bus adapter Abbreviated HBA. A board acting as an interface between the processor and the hard-disk controller in a network server, used by Novell NetWare to relieve the main processor of data-storage and retrieval tasks. Also known as a disk coprocessor board (DCB).

The HBA and its disk subsystems make up a disk channel. NetWare can access five disk channels, with four controllers on each channel, and eight hard-disk drives attached to each controller.

Hot Fix   A Novell NetWare feature that marks defective disk blocks dynamically so that the operating system will not use them. Data is redirected from any faulty blocks to a small portion of disk space set aside as the Hot Fix redirection area. Hot Fix then marks the defective area as bad, and the server will not attempt to store data there again. By default, 2 percent of a disk partition is set aside as the Hot Fix redirection area.

See also fault tolerance.

HotJava   A highly interactive Web browser from Sun Microsystems that is written in the Java programming language.

HP   *See* Hewlett-Packard Company.

HPFS   *See* High-Performance File System.

HP OpenView Certified Consultant   A certification from Hewlett-Packard that recognizes technical competency to both sell and support HP OvenView, a network management system used to monitor and manage networks consisting of equipment and software from multiple vendors.

Three specializations are available:

- Unix
- Windows NT

- Unix and Windows NT combined

HPR   *See* High-Performance Routing.

HP-UX   A version of Unix that runs on Hewlett-Packard computers. HP-UX includes BSD extensions, including the network commands, the Korn shell, and a version of emacs. Visual User Environment (VUE) is HP's graphical user interface, with workspaces for different tasks, drag-and-drop functions, a text editor, a color icon editor, and other productivity tools.

HP-UX also includes System Administration Manager (SAM) for common administrative tasks, such as adding new users, installing and configuring peripherals, managing processes, and scheduling jobs.

HSM   *See* Hierarchical Storage Management.

HSSI   *See* High Speed Serial Interface.

HTML   *See* HyperText Markup Language.

HTTP   *See* Hypertext Transfer Protocol.

hub   A device used to extend a network so that additional workstations can be attached. There are two main types of hubs:

- **Active hubs** amplify transmission signals to extend cable length and ports.

- **Passive hubs** split the transmission signal, allowing additional workstations to be added, usually at a loss of distance.

In some star networks, a hub is the central controlling device.

Huffman coding   In data compression, a method of encoding data on the basis of the relative frequency of the individual elements.

H

Huffman coding is often used with text files; the coding is based on how frequently each letter occurs, because it is a lossless compression method. Huffman coding is used in fax transmissions.

See also data compression; lossless compression; lossy compression.

Hurd   A project from the Free Software Foundation (FSF) to develop and distribute a free version of the Unix operating system for many different hardware platforms. Hurd (or sometimes HURD) is considered a collection of all the GNU software, compilers, editors, and utilities, as well as the operating system.

See also Free Software Foundation; GNU.

hybrid network   A network that uses a collection of different technologies, such as frame relay, leased lines, and X.25.

See also homogeneous network; heterogeneous network.

hybrid organization   In Novell Directory Services (NDS), an organizational strategy that combines two or more of the methods—locational, divisional, and workgroup. A hybrid organization makes most sense in a large organization.

hypermedia   A term used to describe nonsequential applications that have interactive, hypertext links between different multimedia elements— graphics, sound, text, animation, and video.

If an application relies heavily on text-based information, it is known as hypertext; however, if full-motion video,

animation, graphics, and sound are used, the application is considered hypermedia.

hypertext   A method of presenting information so that it can be viewed by the user in a nonsequential way, regardless of how the topics were originally organized.

Hypertext was designed to make a computer respond to the nonlinear way that humans think and access information—by association, rather than according to the linear organization of film, books, and speech.

In a hypertext application, you can browse through the information with considerable flexibility, choosing to follow a new path each time you access the information. When you click a highlighted word, you activate a link to another hypertext document, which may be on the same Internet host or on a completely different system thousands of miles away. These links depend on the care that the document originator used when assembling the document; unfortunately, many links turn into dead-ends.

See also link rot.

HyperText Markup Language   Abbreviated HTML. A standard document formatting language used to create Web pages and other hypertext documents. HTML is a subset of Standardized General Markup Language (SGML).

HTML defines the appearance and placement on the page of elements such as fonts, graphics, text, links to other Web sites, and so on; it has nothing to do with the actual material presented. Hypertext documents often have the filename extension .htm or .html.

The published HTML standards have been revised several times. HTML version 2 was the first version widely used on the World Wide Web and supported by the popular Web browsers of the day. Subsequent revisions to the standard have added new HTML elements such as tables, text flow around images, frames, applets, and style sheets.

Future HTML revisions will be developed by the World Wide Web Consortium (W3C), at least in theory; the manufacturers of the most popular browsers have driven this process in the past by creating their own non-standard HTML elements.

HTML has been vital in the development of the World Wide Web; however, the functions that it performs via the Web browser are becoming restrictive. In part, this has led to the development of other technologies, such as Java, Virtual Reality Modeling Language (VRML), and Extensible Markup Language (XML).

See also Extensible Markup Language; Java; Secure HTTP; Virtual Reality Modeling Language.

Hypertext Transfer Protocol   Abbreviated HTTP. The command and control protocol used to manage communications between a Web browser and a Web server.

When you access a Web page, you see a mixture of text, graphics, and links to other documents or other Internet resources. HTTP is the mechanism that opens the related document when you select a link, no matter where that document is located.

Hz   *See* hertz.

H

I

I2O   *See* Intelligent Input/Output.

IAB   *See* Internet Architecture Board.

IAC   *See* Inter-Application Communication.

IANA   *See* Internet Assigned Numbers Authority.

IBM   *See* International Business Machines Corporation.

IBM 3270   A general name for a family of IBM system components—printers, terminals, and terminal cluster controllers—that can be used with a mainframe computer by an SNA (Systems Network Architecture) link.

Software that emulates a 3270 terminal is available for all major operating systems.

IBM cabling systems   *See* Type 1-9 cable.

IBM Certified Advanced Technical Expert   One of the many certifications from IBM, available in many specializations, including RS/6000 AIX.

IBM Certified AIX User   One of the many certifications from IBM. This one is available to the AIX user.

IBM Certified Expert   One of the many certifications from IBM, available in a range of specializations, including OS/2 Warp Server and OS/2 LAN Server.

IBM Certified Specialist   One of the many certifications from IBM, available in a range of specializations, including:

- AIX System Administration
- AIX Support
- AS/400 Associate System Operator
- AS/400 Professional System Operator
- AS/400 Associate System Administrator
- AS/400 Professional System Administrator
- OS/2 Warp Server Administration
- LAN Server 4 Administration

IBM Certified Systems Expert   One of the many certifications from IBM, available in a range of specializations, including OS/2 Warp and OS/2 Warp 4.

IBM RS/6000   A set of seven or nine separate 32-bit chips used in IBM's line of reduced instruction set computing (RISC) workstations.

With as many as 7.4 million transistors, the RS/6000 uses a superscalar design with four separate 16KB data-cache units and an 8KB instruction cache. The joint venture announced between IBM, Apple, and Motorola in late 1991 specified the development of a single-chip version of the RS/6000 architecture called the PowerPC.

IBM Suite for Windows NT   A software suite from IBM for Microsoft Windows NT that includes five major modules:

- Intel's LANDesk Manager

- Lotus Domino
- IBM's DB2 Universal Database (UDB)
- IBM's eNetwork Communications Server
- IBM's ADSTAR Distributed Storage Manager (ADSM)

The suite is available in both department and enterprise versions.

IBM ThinkPad   A series of innovative and popular notebook computers from IBM. The ThinkPad first introduced the touch-sensitive dual-button pointing stick (called a TrackPoint), the pencil-eraser–like device, found between the G, H, and B keys. It is now included on many portable computers and replaces the mouse.

The top-of-the-line ThinkPad 770 runs a 300MHz Pentium II processor, an 8.1GB hard disk, a 56K modem, a 14.1-inch SVGA screen with resolutions up to 1280×1024, and as much as 320MB of memory.

IC   *See* integrated circuit.

ICA   *See* Independent Computing Architecture.

ICMP   *See* Internet Control Message Protocol.

ICP   *See* Internet Content Provider.

Icon   A general-purpose high-level programming language with a large number of string-processing functions, developed by Ralph Griswold at the University of Arizona. Icon has a C-like syntax and is available both as a compiler and as an interpreter.

icon   In a graphical user interface, a small screen image representing a specific element that the user can manipulate in some way,

selected by moving a mouse or another pointing device.

An icon can represent an application, a document, embedded and linked objects, a hard disk drive, or several programs collected in a group.

IDE   *See* Integrated Drive Electronics.

idle cell   In Asynchronous Transfer Mode, a cell transmitted purely to keep network traffic at a specific level.

See also Asynchronous Transfer Mode.

IDS   *See* Intrusion Detection System.

IDT   *See* Integrated Device Technology, Inc.

IEC   *See* Interexchange Carrier.

IEEE   *See* Institute of Electrical and Electronics Engineers.

IEEE standards   The Institute of Electrical and Electronics Engineers (IEEE), acting as a coordinating body, has established a number of telecommunications standards, including Group 802 as follows:

- **802.1D**   An access-control standard for bridges linking 802.3, 802.4, and 802.5 networks.

- **802.2**   A standard that specifies the Data Link layer for use with 802.3, 802.4, and 802.5 networks.

- **802.3 1Base5**   A standard matching the AT&T StarLAN product with a 1Mbps data transfer rate and a maximum cable-segment length of 500 meters (1640 feet).

- **802.3 10Base2**   An implementation of the Ethernet standard on thin Ethernet cable

169

with a data transfer rate of 10Mbps, and a maximum cable-segment length of 185 meters (600 feet).

- **802.3 10Base-T**   A standard for Ethernet over unshielded twisted-pair wiring, the same wiring and RJ45 connectors used with telephone systems. The standard is based on a star topology, in which each node connects to a central wiring center, with a cable-length limitation of 100 meters (325 feet).

- **802.3 10Broad36**   A standard for long-distance Ethernet with a 10Mbps data rate and a maximum cable-segment length of 3600 meters (11,800 feet).

- **802.4**   A standard for bus topology networks that use token passing to control access and network traffic, running at 10Mbps. Not widely implemented.

- **802.5**   A standard for ring networks that use token passing to control access and network traffic, running at 4Mbps or 16Mbps. It is used by IBM's Token Ring network.

- **802.6**   An emerging standard for metropolitan area networks (MANs) transmitting voice, video, and data over two parallel fiber-optic cables, using signaling rates of up to 155Mbps.

- **802.7**   The Broadband Technical Advisory Committee provides advice on broadband techniques to other IEEE subcommittees.

- **802.8**   The Fiber-Optic Technical Advisory Committee provides advice on fiber-optic technology to other IEEE subcommittees.

- **802.9**   The Integrated Data and Voice (IDV) Networks group is currently working to integrate data, voice, and video to 802 LANs and ISDN. Now more commonly referred to as Iso-Ethernet.

- **802.10**   The Network Security Technical Advisory Group is developing a standard definition of a network security model.

- **802.11**   The Wireless Networking group is developing standards for wireless networks.

- **802.12**   The Demand Priority group is working on standards for the 100Mbps Ethernet standard.

- **802.14**   The Cable Modems group is defining standards for data transport over traditional cable TV networks.

You will also see many of these standards referred to by their ISO reference numbers. IEEE standards 802.1 through 802.11 are also known as ISO standards 8802.1 through 8802.11.

For more information, see the entries on the individual standards.

IETF   *See* Internet Engineering Task Force.

IFS   *See* installable file system.

IGMP   *See* Internet Group Management Protocol.

IGP   *See* Interior Gateway Protocol.

IGRP   *See* Interior Gateway Routing Protocol.

IIOP   *See* Internet Inter-ORB Protocol.

IKE   Abbreviation for Internet Key Exchange.

See ISAKMP/Oakley.

ILEC   *See* Incumbent Local Exchange Carrier.

IMA   *See* Inverse Multiplexing over ATM.

image map   A graphical inline image on a Web page that contains more than one link. Each region of the image map is linked to a different Web resource; you can click a part of the image to retrieve the appropriate resource.

See also inline image.

imaging   The process of capturing, storing, cataloging, displaying, and printing graphical information, as well as scanning paper documents for archival storage. Network users can store and then retrieve imaged documents from large, centralized image-storage systems, using applications such as Lotus Notes or other groupware.

See also document management; high-capacity storage system; optical character recognition.

IMAP   *See* Internet Mail Access Protocol.

impedance   An electrical property of a cable that combines capacitance (the ability to store an electrical charge), inductance (the ability to store energy in the form of a magnetic field), and resistance (the ability to impede or resist the flow of electric current), measured in ohms.

Impedance can be described as the apparent resistance to the flow of alternating current at a given frequency. Mismatches in impedance along a cable cause distortions and reflections. Each transmission protocol and network topology specifies its own standards for impedance.

impersonation attack   An attack in which a hostile computer system masquerades as a trusted computer.

See also brute-force attack; dictionary attack; social engineering

implied security equivalence   In Novell Directory Services, when an object receives the rights of the object's parent, it is said to be security equivalent. Also known as container security equivalence. The Inherited Rights Filter does not affect this.

See also explicit security equivalence; Inherited Rights Filter; Novell Directory Services; security equivalence.

I-Mux   *See* inverse multiplexing.

incremental backup   A backup of a hard disk that consists of only those files created or modified since the last backup.

See also differential backup; full backup.

Incumbent Local Exchange Carrier
Abbreviated ILEC. A term coined from the Telecommunications Act of 1996 to describe the incumbent local telephone company, providing local transmission and switching services.

See also Competitive Local Exchange Carrier.

Independent Computing Architecture
Abbreviated ICA. A presentation service protocol developed by Citrix that transports

171

mouse clicks, keystrokes, and screen updates between a thin client and the server. ICA works with Microsoft Windows, Macintosh, and Unix clients and runs on top of TCP/IP, IPX/SPX, and NetBIOS.

See also thin client.

Independent Software Vendor   Abbreviated ISV. A company that develops and sells computer software but is completely independent of the makers of the hardware upon which the software runs.

Industry Standard Architecture   Abbreviated ISA. The 16-bit bus design first used in IBM's PC/AT computer in 1984. ISA has a bus speed of 8MHz and a maximum throughput of 8MBps. EISA (Extended Industry Standard Architecture) is a 32-bit extension to this bus.

INETCFG   A Novell NetWare 4 NLM used to set up and configure AppleTalk, Internet Protocol (IP) and Internetworking Packet eXchange (IPX) protocols on the server.

infection   The presence of a virus or a Trojan Horse within a computer system; the virus may be active in memory or present on the hard disk.

The infection may remain hidden from the user for a considerable length of time. Some viruses are triggered by particular dates, others by specific events on the system.

See also antivirus program; boot sector virus; file-infecting virus; inoculate; macro

virus; multipart virus; polymorphic virus; stealth virus; Trojan Horse; vaccine; virus.

information node   Abbreviated i-node, sometimes written inode, pronounced "eye-node." In Unix, a data structure on disk that describes a file.

Each directory entry associates a filename with an i-node; although a single file may have several filenames, one for each link , a file has only one i-node. Within a filesystem, the number of i-nodes, and therefore the number of files, is defined when the system is first initialized.

An i-node contains all the information Unix needs to be able to access the file, including the file's length, the times that the file was last accessed or modified, owner and group ID information, access permissions, the number of links to the file, and the disk address of the data blocks that contain the file itself.

See also i-node table.

information warehouse   A central repository containing a company's current and historical data in a form that can be accessed quickly and easily by users to aid in their business decision making. IBM has a large number of products for building fully automated enterprise-wide data warehouses.

Informix-4GL Certified Professional
A professional certification from Informix Software aimed at developers proficient in creating custom database applications using Informix-4GL.

Informix Software, Inc. A major supplier of object-oriented and relational database products, based in Menlo Park, California.

For more information on Informix Software, Inc., see www.informix.com.

Infrared Data Association Abbreviated IrDA. A trade association of more than 150 computer and telecommunications hardware and software suppliers, including Hewlett-Packard, Apple Computer, AST, Compaq, Dell, IBM, Intel, Motorola, Novell, and others.

IrDA is concerned with defining standards for products that use wireless communications.

For more information on IrDA, see www.irda.org.

infrared transmission A method of wireless transmission that uses part of the infrared spectrum to transmit and receive signals.

Infrared transmissions take advantage of a frequency range just below that of visible light, and they usually require a line-of-sight connection between transmitter and receiver.

Infrared transmission can be used to send documents from portable computers to printers, to transmit data between portable computers, to exchange information between computers and cellular telephones and faxes, and to connect to home entertainment systems. Almost every manufacturer of portable devices is implementing infrared communications at some level.

See also Infrared Data Association; mobile computing; wireless communications.

inherited rights Rights (in Novell NetWare) or permissions (in Microsoft Windows 2000) received by an object from its parent object. In Novell NetWare, inherited rights can be blocked by the Inherited Rights Filter or by an explicit assignment.

See also Inherited Rights Filter.

Inherited Rights Filter Abbreviated IRF. In Novell Directory Services (NDS), the mechanism that controls the rights a trustee can inherit from parent directories or container objects.

Inheritance allows an assignment applied at one point to apply to everything below that point in the file and directory structure. The IRF for any file, directory, or object is a part of NetWare's access control information.

In NetWare 3, the IRF was known as the Inherited Rights Mask and applied only to the file system.

See also Inherited Rights Mask; NETADMIN; trustee; trustee assignment.

Inherited Rights Mask Abbreviated IRM. In NetWare 3, the mechanism that controls the rights a trustee can inherit. By default, IRM allows all rights to be inherited. Both files and directories have individual IRM controls.

See also Inherited Rights Filter; trustee; trustee assignment.

initialize 1. To start up a computer.

2. In the Macintosh, the process of preparing a new, blank floppy or hard disk for use.

Initializing completely obliterates any information previously stored on the disk.

3. To assign a beginning value to a variable.

See also formatting.

inline image On a Web page, an image displayed along with accompanying text. The process of placing the image on the page is known as inlining.

inoculate To protect a file against attack from a virus by recording characteristic information about it and then monitoring any changes.

See also antivirus program; boot sector virus; file-infecting virus; infection; macro virus; multipart virus; polymorphic virus; stealth virus; Trojan Horse; vaccine; virus.

i-node *See* information node.

i-node table In Unix, a list of all the i-nodes in a filesystem. Within the i-node table, each i-node is known by a number—the i-number, or index number. If a file is defined by i-node #300, it is said to have an i-number of 300.

See also information node.

in-place migration In Novell NetWare, a method of upgrading an existing NetWare server to NetWare 4, which includes converting the file system and updating the network operating system.

See also across-the-wire migration.

Inprise Corporation Originally known as Borland International, the company changed its name in 1988. Well known for its dBASE database products, the company also markets Delphi Client/Server Suite, a visual rapid applications development environment, and JBuilder, a set of Java programming language development tools.

For more information on Inprise Corporation, see www.inprise.com.

input/output Abbreviated I/O. The transfer of data between the computer and its peripheral devices, disk drives, terminals, and printers.

input/output bound Abbreviated I/O bound. A condition in which the speed of operation of the input/output port limits the speed of program execution. Getting the data into and out of the computer is more time-consuming than actually processing that same data.

See also computation bound.

INSTALL A Novell NetWare server console NetWare Loadable Module (NLM) used for managing, maintaining, and updating NetWare servers. INSTALL can be used for the following tasks:

- Creating, deleting, and managing hard-disk partitions and NetWare volumes on the server

- Installing NetWare and other additional products and updating the license or registration disk

- Adding, removing, checking, and unmirroring hard disks

- Changing server startup and configuration files

install To configure and prepare hardware or software for operation.

Many application packages have their own installation programs, which copy all the required files from the original distribution disks into appropriate directories on your hard disk and then help to configure the program to your own operating requirements. Microsoft Windows programs are installed by a program called Setup.

installable file system Abbreviated IFS. A file system that is loaded dynamically by the operating system when it is needed. Different file systems can be installed to support specific needs, in just the same way as device drivers are loaded to support specific hardware.

installation program A program whose sole function is to install (and sometimes configure) another program.

The program guides the user through what might otherwise be a rather complex set of choices, copying the correct files into the right directories, decompressing them if necessary, and asking for the next disk when appropriate. An installation program may also ask for a person's name and a company name so that the startup screen can be customized. Microsoft Windows programs are installed by a program called Setup.

Institute of Electrical and Electronics Engineers Abbreviated IEEE, pronounced "eye-triple-ee." A membership organization, founded in 1963, including engineers, students, and scientists. IEEE also acts as a coordinating body for computing and communications standards.

For more information in IEEE, see www.ieee.org.

See also IEEE standards.

instruction set The set of machine-language instructions that a processor recognizes and can execute.

An instruction set for reduced instruction set computing (RISC) may only contain a few instructions; a computer that uses complex instruction set computing (CISC) may be able to recognize several hundred instructions.

INT 14 *See* Interrupt 14.

integrated circuit Abbreviated IC, also known as a chip. A small semiconductor circuit that contains many electronic components.

Integrated Device Technology, Inc. Abbreviated IDT. An established manufacturer of SRAM, specialty memory, and embedded microprocessors, who has recently moved into producing clones of Intel microprocessors. IDT's first WinChip, originally known as the C6, shipped in limited quantities in 1997 and 1998, and the company recently announced the WinChip 2 and WinChip 2+.

For more information on Integrated Device Technology, see www.idt.com.

Integrated Drive Electronics Abbreviated IDE. A popular hard-disk interface standard, used for disks in the range of 40MB to 1.2GB, requiring medium to fast data-transfer rates. The electronic control circuitry is located on the drive itself, thus eliminating the need for a separate hard-disk controller card.

See also Enhanced Small Device Interface; Small Computer System Interface; ST506 Interface.

Integrated On-Demand Network

Abbreviated ION. A new high-capacity residential and business service from Sprint that allows customers to simultaneously make a phone call, send/receive a fax, and access the Internet using a single connection.

The service is based on a mixture of broadband technology, such as Asynchronous Transfer Mode (ATM) and Digital Subscriber Line (DSL). Deployment of the network is based on a partnership with three other companies—Cisco Systems, Bellcore, and Radio Shack.

See also Asynchronous Transfer Mode; Digital Subscriber Line.

Integrated Services Architecture

Abbreviated ISA. A proposed extension to the Internet standards that would provide integrated services in support of real-time applications over the Internet.

Using current standards, real-time applications do not work well over the Internet because of variable and unpredictable queuing delays and other losses. To solve this problem, ISA suggests that routers be able to reserve resources for specific data streams called flows. A flow might be video

data from a source to a destination or from a source to multiple destinations.

See also IP over ATM; IP switching; quality of service.

Integrated Services Digital Network

Abbreviated ISDN. A standard for a worldwide digital communications network originally designed to replace all current systems with a completely digital, synchronous, full-duplex transmission system.

Computers and other devices connect to ISDN via simple, standardized interfaces. They can transmit voice, video, and data, all on the same line.

See also Basic Rate ISDN; Broadband Integrated Services Digital Network; Primary Rate ISDN.

integrated software

Application software that combines the functions of several major applications, such as a spreadsheet, a database, a word processor, and a communications program, into a single package. Microsoft Works is an example of integrated software.

Integrated software provides a consistent user interface in all the modules and allows the user to transfer data from one part of the system to another quickly and easily. It is also usually inexpensive. Unfortunately, integrated software packages do not typically offer all the complex features available with their stand-alone counterparts.

See also software suite.

INTEGRATED SERVICES DIGITAL NETWORK

Two 64Kbps B channels

16Kbps D channel

Twenty-three 64Kbps B channels

64Kbps D channel

53-byte cell   53   Broadband ISDN   53-byte cell

Integrated-Private Network-to-Network Interface   Abbreviated I-PNNI. A routing protocol based on the Asynchronous Transfer Mode (ATM) Forum's Private Network-to-Network Interface (PNNI) standard that allows ATM switches to communicate.

See also Private Network-to-Network Interface.

Intel Corporation   The world's largest manufacturer of microprocessors, supplying the processors used in more than 80 percent of the world's personal computers.

Intel has developed a wide range of processors and board-level products that are used in applications as varied as personal computers, automobiles, robots, and supercomputers, as well as the multibus architecture that is used in many industrial and proprietary applications. Intel also manufactures modems, fax modems, memory chips, flash memory products, and other peripheral devices. The name

Intel is a contraction of Integrated Electronics.

For more information on Intel Corporation, see www.intel.com.

Intelligent Input/Output   Abbreviated I2O; pronounced "eye-two-oh." A specification from Intel Corporation that divides the traditional device driver into two parts;

- The part concerned with managing the device

- The part concerned with interfacing to the operating system

By making this distinction, that part of the driver concerned with managing the device now becomes portable across operating systems.

I2O is also designed to work with intelligent input/output subsystems, with support for message passing between multiple independent processors, so that the host system can be relieved of all the interrupt-intensive tasks associated with servicing device drivers.

Several operating system vendors, including SCO, Microsoft, and Novell, have announced support for I2O in future products.

intelligent hub   *See* smart hub.

intelligent terminal   A terminal connected to a large computer, often a mainframe, that has some level of local computing power and can perform certain operations independently from the remote computer, but does not usually have any local disk-storage capacity.

See also dumb terminal.

Interactive Unix   A version of Unix from Sun Microsystems based on AT&T's System V Release 3.2 kernel.

See also Solaris.

Inter-Application Communication

Abbreviated IAC. In the Macintosh operating system, a feature of the System software that allows independent applications to share and exchange information. IAC takes two main forms:

- **Publish-and-subscribe,** which allows users to create documents made of components created by multiple applications.

- **Apple events,** which let one application control another. For example, two programs can share common data, and one program can request that the other perform some action.

IAC is often referred to as program linking in the System manuals.

Interexchange Carrier   Abbreviated IXC; sometimes abbreviated IEC. A term coined from the Telecommunications Act of 1996 to describe voice and data long-distance telephone companies, including AT&T, MCI, Sprint, and Worldcom.

See also Competitive Local Exchange Carrier; Incumbent Local Exchange Carrier; Local Exchange Carrier.

interface   The point at which a connection is made between two hardware devices, between a user and a program or operating system, or between two applications.

In hardware, an interface describes the logical and physical connections, as in

RS-232-C, and is often considered synonymous with the term *port*.

A user interface consists of the means by which a program communicates with the user, including a command line, menus, dialog boxes, online help systems, and so on. User interfaces can be classified as character-based, menu-driven, or graphical.

Software interfaces are application programming interfaces (APIs) and consist of the codes and messages used by programs to communicate behind the scenes.

See also graphical user interface.

interface standard   Any standard way of connecting two devices or elements that have different functions.

Personal computers use many different interface standards. These include Small Computer System Interface (SCSI), Integrated Drive Electronics (IDE), and the Enhanced Small Device Interface (ESDI) for hard disks; RS-232-C and the Centronics parallel interface for serial devices and parallel printers; and the OSI Reference Model for LAN communications over a network.

Interior Gateway Protocol   Abbreviated IGP. The protocol used on the Internet to exchange routing information between routers within the same domain.

See also Border Gateway Protocol; External Gateway Protocol.

Interior Gateway Routing Protocol
Abbreviated IGRP. A distance-vector routing protocol from Cisco Systems for use in large heterogeneous networks.

See also heterogeneous network.

interleaved memory   A method of speeding up access by dividing dynamic RAM (DRAM) into two (or more) separate banks.

DRAM requires that its contents be updated at least every thousandth of a second, and while this update is taking place, it cannot be read by the processor. Interleaved memory divides available memory into banks so that the processor can read from one bank while the other is cycling and so does not have to wait. Because interleaved memory does not require special hardware, it is one of the most cost-effective ways of speeding up system operation.

See also wait state.

internal command   Any operating system command that is not a separate program and is always available to the user. In MS-DOS, DIR, COPY, and TYPE are examples of internal commands.

See also external command.

internal modem   A modem that plugs into the expansion bus of a personal computer or into the PCMCIA connector of a laptop computer.

See also external modem.

internal security   Security measures taken to prevent unauthorized computer access from within an organization.

See also Intrusion Detection System.

International Business Machines Corporation   Abbreviated IBM, also known as "Big Blue." Known originally for its huge range of mainframe computers, IBM introduced the IBM PC, which quickly emerged as an industry standard. Since its introduction in 1981, the PC has seen many changes, and an enormous number of companies worldwide now manufacture or market hardware, software, and peripheral devices for IBM-compatible computers.

IBM also has a huge research effort, owns thousands of patents, and has introduced many innovative products, including the small, touch-sensitive TrackPoint, which replaces the mouse on many portable computers, a 1000MHz chip, and a 3.5-inch hard disk drive capable of storing up to 17GB of information.

For more information on IBM, see www.ibm.com.

See also Advanced Program-to-Program Communications; Advanced Peer-to-Peer Networking; Advanced Interactive Executive; AS/400; Systems Network Architecture.

International Organization for Standardization Sometimes mistakenly referred to as the International Standards Organization, and commonly referred to as ISO, which is not an abbreviation but a derivation of the Greek word *isos,* which means equal and which is a term that was adopted by the International Organization for Standardization. An international standards-making body, based in Geneva, with representatives from more than 100 countries. The ISO establishes global standards for communications and information exchange. ANSI is the U.S. member of the ISO.

The seven-layer OSI Reference Model for computer-to-computer communications is one of the ISO's most widely accepted recommendations in the area of networking.

For more information on ISO, see www.iso.ch.

See also OSI Reference Model.

International Telecommunication Union Abbreviated ITU. The U.N. umbrella organization that develops and standardizes telecommunications worldwide.

The ITU also contains the CCITT, the International Frequency Registration Board (IFRB), and the Consultative Committee on International Radio (CCIR). In popular usage, CCITT standards are being referred to as ITU standards.

For more information on ITU, see www.itu.ch.

Internet The world's largest computer network, consisting of millions of computers supporting tens of millions of users in hundreds of countries. The Internet is growing at such a phenomenal rate that any size estimates are quickly out of date.

The Internet was originally established to meet the research needs of the U.S. defense industry, but it has grown into a huge global network serving universities, academic researchers, commercial interests, government agencies, and private individuals, both in the United States and overseas.

The Internet uses TCP/IP protocols, and Internet computers run many different operating systems, including VMS, Microsoft Windows 2000, and many variations of Unix.

No government agency, single person, or corporate entity controls the Internet; there is no Internet Corporation working behind the scenes. All decisions on methods and standards are made by committees based on input from users.

Internet use falls into several major areas, including:

- **E-mail**   Electronic mail. Well over 80 percent of the people who use the Internet regularly use it for e-mail. You can send e-mail to recipients in more than 150 countries, as well as to subscribers of commercial online services, such as America Online, CompuServe, Delphi, Genie, and Prodigy.

- **IRC chat**   A service that connects large numbers of users in real-time group discussions.

- **Mailing lists**   Private discussion groups accessed by e-mail.

- **Usenet newsgroups**   Larger public discussion groups that focus on a specific subject. Posts and threads in newsgroups are accessed using a newsreader.

- **World Wide Web**   Hypertext-based system for finding and accessing Internet resources; the World Wide Web is one of the fastest growing and most exciting of all Internet applications.

Other Internet applications such as Gopher, FTP and anonymous ftp, and Telnet have either been overshadowed by the growth of the World Wide Web or have seen their function absorbed into the popular Web browsers.

The sheer volume of information available through the Internet is staggering; however, because the Internet is a casual grouping of many networks, there is often no easy way to determine the location of specific information. This has led to the emergence of several prominent portal sites and a number of popular search engines.

Internet access can be via a permanent network connection or by dial-up through one of the many Internet Service Providers (ISP).

See also Internet address; Internet Architecture Board; Internet Assigned Numbers Authority; Internet Engineering Task Force; Internet Research Task Force; Internet Society; portal; Request for Comment; search engine; Usenet; World Wide Web; World Wide Web Consortium.

internet   *See* internetwork.

Internet abbreviations   Like any culture, the Internet world has developed a whole language of abbreviations, acronyms, and slang expressions. The following list describes some of the common terms you are likely to encounter in Usenet newsgroups or in your e-mail.

See also emoticon; smiley.

Abbreviation	Description
aTdHvAaNnKcSe	Thanks in advance
AWTTW	A word to the wise

Internet abbreviations

Abbreviation	Description
BRB	Be right back
BTW	By the way
CU	See you
FAQ	Frequently asked question
FAQL	Frequently asked question list
FOAF	Friend of a friend
F2F	Face to face
FWIW	For what it's worth
GR&D	Grinning, running, and ducking
IMHO	In my (sometimes not very) humble opinion
IWBNI	It would be nice if
IYFEG	Insert your favorite ethnic group
LOL	Laughing out loud
MEGO	My eyes glaze over
MOTAS	Member of the appropriate sex
MOTOS	Member of the opposite sex
MOSS	Member of the same sex
Ob-	Obligatory, as in ob-joke
OTOH	On the other hand

Abbreviation	Description
PD	Public domain
PITA	Pain in the ass
PMFJI	Pardon me for jumping in
RL	Real life
ROTFL	Rolling on the floor laughing
RTFM	Read the (expletive deleted) manual
SO	Significant other
TIA	Thanks in advance
TTFN	Ta ta for now
WRT	With respect to
YMMV	Your mileage may vary
$0.02	My two cents worth

Internet address   A location on the Internet. An Internet address takes the form someone@abc.def.xyz, in which someone is a user's name or part of a user's name, @abc is the network computer of the user, and def is the name of the host organization. The last three letters denote the kind of institution the user belongs to:

edu for educational

com for commercial

gov for government

mil for the military

org for non-profit organizations

net for Internet administrative organizations

See also bang path; IP address.

Internet Architecture Board   Abbreviated IAB. A technical advisory group of the Internet Society (ISOC). The IAB manages the editing and publication of Request for Comments (RFCs), serves as an appeals board, and provides other services to the ISOC.

For more information on the IAB, see www.iab.org/iab.

Internet Assigned Numbers Authority   Abbreviated IANA. A central clearinghouse for the assignment and coordination of Internet protocol parameters, such as Internet addresses, protocol variables and numbers, and domain names.

For more information on the IANA, see www.isi.edu/iana.

Internet Content Provider   Abbreviated ICP. A company that will design and deliver content for your Web site.

See also Internet Service Provider.

Internet Control Message Protocol
Abbreviated ICMP. An error-reporting protocol that works with Internet Protocol (IP) and provides the functions used for network-layer management and control.

Routers send ICMP messages to respond to undeliverable datagrams by placing an ICMP message in an IP datagram and then sending the datagram back to the original source. ICMP is also used by the Ping command.

See also Ping.

Internet Engineering Task Force   Abbreviated IETF. Provides technical and development services for the Internet and creates, tests, and implements Internet standards that are then approved and published by the Internet Society (ISOC). The technical work is done within the IETF working groups.

For more information on IETF, see www.ietf.org.

Internet file types   The Internet offers many opportunities for downloading files from a huge number of Internet hosts. These files may have been generated on different computer systems, so before you spend time downloading a file, it is important to understand the type of file you are dealing with. Table I.1 lists many of the common file types you may encounter.

TABLE I.1   INTERNET FILE TYPES

Filename Extension	Description
tar	A tape archive created by the tar utility.
Z	A file created by the compress utility. You must use uncompress to restore the file before you can use it.
tar.z	A compressed tape archive file.

TABLE I.1 INTERNET FILE TYPES *(CONTINUED)*

z	A file created by the pack utility. You must use unpack to restore the file before you can use it.
zip	A file created by PKZIP or WinZip. You must unzip the file before you can use it.
gz	A file created by the GNU gzip utility. You must decompress the file before you can use it.
hqx	A compressed Macintosh file.
sit	A Macintosh file compressed by StuffIt.
tif/tiff	A graphics file in TIF format.
gif	A graphics file in GIF format.
htm/html	A Web page in HyperText Markup Language.
jpg/jpeg	A graphics file in JPEG format.
mpg/mpeg	A video file in MPEG format.
txt	A text file.
1	An nroff source file.
ps	A PostScript file ready for printing.
uue	A uuencoded file. You must use uudecode before you can use the file.
uue.z	A compressed uuencoded file.
shar	A Usenet newsgroup archive file created by the shar utility.
shar.z	A compressed shar file.

Internet Group Management Protocol Abbreviated IGMP. An Internet protocol used in multicasting.

IGMP allows hosts to add or remove themselves from a multicast group. A multicast group is a collection of computers receiving packets from a host that is transmitting multicast packets with IP Class D addresses. Group members can join the group and leave the group; when there are no more members, the group simply ceases to exist.

See also Class D network; IP Multicast; multicasting.

Internet Inter-ORB Protocol Abbreviated IIOP. That part of the Common Object Request Broker Architecture (CORBA) that allows CORBA-based interaction over TCP/IP networks (including the Internet) by replacing Hypertext Transfer Protocol (HTTP).

See also Common Object Request Broker Architecture.

Internet Key Exchange *See* ISAKMP/Oakley.

Internet Mail Access Protocol Abbreviated IMAP. A protocol that defines how users can access and store incoming e-mail messages.

Internet mail servers use Simple Mail Transfer Protocol (SMTP) to move e-mail from one server to another and then use either IMAP or Post Office Protocol (POP) to manage the e-mail and store messages in the appropriate mailboxes.

IMAP allows users to download mail selectively, to look at a message header, to download only part of a message, to store messages on the server in a hierarchical structure, and to link to documents and Usenet newsgroups. IMAP also has strong authentication features and supports Kerberos. Search commands are also available so that users can locate messages based on their subject or header or based on content .

See also Kerberos; Post Office Protocol; Simple Mail Transfer Protocol

Internet Network File System Abbreviated Internet NFS. A TCP/IP-based protocol from Sun Microsystems used for sharing and accessing files remotely over the Internet.

See also Network File System.

Internet Network Information Center Abbreviated InterNIC. A cooperative venture between AT&T, the National Science Foundation, and Network Solutions, Inc., that provides domain name registration and assigns IP addresses for use on the Internet.

For more information on InterNIC, see www.internic.net.

Internet NFS *See* Internet Network File System.

Internet Protocol Abbreviated IP, IP version 4, and IPv4. The session-layer protocol that regulates packet forwarding by tracking addresses, routing outgoing messages, and recognizing incoming messages in TCP/IP networks and the Internet.

The IP packet header contains the following fields:

- **Version**   Version number of the protocol.

- **IHL (Internet header length)**   Length of the header information. The header length can vary; the default header is five 32-bit words, and a sixth word is optional.

- **TOS (Type of Service)**   Various levels or types of service.

- **Total length**   Length of the datagram in bytes, which can be a minimum of 576 bytes to a maximum of 65,535 bytes.

- **Identification**   Information that the receiving system can use to reassemble fragmented datagrams.

- **Flags**   The first flag bit (DF) specifies that the datagram should not be fragmented and must therefore travel over networks that can handle the size without fragmenting it. The second flag bit (MF) indicates whether this is the last fragment.

- **Fragment Offset**   An indication of where this datagram belongs in the set of fragments; is used during reassembly.

- **Time-to-Live (TTL)**   Originally, the time in seconds that the datagram could be in transit; if this time was exceeded, the datagram was considered lost. Now interpreted as a hop count and usually set to the default value 32 (for 32 hops), this value is decremented by each router through which the packet passes. Once it reaches zero, the datagram is discarded.

- **Protocol**   Identifies the transport-layer process intended to receive the datagram.

A value of 6 indicates Transmission Control Protocol (TCP), and a value of 17 indicates User Datagram Protocol (UDP).

- **Header checksum**   Checksum for the header.

- **Source address**   IP address of the sender.

- **Destination address**   IP address of the recipient.

- **Options/padding**   Optional information and padding.

See also IP multicast; IPv6; Transmission Control Protocol; Transmission Control Protocol/Internet Protocol.

Internet Relay Chat   Abbreviated IRC. An Internet client/server application that allows large groups of people to communicate interactively; developed by Jarkko Oikarinen in Finland.

Specific channels are devoted to a particular subject, from the sacred to the profane, and channels come and go regularly as interest levels change. Each channel has its own name, usually prefaced by the pound sign (#), as in #hottub.

When you join a channel, you can see what others have already typed; when you type a line and press Enter, everyone else sees your text. Most, but not all, of the conversations are in English. If someone asks you for a password during an IRC session, don't be tempted to give it; someone is trying to trick you into divulging important information about your system.

See also listserver; mailing list; newsgroup; Usenet.

INTERNET PROTOCOL FIELDS

Version	IHL	TOS	Total Length	
Identification			Flags	Fragment Offset
Time-to-Live	Protocol		Header Checksum	
Source Address				
Destination Address				
Options/Padding				

Internet Research Task Force   Abbreviated IRTF. An Internet organization that creates long- and short-term research groups concentrating on protocols, architecture, and technology issues.

For more information on IRTF, see www.irtf.org.

Internet Service Provider   Abbreviated ISP. A company that provides commercial or residential customers access to the Internet via dedicated or dial-up connections. An ISP will normally have several servers and a high-speed connection to an Internet backbone. Some ISPs also offer Web site hosting services and free e-mail to their subscribers.

See also Internet Content Provider

Internet Society   Abbreviated ISOC. An international organization that promotes cooperation and coordination for the Inter-

net, Internet applications, and internetworking technologies.

ISOC also coordinates the activities of many other Internet groups, including the Internet Architecture Board (IAB), the Internet Engineering Task Force (IETF), the Internet Assigned Numbers Authority (IANA), and the Internet Research Task Force (IRTF).

For more information on ISOC, see www.isoc.org.

internetwork   Abbreviated internet. Two or more networks using different networking protocols, connected by means of a router. Users on an internetwork can access the resources of all connected networks.

Internetwork Packet eXchange   Abbreviated IPX. Part of Novell NetWare's native protocol stack, used to transfer data between the server and workstations on the network. IPX packets are encapsulated and carried by the packets used in Ethernet and the frames used in Token Ring networks.

IPX packets consist of a 30-byte header which includes the network, node, and socket addresses for the source and the destination, followed by the data area, which can be from 30 bytes (only the header) to 65,535 bytes in length. Most networks impose a more realistic maximum packet size of about 1500 bytes.

The IPX packet header contains the following fields:

- **Checksum**   For data integrity checking..
- **Packet length**   Length of the packet in bytes
- **Transport control**   Number of routers a packet can cross before being discarded
- **Packet type**   The service that created the packet
- **Destination network**   Network address of the destination network
- **Destination node**   Media access control (MAC) address of the destination node
- **Destination socket**   Address of the process running on the destination node
- **Source network**   Network address of the source network
- **Source node**   Media access control (MAC) address of the source node
- **Source socket**   Address of the process running on the source node

See also Sequenced Packet Exchange.

Internetwork Packet Exchange Open Data-Link Interface   Abbreviated IPXODI. In Novell NetWare, the client software that accepts data from the DOS Requester, adds header and address information to each data packet, and transmits the data packet as a datagram.

InterNIC   *See* Internet Network Information Center.

interoperability   The ability to run application programs from different vendors across LANs, WANs, and MANs, giving users access to data and applications across heterogeneous networks. A network user need not know anything about the operating system or the configuration of the network hardware to access data from the file server.

Interoperability is boosted by the increasing availability of products that conform to open standards rather than to specific proprietary protocols. The products work in accordance with national and internationally accepted standards.

interpreter   A programming language translator that converts high-level program source code into machine language statements one line at a time.

Unlike a compiler, which must translate the whole program before execution can begin, an interpreter translates and then executes each line one at a time; this usually means that an interpreted program runs more slowly than a compiled program.

Java is an interpreted language, BASIC was often interpreted, although recent releases have used a compiler instead, and C and C++ are always compiled.

See also compiler; Java; just-in-time compiler.

interprocess communication Abbreviated IPC. A term that describes all the methods used to pass information between two programs running on the same computer in a multitasking operating system or between two programs running on a network, including pipes, shared memory, message queues, sockets, semaphores, and Object Linking and Embedding (OLE).

See also Inter-Application Communication.

Interrupt 14 Abbreviated INT 14. The PC interrupt used to reroute messages from the serial port to the network interface card (NIC); used by some terminal-emulation programs.

interrupt A signal to the processor generated by a device under its control, such as the system clock, that interrupts normal processing.

An interrupt indicates that an event requiring the processor's attention has occurred, causing the processor to suspend and save its current activity and then branch to an interrupt service routine (ISR).

In the PC, interrupts are often divided into three classes:

- Internal hardware
- External hardware
- Software

The Intel family of processors supports 256 prioritized interrupts, of which the first 64 are reserved for use by the system hardware or by the operating system.

See also interrupt request.

interrupt controller A chip used to process and prioritize hardware interrupts. In the PC, a programmable interrupt controller responds to each hardware interrupt, assigns a priority, and forwards it to the main processor.

See also interrupt request.

interrupt handler Special software located in the operating-system kernel that manages and processes system interrupts. Also known as an interrupt service routine (ISR).

When an interrupt occurs, the processor suspends and saves its current activity and then branches to the interrupt handler. This routine processes the interrupt, whether it was generated by the system clock, a keystroke, or a mouse click. When the ISR is complete, it returns control to the suspended process.

Each type of interrupt is processed by its own specific interrupt handler. A table, called the interrupt vector table, maintains a list of addresses for these specific interrupt handlers.

See also hooked vector.

interrupt request Abbreviated IRQ. Hardware lines that carry a signal from a device to the processor.

A hardware interrupt signals that an event has taken place that requires the processor's attention. The interrupt may come from the keyboard, the network interface card (NIC), or the system's disk drives.

See also interrupt controller.

interrupt service routine   *See* interrupt handler.

interrupt vector table   A list of addresses, maintained by the operating-system kernel, for specific software routines known as interrupt handlers.

See also interrupt handler.

intranet   A private corporate network that uses Internet software and TCP/IP networking protocol standards.

Many companies use intranets for tasks as simple as distributing a company newsletter and for tasks as complex as posting and updating technical support bulletins to service personnel worldwide. An intranet does not always include a permanent connection to the Internet.

See also extranet; Internet; internet.

intruder   An unauthorized user of a computer system, usually a person with malicious intent.

See also cracker; firewall; hacker; Intrusion Detection System.

Intrusion Detection System   Abbreviated IDS. A software package designed to detect specific actions on a network that are typical of an intruder or that might indicate an act of corporate espionage.

An IDS package monitors the network or the server for specific "attack signatures" that might indicate an active intruder is attempting to gain access to the network; such actions are carefully documented by the system.

Specific actions, such as opening or renaming certain important files, opening specific applications, downloading large amounts of data from key documents, or sending classified documents out as e-mail attachments, are also monitored by the IDS software.

See also firewall.

inverse multiplexing   Abbreviated I-Mux. In communications, a technique that splits a high-speed data stream into two or more parts for transmission over multiple lower-speed channels. Once at the receiving end of the circuit, the data streams are combined into a single stream.

Inverse multiplexing provides bandwidth on demand, to avoid the high costs associated with a leased line that may not be fully utilized at all times and to take advantage of low-cost low-speed lines.

See also multiplexing.

Inverse Multiplexing over ATM   Abbreviated IMA. A specification defined by the Asynchronous Transfer Mode (ATM) Forum that defines a method of inverse multiplexing ATM over two or more T1 circuits.

See also Asynchronous Transfer Mode; inverse multiplexing.

inverted backbone   A network architecture in which the wiring hub and routers become the center of the network; all the network segments attach to this hub.

See also backbone.

INVERSE MULTIPLEXING

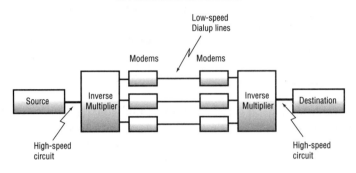

I/O *See* input/output.

I/O bound *See* input/output bound.

Iomega Corporation A major manufacturer of removable storage media, best known for its popular Zip drive, which has shipped more than 12 million units worldwide. Iomega also makes the higher-capacity Jaz drives, the Ditto line of tape-backup products, and Clik! storage devices for digital cameras and hand-held computers.

For more information on Iomega Corporation, see `www.iomega.com`.

ION *See* Integrated On-Demand Network.

IP *See* Internet Protocol.

IP address The unique 32-bit number that identifies a computer on the Internet or some other Internet Protocol network.

An IP address is usually written (in decimal) as four numbers separated by dots or periods and can be divided into two parts. The network address is made up from the high-order bits in the address, and the host address comprises the rest. In addition, the host part of the address can be further subdivided to allow for a subnet address.

These numbers are very difficult for most people to remember, so humans tend to refer to computers by their domain names instead.

See also address classes; domain name; dotted decimal; Internet address; subnet.

IPC *See* interprocess communication.

ipconfig A utility program used to list various Internet Protocol configuration information, including host address, subnet mask, and gateway addresses.

See also IP address; netstat; Ping; subnet mask; tracert.

IP datagram *See* Internet Protocol.

IP Multicast An Internet standard that allows a single host to distribute data to multiple recipients.

IP multicasting can deliver audio and video content in real time so that the person using the system can interact with the data stream. A multicast group is created, and every member of the group receives every datagram. Membership is dynamic; when you join a group, you start to receive the datastream, and when you leave the group, you no longer receive the datastream.

See also Internet Group Management Protocol; multicast backbone; multicasting; streaming.

IPng   *See* IPv6.

I-PNNI   *See* Integrated-Private Network-to-Network Interface.

IP over ATM   A set of proposals that define general methods of integrating Internet Protocol over an Asynchronous Transfer Mode (ATM) network, while preserving the best features of the connectionless IP and connection-oriented ATM.

These proposals have a variety of names, including layer 3 switching, high-speed routing, short-cut routing, and multilayer switching, and come from a variety of sources, including the ATM Forum, the Internet Engineering Task Force, and a vendor collective known as Layer 3 Switching/ Routing Advocates.

See also IP switching.

IPSec   A suite of protocols under development by the Internet Engineering Task Force (IETF) designed to add security provisions to the Internet Protocol (IP). Also known as IP Security.

The Authentication Header (AH) ensures that the datagram has not been tampered with during transmission, and the Encapsulating Security Payload (ESP) defines encryption methods for IP data.

IPSec operates in two modes:

- **Transport mode**   AH or ESP is placed immediately after the original IP datagram header and provides security between two end systems such as a server and a workstation.

- **Tunnel mode**   The original IP datagram is placed inside a new datagram, and AH and ESP are inserted between the IP header of the new packet and the original IP datagram. The new header points to the tunnel endpoint, and the original header points to the final destination of the datagram. Tunnel mode is best suited to Virtual Private Network (VPN) use, securing remote access to your corporate network through the Internet.

See also encapsulation; Internet Protocol; ISAKMP/Oakley; tunneling; Virtual Private Network.

IP security   *See* IPSec.

IP switching   1. A switch, developed by Ipsilon Networks, that combines intelligent Internet Protocol (IP) routing with high-speed Asynchronous Transfer Mode (ATM) switching hardware. The IP protocol stack is implemented on ATM hardware, allowing the system to adapt dynamically to the flow requirements of the network traffic as defined in the packet header.

2. A technique that uses network-layer protocols which provide routing services to add

capabilities to layer 2 switching. IP switching locates paths in a network by using routing protocols and then forwards packets along that route at layer 2. IP switching is designed for networks that use switches rather than networks built around repeater hubs and routers.

See also IP over ATM.

IPv4 *See* Internet Protocol.

IPv6 The next version of the Internet Protocol, also called IP version 6 or IPng for IP next generation.

The most striking feature of IPv6 is that it uses a 128-bit address space rather than the 32-bit system in use today. This provides for a truly astronomical number of possible addresses. The address format consists of 8 sections separated by colons. Each section contains 16 bits expressed as 4 hexadecimal numbers. An address might look like this:

1234:5678:9ABC:DEF0:1234:5678:9ABC :DEF0

In any address, one set of leading zeros can be replaced by two colons.

In addition to the 128-bit address space, IPv6 designates a 128-bit hierarchical address for point-to-point communication called an Aggregatable Global Unicast Ad-dress Format (AGUAF). In this format, a top level aggregator (TLA) is assigned a block of addresses by bodies such as the Internet Assigned Numbers Authority (IANA). In turn, the TLA assigns addresses to a next level aggregator (NLA), which in turn assigns addresses to the site level aggregator (SLA). In turn, the SLA assigns blocks of contiguous addresses to its subscribers. The last level is the host interface ID, which identifies a single host interface. Companies assign host interface IDs by using a unique number on the subnet.

IPv6 assigns addresses to interfaces, and because a node can have multiple interfaces, it can also have multiple IP addresses. A single interface can also have multiple addresses. An address can be multicast, unicast, or anycast, which is a special case of multicast.

The IP datagram header has been simplified, by dropping some fields and making others optional. IPv6 also allows for several types of optional header extensions, some of which might be used for specialized handling instructions. In addition, IPv6 includes the IPSec security extensions.

See also Internet Protocol; IPSec.

IP version 4 *See* Internet Protocol.

IP version 6 *See* IPv6.

IPv6

3bits	13bits	32bits	16bits	64bits
001	TLA ID	NLA ID	SLA ID	Host Interface ID

IPX *See* Internetwork Packet eXchange.

IPX address In Novell NetWare, a network address. Also known as an IPX internetwork address.

The IPX address includes a 4-byte network number assigned to every segment on a LAN (the IPX external network number), a 6-byte node number that identifies a specific system and is usually derived from the interface card address originally assigned by the manufacturer, and a 2-byte socket number.

See also IPX external network number.

IPX external network number In Novell NetWare, a hexadecimal number that identifies a network cable segment, assigned when the NetWare Internetwork Packet eXchange (IPX) protocol is bound to a network interface board in the server. An IPX external network number can have from one to eight digits (1 to FFFFFFFE).

IPX internal network number In Novell NetWare, a hexadecimal number that identifies a NetWare server. Each server on the network must have a unique Internetwork Packet Exchange (IPX) internal network number. The number can have from one to eight digits (1 to FFFFFFFE) and is assigned to the server during NetWare installation.

IPX internetwork address *See* IPX address.

IPXODI *See* Internetwork Packet Exchange Open Data-Link Interface.

IRC *See* Internet Relay Chat.

IrDA *See* Infrared Data Association.

IRF *See* Inherited Rights Filter.

IRM *See* Inherited Rights Mask.

IRQ *See* interrupt request.

IRTF *See* Internet Research Task Force.

ISA *See* Industry Standard Architecture; Integrated Services Architecture.

ISAKMP/Oakley Abbreviation for Internet Security Association and Key Management Protocol/Oakley security key management protocol. Also known as the Internet Key Exchange (IKE).

A security protocol that automatically manages the exchange of secret symmetric keys between sender and receiver.

See also IPSec.

ISDN *See* Integrated Services Digital Network.

ISO 10646 A 4-byte character encoding scheme that includes all the world's national standard character encodings, defined by the International Organization for Standardization (ISO). The 2-byte Unicode characters set maps into a part of ISO 10646.

See also American Standard Code for Information Interchange; double-byte character set; Unicode.

ISO *See* International Organization for Standardization.

ISOC *See* Internet Society.

isochronous service A method of transmitting real-time data using preallocated bandwidth on a communications link, allowing time-synchronized transmissions

195

with very little delay. Isochronous service is required for real-time data such as synchronized voice and video, in which delays in packet delivery would be unacceptable.

Asynchronous Transfer Mode (ATM) can provide isochronous service because its cells are always the same size, so it is possible to guarantee accurate and timely delivery of packets. Other networks can provide isochronous service by using a priority scheme to dedicate bandwidth to video traffic.

Iso-Ethernet   The IEEE standard 802.9a, which describes a combination of Ethernet and Integrated Services Digital Network (ISDN) on the same cable.

As well as providing standard 10Mbps Ethernet connections over Category 3 or Category 5 unshielded twisted-pair wiring, Iso-Ethernet also provides up to 96 ISDN Basic Rate B channels running at 64Kbps connected to internal or external users or systems. One D channel is used for control and signaling information.

The ISDN channels can be accessed over the network via a single point of connection, which in turn is connected to the ISDN service; this removes the need for each workstation to have its own ISDN hardware.

See also Integrated Services Digital Network.

ISO/OSI model   *See* OSI Reference Model.

ISP   *See* Internet Service Provider.

ISR   Abbreviation for interrupt service routine.

See interrupt handler.

ISV   *See* Independent Software Vendor.

ITU   *See* International Telecommunication Union.

IXC   *See* Interexchange Carrier.

J

jabber A continuous and meaningless transmission generated by a network device, usually the result of a user error or a hardware malfunction.

Java A programming language and development environment created by Sun Microsystems, designed to create distributed executable applications for use with a Web browser containing a Java runtime environment.

Java technology has been licensed by literally hundreds of companies, including IBM, Microsoft, Oracle, Hewlett-Packard, and others interested in developing Web-based and platform-independent applications.

The Java programming language is a portable, object-oriented language, loosely modeled after C++, with some of the more troubling C++ constructs such as pointers removed. This similarity to C and C++ is no accident; it means that the huge population of professional programmers can quickly apply their previous C experience to writing code in Java.

Java is designed to support networking and networking operations right from the start and begins with the assumption that it can trust no one, implementing several important security mechanisms.

Java is architecturally neutral, does not care about the underlying operating system, and is portable because it makes no assumptions about the size of data types and explicitly defines arithmetic behavior. Java is also multithreaded to support different threads of execution and can adapt to a changing environment by loading classes as they are needed, even across a network.

Rather than writing code targeted at a specific hardware and operating-system platform, Java developers compile their source code into an intermediate form of bytecode that can be processed by any computer system with a Java runtime environment. The Java class loader transfers the bytecode to the Java Virtual Machine (JVM), which interprets the bytecode for that specific platform. Java class libraries, those files that make up the standard application programming interface (API), are also loaded dynamically. The runtime environment then executes the application, which can run within a Web browser or as a stand-alone application.

See also bytecode; interpreter; Java applet; Java Developer's Kit; Java Virtual Machine; just-in-time compiler; sandbox.

JAVA

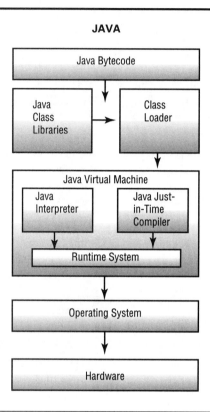

Java Bytecode

Java Class Libraries

Class Loader

Java Virtual Machine

Java Interpreter

Java Just-in-Time Compiler

Runtime System

Operating System

Hardware

Java applet A small program written in the Java programming language designed to add a specific capability to a Web page. The applet is stored on the Web server and is downloaded to and executes within the browser.

Java applets are inserted into a Web page using the <APPLET> tag, which indicates the initial window size for the applet, various parameters for the applet, and the location from which the browser can download the bytecode file.

Stand-alone programs written in the Java programming language that can execute without needing the browser are known as Java applications.

See also bytecode; Java; Java Developer's Kit; Java Virtual Machine; just-in-time compiler; sandbox.

Java Database Connectivity   Abbreviated JDBC. An application programming interface (API) that allows developers to write Java applications that can access a database.

See also Open Database Connectivity.

Java Developer's Kit   Abbreviated JDK. A collection of software-development tools provided by Sun Microsystems for writing Java applications. This kit, distributed free, contains a Java compiler, an interpreter, a debugger, an applet viewer, and documentation.

JavaScript   A simple scripting language created by Netscape Communications and Sun Microsystems that allows developers to add a specific capability to a Web page.

JavaScript is relatively easy to write when compared with the Java programming language, but it is slower in execution and has far fewer application programming interface (API) functions available. A JavaScript-compliant Web browser, such as Netscape Navigator, is necessary to run the JavaScript code.

See also Java; script.

JavaSoft   A subsidiary of Sun Microsystems responsible for developing and promoting the Java programming language and related products.

For more information on JavaSoft, see www.javasoft.com.

Java Virtual Machine   The runtime environment for Java applets and applications; sometimes abbreviated JVM.

The Java Virtual Machine creates a simulated environment that provides the same interface to applications, no matter what hardware and operating system combination is in use.

The Java Virtual Machine consists of two layers:

- The top layer is compatible with all Java applications.
- The bottom layer is compatible with a specific computing platform, such as the Intel family of processors.

See also Java.

JDBC   *See* Java Database Connectivity.

JDK   *See* Java Developer's Kit.

Jini   A technology from Sun Microsystems that is based on Java concepts and that allows spontaneous networking of a large variety of network devices.

Jini creates a federation of Java Virtual Machines on a network and allows users, devices, data, and applications to connect dynamically to share information and to perform tasks without prior knowledge of one another's capabilities.

See also Java.

JIT compiler   *See* just-in-time compiler.

jitter   A type of distortion found on analog communications lines that results in data-transmission errors.

J

job   A unit of work done by a computer, usually in a mainframe environment. A job can be the one-time execution of a single file or the execution of a whole series of programs to accomplish a complex task.

See also job control.

job control   A mechanism used to manage jobs, allowing them to be started, stopped, and moved between the background and the foreground.

Joint Photographic Experts Group

Abbreviated JPEG; also sometimes abbreviated JPG. An image-compression standard and file format that defines a set of compression methods for high-quality images such as photographs, single video frames, or scanned pictures. JPEG does not work very well when compressing text, line art, or vector graphics.

JPEG uses lossy compression methods that result in some loss of the original data. When you decompress the original image, you don't get exactly the same image that you started with, although JPEG was specifically designed to discard information not easily detected by the human eye.

JPEG can store 24-bit color images in as many as 16 million colors; files in Graphics Interchange Format (GIF) form can only store 256 colors.

See also Graphics Interchange Format; lossy compression.

JPEG   *See* Joint Photographic Experts Group.

JPG   *See* Joint Photographic Experts Group.

jukebox   A high-capacity storage device that uses an autochanger mechanism to mount or dismount disks automatically. A jukebox typically contains as many as 50 disks and a mechanism that picks up disks from a bay and loads them into the drives as they are needed.

See also high-capacity storage system.

Julian date   A method of representing the date that is often used in computer systems. The first digit represents the year, and the remaining digits represent the day of the year, counting from January 1.

See also Y2K problem.

jumper   A small plastic and metal connector that completes a circuit, usually to select one option from a set of several user-definable options. Jumpers are often used to select one particular hardware configuration from a choice of configurations.

just-in-time compiler   Sometimes abbreviated JIT compiler. A compiler that receives the bytecode of a Java application and compiles the bytecode on the fly.

Java bytecode processed by a just-in-time compiler executes faster than the same bytecode processed by a Java Virtual Machine.

See also Java; Java Virtual Machine.

JVM   *See* Java Virtual Machine.

K

K *See* kilo-.

K56Flex   A modem technology from Rockwell Semiconductor Systems and Lucent Technologies that provides up to 56Kbps downstream and up to 40Kbps upstream. Replaced by the V.90 standard. *See also* V.90; X2.

Kb *See* kilobit.

KB *See* kilobyte.

Kbit *See* kilobit.

Kbps *See* kilobits per second.

Kbyte *See* kilobyte.

keep-alive signal   A signal transmitted to maintain a communications circuit during periods of idleness and to prevent the circuit from timing out and terminating the connection.

Kerberos   A network security system developed as a part of Project Athena at MIT. Kerberos is used to authenticate a user who is asking for permission to use a particular network service.

Kerberos can be used to control the initial connection to a server or to authenticate every single request between a client and the server. It grants tickets to a client to allow the use of a specific service and is secure even on a nonsecure network.

Kerberos takes the following precautions:

- Passwords are never sent over the network unencrypted, making it impossible for network snoopers to capture passwords.

- All Kerberos messages are timestamped so that they cannot be captured and then replayed at a later time; Kerberos does not accept old messages.

- When you request access to a service, to access a file server, for example, Kerberos gives you a "ticket" that is valid for access to the file server but not valid for any other service. When you try to connect to the server, you send your ticket with the request. Once the server knows who you are, the server decides whether to grant you access. Tickets also expire, and if your session lasts longer than the predefined limit, you will have to reauthenticate yourself to Kerberos to get a new ticket.

Kerberos is named after the three-headed dog Cerberus, who guards the gates of the underworld in Greek mythology.

See also authentication; certificate; digital signature.

K

Kermit   A file-transfer protocol developed at Columbia University and placed in the public domain that is used to transfer files between PCs and mainframe computers over standard telephone lines.

Data is transmitted in variable-length blocks up to 96 characters in length, and each block is checked for transmission errors. Kermit detects transmission errors and initiates repeat transmissions automatically.

See also Xmodem; Ymodem; Zmodem.

kernel   The fundamental part of an operating system. The kernel stays resident in memory at all times, often hidden from the user, and manages system memory, the file system, and disk operations.

The kernel also runs processes and provides interprocess communications between those processes, including synchronizing events, scheduling, passing messages, managing input and output routines, and managing memory.

See also Linux; Mach, microkernel, shell.

key   **1.** An entry in the Microsoft Windows Registry that contains an element of configuration information. A key may also be empty and have no value set.

2. In encryption, a mechanism used to encode a message.

3. In a database system, a unique value used to identify data records. Also known as a primary key.

See also public key encryption; sub-key.

keyboard buffer   A small amount of system memory used to store the most recently typed keys, also known as the type-ahead buffer. Some utilities or shells let you collect a number of keystrokes or commands and edit or reissue them.

keyboard template   A plastic card that fits over certain keys (usually the function keys) on the keyboard as a reminder of how to use them. These templates are specific to an application, and they can be a useful reminder for new or occasional users.

key combination   In menu-driven and graphical user interfaces, some menu commands can be executed by certain combinations of keystrokes, also known as shortcut keystrokes. By using key combinations, users can bypass the menus and so speed up operations.

keypass attack   *See* brute-force attack.

keyspace attack   *See* brute-force attack.

key redefinition   The ability of an application to assign different functions to specific keys.

keystroke   The action of pressing and then releasing a key on the keyboard to initiate some action or enter a character.

keyword   Any of the words, sometimes known as reserved words, that make up the vocabulary of a particular programming language or set of operating system commands and utilities.

kilo-   A prefix indicating 1000 in the metric system. Because computing is based on powers of 2, kilo usually means 2^{10}, or 1024. To differentiate between these two uses, a lowercase k is used to indicate 1000 (as in kHz), and an uppercase K is used to indicate 1024 (as in KB).

See also mega-.

kilobaud   One thousand baud. A unit of measurement of the transmission capacity of a communications channel.

See also baud.

kilobit   Abbreviated Kb or Kbit. 1024 bits (binary digits).

See also gigabit; megabit.

kilobits per second   Abbreviated Kbps. The number of bits, or binary digits, transmitted every second, measured in multiples of 1024 bits per second. Used as an indicator of communications transmission rates.

See also megabits per second.

kilobyte   Abbreviated K, KB, or Kbyte. 1024 bytes.

See also exabyte; gigabyte; megabyte; petabyte; terabyte.

kluge   Pronounced "klooj." A program that doesn't work as well as it should, is not carefully designed, and is not well written. A kluge may also be a program that works, but for all the wrong reasons, or only under very specific, highly unrealistic conditions.

See also hack.

Korn shell   An upward-compatible extension to the original Unix shell, written by David Korn and released as part of System V.

The Korn shell is now the default shell on many Unix systems, particularly those based on System V, including UnixWare and many others.

Because the Korn shell is an extension of the Bourne shell, everything that works in the Bourne shell also works in the Korn shell. The Korn shell also adds the following:

- Interactive editing of the command line with either vi or emacs

- Better function definitions providing local variables and the ability to create recursive functions

- Extensive pattern matching for filenames, similar to regular expressions

Several features were adapted from the C shell, including:

- Command history allowing retrieval and reuse of previous commands

- Job control and the mechanism for moving jobs between the background and the foreground

- Aliases for abbreviated command names

- The tilde (~) used as a shorthand for the name of the home directory

See also Bash shell; Bourne shell; C shell; Unix shell.

K

L

L2 Cache   *See* secondary cache.

L2TP   *See* Layer 2 Tunneling Protocol.

LAN   *See* local-area network.

LANalyzer for Windows   A Microsoft Windows-based software product from Novell used to troubleshoot and monitor network performance and activity.

The LANalyzer main screen is a dashboard of gauges displaying real-time statistics, including LAN utilization, packets per second, and errors per second. User-specified alarms can also be set on these gauges, and detailed statistics screens plot frame rate, utilization, and error rate over time.

LAN-aware   An application that contains mechanisms for file and record locking to prevent multiple simultaneous access when used on a network. The term is often applied in a broader sense to any application capable of running in a networked environment.

LANDesk Management Suite   A package of network management utilities from Intel Corporation that includes hardware and software inventory, server monitoring, client monitoring and control, network traffic monitoring, virus protection, remote access, remote control, and print-queue management.

LANDesk also includes a Desktop Management Interface (DMI) remote management console and DMI desktop agents or service layers for MS-DOS and Windows clients. *See also* Desktop Management Interface.

LAN Distance   A hardware/software combination product from Network Communications Corp. used to troubleshoot and monitor performance and activity on Ethernet and token-ring LANs.

The LAN Distance hardware includes an on-board processor and a large buffer for packet capturing. The package can decode most LAN protocols in common use, including NetWare, TCP/IP, DECnet, Banyan, Network File System (NFS), AppleTalk Filing Protocol (AFP), Open Systems Interconnect (OSI), Systems Network Architecture (SNA), NetBEUI, Xerox Network Services (XNS), and Server Message Block (SMB).

LANE   *See* LAN Emulation.

LAN Emulation   Abbreviated LANE. An Asynchronous Transfer Mode (ATM) specification that defines ways of connecting legacy local-area networks such as Ethernet and token ring to an ATM backbone, allowing ATM to replace older and slower backbone circuits.

LANE provides the translation services needed between the two types of networks and is totally transparent to the high-level protocols. LANE consists of four major components:

- Broadcast and unknown server (BUS), which manages address resolution.

- LAN Emulation Client (LEC), which runs on all nodes connected to the ATM network, initiates data transfers between other clients, and makes mapping requests between MAC (media access control) addresses and ATM addresses.

- LAN Emulation Configuration Server (LECS), which provides configuration information and tracks on which virtual LAN each LAN Emulation Client operates.

- LAN Emulation Server (LES), which provides address mapping between MAC addresses and ATM addresses and usually runs on the same node as the BUS.

See also Asynchronous Transfer Mode; Integrated-Private Network-to-Network Interface; IP over ATM; IP switching.

LANRover A remote access package from Shiva Corporation that lets network users log in from their PC or portable computer when away from the office.

LAN Server An IBM network operating system, based on a version of OS/2, that runs on Intel processors as well as on the PowerPC.

LAN Server supports Microsoft Windows, MS-DOS, OS/2, and Macintosh clients as well as AppleTalk, IPX/SPX, TCP/IP, and NetBIOS protocols. LAN Server supports domain directory services and encrypted passwords, but does not include C-2 level certification.

LANtastic A popular peer-to-peer network operating system, from Artisoft, Inc., that runs with MS-DOS, OS/2, or Microsoft

Windows and supports Microsoft Windows, MS-DOS, OS/2, Macintosh, and Unix clients.

The network can be run with all stations sharing files with all other stations or, for enhanced performance, with one PC acting as a dedicated file server. LANtastic supports an unlimited number of users, includes built-in CD-ROM, network e-mail, and network fax support, scheduling and network management, file-level security, and Internet access and can connect easily into the NetWare environment.

LAN WorkGroup Novell's connectivity package that is located and managed centrally from the NetWare file server.

The system includes transparent file sharing, terminal emulation, remote command execution, and printer-redirection features for both MS-DOS and Windows clients. The LAN WorkGroup differs from its stand-alone counterpart, LAN WorkPlace, in that it can be managed from the file server.

See also LAN WorkPlace.

LAN WorkPlace Novell's connectivity software for MS-DOS and Windows clients. Features include terminal emulation, transparent Network File System (NFS) file sharing, and a Web browser.

See also LAN WorkGroup.

LAP *See* Link Access Procedure.

LAP-B *See* Link Access Procedure-Balanced.

LapLink A popular communications package from Traveling Software, used to

L

transfer and synchronize files between a laptop computer and a desktop or networked computer.

LAPM   *See* Link Access Procedure for Modems.

laptop computer   A small, portable computer that is light enough to carry comfortably, with a flat screen and keyboard that fold together.

Advances in battery technology allow laptop computers to run for many hours between charges. Laptop computers often have a thin, backlit or sidelit liquid-crystal display (LCD) or a plasma screen. Some models can mate with a docking station to perform as a full-sized desktop system back at the office, and many new laptop computers allow direct connection to the network with PCMCIA network interface cards. In some laptop computers, a set of business applications is built in to ROM.

See also hand-held computer; mobile computing; notebook computer; PC Memory Card International Association; port replicator; wireless communications.

Large Internet Packet   Abbreviated LIP. A mechanism that allows the Novell NetWare internetwork packet size to be increased from the default 576 bytes, thus increasing throughput over bridges and routers.

LIP allows workstations to determine the packet size based on the largest packet supported by the router; the larger packet size is also supported by Ethernet and token-ring networks.

last known good configuration   In Microsoft Windows NT, the last configuration that was used to boot the computer successfully. Windows NT saves this configuration and offers it as a startup option during the boot process.

last mile   A term, not to be taken too literally, that describes the link between a customer site and the telephone company's central office. This link is often the most expensive and least efficient connection in the telephone company's system and is often a barrier to high-speed services.

latency   The time delay involved in moving data traffic through a network. Latency can arise from several sources:

- Propagation delay, which is the time it takes the data to travel the length of the line.

- Transmission delay, which is the time it takes to move the data across the network media.

- Processing delay, which is the time it takes to establish the route, encapsulate the data, and take care of other switching tasks.

See also propagation delay.

Layer 2 Tunneling Protocol   Abbreviated L2TP. A proposed standard for a secure, high-priority, temporary communications path through the Internet.

L2TP is based on Cisco's Layer 2 Forwarding (L2F) protocol and includes features from Microsoft's Point-to-Point Tunneling Protocol (PPTP). A tunnel is established from an Internet Service Provider (ISP) to a corporate site, and information is transmitted through the tunnel. Once L2TP is set up, the user communicates with the corporate system through what seems to be a direct dial-up connection; the ISP is effectively removed from the picture.

See also tunneling.

LCD *See* liquid-crystal display.

LCD monitor A monitor that uses liquid-crystal display (LCD) technology. Many laptop and notebook computers use LCD monitors because of their low power requirements.

LDAP *See* Lightweight Directory Access Protocol.

leaf object In Novell NetWare Directory Services (NDS), an object that cannot contain any other objects; also known as a noncontainer object. Leaf objects can be printers, servers, print queues, or even users.

See also container object.

Learning Tree International A major provider of training classes and computer-technology certifications. Learning Tree International offers more than 150 networking and computer-related training classes in the United States, Europe, and Asia, as well as 27 professional certification programs.

For more information about Learning Tree International, see `www.learningtree.com`.

Learning Tree International Certified Professional A professional certification from Learning Tree International, available with a large number of subject specializations, including Local Area Networks,

Wide Area Networks, Internetworking, PC Service and Support, and Unix Systems.

See also Learning Tree International.

leased line A communications circuit or telephone line reserved for the permanent use of a specific customer; also called a private line.

See also dedicated line.

LEC *See* Local Exchange Carrier.

legacy application An application designed to run on what has now become a legacy system and that continues to be used.

A legacy application may perform admirably and provide little reason to upgrade to a more up-to-date system, or it may be inefficient, perform poorly, and continue in use because replacing it is simply too expensive.

See also legacy system; legacy wiring.

legacy system A computer system, developed to solve a particular business need, which, due to the passage of time, has become obsolete.

Legacy systems do not conform to the technical standards or performance standards of up-to-date systems. There is usually a requirement to maintain backward compatibility with or connections to legacy systems.

legacy wiring Preinstalled wiring that may or may not be suitable for use with a network.

See also legacy system.

L

Lempel-Ziv-Welch   Abbreviated LZW, an algorithm used in data compression, developed by Abraham Lempel, Jacob Ziv, and Terry Welch.

LZW is a general-purpose compression algorithm suitable for use on almost any type of data. It is fast in both compressing and decompressing data and does not require the use of floating-point operations.

LZW is a lossless compression method and is used in several image formats such as Graphics Interchange Format (GIF) and Tag Image File Format (TIFF), as well as a part of the V.32 bis modem compression standard and PostScript Level 2.

The patent for LZW compression is held by Unisys, which levies a fee on any application that uses the LZW compression algorithm.

See also lossless compression; lossy compression.

level 2 cache   A secondary static RAM cache located between the primary cache and the rest of the system. A level 2 cache is often larger than the primary cache, and it is usually slower. In Intel's Pentium II processor, the level 2 cache is implemented as a part of the package that holds the CPU.

See also cache; memory cache.

Lexmark International, Inc.   A major manufacturer of printers, based in Lexington, Kentucky; spun off from IBM in 1991. Lexmark markets laser and ink jet printers for both home and office use, as well as laser-printer management software for servers.

For more information on Lexmark International, Inc., see www.lexmark.com

LF   *See* line feed.

light-wave communications   Usually refers to communications using fiber-optic cables and light generated by light-emitting diodes (LEDs) or lasers.

Lightweight Directory Access Protocol   Abbreviated LDAP. A directory services specification that has recently gained wide acceptance.

A directory service provides "white page" service for an organization to help people find other people and network services and can also be used over the Internet. A directory service is a database that can be manipulated in a variety of ways to provide this information.

LDAP can be used as a directory service by itself, or it can be used for "lightweight" access to an X.500-compliant directory service. LDAP is a subset of X.500 that runs over TCP/IP; X.500 runs on OSI-compliant systems. Many companies have announced their intention to support LDAP in upcoming products.

See also Active Directory; Novell Directory Services; X.500.

LIM EMS   *See* Expanded Memory Specification.

limited-distance modem   *See* line driver.

line adapter   In communications, a device that converts a signal into a form suitable for transmission over a communications channel.

A modem is a specific type of line adapter used to convert the computer's digital signals into analog form so that they can be transmitted over a telephone line.

line analyzer   Any device that monitors and displays information about a transmission on a communications channel. A line analyzer is used for troubleshooting and load monitoring.

line-of-business application   *See* mission-critical application.

line driver   In communications, a hardware device used to extend the transmission distance between computers that are connected using a serial interface based on the RS-232 standard. A line driver is required at each end of the line. Also known as a baseband modem, limited-distance modem, or short-haul modem.

See also short-haul modem.

line feed   Abbreviated LF. A printer command that advances the paper in the printer by one line, leaving the print head in the same position. In the ASCII character set, a line feed has a decimal value of 10.

See also American Standard Code for Information Interchange; carriage return; Extended Binary Coded Decimal Interchange Code.

line printer   Any high-volume printer that prints a complete line at a time, rather than printing one character at a time (as a dot-matrix printer or a daisy-wheel printer does) or one page at a time (as a laser printer does).

Line printers are very high-speed printers and are common in mainframe environments.

line-sharing device   A small electronic mechanism that allows a fax machine and a telephone answering machine to share the same phone line. The device answers the call and listens for the characteristic high-pitched fax carrier signal. If this signal is detected, the call is routed to the fax machine; if it is not present, the call is sent to a telephone or answering machine.

line-of-sight   An unobstructed path between the transmitter and receiver. Laser, microwave, and infrared transmissions usually require a clear line-of-sight.

See also wireless communications.

line speed   In communications, the transmission speed that a line will reliably support for any given grade of service.

See also connection speed; data-transfer rate.

link   On a Web page or a hypertext document, a connection between one element and another in the same or in a different document.

Link Access Procedure   Abbreviated LAP. The link-level protocol specified by the CCITT X.1 recommendation used for communications between DCE (data communications equipment) and DTE (data terminal equipment).

See also Consultative Committee for International Telephony and Telegraphy; Link Access Procedure-Balanced.

Link Access Procedure-Balanced   Abbreviated LAP-B. A common CCITT bit-oriented, data-link layer protocol used to

L

link terminals and computers to packet-switched networks. It is equivalent to the HDLC (High-level Data Link Control) asynchronous balanced mode, in which a station can start a transmission without receiving permission from a control station.

Link Access Procedure for Modems

Abbreviated LAPM. The data-link protocol used by V.32 error-correcting modems.

When two LAPM modems connect, they transmit data in frames using bit-oriented synchronous techniques, even though the attached computer communicates with the modem as a standard asynchronous device.

See also Link Access Procedure.

link level

Part of the CCITT's X.25 standard that defines the link protocol. LAP (Link Access Procedure) and LAP-B (Link Access Procedure-Balanced) are the link access protocols recommended by CCITT.

See also Consultative Committee for International Telephony and Telegraphy.

link rot

A slang expression used to describe an out-of-date URL on a Web page. Link rot occurs when the page indicated by the link is moved or erased.

See also link; Uniform Resource Locator.

link-state routing algorithm

A routing algorithm in which each router broadcasts information about the state of the links to all other nodes on the internetwork. This algorithm reduces routing loops but has greater memory requirements than the distance vector algorithm.

See also distance vector algorithm; Open Shortest Path First.

link-support layer

Abbreviated LSL. An implementation of the Open Datalink Interface (ODI) that works between the NetWare server's LAN drivers and communications protocols, such as IPX (Internet Packet eXchange) or TCP/IP, allowing network interface cards to service one or more protocol stacks. LSL is also used on workstations.

See also multiple-link interface driver; Open Data-link Interface/Network Driver Interface Specification Support.

Linux

A free, Unix-compatible, 32-bit operating system developed in 1991 by Linus Torvalds while at the University of Helsinki in Finland.

Strictly speaking, Linux is the name of the operating system kernel, the central part of the operating system that manages system services, but many people use the name to refer to the complete operating system package, including utilities, editors and compilers, games, and networking components. Many of these important elements are actually part of the Free Software Foundation's GNU Project, and others have been written and released by volunteers.

Linux is supported and distributed by companies such as Red Hat Software, Caldera Software, Workgroup Solutions, Walnut Creek Software, and S.u.S.E. of Germany.

With the increasing use of Linux in the corporate world, several major companies have announced some level of support for the operating system, including Hewlett-Packard, Silicon Graphics, Sun Microsystems, and Intel, and several major applications packages have been ported to Linux, including Oracle's Oracle8, Adaptive Server Enterprise from Sybase, and IBM's DB2.

See also Free Software Foundation; open source software.

LIP   *See* Large Internet Packet.

liquid-crystal display   Abbreviated LCD. A display technology common in portable computers that uses electric current to align crystals in a special liquid.

The rod-shaped crystals are contained between two parallel, transparent electrodes. When current is applied, the electrodes change their orientation, creating a dark area. Many LCD screens are also backlit or sidelit to increase visibility and reduce eyestrain.

LISTSERV   A mailing list product available from L-Soft International, Inc. LISTSERV runs on Unix, Microsoft Windows, and several other operating systems.

See also listserver; mailing list.

listserver   An automatic mailing system available on the Internet.

Rather than sending e-mail on a particular topic to a long list of people, you send it to a special e-mail address, where a program automatically distributes the e-mail to all the people who subscribe to the mailing list.

Several programs have been written to automate a mailing list; the most common is called LISTSERV, but you may also encounter mailserv, majordomo, or almanac.

Mailing lists are usually devoted to a specific subject, such as training dogs or playing obscure types of bagpipes, rather than to general interest communications.

See also LISTSERV; mailing list; newsgroup; Usenet.

little endian   A computer architecture in which the least significant byte has the lowest address and so is stored little end first.

Many processors, including those from Intel, the PDP-11, and the VAX family of computers, are all little endian. The term comes from Swift's *Gulliver's Travels*, in which wars were fought over whether boiled eggs should be opened at the big end or the little end.

See also big endian; holy wars.

liveware   A slang term for the people who use computers, as distinct from hardware, firmware, or software.

LLC   *See* logical link control.

loadable module   In Novell NetWare, a program that can be loaded and unloaded from the server or workstation while the operating system is running.

Two common types of loadable modules are NetWare Loadable Modules (NLMs), which are run on the server, and Virtual Loadable Modules (VLMs), which run on a workstation.

See also NetWare Loadable Module; Virtual Loadable Module.

load average   One measure of how much work the CPU is doing; defined as the average number of jobs in the run queue plus the number of jobs that are blocked

L

while waiting for a disk access. This measurement is usually taken at 1-, 5-, and 15-minute intervals during a 24-hour period to give useful information.

See also uptime.

load balancing   A technique that distributes network traffic along parallel paths to make the most efficient use of the available bandwidth while also providing redundancy. Load balancing will automatically move a user's job from a heavily loaded network resource to a less-loaded resource.

See also clustering.

load sharing   The ability of two or more remote bridges to share their load in a parallel configuration. If a bridge fails, traffic is routed to the next parallel bridge.

local-area network   Abbreviated LAN. A group of computers and associated peripheral devices connected by a communications channel, capable of sharing files and other resources among several users.

See also file server; metropolitan-area network; peer-to-peer network; wide-area network; zero-slot LAN.

local bus   A PC bus specification that allows peripheral devices to exchange data at a rate faster than the 8MBps allowed by the ISA (Industry Standard Architecture) definition and the 32MBps allowed by the EISA (Extended Industry Standard Architecture) definition.

Local bus capability must be built into the system's motherboard right from the start; it is not possible to convert an ISA-, EISA-,

or MCA (Microchannel Architecture)-based computer into a local-bus system.

local disk   In networking, a disk drive on your workstation or PC, rather than a drive available to you over the network.

See also network drive.

local drive   *See* local disk.

Local Exchange Carrier   Abbreviated LEC. A term coined from the Telecommunications Act of 1996 to describe the local telephone company that provides local transmission and switching services.

See also Competitive Local Exchange Carrier; Incumbent Local Exchange Carrier.

local group   In Microsoft Windows NT Server, a group granted rights and permissions to only the resources on the servers of its own domain.

See also global group.

local loop   That part of a communications circuit that connects subscriber equipment to equipment in a local telephone exchange. This link is often the most expensive and least efficient connection in the telephone company's system and is often a barrier to high-speed services.

See also last mile.

local printer   In networking, a printer attached to a workstation or a PC, rather than to the file server or a print server.

Local Procedure Call   Abbreviated LPC. An interprocess communications method used in multitasking operating systems that allows tasks running concurrently to talk to each other. LPCs allow tasks to share memory space, synchronize tasks, and pass messages to one another.

See also interprocess communication; pipe; Remote Procedure Call; socket.

local security authority   In Microsoft Windows NT, a security subsystem that manages the security policy on the local computer and provides user authentication services to other operating system components that need access to that information.

LocalTalk   The shielded twisted-pair (STP) wiring and connectors available from Apple for connecting Macintosh computers using the built-in AppleTalk network hardware.

See also AppleTalk.

local user profile   A user profile that is specific to the computer upon which it was created; a local user profile does not follow the user if he or she logs on to a different computer.

See also mandatory user profile; roaming user profile.

locational organization   A way of organizing the Novell Directory Services (NDS) Directory tree that divides it into Organizational Units for each geographical location in a company.

See also Organizational Unit.

locked file   A file that you can open and read, but not write to, delete, move, rename, or change in any way.

logical drive   The internal division of a large hard disk into smaller units. One single physical drive may be organized into several logical drives for convenience, with each one appearing to the user as a separate drive.

logical link control   Abbreviated LLC. The upper component of the data-link layer that provides data repackaging functions for operations between different network types.

The media access control is the lower component that gives access to the transmission medium itself.

See also data-link layer; media access control.

logical unit   Abbreviated LU. A suite of protocols developed by IBM to control communications in an SNA (Systems Network Architecture) network, as follows:

- LU type 0   Uses SNA transmission control and flow-control layers.

- LU type 1, LU type 2, and LU type 3 Control host sessions for IBM 3270 terminals and printers.

- LU type 4   Supports peer-to-peer and host-to-device communications between peripheral nodes.

- LU type 6.1   Supports a communications session for IBM databases and transaction management systems.

- LU type 6.2   The peer-to-peer protocol of Advanced Program-to-Program Communications. It also features comprehensive end-to-end error processing and a generalized application program interface (API).

L

• **LU type 7** Data Stream terminals used on AS/400 systems.

See also Advanced Program-to-Program Communications; physical unit.

logical unit number Abbreviated LUN. The logical address of a Small Computer System Interface (SCSI) device when several devices are attached to a single SCSI device ID. The LUN is usually set to zero unless the SCSI adapter supports multiple LUNs on a single SCSI device ID.

See also Small Computer System Interface.

logic bomb A sabotage attack on a system timed to go off at some time in the future; essentially a Trojan Horse with a fuse.

A logic bomb goes off at a certain time or when triggered by a certain event and then performs some operation. It might release a virus, delete files, or send comments to a terminal. An unhappy programmer may plant a logic bomb on a system and time it to go off long after she has left the company so as to avoid suspicion.

See also boot sector virus; file-infecting virus; macro virus; multipart virus; polymorphic virus; stealth virus; Trojan Horse; vaccine.

log in *See* log on.

LOGIN directory In Novell NetWare, the SYS:LOGIN directory, created during the network installation, that contains the LOGIN and NLIST utilities used to support users who are not yet authenticated.

login script A small file or macro that executes the same set of instructions every time a user logs on to a computer system or network. Sometimes called a logon script.

Login scripts can map drives, display messages, set environment variables, and run programs and are critical for proper configuration of each user's network environment.

A communications script may send the user-identification information to an online information service each time a subscriber dials up the service.

See also script.

log off To terminate a session and sign off a computer system by sending an ending message. Also known as logoff and log out.

The computer may respond with its own message, indicating the resources consumed during the session or the period between log on and log off. Logging off is not the same as shutting down or turning off the computer.

See also log on.

log on To establish a connection to a computer system or online information service; also known as logon and log in. Many systems require the entry of an identification number or a password before the system can be accessed.

See also log off; password protection.

logon script *See* login script.

log out *See* log off.

long filename Any filename longer than the eight-character plus three-character filename extension allowed by MS-DOS.

In many of today's operating systems, including Unix, Microsoft Windows, and the Macintosh, filenames can be more than 200 characters and can include upper- and lowercase letters and spaces.

long-haul modem   A modem or other communications device that can transmit information over long distances.

See also line driver; short-haul modem.

loopback   A troubleshooting test in which a signal is transmitted from a source to a destination and then back to the source again so that the signal can be measured and evaluated or so that the data contained in the signal can be examined for accuracy and completeness.

lossless compression   Any data-compression method that compresses a file by rearranging or recoding the data that it contains in a more compact fashion.

With lossless compression, no original data is lost when the file is decompressed. Lossless compression methods are used on program files and on images such as medical X rays, when data loss cannot be tolerated, and can typically reduce a file to 40 percent of its original size.

Many lossless compression programs use a method known as the Lempel-Ziv-Welch (LZW) algorithm, which searches a file for redundant strings of data and converts them to smaller tokens. When the compressed file is decompressed, this process is reversed.

See also Lempel-Ziv-Welch; lossy compression.

lossy compression   Any data-compression method that compresses a file by discarding any data that the compression mechanism decides is not needed.

Original data is lost when the file is decompressed. Lossy compression methods may be used for shrinking audio or image files when absolute accuracy is not required and the loss of data will not be noticed; however, this technique is unsuitable for more critical applications in which data loss cannot be tolerated, such as with medical images or program files. Lossy compression can typically reduce a file to as little as 5 percent of its original size.

See also Joint Photographic Experts Group; lossless compression; Moving Pictures Experts Group.

Lotus cc:Mail   An e-mail and messaging package originally developed by Lotus Development Corporation and now supported by IBM.

cc:Mail works with MS-DOS, Macintosh, Microsoft Windows, Unix, and OS/2 networks and includes built-in discussion groups and connections to the Internet.

Lotus Domino   A server technology from Lotus Development Corporation that turns the popular Lotus Notes groupware product into an Internet application server.

With Lotus Domino, users can access the Notes environment, including dynamic data and applications on Notes servers, and use a Web browser. Application developers can use the Notes environment to develop Web-based applications.

See also Lotus Notes.

L

Lotus Notes   A popular groupware product originally developed by Lotus Development Corporation and now supported by IBM.

Lotus Notes is the defining force behind the entire groupware market and is the target toward which all other developers aim. Notes includes a flexible database that can contain a variety of data types with none of the restrictions that normally apply, such as fixed field lengths. A Notes field can contain text, scanned images, OLE embedded objects, and even hypertext links to other Notes documents.

This database is closely linked with an e-mail system that allows users to forward any document in any Notes database to any other Notes database; a user can send e-mail to the database, and an application can even send e-mail to an individual user. Notes can also maintain multiple copies of the database, perhaps on the LAN or on remote workstations, and can synchronize these copies using background dial-up modem connections, IPX/SPX, or TCP/IP.

Notes is supported by a large number of networks, including AppleTalk, Banyan VINES, IBM APPC, Novell NetWare, TCP/IP, and X.25.

See also Lotus Domino; workflow software.

Lotus SmartSuite   A popular software suite originally developed by Lotus Development Corporation and now supported by IBM.

SmartSuite consists of the 1-2-3 spreadsheet, WordPro word processor (previously known as Ami Pro), Approach database, Freelance Graphics, and the Organizer personal information manager.

SmartSuite is also available in a version called NotesSuite, which is integrated with Lotus Notes for groupware applications.

low-end   Describes any inexpensive product, from the bottom of a company's product list, that includes a reduced set of capabilities.

See also high-end.

low-level language   A hardware-specific programming language close to machine language. All assembly languages are considered low-level languages.

See also high-level language.

LPC   *See* Local Procedure Call.

LPT ports   In MS-DOS, the device name used to denote a parallel communications port, often used with a printer.

LSL   *See* link-support layer.

LU6.2   *See* logical unit.

LU   *See* logical unit.

Lucent Technologies, Inc.   A major manufacturer of networking switches and routing products, spun off from AT&T in 1996.

Lucent Technologies provides products for the wired, wireless, and voice/data/video markets, as well as voice and fax messaging systems, Gigabit Ethernet, and Asynchronous Transfer Mode (ATM) products. In 1999, Lucent bought Ascend Communications, Inc.

For more information on Lucent Technologies Inc, see www.lucent.com

LUN   *See* logical unit number.

lurking   The practice of reading an Internet mailing list or Usenet newsgroup without posting anything yourself. In the online world, lurking is not considered particularly antisocial; in fact, it is a good idea to lurk for a while when you first subscribe so that you can get a feel for the tone of the discussions in the group and come up to speed on recent history.

LZW   *See* Lempel-Ziv-Welch.

L

M

M *See* mega-.

m *See* milli-.

MAC *See* media access control.

Mac *See* Macintosh.

MacBinary In the Macintosh, a file transfer protocol that ensures a proper transfer of Macintosh files and related data over a modem, including the file itself, the file's resource fork, data fork, and Finder information block.

Most Macintosh communications programs support sending and receiving files in MacBinary, but the protocol is not often supported in other environments.

Mach An operating system created from scratch at Carnegie-Mellon University, designed to support advanced features such as multiprocessing and multitasking.

Mach has its roots in the Unix world and was originally based on BSD 4.4; however, its most notable feature is that it employs a relatively small microkernel rather than a conventional monolithic kernel.

The microkernel is designed to manage only the most fundamental operations, including interrupts, task scheduling, messaging, and virtual memory; other modules can be added as necessary for file management, network support, and other tasks.

See also microkernel.

machine code *See* machine language.

machine collating sequence The sequence in which the computer orders characters. Because most systems use ASCII, except the large IBM systems that use EBCEDIC, the machine collating sequence is usually based on the ordering of characters in the ASCII character set; see Appendix C for details.

See also American Standard Code for Information Interchange; Extended Binary Coded Decimal Interchange Code.

machine language The native binary language used internally by the computer; also known as machine code.

Machine language is difficult for humans to read and understand. Programmers create applications using high-level languages, which are translated into a form that the computer can understand by an assembler, a compiler, or an interpreter. Whichever method is used, the result is machine language.

See also assembly language; compiler; interpreter; microcode.

Macintosh Abbreviated Mac. A range of personal computers first introduced in 1984 by Apple Computer, Inc., featuring a popular and easy-to-use graphical user interface. The computer was based on the Motorola 68000 series of microprocessors and used a proprietary operating system to simulate the user's desktop on the screen.

The original Mac was a portable, self-contained unit with a small monochrome screen, 128KB of memory, two serial ports, extended sound capabilities, and a single 400KB, 3.5-inch floppy disk. The computer was an instant success, and users quickly began to demand more power and additional features.

Apple released many new models over the years, expanding the range to include Macs based on the 68020, 68030, and 68040 processors and adding color, more memory, a built-in SCSI interface, built-in networking, a 32-bit bus, and larger and faster hard disks.

Introduced in 1991, the PowerBook series of notebook computers offered both power and convenience in a very small package, posing a real challenge to the MS-DOS–based laptops.

During the 1990s, the Mac lost overall market share, but remained popular in the desktop-publishing, music, and graphics-related fields.

The iMac, introduced in 1998, was an instant success with its sleek new shape and bold color schemes; the one criticism was that it lacked a floppy disk drive.

Macintosh client Any Macintosh computer attached to a network. A Macintosh client can store and retrieve information from a NetWare server running NetWare for Macintosh modules and can run executable Macintosh network files.

Macintosh File System Abbreviated MFS. In the Macintosh, an older system that stored files in a flat structure rather than the hierarchical system used in more recent versions. All current Macintosh models can read disks created using MFS.

See also Hierarchical File System.

MacOS The operating system that runs on Macintosh computers. MacOS contains the famous Mac graphical user interface, it is multithreaded to allow execution of multiple concurrent tasks, and it includes Internet access in the form of TCP/IP and a Web browser.

MacOS 8.5 requires a PowerPC processor and so will not run on Macs based on earlier Motorola 680x0 processors; you will also need 16MB of physical RAM and virtual memory set to at least 24MB.

macro A stored group of keystrokes or instructions that can automate a complex or repetitive sequence of application commands.

Many of the major spreadsheet, word-processing, and database programs let users create and edit macros to speed up operations. Some macros can incorporate control structures, such as DO/WHILE loops and IF/THEN branching statements.

See also login script; script.

macro virus An executable program that attaches itself to a document created in Microsoft Word or Excel. When you open the document and execute the macro, the virus runs and does whatever damage it was programmed to do.

See also boot sector virus; file-infecting virus; multipart virus; polymorphic virus; stealth virus; vaccine; virus.

M

magic A substance that is sprinkled or a phrase that is chanted by a guru to make something work.

A magic character is one with special, often hard to understand capabilities, used at every opportunity by gurus wanting to demonstrate their powers.

A magic number is one that represents a particular condition, but whose value is unusual, given the conditions, and which would certainly never be guessed by anyone who is not a guru.

See also guru.

Magneto-optical storage Abbreviated MO. A high-capacity network storage device capable of storing 5.2GB on a 5.25-inch removable cartridge.

The data on the cartridge is highly stable, and so MO storage is suitable for use as backup and archival storage. MO offers access speeds of 35ms, compared with CD-RW and DVD-R, which offer speeds of between 100 and 200ms.

See also CD ReWritable; digital video disc-recordable.

mail In the networking world, e-mail, rather than the postal service.

See also electronic mail.

mail-aware application Any application with the ability to send and receive e-mail. Applications in the document management, groupware, and workflow categories all use e-mail to interconnect users and help with the flow of information. This integration of e-mail is made possible in part by APIs such as Microsoft's Messaging API and Novell's Message Handling Service.

Sometimes known as a message-enabled application.

See also groupware; Lotus Notes; workflow software.

mail bombing To send a huge number of long e-mail messages to the same e-mail address, effectively bringing the e-mail server to a halt. A variation on the denial of service attack, but one that can be aimed at a specific person.

This kind of attack is relatively easy to carry out and does not require actual access to the server. A malicious person can easily write a program to send a huge e-mail message to the same address a few hundred thousand times, overwhelming the server and annoying the recipient.

See also denial of service attack.

mailbox In e-mail systems, an area of hard-disk space used to store e-mail messages until users can access them. An on-screen or audio message often tells users that they have mail.

MAIL directory In Novell NetWare, a default directory created during installation for the use of e-mail applications.

mail-enabled application Any application that includes an e-mail function but that also provides additional services, such as contact-management software, intelligent mail handling, and workflow automation. Also known as message-enabled application.

See also groupware; Lotus Notes; mail-aware application; workflow software.

mailer A program used for sending and receiving e-mail.

mailing list On the Internet, a group of people who share a common interest and who automatically receive all the e-mail posted to the listserver or mailing-list manager program.

Contributions are sent as e-mail to the listserver and then distributed to all subscribers. Mailing lists are private or by invitation only; Usenet newsgroups, by contrast, are open to everyone.

See also LISTSERV; listserver; newsgroup; Usenet.

mail reflector On the Internet, a program that manages a mailing list.

See also LISTSERV; listserver; newsgroup; Usenet.

mailslots In Microsoft Windows NT, a connectionless interprocess communications mechanism that provides one-to-many and many-to-one communications, suitable for broadcasting a message to multiple processes.

In Windows NT, mailslots are implemented via the Mailslot File System, which manages all mailslot access and connections. Mailslots are used for browse requests and logon authentication.

See also named pipe; pipe; semaphore; shared memory; socket.

mailto An HTML attribute that creates a link to an e-mail address. If a user clicks on the mailto link, the browser opens a window for composing an e-mail message to this address.

See also HyperText Markup Language.

mail transport agent A program that manages the transportation and delivery of e-mail. The mail transport agent accepts the message from a mail user agent or client, performs any translations required, and then routes the message.

See also mail user agent; Simple Mail Transfer Protocol.

mail user agent A client program that provides a user interface for sending and receiving e-mail, as well as all the other features required by any e-mail application, including creating, reading, forwarding, and deleting messages.

mainframe computer A large, fast, multiuser computer system, often utilizing multiple processors, designed to manage huge amounts of data and complex computing tasks.

Mainframes are normally found in large corporations, universities, or military installations and can support thousands of users.

M

The feature that distinguishes mainframe computers from other types is that they perform all processing at one central location; the terminals accessed by users have no local computing power of their own.

See also dumb terminal; minicomputer; network computer; thin client.

maintenance release   A software upgrade that corrects minor bugs or adds a few small features. This type of release is usually distinguished from a major release by an increase in only the decimal portion of the version number; for example, from 3.1 to 3.11 rather than from 3.1 to 4.0.

See also service pack.

male connector   Any cable connector with pins designed to engage the sockets on the female connector.

See also female connector.

MAN   *See* metropolitan-area network.

Management Information Base   Abbreviated MIB. A database of network configuration information used by Simple Network Management Protocol (SNMP) and Common Management Information Protocol (CMIP) to monitor or change network settings. MIB provides a logical naming of all resources on the network related to the network's management.

See also Common Management Information Protocol; MIB variables; Simple Network Management Protocol.

Management Information System   Abbreviated MIS. A computer-based information system that integrates data from all the departments that it serves, to provide company management with the information it needs to make timely decisions, track progress, and solve problems.

Manchester encoding   In communications, a method used to encode data and timing signals in the same transmitted data stream. The signal state during the first half of the bit period indicates its data value (1 is high; 0 is low). A transition to the opposite state in the middle of the bit period acts as the timing signal.

See also 4B/5B encoding.

mandatory user profile   In Microsoft Windows NT, a user profile created and managed by the Administrator and stored on the server and downloaded to the workstation when the user attempts to log on to the network.

The profile is saved with a special extension (.man) so that the user cannot change or alter the profile in any way. Mandatory user profiles can be assigned to a single user or to a group of users.

See also local user profile; roaming user profile.

man pages   Short for manual pages. In Unix, the online documentation.

Each man page treats a single topic; some are short, and others are quite long. They are all organized in a standard format using these headings: Name, Synopsis, Description, Files, See Also, Diagnostics, and Bugs.

See also permuted index.

MALE CONNECTOR

Manufacturing Automation Protocol
Abbreviated MAP. A protocol that was originally developed by General Motors and was designed for use in a manufacturing environment.

See also Technical and Office Protocol.

map **1.** To direct a request for a file or a service to an alternative resource. For example, in a virtual memory system, an operating system can translate or map a virtual memory address into a physical address; in a network, drive letters are assigned to specific volumes and directories.

2. An expression of the structure of an object. For example, a memory map describes the use and layout of physical memory.

MAP *See* Manufacturing Automation Protocol.

MAPI *See* Messaging API.

Marimba, Inc. A company founded by four of the original Sun Microsystems Java team to develop products for the creation and deployment of network-managed applications across the Internet and across corporate intranets.

For more information on Marimba, Inc, see `www.marimba.com`.

See also Castanet.

mark parity *See* parity.

marquee A scrolling banner on a Web page, usually containing advertising material.

mask A binary number that is used to remove bits from another binary number by use of one of the logical operators (AND, OR, NOT, XOR) to combine the binary number and the mask. Masks are used in IP addresses and file permissions.

See also IP address; subnet mask.

Master Business Continuity Professional Abbreviated MBCP. A certification from Disaster Recovery Institute International (DRII) that covers advanced information on business continuity planning, disaster recovery, and associated work experience and board certification.

See also Associate Business Continuity Professional; Certified Business Continuity Professional.

M

223

Master Certified Novell Engineer Abbreviated Master CNE. A Novell certification program for CNEs who want to focus on the support of enterprise-wide networks. Previously known as Enterprise CNE.

Many consider the Master CNE program the advanced degree of NetWare certification, because candidates must demonstrate proficiency in specialized networking technologies, as well as an in-depth knowledge of the NetWare operating system.

Specializations are available in the general categories of Management, Connectivity, Messaging, and Internet/Intranet Solutions and in the client categories of AS/400 Integration, Unix Integration, and Windows NT Integration.

See also Certified Novell Engineer.

Master Certified Novell Instructor
Abbreviated MCNI. An advanced Novell certification program for trainers who want to teach Novell courses. An MCNI must have at least two years of teaching experience and be certified as a Master CNE; in addition, an MCNI must also complete an Annual Update Requirement to keep their skills up-to-date.

See also Certified Novell Instructor.

Master CNE *See* Master Certified Novell Engineer.

master replica In Novell NetWare, the main replica for a partition. The master replica must be available during major changes such as partition splitting or merging. Another replica can be assigned as the master replica if the original is lost or damaged.

MAU *See* medium attachment unit; Multi-station Access Unit.

MB *See* megabyte.

Mb *See* megabit.

MBCP *See* Master Business Continuity Professional.

Mbone *See* multicast backbone.

MBps *See* megabytes per second.

Mbps *See* megabits per second.

MCA *See* Microchannel Architecture.

McAfee Associates, Inc. A major provider of antivirus, help desk, security, and encryption software. Merged with Network General Corporation to form Network Associates in 1997.

See also Network Associates, Inc.

MCI *See* Media Control Interface.

MCNE *See* Master Certified Novell Engineer.

MCNI *See* Master Certified Novell Instructor.

MCP *See* Microsoft Certified Professional.

MCSD *See* Microsoft Certified Solutions Developer.

MCSE *See* Microsoft Certified Systems Engineer.

MCT *See* Microsoft Certified Trainer.

mean time between failures Abbreviated MTBF. The statistically derived average length of time for which a system component operates before failing. MTBF is expressed in thousands or tens of thousands of hours, also called power-on hours, or POH.

See also mean time to repair.

mean time to repair Abbreviated MTTR. The statistically derived average length of time, expressed in hours, that it takes to make a system-level repair.

See also mean time between failures.

media access control Abbreviated MAC. The lower component of the data-link layer that governs access to the transmission medium. The logical link control layer is the upper component of the data-link layer. MAC is used in CSMA/CD and token-ring LANs as well as in other types of networks.

media access control protocol *See* access control list.

Media Control Interface Abbreviated MCI. A standard interface used for controlling multimedia files and devices. Each device has its own device driver that implements a standard set of MCI functions, such as stop, play, and record.

media filter A device used to convert the output signal from a token-ring adapter board to work with a specific type of wiring. For example, a media filter can link 16Mbps token-ring network interface cards with unshielded twisted-pair (UTP) wiring, thus saving the expense of additional cable runs.

THE MAC SUBLAYER

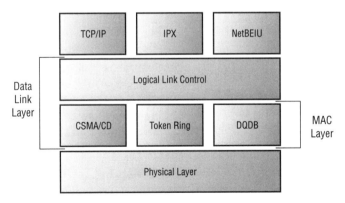

medium attachment unit Abbreviated MAU. A transceiver that attaches to the AUI (Attachment Unit Interface) port on an Ethernet adapter and provides electrical and mechanical attachments to fiber-optic cable, twisted-pair cable (TP), or other media types.

meg A common abbreviation for megabyte.

mega- Abbreviated M. A prefix meaning one million in the metric system. Because computing is based on powers of 2, mega usually means 2^{20}, or 1,048,576; the power of 2 closest to one million.

megabit Abbreviated Mbit. Usually 1,048,576 binary digits or bits of data. Often used as equivalent to 1 million bits.

See also bit; megabits per second.

megabits per second Abbreviated Mbps. A measurement of the amount of information moving across a network or communications link in one second, measured in multiples of 1,048,576 bits.

megabyte Abbreviated MB. Usually 1,048,576 bytes. Megabytes are a common unit of measurement for computer memory or hard-disk capacity.

megabytes per second Abbreviated MBps. A measurement of the amount of information moving across a network or communications link in one second, measured in multiples of 1,048,576 bytes.

megahertz Abbreviated MHz. One million cycles per second. A processor's clock speed is often expressed in megahertz.

The original IBM PC operated an Intel 8088 processor running at 4.77 MHz; today's Pentium processor runs at 450 MHz; and IBM has announced an experimental processor capable of speeds of 1000 MHz.

member server In Microsoft Windows NT, a server that participates in a security domain, but that does not act as a domain controller and does not store domain user accounts.

A member server can be used to store shared data, but a user must be authenticated by a primary or a backup domain controller before gaining access to the member server.

memory The primary physical RAM installed in the computer. The operating system copies applications from disk into memory, where all program execution and data processing take place, and then writes the results back to disk. The amount of memory installed in the computer can determine the size and number of programs that it can run, as well as the size of the largest data file.

See also dynamic RAM; static RAM; swapping; virtual memory.

memory address The exact location in memory that stores a particular data item or program instruction.

memory board A printed circuit board containing memory chips. When all the sockets on a memory board are filled and the board contains the maximum amount of memory that it can manage, it is said to be "fully populated."

memory cache   An area of high-speed memory on the processor that stores commonly used code or data obtained from slower memory, eliminating the need to access the system's main memory to fetch instructions.

The Intel 82385 cache controller chip was used with fast static RAM on some systems to increase performance, but more up-to-date processors include cache-management functions on the main processor.

The Intel Pentium contains two separate 512KB caches, one each for data and instructions.

See also cache; level 2 cache.

memory chip   A chip that holds data or program instructions. A memory chip may hold its contents temporarily, as in the case of RAM, or permanently, as in the case of ROM.

memory leak   A programming error that causes a program to request new areas of computer memory rather than reusing the memory already assigned to it. This causes the amount of memory in use by the program to increase as time goes on. In a worst case, the application may consume all available memory and stop the computer.

memory management   The way in which the operating system handles the use of memory, usually as a combination of physical memory and virtual memory.

When applications are loaded, they are assigned space in which to run and store data.

As they are removed, the memory space they occupied is released for use by the next program to run.

See also memory leak.

memory management unit   Abbreviated MMU. The part of the processor that manages the mapping of virtual memory addresses to actual physical addresses.

In some systems, such as those based on early Intel or Motorola processors, the MMU was a separate chip; however, in most of today's systems, the MMU is integrated into the processor itself.

memory map   The organization and allocation of memory in a computer. A memory map indicates the amount of memory used by the operating system, as well as the amount remaining for use by applications.

memory-resident   Always located in the computer's memory and available for use; not swapped out.

Merge   An MS-DOS emulator from Locus Computing that runs MS-DOS and Windows applications under Unix.

Merge provides a complete MS-DOS environment and acts as though your system is running only MS-DOS. Merge is available for UnixWare, SCO, and other systems.

mesh network   A network topology in which every device is connected by a cable to every other device on the network. Multiple links to each device are used to provide network link redundancy.

M

227

MESH NETWORK

message channel   A form of interprocess communication found in multitasking operating systems. Interprocess communications allow two programs running in the same computer to share information.

See also pipe; queue; semaphore.

message-enabled application   *See* mail-aware application.

Message Handling Service   Abbreviated MHS. A protocol for e-mail storage, management, and exchange, originally created by Action Technologies and then licensed by Novell. MHS can collect, route, and deliver e-mail and other files by using store-and-forward technology.

Message Handling System   The CCITT X.400 standard protocol for global store-and-forward messaging. The X.400 standard specifies everything from the type of data that a message can contain to rules for converting between different message types, such as from fax to text or vice versa.

See also Consultative Committee for International Telephony and Telegraphy; X.500.

message switching   A routing method that uses store-and-forward techniques. Each message contains a destination address and is passed from source to destination through a series of intermediate nodes.

At each intermediate node, the message is stored briefly, reviewed, and then forwarded to the next node. Message switching allows a network operating system to regulate traffic and to use the available communications links effectively.

Messaging API Abbreviated MAPI. An interface used to add messaging capabilities to any Microsoft Windows application. MAPI handles the details of message storage and forwarding and directory services.

Originally developed by Microsoft, MAPI has become a widely supported industry standard.

MAPI Version 3.2 provides for cross-platform messaging independent from the operating system.

See also mail-aware application; Vendor Independent Messaging.

Messenger service In Microsoft Windows NT, a service that sends and receives messages sent by the system administrator or by the Alerter service.

See also Alerter service; service.

metafile A file that contains both data and output control information. For example, a graphics metafile contains not only a graphical image of some kind, but also information on how the image is to be displayed. Use of a metafile allows one single version of the image to be output to a variety of display devices.

metering The process of tracking application software use and availability across a network to ensure that the terms of the license are being met. Metering can also be used to predict when a license will expire and require renewal.

metropolitan-area network Abbreviated MAN. A public, high-speed network, capable of voice and data transmission over a distance of up to 80 kilometers (50 miles). A MAN is smaller than a wide-area network (WAN) but larger than a local-area network (LAN).

MFS *See* Macintosh File System.

MHS *See* Message Handling Service.

MHz *See* megahertz.

MIB *See* Management Information Base.

MIB variables The information stored in a Management Information Base (MIB) database, which can be accessed and managed by network management protocols such as Simple Network Management Protocol (SNMP).

See also Management Information Base; Simple Network Management Protocol.

Microchannel Architecture Abbreviated MCA. A 32-bit, proprietary expansion bus, first introduced by IBM in 1987 for the IBM PS/2 range of computers and also used in the IBM RS/6000 series.

MCA was designed for multiprocessing. It allows expansion boards to identify themselves, thus eliminating many of the conflicts that arose through the use of manual settings in the original bus. The MCA bus can also be driven independently by multiple bus master processors.

M

229

MCA is physically and electronically incompatible with expansion boards that follow the earlier 16-bit AT bus standard; the boards are about 50 percent smaller, and the bus depends on proprietary integrated circuits.

See also Extended Industry Standard Architecture; Industry Standard Architecture; local bus; Peripheral Component Interconnect local bus.

microcode   Low-level instructions that define how a particular microprocessor works by specifying what the processor does when it executes a machine-language instruction.

See also machine language.

Microcom Networking Protocol   Abbreviated MNP. A set of communications protocols from Microcom, Inc., that has become the standard for data compression and error detection and correction, as follows:

- MNP 1 to 4 define hardware error control.

- MNP 5 describes a method of data compression that achieves a 2-to-1 compression ratio.

- MNP 6 describes a communication protocol that begins with V.22 bis modulation and then switches to V.29 when possible.

- MNP 7 describes a method of data compression that achieves a 3-to-1 compression ratio.

- MNP 8 is based on MNP 7 and adds a V.29 technique that lets half-duplex devices operate as full-duplex.

- MNP 9 contains a proprietary technique that provides good performance over a wide variety of link types.

- MNP 10 describes an extremely rigorous error control protocol that is well suited for use on extremely noisy links. MNP 10 has been adopted for use in cellular modems.

These days the CCITT V standards are implemented in modems due to their worldwide acceptance; however, some modem manufacturers offer both.

For more information on Microcom, Inc., see www.microcom.com

See also Consultative Committee for International Telephony and Telegraphy.

microcomputer   Any computer based on a single-chip processor. Many of today's microcomputers are as powerful as mainframe models designed just a few years ago; they are also smaller and cheaper.

See also workstation.

microkernel   An alternative operating-system kernel design developed by researchers at Carnegie-Mellon University and implemented in the Mach operating system.

Traditionally, the kernel has been a monolithic piece of the operating system, resident in memory at all times. It takes care of operations as varied as virtual memory management, network support, file input/output, and task scheduling.

The microkernel is a stripped-down kernel that is only concerned with loading, running, and scheduling tasks. All other operating system functions (virtual memory management, disk input/output, and so on) are implemented and managed as tasks running on top of the microkernel.

micron   A unit of measurement. One millionth of a meter, corresponding to approximately 1/25,000 of an inch. The core diameter of fiber-optic cable for networks is often specified in terms of microns; 62.5 microns is a common size.

Micron Technology, Inc.   A major manufacturer of DRAM (dynamic RAM) components, flash memory, synchronous SRAM (static RAM), and graphics DRAM. Micron Technology also owns a majority interest in Micron Electronics, a manufacturer of direct-sales PCs and servers for the consumer, government, business, and education markets.

For more information on Micron Technology, see `www.micronpc.com`.

microprocessor   A central processor unit on a single chip, often referred to as the processor.

The first microprocessor was developed by Intel in 1969. The microprocessors most often used in Apple Macintosh computers are manufactured by Motorola, and Intel microprocessors are commonly used in the PC.

microsegmentation   The division of a network into smaller segments, usually with the aim of increasing bandwidth.

Microsoft Access   A popular relational database program from Microsoft.

Microsoft BackOffice   A network software suite from Microsoft that runs on Windows NT Server and consists of Microsoft Exchange Server, Microsoft SQL Server, Microsoft Site Server, Microsoft SNA Server, Microsoft Proxy Server, and Microsoft System Management Server.

See also Microsoft Office.

Microsoft Certified Product Specialist   *See* Microsoft Certified Professional.

Microsoft Certified Professional   Abbreviated MCP. A basic certification from Microsoft designed to establish expertise with at least one Microsoft operating system. Previously known as the Microsoft Certified Product Specialist.

An MCP+Internet certification is also available and covers the use of Internet Explorer, designing and building a Web site, and configuring and troubleshooting Microsoft's implementation of TCP/IP.

Microsoft Certified Solutions Developer   Abbreviated MCSD. An advanced certification from Microsoft for computer professionals who develop custom applications using Microsoft products and computer programming language packages. Three core exams focus on operating system architecture, and two elective exams concentrate on programming and database concepts and skills.

Microsoft Certified Systems Engineer   Abbreviated MCSE. An advanced certification from Microsoft that requires passing four core and two elective exams. The core exams cover the basic

M

concepts and skills involved in installing, using, maintaining, and troubleshooting a Windows NT Server network, and the elective exams cover other server topics and advanced networking concepts.

An MCSE+Internet certification is also available and covers the use of Internet Explorer, designing and building a Web site using Internet Information Server, and configuring and troubleshooting Microsoft's implementation of TCP/IP.

Microsoft Certified Trainer   Abbreviated MCT. A certification from Microsoft for technical trainers. An MCT certification is required before you can teach Microsoft Official Curriculum courses at Microsoft Authorized Technical Education Centers.

Microsoft Corporation   The world's largest and most successful software company, founded in 1975 by Bill Gates and Paul Allen.

Microsoft's great initial success was in supplying IBM with the PC-DOS operating system for the IBM PC and then providing versions of MS-DOS to the clone manufacturers. Microsoft released Windows 3 in May 1990 and continued to upgrade Windows regularly. The release of Windows NT during 1993 consolidated Microsoft's position as a leading developer of operating systems, and Windows 2000 will continue this trend.

In addition to operating systems and its extensive computer language products, Microsoft markets a wide range of applications, including Microsoft Word, a word processor; Microsoft Excel, a spreadsheet; Microsoft Access, a database program;

Microsoft Publisher, a desktop publishing program; and Microsoft Office, an integrated software suite. Microsoft also provides an extensive set of Internet-related products, including Internet Explorer, FrontPage, and Internet Information Server.

The Microsoft consumer division now has more than 50 products, including popular multimedia titles such as Encarta and Cinemania, an interactive movie guide. Microsoft Press publishes and distributes computer-related books and CD-ROM products to bookstores.

For more information on Microsoft, see `www.microsoft.com`.

Microsoft Disk Operating System
Abbreviated MS-DOS. A single-user, single-tasking operating system, with either a command-line or shell interface, for use on Intel processors, first introduced in 1981.

Microsoft Excel   A popular spreadsheet program from Microsoft.

Microsoft Exchange Server   A client/server message-management system from Microsoft. Exchange Server provides enterprise-wide message exchange by integrating e-mail, scheduling, document sharing, and electronic forms and also connects to the Internet and other networks outside the enterprise allowing global messaging. Exchange uses Microsoft Outlook as the client. Exchange Server is a component of Microsoft BackOffice.

Microsoft FrontPage   An HTML editor from Microsoft that combines Web-page creation with graphical Web site publication and management.

Microsoft Internet Explorer   A popular Web browser from Microsoft, which is also integrated into Windows 98.

Microsoft Internet Information Server   A powerful and capable Web server package from Microsoft that runs on Windows NT Server.
See also Microsoft Site Server.

Microsoft LAN Manager   A network operating system, developed by Microsoft and 3Com, based on a version of OS/2; client PCs can run OS/2, MS-DOS, Unix, or Macintosh. Disk mirroring, disk duplexing, and UPS (uninterruptible power supply) monitoring functions are available. The network operating system supports IPX/SPX, TCP/IP, and NetBEUI. LAN Manager interoperates with, and has largely been superseded by, Windows NT Server.

Microsoft NetMeeting   An Internet-based audio- and video-conferencing application from Microsoft.

Microsoft NetShow   A client/server streaming audio and video application from Microsoft. The NetShow server runs on Windows NT and streams audio, video, and animation to the client, a multimedia player.

Microsoft Office   A popular business software suite from Microsoft that runs on Microsoft Windows and the Macintosh and includes Microsoft Word, Microsoft Excel, Microsoft PowerPoint, Microsoft Outlook, Microsoft Access, Microsoft Publisher, Microsoft FrontPage, and Microsoft PhotoDraw.
See also Microsoft BackOffice.

Microsoft Office Expert   Abbreviated MOE. An advanced certification from Microsoft that demonstrates complete familiarity with the Microsoft Office suite of applications, both individually and as a group.

Microsoft Office Expert Specialist   Abbreviated MOES. A middle-level certification from Microsoft that demonstrates familiarity with more complex tasks in the Microsoft Office suite of applications.

Microsoft Office Proficient Specialist   Abbreviated MOPS. A basic certification from Microsoft that demonstrates familiarity with basic tasks in Microsoft Word or Microsoft Excel.

Microsoft Outlook   A popular e-mail application from Microsoft, which also includes scheduling and calendar functions, a contact-management module, and a simple project-management tool.

Microsoft Outlook Express   An easy-to-use e-mail application, distributed with Internet Explorer; both are available from Microsoft.

Microsoft Services for Macintosh   Software that allows a Macintosh client to share files on a Windows NT server.

Microsoft Services for NetWare   Software for NetWare servers that allows NetWare clients to access Windows NT services.

Microsoft Site Server   A Microsoft package of tools for creating and managing Internet or intranet Web sites.

M

Site Server includes Site Analyst, Usage Analyst, Personalization System, Commerce Server, Publishing Solution, Knowledge Management Solution, and the Analysis Solution.

See also Microsoft Internet Information Server.

Microsoft SNA Server   A server component from Microsoft that provides Windows, Macintosh, MS-DOS, and OS/2 clients with access to IBM's AS/400 and mainframe systems using System Network Architecture (SNA).

Microsoft SQL Server   A Windows NT Server–based relational database management system from Microsoft that also includes development tools, system management tools, data replication processes, and an open development environment.

Microsoft Systems Management Server   A set of network management tools from Microsoft, designed to provide a single point for managing network and client hardware and software (SMS hardware and software inventory functions track more than 200 properties for each desktop), software distribution, application metering and licensing, and troubleshooting.

Microsoft Terminal Server   A software package that provides clients with access to Windows-based applications running on the server rather than on the local system.

The server receives and processes all keystrokes and mouse clicks sent from the client and sends the output back to the appropriate client. The server manages all resources for each connected client and provides each logged-in user with his or her own environment.

Microsoft Transaction Server   Often abbreviated MTS. A package from Microsoft for developing and deploying distributed transaction-processing applications.

See also online transaction processing.

Microsoft Visual Basic   Often abbreviated VB. A version of the BASIC programming language that allows developers to create Windows applications quickly and easily.

Microsoft Windows   A general name for the family of operating systems available from Microsoft that includes Windows CE, Windows 95/98, and Windows 2000.

Microsoft Windows 2000   A family of powerful operating systems from Microsoft, based on Windows NT, including Windows 2000 Professional for workstation users, Windows 2000 Server, and Windows 2000 Advanced Server. Windows 2000 Datacenter Server is a 64-bit version capable of addressing 64GB of physical RAM and managing 16 processors.

Microsoft Windows 3.1   A 16-bit graphical operating environment that runs on top of MS-DOS on Intel-based PCs, featuring overlapping windowed areas, drop-down menus, and mouse support. The three main elements of Windows 3.1 are the File Manager (used to manage files, directories, and disks), the Program Manager (which manages applications), and the Print Manager (which coordinates printers and printing).

Microsoft Windows 95   A 32-bit, multitasking, multithreaded desktop operating system capable of running MS-DOS, Windows 3.1, and Windows 95 applications. It supports Plug and Play (on the appropriate hardware) and adds an enhanced FAT file system in the Virtual FAT, which allows filenames of up to 255 characters while also supporting the MS-DOS 8.3 filenaming conventions.

Applets include WordPad (a word processor), Paint, and WinPad (a personal information manager), as well as system tools such as Backup, ScanDisk, Disk Defragmenter, and DriveSpace. The Start button and desktop Taskbar make application management easy and straightforward.

Windows 95 supports TCP/IP, IPX/SPX, NetBEUI, NDIS, FTP, SLIP, and PPP communications and networking protocols.

See also protocol.

Microsoft Windows 98   An evolutionary upgrade to Windows 95; includes an integrated Web browser, several other Web-based tools for conferencing, e-mail, Web page creation, and Web publishing.

Windows 98 also includes a complete set of capable and easy-to-use tools for tasks such as defragmenting hard disks, compressing

files, testing disks, and monitoring the system and supports new multimedia hardware and entertainment technologies.

You can choose between the classic Windows interface familiar to Windows 95 users and the Active Desktop.

Microsoft Windows CE   A small, 32-bit operating system for hand-held portable computers and other specialized devices such as telephones, cable decoder boxes, and television sets.

Microsoft Windows NT Server   Microsoft's flagship 32-bit network operating system, which provides high levels of security, manageability, reliability, and performance. Runs on servers based on Intel, Alpha, and MIPS processors, includes preemptive multitasking and multiple threads of execution, and supports all major networking protocols.

NT Server supports fault tolerance with disk mirroring, disk duplexing, RAID (redundant array of inexpensive disks), and UPS (uninterruptible power supply) monitoring.

The user interface is similar to those available in other members of the Windows family. The latest version of NT Server includes Internet Information Server (a Web server), DNS Server, and multiprotocol router support. All popular interprocess communications protocols for distributed computing are available, including Windows Sockets and Remote Procedure Calls (RPCs).

See also Microsoft Windows 2000.

M

Microsoft Windows NT Workstation
Microsoft's high-end 32-bit operating system, which provides high levels of security, manageability, reliability, networking, and performance. Runs on workstations based on Intel, Alpha, and MIPS processors and supports preemptive multitasking and multiple threads of execution. The user interface is similar to those available in other members of the Windows family.

See also Microsoft Windows 2000.

Microsoft Word   A popular and fully featured word processor from Microsoft. Wizards help users with tasks such as mail merge and formatting, and you can customize the various toolbars and menu bars to suit your individual needs. Word also supports a powerful macro language

micro-to-mainframe   Any form of connection that attaches a PC to a mainframe-based network. Often used to describe software (called terminal-emulation software) that allows the microcomputer to access data and applications on the mainframe system.

See also terminal emulation.

microwave   A method of radio transmission that uses high-frequency waves (in the range of 1 to 30 gigahertz) for line-of-sight broadband communications. It requires a repeater station every 20 miles or so because of the curvature of the earth. Microwaves are used for satellite communications, for communications between two buildings in a metropolitan area, and across large open areas such as lakes and rivers where laying a cable may be impractical.

See also broadband network; repeater.

middleware   A category of software that shields an application from the underlying mechanics of a network so that the developers of an application do not have to know in advance which network and communications protocols will be used.

Middleware is often implemented in a client/server environment in which it allows systems to exchange information or connect, even though they use different interfaces.

midsplit   A special type of broadband cable system that divides the available frequencies into two groups: one for transmission and the other for reception.

See also broadband network.

migration   In Novell NetWare, the process of upgrading bindery and other information to a newer version of the network operating system.

See also bindery.

Migration Tool for NetWare   A Microsoft Windows NT utility loaded with the Gateway Service for NetWare that duplicates user account and group and security information from a NetWare server onto a Windows NT server, allowing a migration from NetWare to NT.

milli-   Abbreviated m. A prefix meaning one-thousandth in the metric system, often expressed as 10^{-3}.

millisecond Abbreviated ms or msec. A unit of measurement equal to one-thousandth of a second. In computing, hard disk and CD-ROM drive access times are often described in milliseconds; the higher the number, the slower the disk system.

millivolt Abbreviated mv. A unit of measurement equal to one-thousandth of a volt.

MIME *See* Multipurpose Internet Mail Extension.

MIME Content Type Information contained in a Multipurpose Internet Mail Extension (MIME) message header indicates the content type of the data contained in the next part of the message. Table M.1 lists the seven major content types as well as the subtypes. *See also* Secure MIME.

TABLE M.1 MIME CONTENT TYPES

Content Type	Subtype	Description
Text	Plain	Unformatted text.
	Rich Text	Formatted text.
Multipart	Mixed	Multiple parts of different types.
	Alternative	Multiple parts containing the same data in different formats.
	Digest	Message digest with multiple parts all in the same format.
	Parallel	Multiple parts to be viewed simultaneously, such as audio and video data.
Message	RFC822	E-mail message.
	Partial	Message was fragmented for transmission as the original was larger than 64Kb.
	External-body	External data should be referenced, such as data at an ftp site.

M

TABLE M.1 MIME CONTENT TYPES *(CONTINUED)*

Content Type	Subtype	Description
Application	Octet-stream	Binary data associated with no known application.
	PostScript	PostScript document ready for printing.
	SGML	SGML data.
Image	JPEG	JPEG image data.
	GIF	GIF image data.
Audio	Basic	Audio data.
Video	MPEG	MPEG video data.

minicomputer   A medium-sized computer running a multitasking operating system capable of managing more than 100 users simultaneously, suitable for use in a small company or a single corporate or government department.

See also mainframe computer; workstation.

mini-hard disk   A hard disk mounted on a Type III PC Card.

See also PC Memory Card International Association.

MIPS   Acronym for millions of instructions per second. A measure of the processing speed of a computer's CPU.

See also benchmark program.

mirroring   The process of duplicating stored information in real time to protect vital data from unexpected hardware failures. *See also* clustering; disk duplexing; disk mirroring; fault tolerance; redundant array of inexpensive disks.

mirror site   **1.** A duplicate Web site. A mirror site contains the same information as the original Web site and reduces traffic on that site by providing a local or regional alternative.

2. A duplicate data center. Large companies running mission-critical applications often mirror their entire data center so that the company can continue to function if the main center is hit by a natural disaster.

MIS   *See* Management Information System.

mission-critical application   A computer application whose function is vital to the operation of the corporation using it; also called line-of-business application.

MJ   *See* modular jack.

MLID   *See* multiple-link interface driver.

MMJ   *See* modified modular jack.

MMU   *See* memory management unit.

mnemonic   Pronounced "nee-monic." A name or abbreviation used to help you remember a long or complex instruction. Programming languages use many mnemonics to represent complex instructions.

MNP   *See* Microcom Networking Protocol.

MO   *See* Magneto-optical storage.

mobile computing   **1.** The daily use of a portable or laptop computer as a normal part of the workday.

2. Techniques used to establish links to a network by employees who move from one remote location to another, such as members of a sales staff or telecommuters who work from home. Once the connection is made, users log in and access network resources as easily as if they were working from a computer in the corporate office.

See also docking station; laptop computer; portable computer; port replicator; wireless communications.

mobile IP   A mechanism that allows mobility on the Internet by allowing a computer to use the same IP address as it moves from one location to another. Mobile IP also allows a user to change from one medium, such as Ethernet, to another, perhaps a wireless connection.

See also Ethernet; Internet Protocol.

modem   Contraction of modulator/demodulator; a device that allows a computer to transmit information over a telephone line.

The modem translates between the digital signals that the computer uses and analog signals suitable for transmission over telephone lines. When transmitting, the modem modulates the digital data onto a carrier signal on the telephone line. When receiving, the modem performs the reverse process to demodulate the data from the carrier signal.

Modems usually operate at speeds up to 56Kbps over standard telephone lines and at higher rates over leased lines.

See also baud rate; external modem; internal modem.

modem eliminator   A device that allows two computers to be linked without using modems. In an asynchronous system, in which the serial ports of two PCs are connected, the modem eliminator is a null-modem cable. In synchronous systems, a modem eliminator must also provide timing functions to synchronize communications.

modem server   A LAN server that allows a network user to dial out of the network into the Public Switched Telephone System or to access leased lines for asynchronous communications. Also called an asynchronous communications server or a dial-in/dial-out server.

M

moderated newsgroup On the Internet, a Usenet newsgroup or mailing list that is managed by one or more people in an attempt to maintain standards.

All posts to the newsgroup are reviewed by the moderator to make sure they meet the standards the group has set for subject matter and commercial content before being passed on to the whole group. Moderation is not censorship but an attempt to avoid some of the more extreme antics of those who enjoy flame wars.

See also flame war; listserver; mailing list; moderator.

moderator A person or small group of people who review the contents of all posts to a Usenet newsgroup or Internet mailing list to ensure that the postings meet the standards set by the group. Moderators are almost always volunteers, so be nice to them.

See also moderated newsgroup.

modified modular jack Abbreviated MMJ. A six-pin connector developed by Digital Equipment Corporation used to connect serial lines to terminal devices. MMJ jacks have a side-locking tab and so can be distinguished from RJ-11 jacks, which have a center-mounted tab.

See also modular jack; RJ-11.

modular jack Abbreviated MJ. The jack used to connect telephone cables to a wall-mounted face plate.

See also modified modular jack; RJ-11.

modulation In communications, the process used by a modem to add the digital signal onto the carrier signal so that the signal can be transmitted over a telephone line. The frequency, amplitude, or phase of a signal may be modulated to represent a digital or an analog signal.

See also carrier signal; demodulation.

module In programming, a self-contained portion of a larger program written, tested, and compiled separately. Normally, a module performs only one specific operation.

See also NetWare Loadable Module; Virtual Loadable Module.

MOE *See* Microsoft Office Expert.

MOES *See* Microsoft Office Expert Specialist.

MONITOR A Novell NetWare server utility that displays information about the server, including the time elapsed since the server was booted, percent utilization of the server's processor, number of disk blocks available, the number of blocks waiting to be written to disk, the number of connections to the server, and the number of files being accessed. It also provides information about server disks, LAN drivers, and other attached mass-storage devices.

See also SERVMAN; SET.

Monitrix for NetWare A package of network management utilities from Cheyenne Software, Inc., that includes hardware and software inventory, server monitoring, traffic monitoring, and virus protection. The package also includes automatic task-scheduling and reporting functions.

Moore's Law   States that the number of transistors on a chip of a given size doubles approximately every 18 months. Named for Intel's Gordon Moore, who first made this statement in 1965.

MOPS   *See* Microsoft Office Proficient Specialist.

Mosaic   A Web browser, released on the Internet in 1993 by the National Center for Supercomputing Applications (NCSA) at the University of Illinois, and placed in the public domain.

Although Mosaic was one of the first graphical Web browsers and was available free for most computing platforms, it has been overtaken by Netscape Navigator and Microsoft Internet Explorer.

motherboard   The main printed circuit board in a computer, containing the central processing unit, appropriate coprocessor and support chips, device controllers, and memory. It may also include expansion slots to give access to the computer's internal bus.

Motorola, Inc.   A major manufacturer of microprocessors, including those used in Macintosh computers, founded in 1928 in Chicago. Motorola is also extensively involved in radio and data communications and in automotive and industrial products.

For more information on Motorola, see www.motorola.com.

mount   **1.** The method by which nodes access network resources in the Network File System (NFS) and other networks.

2. To load a disk volume or tape archive so that users can access files and other resources.

mouse   A small input device with one or more buttons used with graphical user interfaces. As the mouse moves, an on-screen mouse cursor follows; all movements are relative. Once the pointer is in the correct position on the screen, you press one of the mouse buttons to initiate an action or operation. *See also* trackball.

Moving Pictures Experts Group   Abbreviated MPEG. A set of image-compression standards and file formats that defines a compression method for desktop audio, animation, and video.

MPEG is a lossy compression method that results in some data loss when a video clip is compressed. The following standards are available:

- **MPEG-1**   The original MPEG standard, designed for CD-ROM use, with a bandwidth of 1.5Mbps, two audio channels, and non-interlaced video.

- **MPEG-2**   An extension to MPEG-1, designed for broadcast television, including HDTV (High-Definition Television), with a bandwidth of up to 40Mbps, five audio channels, interlaced video, and a wider range of frame sizes.

- **MPEG-3**   A standard designed for HDTV until it was discovered that MPEG-2 covered HDTV. This standard is no longer used.

- **MPEG-4**   A standard designed for video phones and multimedia applications, with a bandwidth of up to 64Kbps.

M

See also lossy compression.

MPEG   *See* Moving Pictures Experts Group.

MPOA   *See* Multiprotocol over ATM.

MPPP   *See* PPP Multilink.

ms   *See* millisecond.

MSAU   *See* Multi-station Access Unit.

MS-DOS   *See* Microsoft Disk Operating System.

MS-DOS prompt   A visual confirmation that MS-DOS is ready to receive input from the keyboard. The default prompt includes the current drive letter followed by a colon and a greater-than symbol, as in C:>. You can customize the MS-DOS prompt by using the PROMPT command.

See also command line; command prompt.

msec   *See* millisecond.

MTBF   *See* mean time between failures.

MTTR   *See* mean time to repair.

multicast   **1.** A special form of broadcast in which copies of a message are delivered to multiple stations but not to all possible stations.

2. A data stream from a server from which multiple viewers can simultaneously watch a video.

See also broadcast; multicasting; unicast.

multicast backbone   Abbreviated Mbone. A method of transmitting digital video over the Internet in real time.

The TCP/IP protocols used for Internet transmissions are unsuitable for real-time audio or video; they were designed to deliver text and other files reliably, but with some delay. MBONE requires the creation of another backbone service with special hardware and software to accommodate video and audio transmissions; the existing Internet hardware cannot manage time-critical transmissions.

See also IP Multicast; multicasting; Real-time Transport Protocol; Resource Reservation Protocol; unicast.

multicasting   An Internet standard that allows a single host to distribute data to multiple recipients.

Multicasting can deliver audio and video content in real time so that the person using the system can interact with the data stream. A multicast group is created, and every member of the group receives every datagram. Membership is dynamic; when you join a group, you start to receive the datastream, and when you leave the group, you no longer receive the datastream.

See also broadcast; IP Multicast; unicast.

multidrop line   A circuit connecting several stations or nodes on a single logical link; also called a multipoint line.

A multidrop line is often used in IBM's SNA (Systems Network Architecture). It is controlled by a primary station, and the other nodes are considered secondary.

multihomed computer   Any computer system that contains multiple network interface cards and is attached to several physically separate networks; also know as a multihomed host. The term can also be applied to a computer configured with multiple IP addresses for a single network interface card.

multihomed host   *See* multihomed computer.

multilayer   A printed circuit board that contains several layers of circuitry. The layers are laminated together to make a single board, onto which the other discrete components are added.

multilink   In Microsoft Windows NT Server Remote Access Server, the ability to combine several slower data streams into one network connection. For example, you can use two 28.8Kbps modems to form a single 57.6Kbps connection.

Multilink Point-to-Point Protocol   *See* PPP Multilink.

Multimaster Replication   In Microsoft Active Directory, the process by which Active Directory domains replicate and resolve conflicting updates as peers.

All Active Directory domain controllers maintain a writable copy of the domain database, and updating any record on any domain controller will ensure that all other domain controllers are eventually updated.

See also Active Directory.

multimedia   A computer technology that displays information using a combination of full-motion video, animation, sound, graphics, and text, with a high degree of user interaction.

multimode fiber   A fiber-optic cable with a wide core that provides multiple routes for light waves to travel.

Its wider diameter of between 25 to 200 microns prevents multimode fiber from carrying signals as far as single-mode fiber due to modal dispersion.

See also single-mode fiber.

multipart virus   A form of virus that infects both the boot sector of a hard disk and executable files. Multipart viruses are difficult to locate because they use stealth and polymorphic techniques to avoid detection.

See also boot sector virus; file-infecting virus; macro virus; polymorphic virus; stealth virus; vaccine; virus.

multiple-link interface driver   Abbreviated MLID. A Novell Open Datalink Interface (ODI) device driver that manages the sending and receiving of packets to and from the physical network medium.

See also link-support layer; Open Data-link Interface/Network Driver Interface Specification Support.

Multiple Virtual Storage   Abbreviated MVS. IBM's standard operating system for large mainframe computers.

See also virtual machine.

multiplexer   Often abbreviated mux. A device that merges several lower-speed transmission channels into one high-speed channel

M

at one end of the link. Another multiplexer reverses this process at the other end of the link to reproduce the low-speed channels.

See also frequency-division multiplexing; inverse multiplexing; statistical multiplexing; time-division multiplexing.

multiplexing   A technique that transmits several signals over a single communications channel. Frequency-division multiplexing separates the signals by modulating the data into different carrier frequencies. Time-division multiplexing divides the available time among the various signals. Statistical multiplexing uses statistical techniques to dynamically allocate transmission space depending on the traffic pattern.

See also inverse multiplexing.

multipoint line   *See* multidrop line.

multiprocessing   The ability of an operating system to use more than one processor in a single computer.

Symmetrical multiprocessing refers to the operating system's ability to assign tasks dynamically to the next available processor. Asymmetrical multiprocessing requires that the original program designer choose the processor to use for a given task when writing the program.

Multiprotocol over ATM   Abbreviated MPOA. A proposal to allow layer three network routing protocols over an Asynchronous Transfer Mode Switched network. Multiprotocol over ATM allows corporations to take advantage of ATM's benefits while still maintaining legacy LANs.

See also Integrated-Private Network-to-Network Interface; IP over ATM; LAN Emulation.

Multipurpose Internet Mail Extension   Abbreviated MIME. An Internet specification that allows users to send multiple-part and multimedia messages, rather than simple text messages. A MIME-enabled e-mail application can send PostScript images, binary files, audio messages, and digital video over the Internet.

See also MIME Content Type; Secure MIME; uudecode; uuencode.

MULTIPLEXER

multiserver network   A network that uses two or more file servers.

Multi-station Access Unit   Abbreviated MAU; sometimes abbreviated MSAU. A multiport wiring hub for token-ring networks that can connect as many as eight lobes to a ring network. IBM refers to an MAU that can be managed remotely as a Controlled Access Unit.

multitasking   The simultaneous execution of two or more programs in one computer.

multithreading   The concurrent processing of several tasks or threads inside the same program. Because several threads can be processed in parallel, one thread does not need to wait for another to finish before starting.

multiuser   Describes an operating system that supports more than one simultaneous user. MS-DOS and Windows are single-user operating systems. Unix and its derivatives and networking operating systems are multiuser systems.

mux   *See* multiplexer.

mv   *See* millivolt.

MVS   *See* Multiple Virtual Storage.

M

N

n *See* nano-.

NAEC *See* Novell Authorized Education Center.

NAK *See* negative acknowledgment.

named pipe A communications API used by applications running on a network. Named pipes provide connection-oriented messaging between a client and a server using routines similar to those used in normal operations for opening, reading, and writing to files.

See also mailslots; pipe; semaphore; shared memory; socket.

name resolution The process of translating the appropriate numerical IP address, which is required by a computer, into a name that is more easily understood and remembered by a person.

In the TCP/IP (Transmission Control Protocol/Internet Protocol) environment, names such as www.sybex.com are translated into their IP equivalents by the Domain Name Service (DNS). In a Microsoft Windows environment, NetBIOS names are resolved into IP addresses by Windows Internet Naming Service (WINS).

namespace In Microsoft Active Directory, a collection of unique domain names.

A namespace can be contiguous or disjointed. In a contiguous namespace, a child domain always contains the name of the parent, for example, accounting.sybex.com as a subdomain of sybex.com. In a disjointed namespace, a child domain does not share its parent's name, as in sybex.com and sybexnet.com.

name space In Novell NetWare, the ability of a NetWare volume to support files from non–MS-DOS clients.

Each client sees files on the server in its own format; a Macintosh client sees files as Macintosh files, and a Unix client sees files as Unix files. Name space support is enabled per NetWare volume.

See also name-space NLM.

name-space NLM A specific type of NetWare Loadable Module (NLM) that allows non–MS-DOS filenaming conventions, such as those used in OS/2, Unix, or the Macintosh system, to be stored in NetWare's directory and filenaming systems.

NAMPS *See* Narrowband Advanced Mobile Phone Service.

nano- Abbreviated n. A prefix meaning one-billionth in the American numbering scheme, and one thousand millionth in the British system.

nanosecond Abbreviated ns. One-billionth of a second. The speed of computer memory and logic chips is measured in nanoseconds.

narrowband   In communications, a voice-grade transmission channel of 2400 bits per second or less.

Narrowband Advanced Mobile Phone Service   Abbreviated NAMPS. A proposed standard from Motorola that combines the AMPS (Advanced Mobile Phone Service) cellular standard with digital signaling information. NAMPS is designed to provide a higher level of performance, reduce the number and incidence of dropped calls, and greatly increase communications capabilities.

See also Advanced Mobile Phone Service; Code Division Multiple Access; Time Division Multiple Access.

Narrow SCSI   A Small Computer System Interface (SCSI) or SCSI-2 interface capable of transferring only 8 bits of data at a time

See also Fast SCSI; Fast/Wide SCSI; Wide SCSI.

NAS   *See* network attached storage.

NAT   *See* network address translation.

National Center for Supercomputing Applications   Abbreviated NCSA. At the University of Illinois at Urbana-Champaign, NCSA is credited with the creation of Mosaic, the first ever graphical Web browser.

National Computer Security Center   Abbreviated NCSC. A branch of the U.S. National Security Agency that defines security for computer products. The Department of Defense Standard 5200.28, also known as the Orange Book, specifies several levels of increasingly complex security measures.

See also C2; Orange Book.

National Information Infrastructure   Abbreviated NII. A planned, high-speed, public-access information service, designed to reach millions of schools, homes, and businesses throughout the United States.

National Semiconductor Corp.   A major manufacturer of semiconductor products based in Santa Clara, California. In 1997, National spun off its Fairchild Semiconductor division, and in 1998 acquired Mediamatics, a manufacturer of audio/video decoders, as well as chip maker Cyrix.

For more information on National Semiconductor, see www.national.com.

nbtstat   A utility program used to show active TCP/IP (Transmission Control Protocol/Internet Protocol) connections and statistics for NetBIOS over TCP/IP.

See also ipconfig; netstat; Ping; subnet mask; tracert.

NC   *See* network computer.

NCB   *See* Network Control Block.

NCIP   *See* Novell Certified Internet Professional.

NCP   *See* NetWare Core Protocol; network control program.

NCP packet signature   In Novell NetWare, a security feature that allows each workstation to add a special signature to each NetWare Core Protocol (NCP) packet going to the server. This signature changes dynamically for each packet, protecting both the server and the workstation against unauthorized access or any attempt to use unauthorized network privileges.

See also NetWare Core Protocol.

NCSA *See* National Center for Super-computing Applications.

NCSC *See* National Computer Security Center.

NDD *See* NetWare Directory Database.

NDIS *See* Network Driver Interface Specification.

NDPS See Novell Distributed Print Services.

NDS *See* Novell Directory Services.

NDS for NT An add-on product from Novell that allows the management and integration of Windows NT domains from within NetWare Administrator.

NDS tree In Novell Directory Services (NDS), the container objects and all the leaf objects that make up the hierarchical structure of the NDS database. Also known as the Directory Tree.

See also container object; leaf object; Novell Directory Services.

NEAP *See* Novell Education Academic Partner.

near-end crosstalk Abbreviated NEXT. Any interference that occurs close to a connector at either end of a cable. NEXT is usually measured near the source of the test signal.

See also crosstalk; far-end crosstalk.

NEC Corporation Major manufacturer of a wide range of electronic products, including semiconductors, communications equipment, the MultiSynch line of monitors, LCD flat-panel monitors, plasma displays, and PCs.

For more information on NEC Corporation, see www.nec.com.

See also Packard Bell NEC.

negative acknowledgment Abbreviated NAK. In communications, a control code, ASCII 21, sent by the receiving computer to indicate that the data was not properly received and should be sent again.

See also acknowledgment.

NETADMIN A Novell NetWare 4 utility used to manage NetWare Directory Services (NDS) objects. This utility has many of the same features and controls many of the same functions as the Windows-based program NWADMIN.

NETADMIN replaces the functions found in several NetWare 3.*x* utilities, including DSPACE, SECURITY, SYSCON, and USERDEF, and has itself been replaced in NetWare 5 by NetWare Administrator.

See also NetWare Administrator.

NetBEUI *See* NetBIOS Extended User Interface.

NETBIOS A Novell NetWare 3.*x* workstation utility used to determine if the client software NETBIOS.EXE is loaded and, if so, which interrupts it is using.

NetBIOS   *See* network basic input/output system.

NetBIOS Extended User Interface. Abbreviated NetBEUI, pronounced "net-boo-ee." A network device driver for the transport layer supplied with Microsoft's LAN Manager, Windows for Workgroups, and Windows NT. NetBEUI communicates with the network interface card via the NDIS (Network Driver Interface Specification).

NetBEUI is a small protocol with no networking layer and therefore no routing capability. It is suitable only for small networks; you cannot build internetworks using NetBEUI, and so it is often replaced with TCP/IP.

Microsoft has added extensions to NetBEUI in Windows NT to remove the limitation of 254 sessions per node and calls this extended NetBEUI the NetBIOS Frame (NBF).

See also network basic input/output system; Transmission Control Protocol/Internet Protocol.

NetBSD   An implementation of Unix derived from the BSD series of releases; designed to run on Intel processors. The distribution is usually free, although there may be a small charge to cover the distribution media and packaging.

NetBSD emphasizes multiple platform support and so has been ported to several non-Intel systems.

See also FreeBSD; Linux.

netcasting   A method used to deliver Web content automatically to the desktop. Netcasting is referred to as push technology because content is pushed from a Web site to those users who requested receipt of the content. Content can include weather forecasts, stock market quotes, or software updates.

See also Castanet; Marimba, Inc.; PointCast, Inc.; server push.

NET.CFG   A Novell NetWare workstation configuration file that contains information used to configure the client software on the workstation. The file is read once, during startup of the network files.

For normal network use, the default values established in this file usually work. In some cases, the NET.CFG values must be adjusted to work with particular applications or in certain configurations.

NetDDE   *See* Network Dynamic Data Exchange.

netiquette   A contraction of *network etiquette*. The set of unwritten rules governing the use of e-mail and other computer and network services.

Like any culture, the online world has its own rules and conventions, and if you understand and observe these conventions, you can take your place in the online community without problems. Here are a few tips:

• Remember that the people reading your post are human; if you wouldn't say it to their face, don't post it in your e-mail.

• Lurk before you leap. Spend a few days reading the posts in a newsgroup or mailing list before you post anything of your own.

- If you use a signature file to close your e-mail, remember to keep it short; people don't want to read lots of cute stuff every time you post.

- Don't post messages in uppercase as it is the e-mail equivalent of YELLING; to add emphasis, place an asterisk before and after a word.

- Don't flame or mount personal attacks on other users.

- Check your grammar and spelling before you post.

- Don't be shy; if you are an expert, share your knowledge with others.

NetPC An initiative from Compaq, Dell, Hewlett-Packard, Intel, and Microsoft describing a networked PC designed to give system administrators greater control and security than a traditional PC.

NetPC is based on a minimum configuration of a 133MHz Pentium with at least 16MB of memory, running a Windows operating system, with a hard disk and the capability to run applications locally. The computer case is sealed and lockable, and floppy disks and CD-ROM drives are optional. All software distribution is centralized.

See also network computer; thin client; total cost of ownership; Zero Administration for Windows.

Netscape Catalog Server A server for Microsoft Windows NT and Unix systems that allows the publication of complex, hierarchically organized documents stored on the Internet or on a corporate intranet; based on the popular freeware application Harvest.

Netscape Certificate Management System A server for Microsoft Windows NT and Unix systems that manages digital certificates and allows the server to become a certificate authority.

See also certificate authority.

Netscape Collabra Server A Network News Transfer Protocol (NNTP) server for Microsoft Windows NT and Unix systems that allows the creation and management of private and secure newsgroups.

Netscape Commerce Server A server for Microsoft Windows NT and Unix systems that manages electronic commerce on the Internet.

Netscape Communications Corporation A major publisher of software development tools, Web browsers, and Web-server software; based in Menlo Park, California, and founded in 1994 by Jim Clark and Marc Andreessen. Its Web browser, Netscape Navigator, was initially very popular, but later lost market share to Microsoft's Internet Explorer.

In 1998, America Online bought Netscape Communications and spun off the server-based products to Sun Microsystems.

For more information on Netscape Communications, see www.netscape.com.

Netscape Communicator A package that includes the Netscape Navigator Web browser, e-mail support, a newsreader, and Netscape Page composer, an HTML editor. Netscape Communicator is available for Microsoft Windows, the Macintosh, and Unix.

Netscape Directory Server   A general-purpose Lightweight Directory Access Protocol (LADP) directory server that stores, publishes, and manages user, group, and other information in one location on a network and makes this information available to the Netscape SuiteSpot servers.

See also Netscape SuiteSpot.

Netscape Enterprise Server   A high-performance and very popular Web server for Microsoft Windows NT, Novell NetWare, and Unix systems that is specifically designed to support large Web sites on the Internet or on a corporate intranet.

Enterprise Server supports standard CGI (Common Gateway Interface), and for application creation, also offers Netscape Server API (NSAPI) for in-process server applications. The LiveWire runtime environment supports server-side JavaScript applications, and for Java developers, the Sun Java Servlet API is also available.

Enterprise Server is administered using a Web-based application called Server Manager, giving access to server settings such as security, users, and groups, as well as Web site content management.

Netscape FastTrack Server   A Web server for Microsoft Windows NT and Unix systems. Designed for non-programmers, it lets users establish a Web presence or an intranet quickly and easily.

Netscape Messaging Server   An e-mail server for Microsoft Windows NT and Unix systems that supports Lightweight Directory Access Protocol (LADP), Simple Mail Transfer Protocol (SMTP), as well as Post Office Protocol 3 (POP3) and Internet Mail Access Protocol (IMAP).

Netscape Navigator   A popular Web browser that runs under Windows and Unix and on the Macintosh. Netscape is distributed free by Netscape Communications Corporation, and in an unusual move for a commercial software developer, Netscape has made the source code to Navigator available on the Internet.

Netscape SuiteSpot   A popular package of integrated server components designed to provide groupware services, document publishing and management, messaging and e-mail, directory services, and security for corporate intranets. SuiteSpot is available in a Standard Edition and a Professional Edition.

The Standard Edition includes Communicator, Enterprise Server, Messaging Server, Calendar Server, Collabra Server, and Directory Server. The Professional Edition includes all the components found in the Standard Edition and adds Compass Server, Certificate Server, Proxy Server, and Netscape Mission Control Desktop for centralized network management.

netstat   A utility program used to show server connections running over TCP/IP (Transmission Control Protocol/Internet Protocol) and statistics, including current connections, failed connection attempts, reset connections, segments received, segments sent, and segments retransmitted.

See also ipconfig.

NETSYNC   In Novell NetWare, two utility programs for NetWare 3 (NETSYNC3) and NetWare 4 (NETSYNC4) servers that allow NetWare 3 servers to be managed by Novell Directory Services (NDS).

See also Novell Directory Services.

NETUSER   In Novell NetWare 4.*x*, a workstation utility that offers a menu system for performing simple user tasks, including managing print jobs, sending messages to other users, mapping network drives, capturing ports to printers or print queues, and changing the login script and password.

NETUSER replaces the NetWare 3.*x* utility SESSION and can be invoked from either the workstation or the server.

This utility has many of the same features and controls many of the same functions as the Windows-based program NWUSER.

NetVIEW   IBM SNA (Systems Network Architecture) management software that provides monitoring and control functions for SNA and non-SNA devices. This system relies heavily on mainframe data-collection programs, but it also incorporates Token Ring networks, Rolm CBXs, non-IBM modems, and PC-level products.

NetWare   *See* Novell NetWare.

NetWare Administrator   In Novell NetWare, the main utility used for performing NetWare 4 and higher supervisory and administrative tasks. A graphical application, NetWare Administrator can be run from within Windows or OS/2.

NetWare Client32   A set of 32-bit client software packages released with Novell NetWare 5. Client32 software is available for Windows 3.*x*, Windows 95, Windows 98, and Windows NT.

See also NetWare DOS Requester; NETx.COM.

NetWare Client for DOS and MS Windows   Client software that allows MS-DOS and Windows workstations to connect to a Novell NetWare server and access network resources.

See also NetWare Client32; NetWare DOS Requester; NETx.COM.

NetWare Client for OS/2   Client software that allows OS/2 workstations to connect to a Novell NetWare server and access network resources.

NetWare command files   Text files created by the network administrator containing a series of Novell NetWare commands and the appropriate modifying parameters.

NetWare command files execute just as though you typed the commands at the NetWare console, and they have the filename extension .NCF. For example, AUTOEXEC.NCF contains server configuration information used by SERVER.EXE when starting the server.

NetWare Connect   *See* NetWare Internet Access Server.

NetWare Core Protocol   Abbreviated NCP. In Novell NetWare, a presentation-layer procedure used by a server when responding to workstation requests. It includes routines for manipulating directories and files, opening semaphores, printing, and creating and destroying service connections.

NetWare Directory Database Abbreviated NDD. In Novell NetWare, a system database that holds the information on all the objects in a Novell Directory Services (NDS) tree. Often referred to as the Directory or the Directory tree.

NetWare Directory Services Abbreviated NDS. In Novell NetWare, a global naming service that maintains information on, and provides access to, every resource on the network, including users, groups, printers, volumes, and servers.

NDS manages all network resources as objects in the NetWare Directory Database (NDD), independent of their actual physical location, and presents them in a hierarchical tree structure. NDS is global to the network, and information is replicated so that a local failure cannot bring down the whole system.

NDD replaces the bindery, the system database for earlier releases of NetWare. The bindery managed the operation of a single NetWare server; NDS supports the whole network, including multiserver networks. Bindery emulation provides compatibility with previous versions of NetWare.

NDS is based on the 1988 CCITT X.500 standard.

See also Consultative Committee for International Telephony and Telegraphy.

NetWare DOS Requester A group of Virtual Loadable Modules (VLMs) that provide NetWare 3.*x* and 4.*x* support for MS-DOS and Windows workstations. The Requester replaces the NetWare shell used by earlier versions of NetWare.

NetWare Hub Services A software package from Novell that supports the management of any hub card that complies with the NetWare Hub Management Interface (HMI) standard.

NetWare Internet Access Server Abbreviated NIAS. In Novell NetWare, the server software that translates data requests from a client using Internetwork Packet eXchange (IPX) into TCP/IP (Transmission Control Protocol/Internet Protocol) for connection to the Internet or other TCP/IP host. Previously known as NetWare Connect.

NetWare/IP A set of NetWare Loadable Modules (NLMs) that provide IP support for NetWare 3.*x* and 4.*x* servers by encapsulating the IPX information inside an IP datagram. Native TCP/IP support is available in Novell NetWare 5.*x*, so this capability is not needed in a pure NetWare 5 environment. NetWare/IP allows a Novell NetWare server to act as a gateway between NetWare and a TCP/IP network.

See also Internet Protocol; Internetwork Packet eXchange; Transmission Control Protocol/Internet Protocol.

NetWare Licensing Services Abbreviated NLS. In Novell NetWare, a service that allows system administrators to monitor and manage the execution of licensed application software.

NetWare Link Services Protocol Abbreviated NLSP. The Novell NetWare IPX (Internetwork Packet eXchange) link-state protocol used by IPX routers to share information about their routes with other devices on the network.

Once the network map is built, information is transferred between routers only when the network changes. NLSP allows large or small internetworks to be connected without causing routing inefficiencies.

See also Routing Information Protocol.

NetWare Loadable Module Abbreviated NLM. Server management programs and LAN drivers that run on a server under Novell NetWare's network operating system. NLMs can be loaded and unloaded dynamically, without interrupting the server, and provide better service than applications that run outside the core operating system. Several kinds of NLMs are available:

- Utilities and application modules allow you to look at or change various configuration options. These NLMs have the .NLM filename extension.

- Name-space modules allow non-DOS filenaming conventions to be used when storing files. These NLMs have the .NAM filename extension.

- Disk drivers give access to hard disks; they have the .DSK filename extension.

- LAN drivers control communications between the network operating system and the network interface cards; they have a .LAN filename extension.

See also NetWare Peripheral Architecture; Virtual Loadable Module.

NetWare for Macintosh A set of NetWare Loadable Modules (NLMs) used to provide file handling, printing, and Apple-Talk routing for Macintosh clients on a NetWare network.

See also AppleTalk.

NetWare Management System A network management system for Novell NetWare servers that has been replaced by ManageWise.

See also Novell ManageWise.

NetWare Mobile Services In Novell NetWare, a dial-in remote access client for Windows 3.x and Windows 95.

NetWare Multiprotocol Router PC-based software from Novell that allows network administrators to connect LANs using IPX, TCP/IP, or AppleTalk Filing Protocol (AFP) over a wide range of LANs and WANs. The NetWare Multiprotocol Router supports Ethernet, Fast Ethernet, token ring, FDDI, and ARCnet network architectures.

See also Fiber Distributed Data Interface; Internetwork Packet eXchange; PC-based router; Transmission Control Protocol/Internet Protocol.

NetWare Multiprotocol Router Plus PC-based software from Novell that provides wide-area connectivity for dispersed heterogeneous networks over T1, fractional T1, X.25, and low-speed synchronous leased lines. NetWare Multiprotocol Router Plus replaces three earlier products: NetWare Link/64, NetWare Link/T1, and NetWare Link/X.25.

See also PC-based router.

NetWare NFS A Novell NetWare Loadable Module (NLM) that adds NFS (Network File System) server capability to an existing NetWare file server. Once loaded,

Unix NFS clients see the NetWare server as another NFS server.

See also Network File System.

NetWare NFS Gateway A Novell NetWare Loadable Module (NLM) that lets a NetWare server mount a Unix file system as a NetWare volume. Complete NetWare security is maintained, and access to the Unix system is based on the NetWare client's privileges.

NetWare Peripheral Architecture Abbreviated NPA or NWPA. A feature of NetWare that allows developers to add and support new storage devices and their associated controllers. NPA consists of the following components:

- **Host Adapter Module (HAM)** The adapter-specific driver that controls the interaction between the operating system and the hardware; provided by Novell or by the manufacturer of the adapter, with the filename extension .HAM. There will be one HAM for each adapter on the server.

- **Host Adapter Interface (HAI)** An API within NPA for communication between the HAM and the NetWare database that tracks the storage devices and media available on the server.

- **Custom Device Module (CDM)** The software that controls the devices attached to the adapter, usually provided by the manufacturer, with the filename extension .CDM. There may be multiple CDMs for a single adapter as each device connected to the adapter needs its own CDM.

- **Custom Device Interface (CDI)** An API within NPA for communication between the CDM and the NetWare database that tracks the storage devices and media available on the server.

The NPA replaces many of the functions found in the NetWare Loadable Module drivers used to control hard disks; the .DSK drivers controlled the hard-disk controller and all the devices attached to that controller.

See also NetWare Loadable Module; Virtual Loadable Module.

NetWare Requester for OS/2 A group of Virtual Loadable Modules (VLMs) that provide NetWare 4.*x* support for OS/2-based workstations.

NetWare Runtime A single-user version of Novell NetWare, often used as a communications server or applications server that provide its own authentication.

NetWare shell The Novell NetWare program loaded into each workstation's memory that allows the workstation to access the network.

The shell captures the workstation's network requests and forwards them to a NetWare server. In earlier versions of NetWare, the shell program was specific to the version of MS-DOS or Windows in use. The term *shell* is not used in recent versions of NetWare.

See also NetWare Client32; NetWare DOS Requester; NetWare Requester for OS/2; NET*x*.COM.

NetWare for SNA   A set of NetWare Loadable Modules (NLMs) used to provide connectivity to an IBM Systems Network Architecture (SNA) network. With the right access permissions, MS-DOS, Macintosh, Unix, and Windows clients can run applications on the IBM mainframe.

NetWare System Fault Tolerance   *See* System Fault Tolerance.

NetWare Tools   Novell NetWare utilities that allow users to perform a variety of network tasks, such as accessing network resources, mapping drives, managing printing, and sending messages to other network users.

NetWare Tools programs are installed separately from the server installation program, and they are available for MS-DOS, Windows, and OS/2 workstations.

NetWare for Unix   A software package that allows Unix clients to access a Novell NetWare server.

NetWare Users International   Abbreviated NUI. An organization created to support distributed NetWare user groups, first formed in the mid-1980s.

NUI now has 150 regional chapters and more than 140,000 members worldwide. Users can present a united voice to Novell, giving feedback on new products and how to support and improve existing products. Although supported by Novell, NUI is completely independent from the company.

NetWire   Novell's online information service accessed through the commercial service CompuServe. It provides product information, press releases, technical support, downloadable patches, upgrades, and utilities. All the material available through NetWire on CompuServe is also available on the Novell ftp site at ftp.novell.com and on the Web at www.novell.com.

network   A group of computers and associated peripheral devices connected by a communications channel capable of sharing files and other resources among several users.

A network can range from a peer-to-peer network connecting a small number of users in an office or department, to a LAN connecting many users over permanently installed cables and dial-up lines, to a MAN or WAN connecting users on several networks spread over a wide geographic area.

network adapter   *See* network interface card.

network address translation   Abbreviated NAT. A term used to describe the process of converting between IP addresses on an intranet or other private network and Internet IP addresses.

See also name resolution.

network administrator   The person responsible for the day-to-day operation and management of a network; also known as a system administrator. Duties of the network administrator can include the following:

- Planning for future expansion

- Installing new workstations and network peripheral devices

- Adding and removing authorized users

- Backing up the system and archiving important files

- Assigning and changing passwords

- Troubleshooting network problems

- Monitoring system performance

- Evaluating new products

- Installing hardware and software updates

- Training users

See also configuration management.

network analyzer   Any device that decodes and analyzes data transmitted over the network. A network analyzer may be hardware, software, or a combination of the two. Some analyzers troubleshoot network problems by decoding packets; others create and transmit their own packets.

See also protocol analyzer; sniffer.

network architecture   The design of a network, including the hardware, software, access methods, and the protocols in use.

Several well-accepted network architectures have been defined by standards committees and major vendors. For example, the International Organization for Standardization (ISO) developed the seven-layer OSI Reference Model for computer-to-computer communications, and IBM designed SNA (Systems Network Architecture). Both architectures organize network functions into layers of hardware and software, with each layer building on the functions provided by the previous layer.

The ultimate goal is to allow different computers to exchange information freely in as transparent a fashion as possible.

Network Associates, Inc.   Formed in 1997 by the merger of Network General and McAfee Associates, Network Associates provides virus detection and protection software, encryption software, help desk systems, and network management products.

For more information on Network Associates, see www.networkassociates.com.

network attached storage   Abbreviated NAS. A collection of mass-storage devices contained in a single chassis with a built-in operating system.

Ethernet connectors allow the NAS to connect directly to the network. A NAS might contain a large hard disk as well as a set of SCSI connectors to attach additional disks, CD-ROM drives, tape drives, or Iomega Zip and Jaz drives. Because the NAS is managed by its own embedded operating system, adding one to a network adds little in the way of overhead.

See also storage area network.

network backbone   *See* backbone.

network basic input/output system
Abbreviated NetBIOS, pronounced "net-bye-os." A session-layer network protocol, originally developed in 1984 by IBM and Sytek to manage data exchange and network access.

NetBIOS provides an API (application programming interface) with a consistent set of commands for requesting lower-level network services to transmit information from node to node, thus separating applications from the underlying network operating system. Many vendors provide either their own version of NetBIOS or an emulation of its communications services in their own products.

See also WinSock.

network board   *See* network interface card.

network-centric   An imprecise term often used to describe an approach to software design and development that includes a strong client/server component.

Network+ certification   A certification program from the CompTIA (Computer Technology Industry Association) designed to measure competence in basic networking concepts; aimed at the computer technician.

network computer   Abbreviated NC. An initiative from Apple, IBM, Netscape, Oracle, and Sun Microsystems describing a networked computer designed to give system administrators greater control and security than a traditional PC provides.

The network computer is based on a minimum configuration of a 25MHz Intel i960 with at least 32MB of memory, running a Java Virtual Machine, and downloads applications from the server and runs them locally. Hard disk, floppy disk, and CD-ROM drives and expansion slots are not required.

The initiative fizzled out, in part at least because conventional PCs can do the same job, but also due to Compaq (and other manufacturers) creating the sub-$1,000 PC.

See also NetPC; thin client; total cost of ownership; Zero Administration for Windows.

Network Control Block   Abbreviated NCB. The packet structure used by the NetBIOS transport protocol.

network control program   Abbreviated NCP. In an IBM Systems Network Architecture (SNA) environment, performs the routing, error control, testing, and addressing of SNA devices.

network device driver   Software that controls the physical function of a network interface card, coordinating between the card and the other workstation hardware and software.

See also Network Driver Interface Specification.

network directory   A directory located on a computer other than the one currently being used. Depending on access privileges, the rest of the disk may or may not be available to the user. On the Macintosh, a network directory is often referred to as a shared folder.

See also network drive; shared folder.

network drive   A drive located on a computer other than the one currently being used and that is available to users on the network.

See also local disk; network directory.

Network Driver Interface Specification   Abbreviated NDIS. A device driver specification, originally developed by Microsoft and 3Com in 1990, that is independent of both the underlying network interface card hardware and the protocol being used. NDIS also allows multiple protocol stacks to be used at the same time in the same computer.

Windows NT includes the latest version, NDIS 3, which is backward-compatible with the original NDIS and NDIS 2.

See also Open Data-link Interface; Open Data-link Interface/Network Driver Interface Specification Support.

Network Dynamic Data Exchange
Abbreviated NetDDE. A version of Microsoft's DDE that uses NetBIOS to extend DDE features over a network.

Using NetDDE, two or more applications running on networked workstations can dynamically share data.

See also Component Object Model; Distributed Component Object Model; Dynamic Data Exchange; Object Linking and Embedding.

Network File System Abbreviated NFS. A distributed file-sharing system developed well over a decade ago by Sun Microsystems, Inc.

NFS allows a computer on a network to use the files and peripheral devices of another networked computer as if they were local, subject to certain security restrictions. Using NFS, you can share files on your system with other computers running MS-DOS, MacOS, Unix, Novell NetWare, VMS, and many other operating systems, in both local and global environments.

NFS is platform-independent and runs on mainframes, minicomputers, RISC-based workstations, diskless workstations, and personal computers. NFS has been licensed and implemented by more than 300 vendors.

See also Andrews File System; Common Internet File System; WebNFS.

Network Information Service Abbreviated NIS. A recent name for the security and file-access databases on Unix systems, previously known as the Yellow Pages. The NIS for most Unix systems comprises the Unix host files /etc/hosts, /etc/passwd, and /etc/group.

network interface card Abbreviated NIC. In networking, the PC expansion board that plugs into a personal computer or server and works with the network operating system and the appropriate device drivers to control the flow of information over the network.

The network interface card is connected to the network media (twisted pair, coaxial, or fiber-optic cable) and is designed for a specific type of network such as Ethernet, token ring, FDDI (Fiber Distributed Data Interface), or ARCnet.

Novell NetWare documentation uses the term *network board* rather than the more common term *network interface card*.

Network support is built in to Macintosh computers and does not require an additional expansion board.

network layer The third of seven layers of the OSI Reference Model for computer-to-computer communications. The network layer defines protocols for data routing to ensure that the information arrives at the correct destination node and manages communications errors.

See also OSI Reference Model.

Network Management Protocol Abbreviated NMP. A set of protocols developed by AT&T, designed to control certain network devices, such as modems and T1 multiplexers.

Network Monitor   In Microsoft Windows NT Server, a graphical utility program used to monitor and troubleshoot network-related problems.

Network Monitor tracks information up to the network layer, filters packets according to the protocol or the source or the destination machine, and performs packet analysis.

A more capable version of Network Monitor is available as part of Microsoft's Systems Management Server package.

Network News Transfer Protocol   Abbreviated NNTP. An Internet protocol used for posting, retrieving, and managing posts to newsgroups.

network operating system   Abbreviated NOS. In typical client/server architecture LANs, the NOS consists of two parts. The largest and most complex part is the system software running on the file server. This system software coordinates many functions, including user accounts and network access information, security, resource sharing, administration, UPS and power monitoring, data protection, and error detection and control. A much smaller component of the NOS runs on each of the networked PCs or workstations attached to the network.

Network operating systems are available from Banyan (VINES), IBM (OS/2 Warp Server), Microsoft (Windows NT Server and Windows 2000), Novell (IntraNetWare and NetWare), and Sun Microsystems (Solaris),

and, of course, many versions of Unix are available.

In peer-to-peer networks, a part of the NOS is installed on each PC or workstation attached to the network and runs on top of the PC operating system. In some cases, the NOS may be installed on one PC designated as a file server, but this PC is not dedicated to the file-server function; it is also available to run applications.

network printer   A printer attached to and accessible from the network. A network printer may be attached to a file server or a printer server, or it may have its own direct connection to the network.

See also local printer.

Network Service Access Point   Abbreviated NSAP. A 20-octet addressing scheme used in Asynchronous Transfer Mode (ATM) networks for private network addresses.

network topology   *See* topology.

NETx.COM   The workstation shell software used in Novell NetWare 2.x and 3.x networks. This program is loaded into memory on the workstation and begins transmission when the workstation requests network resources.

In earlier versions of NetWare, NETx.COM was specific to the version of MS-DOS running on the workstation. The only way to unload NETx.COM from memory is to reboot the workstation.

See also NetWare Client32; NetWare DOS Requester.

newsgroup   A Usenet e-mail discussion group devoted to a single topic. Subscribers to a newsgroup post articles that can be read by all the other subscribers.

Newsgroup names fit into a formal structure in which each component of the name is separated from the next by a period. The leftmost portion of the name represents the category of the newsgroup, and the name gets more specific from left to right.

The major top-level newsgroup categories are:

- **alt**   Newsgroups outside the main structure outlined below

- **comp**   Computer science and related topics, including information about operating systems and hardware, as well as more advanced topics such as graphics and robotics

- **misc**   Anything that does not fit into any of the other categories

- **news**   Information on Usenet and newsgroups

- **rec**   Recreational activities, such as hobbies, the arts, movies, and books

- **sci**   Discussion groups on scientific topics, including math, physics, and biology

- **soc**   Groups that address social and cultural issues

- **talk**   Groups that concentrate on controversial subjects

Private newsgroups are often available on corporate intranets, where organization,

structure, and subject matter are decided by the system administrator.

See also newsreader; Usenet.

newsreader   An application used to read articles posted to Usenet newsgroups. Newsreaders are of two kinds:

- Threaded newsreaders group the posts into threads of related articles.

- Unthreaded newsreaders present articles in their original order of posting without regard for the subject.

Of the two, threaded newsreaders are much easier to use.

See also newsgroup; thread; Usenet.

New Technology File System   Abbreviated NTFS; sometimes NT File System. The native file system used by Microsoft Windows NT, which supports long filenames, reduced file fragmentation, improved fault tolerance, increased system security, and much better recovery after a system crash.

NEXT   *See* near-end crosstalk.

Next Hop Resolution Protocol   Abbreviated NHRP. An Internet name resolution protocol designed to route IP datagrams across nonbroadcast multiple access networks such as Asynchronous Transfer Mode (ATM), frame relay, Switched Multimegabit Data Service (SMDS), and X.25.

See also Asynchronous Transfer Mode ; IP over ATM; IP switching.

NFS   *See* Network File System.

NHRP   *See* Next Hop Resolution Protocol.

NIAS   *See* NetWare Internet Access Server.

NIC   *See* network interface card.

NII   *See* National Information Infrastructure.

NIS   *See* Network Information Service.

NLM   *See* NetWare Loadable Module.

NLS   *See* NetWare Licensing Services.

NLSP   *See* NetWare Link Services Protocol.

NMP   *See* Network Management Protocol.

NNTP   *See* Network News Transfer Protocol.

node   Any device attached to the network capable of communicating with other network devices. In Novell NetWare documentation, a workstation is often called a node.

node number   The number that uniquely identifies a network interface card and distinguishes it from all others.

Node numbers can be assigned in different ways. Ethernet node numbers are factory-set, so no two Ethernet boards have the same number. On other network interface cards, node numbers are set by jumpers or switches.

noise   In communications, extraneous signals on a transmission channel that de-

grade the quality or performance of the channel. Noise is often caused by interference from nearby power lines, electrical equipment, or spikes in the AC line voltage. *See also* crosstalk; far-end crosstalk; near-end crosstalk.

nominal velocity of propagation   The speed at which a signal moves through a cable, expressed as a percentage or fraction of the speed of light in a vacuum. Some cable testers use this speed, along with the time it takes for a signal to return to the testing device, to calculate cable lengths.

nondedicated server   A server upon which applications are available, while network management software runs in the background. Nondedicated servers are common in peer-to-peer networks.

non-preemptive multitasking   Any form of multitasking in which the operating system cannot preempt a running task and move to the next task in the queue.

Programs are easy to write for this environment; however, a single badly written program can take over the whole system. By refusing to relinquish the processor, such a program can cause serious problems for other programs running at the same time. Poorly written non-preemptive multitasking can produce a kind of stuttering effect on running applications, depending on how the programs behave.

See also preemptive multitasking; time-slice multitasking.

nonvolatile memory   Any form of memory that holds its contents when the power is removed. ROM (read-only memory),

EPROM (erasable programmable read-only memory), and EEPROM (electrically erasable programmable read-only memory) are all forms of nonvolatile memory.

no parity *See* parity.

NOS *See* network operating system.

notebook computer A small, portable computer, about the size of a computer book, with a flat screen and a keyboard that fold together.

A notebook computer is lighter and smaller than a laptop computer. Recent advances in battery technology allow them to run for many hours between charges. Some models use flash memory rather than conventional hard disks for program and data storage; other models offer a range of business applications in ROM . Many offer PCMCIA expansion connections for additional peripheral devices, such as modems, fax modems, and network connections.

See also laptop computer; PC Memory Card International Association.

Novell Application Launcher In Novell NetWare, a utility used with applications for NetWare clients.

The NetWare administrator decides which applications are appropriate and creates an icon group for the users; additional startup and shutdown scripts can be used to add more application control. Novell Application Launcher uses the Universal Naming Convention (UNC) for ease and clarity.

See also Universal Naming Convention.

Novell Authorized Education Center Abbreviated NAEC. A private organization that provides Novell-approved training courses.

See also NEAP.

Novell BorderManager A network protection package from Novell that provides a firewall, circuit-level gateways, proxy services, and Internet access.

Novell Certified Internet Professional Abbreviated NCIP. A certification system from Novell structured for professionals who design, build, and maintain Web sites. The following specializations are available: Internet Business Strategist, Web Designer, Intranet Manager, Internet Architect, and Web Developer.

Novell Connect An add-on product from Novell that allows remote users to dial in and access network resources.

See also Novell Connect Services,

Novell Connect Services A collection of network products from Novell that are designed to simplify WAN administration; includes Novell NetWare, Novell Directory Services, ManageWise, Novell Connect, and NetWare Multiprotocol Router.

Novell Directory Services Abbreviated NDS. A distributed directory system from Novell, similar in scope and concept to the X.500 directory services specification.

Originally designed for use with Novell NetWare, NDS is now available for several other platforms, including Microsoft Windows NT.

263

NDS uses a distributed database known as the NetWare Directory Database (NDD) to keep track of all network objects, including servers, users, groups, printers, and other networked resources. This information is presented to the user as a collection of containers, arranged in a hierarchical structure according to the organization or corporation structure, and is known as the Directory Tree or simply as the Directory.

Users no longer log in to a single server; they are authenticated by the network through NDS.

See also container object; leaf object; Root object.

Novell Distributed Print Services   Abbreviated NDPS. A set of printer services available for Novell NetWare that standardizes and centralizes use and management of printers and printing on a network.

NDPS was developed jointly by Novell, Xerox, and Hewlett-Packard and allows bidirectional communications with newer printers, supports drag-and-drop printing for text and PostScript files without opening the creating application, and supports ISO 10175 Document Printing Architecture, Simple Network Management Protocol (SNMP), Management Information Base (MIB), and automatically downloadable printer drivers.

Networked printers are administered using the NetWare Administrator program.

Novell Education Academic Partner   Abbreviated NEAP. A college or university that provides Novell-approved training courses as a part of its standard curriculum.

See also Novell Authorized Education Center.

Novell GroupWise   A groupware software package from Novell that includes e-mail, group scheduling, task management, personal calendaring, document management, workflow routing, and support for threaded discussions.

GroupWise also includes Internet Mail Access Protocol (IMAP), Post Office Protocol 3 (POP3), and Lightweight Directory Access Protocol (LDAP) support.

Novell, Inc.   A leading developer of network operating system software, groupware, network management tools, Internet and intranet tools, and security products, based in Orem, Utah.

Best known for its Novell NetWare network operating systems, Novell is moving toward more open systems, the Internet, and corporate intranets and sees Novell Directory Services (NDS) as a significant advance in this direction.

For more information on Novell, see www.novell.com.

Novell IntraNetWare   An intranet software package from Novell that includes the NetWare operating system, the Netscape Navigator Web browser, the NetWare Web server, the Multiprotocol Router (MPR), Novell Directory Services (NDS), and the

IPX/IP Gateway—also known as Novell Internet Access Server (NAIS).

Novell LANalizer   A network monitoring and analysis package from Novell used for troubleshooting Ethernet and token-ring networks.

Novell ManageWise   A software package from Novell for managing NetWare and Microsoft Windows NT servers. ManageWise includes server and desktop management, network analysis, software management, virus protection, and automatic network inventory. ManageWise replaces NetWare Management System on Novell servers.

See also Novell Z.E.N.works.

Novell NDS for NT   An add-on product for Microsoft Windows NT Server from Novell that allows the integration of Windows NT domains with Novell Directory Services (NDS) and their joint management from within NetWare Administrator.

Novell NetWare   A general term for the family of network operating systems available from Novell.

Novell NetWare 3.x   A 32-bit network operating system that is designed to take advantage of the features of the Intel 80386 (and later) processors and is suitable for larger, multisegment networks, with up to 250 nodes per server.

NetWare 3.x provides enhanced security, performance, and flexibility and can access up to 4GB of RAM and up to 32TB of storage. A maximum of 100,000 files can be open concurrently on the file server, and

the maximum file size is 4GB. Disk mirroring, disk duplexing, support for optical disks, and UPS-monitoring functions are all available.

Novell NetWare 4.x   A 32-bit network operating system from Novell announced in 1993 that builds on the successes of Novell NetWare 3.x.

Its most significant feature was the inclusion of Novell Directory Services (NDS), which allowed system administrators to organize users and network resources such as printers and servers the way people naturally access them. NDS is based on the CCITT X.500 directory standard and replaces the bindery database in earlier versions of NetWare.

NetWare 4.x also adds support for optical disks, CD-ROMs, data compression, and improved login security mechanisms. NetWare 4.1 is the first version of NetWare to integrate Message Handling Service with the directory, and it also adds System Fault Tolerance. NetWare 4.x is suitable for larger, multisegment internetworks, supporting up to 1000 nodes per server. It includes a set of user and administrator utilities featuring a graphical user interface, and it is available in several languages.

Novell NetWare 4.x SFT III   A network software package from Novell that provides fault tolerance and protects against downtime by integrating two physically separate servers; if one of the servers fails for whatever reason, the other takes over and continues to support users.

Novell NetWare 5   A 32-bit network operating system from Novell. NetWare 5 continues Novell's transition into open systems, with native TCP/IP support, a Java Virtual Machine that runs on the server, and an enhanced file system.

Improvements have been made to Novell Directory Services (NDS), including the addition of Lightweight Directory Access Protocol (LADP), as well as to the Remote Access Services for dial-in users. NetWare 5 also includes WAN Traffic Manager, Secure Sockets Layer (SSL), Novell's Public Key Infrastructure Services, Storage Management Services, Netscape's FastTrack Web server, DNS/DHCP services, and a Z.E.N.works starter pack.

Novell NetWare Connect   *See* NetWare Internet Access Server.

Novell NetWare Navigator   An automated software distribution package from Novell.

Novell Support Connection   A technical information service available by subscription from Novell.

Two update CDs in a searchable format are issued periodically, containing all the latest files, patches, device drivers, and technical information, including product documentation, Novell Appnotes, Novell Developer Notes, and Novell Labs Certification Bulletins.

Novell Z.E.N.works   A software management package from Novell that provides desktop management, including hardware inventory, and adds flexibility to the desktop policy capabilities built into Microsoft Windows. Z.E.N.works can also control the applications a client can run and can operate the client remotely.

Z.E.N.works maintains a hardware inventory for each client, which is updated each time the client logs on to the network, and includes the desktop operating system, the amount of RAM in the workstation, the capacity of the local hard disk, and any connected peripherals.

Z.E.N.works also removes the need to log on twice—once to the operating system and once to the network—under Windows.

See also Novell ManageWise.

NPA   *See* NetWare Peripheral Architecture.

ns   *See* nanosecond.

NSAP   *See* Network Service Access Point.

NTFS   *See* New Technology File System.

NT File System   See New Technology File System.

NUI   *See* NetWare Users International.

null   A character that has all the binary digits set to zero (ASCII 0) and therefore has no value.

In programming, a null character is used for several special purposes, including padding fields or serving as a delimiter character. In the C programming language, for example, a null character indicates the end of a character string.

null modem A short serial cable that connects two personal computers so that they can communicate without the use of modems.

The cable connects the two computers' serial ports, and certain lines in the cable are crossed over so that the wires used for sending by one computer are used for receiving data by the other computer.

See also modem eliminator.

NWADMIN A Novell NetWare workstation utility that provides most of the functions needed to administer a Novell NetWare network.

Referred to as the Network Administrator in the Novell documentation, NWADMIN

allows you to create users and groups, create, move, delete, and rename Novell Directory Services (NDS) objects, and manage NDS partitions and volumes.

NWLink IPX/SPX In Microsoft Windows NT, a protocol that implements Novell's IPX/SPX protocol.

See also Internetwork Packet eXchange; Sequenced Packet Exchange.

NWLink NetBIOS In Microsoft Windows NT, a protocol that enables Novell NetBIOS packets to be sent between a Novell server running NetBIOS and a Windows NT computer.

See also network basic input/output system.

NULL MODEM

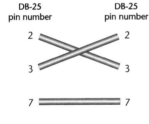

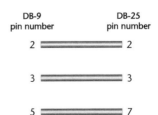

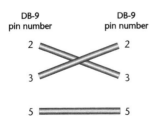

NWPA   *See* NetWare Peripheral Architecture.

NWUSER   A Novell NetWare workstation utility that lets users display or modify their workstation's drive mappings, server attachments, and print queues using a simple graphical user interface.

Object   **1.** In Novell Directory Services (NDS), a representation of a logical or physical network resource, including users, computers, and printers. An Object has both properties and values and may be a Root, leaf, or container object.

2. In Microsoft's Active Directory, a representation of a network resource, including users, computers, and printers. Objects contain properties for definition and configuration.

See also Active Directory; container object; leaf object; Organizational Unit; Root object; Schema.

object   **1.** Any distinct entity. Program objects can represent applications such as word processors, spreadsheets, and so on. Folder objects can represent a directory and contain a group of files, a group of programs, or a group of other folders. Data-file objects can include information such as text, memos, letters, spreadsheets, video, and sound. Device objects can be printers, fax modems, plotters, servers, and CD-ROMS.

2. In Object Linking and Embedding (OLE), an object can be any user-selected group of data, such as a block of text, a set of spreadsheet cells, a chart, a sound, or a graphical image. This data can be embedded in or linked to another document created by a different OLE application.

3. In object-oriented programming, a program consists of a set of related but self-contained objects that can contain both code and data.

See also container object; leaf object; NetWare Directory Services.

Object Linking and Embedding   Abbreviated OLE, pronounced "oh-lay." A Microsoft protocol for application-to-application exchange and communications using data objects. From a user standpoint, the main benefit to OLE is that it allows any OLE-compliant application to display information created in a different application.

Data objects can be either embedded or linked. If the source data in its original form is actually stored inside the other application program's data file, the data is embedded. In this case, there are two separate copies of the data: the original data and the embedded copy. Any changes made to the original document will not be made in the compound document unless the embedded object is updated.

If the data still exists in a separate file and a set of pointers to this data is stored in the other application program's data file, the data is linked. In this case, only one copy of the data exists; any changes made in the original document will be made automatically in the compound document.

To determine whether an application supports OLE, check the Edit menu for commands such as Paste Link, Paste Special, and Insert Object. If these commands are present, the application supports OLE.

See also OpenDoc.

object-oriented   An over-used term that can be applied to any computer system, operating system, programming language, application, or graphical user interface that supports the use of objects.

See also object-oriented programming.

object-oriented graphics   Graphics that are constructed from individual components, such as lines, arcs, circles, and squares.

The image is defined mathematically rather than as a set of dots, as in a bitmapped graphic. Object-oriented graphics are used in illustration, drawing, and CAD (computer-aided design) programs and are also known as vector graphics or structured graphics.

Object-oriented graphics allow the user to manipulate a part of an image without redrawing. Unlike bitmapped graphics, all or parts of object-oriented graphics can be resized or rotated without introducing any distortion.

object-oriented programming   Abbreviated OOP. A programming model that views a program as a set of self-contained objects.

These objects interact with other objects by passing messages. Object-oriented programming also lets you create procedures that work with objects whose exact type may not be known until the program actually runs.

In object-oriented programming, each object contains both data and code and is completely self-contained. The program incorporates an object by making it part of a layered hierarchy. Object-oriented programming is the result of many years of theoretical development, and many consider it the current extension of the theory behind modular programming, in which code is combined into reusable modules.

Object Request Broker   Abbreviated ORB. A communications mechanism used in an object-oriented distributed computing environment in which program modules can be written in any programming language and still provide services to other applications.

An object makes a request and sends it to the ORB. The ORB locates the requested object and establishes communications between client and server. The receiving object then responds to the request and sends a response to the ORB, which, in turn, sends the response to the original requester.

The physical location of the object that provides the response is unimportant, and to the user, the application appears seamless, even though the various services may be coming from several different parts of the network.

The ORB standard is defined by the Object Management Group, an industry consortium developing middleware standards based on distributed-object architecture.

See also Common Object Request Broker Architecture; Distributed Component Object Model; middleware.

object rights In Novell Directory Services (NDS), rights granted to a trustee over an object. For example, the Create object right for a container object allows a trustee to create new objects in that container.

See also Object.

OC *See* Optical Carrier.

occupant In Novell Directory Services (NDS), a user who has been assigned to an Organizational Role object. Each Organizational Role object can have multiple occupants.

OCR *See* optical character recognition.

octet The Internet's own term for a unit of data containing exactly eight bits. Some of the computer systems attached to the Internet use bytes with more than eight bits; hence, the need for this term.

See also byte.

ODBC *See* Open Database Connectivity.

odd parity *See* parity.

ODI *See* Open Data-link Interface.

ODI/NDIS Support *See* Open Data-link Interface/Network Driver Interface Specification Support.

ODINSUP *See* Open Data-link Interface/ Network Driver Interface Specification Support.

ODSI *See* Open Directory Services Interface.

OEM *See* original equipment manufacturer.

offline Describes any device that is not in ready mode and is therefore unavailable for use.

See also online.

offline reader An application that lets you read postings to Usenet newsgroups without having to stay connected to the Internet.

The program downloads all the newsgroup postings you have not read and disconnects from your Internet Service Provider. You can then read the postings at your convenience without incurring online charges or tying up your telephone line. If you reply to any of these postings, the program will automatically upload them to the correct newsgroup the next time you connect to your service provider.

See also newsgroup; newsreader; Usenet.

OLAP *See* online analytical processing.

OLE *See* Object Linking and Embedding.

OLTP *See* online transaction processing.

online 1. Most broadly, any work done on a computer instead of by more traditional manual means.

2. Any function available directly on a computer, such as an application's help system.

3. Describes a peripheral device, such as a printer or a modem, when it is directly connected to a computer and ready to operate.

O

4. In communications, describes a computer connected to a remote computer over a network or a modem link.

See also offline.

online analytical processing Abbreviated OLAP. A category of software used to analyze historical business data to find previously hidden patterns.

Analysts use OLAP software to view data in a multidimensional form, rather than in the more usual two-dimensional row and column format. In a multidimensional format, the intersection of important data is much more obvious, and data is easier to group and categorize.

See also data mining; data warehousing.

online service A service that provides an online connection via modem for access to various services. Online services fall into these main groups:

- **Commercial services** Services such as America Online charge a monthly membership fee for access to online forums, e-mail services, software libraries, and online conferences.

- **Internet** The Internet is a worldwide network of computer systems and is not always easy to use, but the wealth of information available is staggering. The main problem for casual users is that there is no central listing of everything that is available.

- **Specialist databases** Specific databases aimed at researchers can be accessed through online services such as Dow Jones News/Retrieval for business news and

Lexis and Nexis for legal information and news archives.

online transaction processing Abbreviated OLTP. A business system that operates in real time, collecting and posting transaction-related data and making changes to shared databases.

A transaction is a single, discrete unit of work, which is normally part of a business process. Examples of OLTP systems include airline and hotel reservation systems, inventory control systems, and banking systems.

See also transaction processing.

OOP *See* object-oriented programming.

open architecture A vendor-independent design that is publicly available and well understood within the industry.

See also closed architecture.

Open Database Connectivity Abbreviated ODBC. An application program interface (API) from Microsoft that allows a single application to access many types of database and file formats.

ODBC uses Structured Query Language (SQL) for operations that access a database, and the client does not need to know the location of the database or its type or the method used to access the data; all these details are managed by ODBC. Data sources can range from a simple spreadsheet all the way up to very large relational databases.

Open Data-link Interface Abbreviated ODI. A Novell specification, released in 1989, that allows multiple network interface card device drivers and protocols to share a single network interface card without conflict.

ODI defines an interface that separates device drivers from protocol stacks and lets multiple protocol stacks share the same network hardware. Here are the main components:

- The multiple-link interface driver (MLID) manages the sending and receiving of packets to and from the network.

- The link-support layer (LSL) is the interface layer between the device driver and the protocol stacks. Any ODI LAN driver can communicate with any ODI protocol stack via the LSL.

- The MLI (Multiple-Link Interface) communicates with the network interface cards through an MLID and consists of three main components:

  - The media-support module (MSM), which manages the details of interfacing ODI MLIDs to the LSL and to the operating system.

  - The hardware-specific module (HSM), which is specific to a particular network interface card. It handles adapter initialization, reset, shutdown, packet reception, timeout detection, and multicast addressing.

  - The topology-specific module (TSM), which manages operations that are specific to a particular media type, such as Ethernet or token ring.

See also Network Driver Interface Specification; Open Data-link Interface/Network Driver Interface Specification Support.

Open Data-link Interface/Network Driver Interface Specification Support

Abbreviated ODINSUP; also written as ODI/NDIS Support. A Novell interface that allows the coexistence of two network driver interfaces:

- Microsoft's NDIS (Network Driver Interface Specification)

- Novell's ODI (Open Data-link Interface)

ODINSUP allows an MS-DOS or Microsoft Windows workstation to connect to dissimilar networks through a single network interface card and to use them as if they were a single network.

ODINSUP also allows NDIS protocol stacks to communicate through the ODI's link-support layer (LSL) and multiple-link interface driver (MLID) so that ODI and NDIS protocol stacks can coexist in the same system, using a single ODI MLID.

Open Desktop   A graphical user interface from SCO that provides access to files and system utility functions on the desktop. Files, directories, and applications are represented by icons and displayed in windows.

See also OpenServer; Santa Cruz Operation, Inc.; UnixWare.

Open Directory Services Interface

Abbreviated ODSI. A standard from Microsoft that enables client software to query Internet directories by providing a common API for naming.

O

OPEN DATA-LINK INTERFACE

OpenDoc   A specification for creating compound documents, from Apple, IBM, Borland, and Novell. OpenDoc manages text, spreadsheets, graphics, sound, and video as objects that can be created in one application and then inserted into another.

OpenDoc is similar in many respects to Microsoft's Object Linking and Embedding (OLE) specification, but OpenDoc provides for greater network support and also includes a certification process to ensure that applications work together.

OpenGL   *See* Open Graphics Library.

Open Graphics Library   Abbreviated OpenGL. A set of graphics libraries originally developed by Silicon Graphics and now supported by IBM, Intel, Microsoft, and many other companies.

OpenGL lets developers create 3-D graphical applications for workstations running the Programmers Hierarchical Interactive

Graphics System (PHiGS) extensions to the X Window system.

See also X Window.

Open Group   An international consortium of vendors, educational institutions, and government agencies that develops standards for open systems. Formed in 1996 as an umbrella organization to bring together the Open Software Foundation (OSF) and X/Open Company Limited.

For more information on Open Group, see www.opengroup.com.

OpenServer   A scalable set of Unix-based products from SCO, including the Desktop System, Host System, and Enterprise System, based on SVR2 but containing many significant SVR4 enhancements.

The Desktop System is a single-user, multi-tasking system with MS-DOS and Windows emulations, TCP/IP, and Internet connectivity.

The Host and Enterprise systems provide high-performance scalable servers for Intel-based platforms, supporting more than 8,000 applications, and with extensive networking support, UPS (uninterruptible power supply), and advanced power management support.

See also Open Desktop.

Open Shortest Path First   Abbreviated OSPF. A routing protocol used on TCP/IP networks that takes into account network loading and bandwidth when routing information over the network. Routers maintain a map of the network and swap information on the current status of each network link. OSPF incorporates least-cost routing, equal-cost routing, and load balancing.

See also Routing Information Protocol.

open source software   Any software package that includes the original source code from which the product was originally created.

Open source software allows knowledgeable users to make changes to the way the software actually works, unlike products from mainstream software developers which never include the source code. And while this mainstream software is certainly configurable, it is basically a take-it-or-leave-it package.

See also Free Software Foundation; Linux.

Open Systems Interconnect   *See* OSI Reference Model.

OpenView   A popular network management package from Hewlett-Packard that includes Network Node Manager, Event Correlation Services, a Java-based Web user interface, Open Database Connectivity (ODBC) integration, and other support services. OpenView is available on HP-UX, a Unix variant, and on Microsoft Windows NT.

operating system   Abbreviated OS. The software responsible for allocating system resources, including memory, processor time, disk space, and peripheral devices such as printers, modems, and monitors. All applications use the operating system to gain access to these resources as necessary. The operating system is the first program loaded into the computer as it boots, and it remains in memory throughout the session.

See also kernel; microkernel; network operating system.

Optical Carrier   Abbreviated OC. A set of Synchronous Optical Network (SONET) hierarchies that define how digital signals are multiplexed over fiber-optic cable.

SONET is the physical-layer standard used by telephone carriers to connect long-distance services. Table O.1 lists the OC levels and related data rates.

See also digital signal; Synchronous Optical Network; Synchronous Digital Hierarchy.

O

optical character recognition

TABLE O.1 OC LEVELS

OC Level	Data Rate (Mbps)
OC-1	51.84
OC-3	155.52
OC-6	311.04
OC-9	466.56
OC-12	622.08
OC-18	933.12
OC-24	1244.16
OC-36	1866.24
OC-48	2488.32
OC-96	4976.00
OC-192	9952.00

optical character recognition Abbreviated OCR. The computer recognition of printed or typed characters. OCR is usually performed using a standard optical scanner and special software, although some systems use special readers. The text is reproduced just as though it had been typed. Certain advanced systems can even resolve neatly handwritten characters.

See also document management.

optical drive A high-capacity disk-storage device that uses a laser to read and write information.

Because optical drives are relatively slow, they are used for archiving information and for other applications for which high access speed is not critical.

See also high-capacity storage system; jukebox; Magneto-optical storage.

Oracle Corporation   A major developer of powerful relational database software, client/server development tools, and other related products for multiuser enterprise computing.

For more information on Oracle, see www.oracle.com.

Oracle NCA   *See* Oracle Network Computing Architecture.

Oracle Network Computing Architecture   Abbreviated Oracle NCA. A set of technologies from Oracle Corporation designed to allow clients to access information from Web servers, database servers, and other systems. NCA includes open Internet standards and special components called *cartridges* that provide a connection between proprietary applications.

Orange Book   Lay term for the National Security Agency document called "Trusted Computer System Evaluation Criteria," or TCSEC, which specifies security levels that vendors must comply with to achieve Department of Defense security standards; so called because of the color of its cover.

This publication details standards for security levels used to control access to computer systems from Class A1, the highest verifiable security level, to Class D, the lowest, which has no security.

Class C2 is the security level most appropriate to the business world; higher levels of security tend to intrude too much into normal commercial working patterns. C2 security requires that the operating system provide individual logins with separate accounts and a verifiable audit trail, that re-

sources have owners, and that files and other system resources be protected from other processes that might corrupt them.

According to the standard, a C2 compliant workstation cannot be connected to a network. Secure networking is defined in "Trusted Network Interpretation," which is known as the Red Book.

See also security.

ORB   *See* Object Request Broker.

Organization object   In Novell Directory Services (NDS), a container object below the Country object and above the Organizational Unit object that helps to organize other objects in the tree. You must have at least one Organization object, usually the name of your company or department, and you can use multiple Organization objects if you wish.

See also leaf object; Novell Directory Services.

Organizational Role object   In Novell Directory Services (NDS), a container object used to specify a role within an organization such as Workgroup Leader or Department Manager who has access to certain NDS objects or files. The Organizational Role object is often used for container administrators.

See also occupant.

Organizational Unit   In Microsoft's Active Directory, an object that can contain other objects, such as other Organizational Units, users, groups, or Distributed File System (DFS) shares.

See also Active Directory.

Organizational Unit object In Novell Directory Services (NDS), a container object below the Organization object. The Organizational Unit object can contain other Organizational Unit objects or leaf objects. This container is not a required container, but its use allows better management of workgroups or project teams.

original equipment manufacturer Abbreviated OEM. The original manufacturer of a hardware subsystem or component. For example, Canon makes the print engine used in many laser printers, including those from Hewlett-Packard (HP); in this case, Canon is the OEM, and HP is a value-added reseller (VAR).

OS *See* operating system.

OS/2 A 32-bit multitasking operating system from IBM that runs on Intel processors.

OS/2 was developed jointly by Microsoft and IBM as the successor to MS-DOS, with Windows as a stop-gap measure until OS/2 was ready. When Microsoft chose to back Windows, placing considerable resources behind the breakthrough release of Windows 3, IBM took control of OS/2 development.

The current version of OS/2 Warp includes voice-recognition software, Internet access, and peer-to-peer networking. It supports Novell Directory Services (NDS) and includes IBM Personal Communications/3270, a package used to communicate with Systems Network Architecture (SNA) systems over TCP/IP networks.

IBM's server for network environments is OS/2 Warp Server.

OS/2 client Any computer running OS/2 that connects to a network server. OS/2 client workstations support TCP/IP, IPX/SPX, NetBIOS, and named pipes.

OS/2 Warp Server A network operating system, based on LAN Server 4, from IBM. It provides network services, system management services, remote access, standard file-sharing and network print services, support for up to 1,000 users, and secure Internet access.

As an application server, OS/2 Warp Server supports Microsoft Windows and Windows NT applications and can support OS/2, MS-DOS, Windows, Windows NT, AIX, and Macintosh clients. All the important network protocols are available, including TCP/IP, NetBIOS, and IPX.

OSF Abbreviation for Open Software Foundation. *See* Open Group.

OSI Reference Model A networking reference model defined by the ISO (International Organization for Standardization) that divides computer-to-computer communications into seven connected layers. Such layers are known as a protocol stack.

Each successively higher layer builds on the functions of the layers below, as follows:

- **Application layer 7** The highest level of the model. It defines the manner in which applications interact with the network, including database management, e-mail, and terminal-emulation programs.

- **Presentation layer 6** Defines the way in which data is formatted, presented, converted, and encoded.

- **Session layer 5** Coordinates communications and maintains the session for as long as it is needed, performing security, logging, and administrative functions.

- **Transport layer 4** Defines protocols for structuring messages and supervises the validity of the transmission by performing some error checking.

- **Network layer 3** Defines protocols for data routing to ensure that the information arrives at the correct destination node.

- **Data-link layer 2** Validates the integrity of the flow of data from one node to another by synchronizing blocks of data and controlling the flow of data.

- **Physical layer 1** Defines the mechanism for communicating with the transmission medium and interface hardware.

OSPF *See* Open Shortest Path First.

OSx A version of Unix from Pyramid Technology that includes elements of both AT&T and BSD systems.

THE OSI REFERENCE MODEL

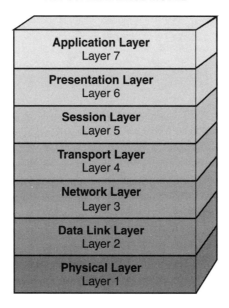

out-of-band signaling The transmission of control information on frequencies outside the bandwidth available for a voice or data transfer. The separation is usually accomplished by means of a filter.

output Computer-generated information that is displayed on the screen, printed, written to disk or tape, or sent over a communications link to another computer.

See also input/output.

outsourcing To subcontract a company's data processing operations to outside contractors rather than maintain corporate hardware, software, and staff. Outsourcing is often used as a cost-cutting mechanism, although the cost savings can be difficult to quantify.

See also downsizing.

oversampling A time-division multiplexing (TDM) technique in which each bit from each channel is sampled more than once.

See also time-division multiplexing.

P *See* peta-.

PABX *See* private automatic branch exchange.

PACE *See* Priority Access Control Enabled.

Packard Bell NEC Major manufacturer of PCs and servers; manages all NEC Corporation's computer manufacturing outside Japan. Packard Bell has recently established a configure-it-yourself direct sales promotion known as NEC Now.

For more information on Packard-Bell, see www.packardbell.com.

See also NEC Corporation.

packet Any block of data sent over a network or communications link.

Each packet may contain sender, receiver, and error-control information, in addition to the actual message, which may be data, connection management controls, or a request for a service. Packets may be fixed- or variable-length, and they will be reassembled if necessary when they reach their destination. The actual format of a packet depends on the protocol that creates the packet; some protocols use special packets to control communications functions in addition to data packets.

See also datagram; frame; packet switching.

packet assembler/disassembler Abbreviated PAD. A device that is connected to a packet-switched network and that converts a serial data stream from a character-oriented device, such as a bridge or a router, into packets suitable for transmission. It also disassembles packets back into characters for transmission to the character device. PADs are often used to connect a terminal or computer to an X.25 packet-switched network.

Packet Burst Protocol Abbreviated PBP. A Novell NetWare protocol built on top of IPX that speeds up the transfer of multipacket NetWare Core Protocol (NCP) data transfers between a workstation and a server by removing the need to sequence and acknowledge every packet. Using PBP, a workstation or server can transmit a burst of packets before requiring an acknowledgment, thus reducing network traffic.

See also Internetwork Packet eXchange.

packet filtering A process used by bridges to limit protocol-specific traffic to one segment of the network, to isolate e-mail domains, and to perform other traffic-control functions. The network administrator sets the packet-filtering specifications for each bridge. If a packet matches the specifications, the bridge can either accept it or reject it.

See also application-level filter; firewall.

packet-level filter   A category of firewall that provides a high degree of convenience, but a relatively low level of security.

A packet-level filter blocks or forwards a packet solely on its merits, without taking into account past history; the filter may also look at the source and destination address information contained in the packet.

This kind of filter is easy to implement, has little effect on network operations, but can be bypassed by encapsulating a blocked protocol within an allowed protocol.

See also application-level filter; firewall.

Packet-level Procedure   Abbreviated PAP. An X.25 full-duplex protocol for the transfer of packets between a computer and a modem.

packet signature   *See* NCP packet signature.

packet sniffer   A program used by an intruder to monitor a data stream for a pattern such as a password or credit card number.

Packet sniffers also have a more salutary purpose when used for network analysis and troubleshooting by the system administrator.

See also network analyzer; protocol analyzer.

packet-switched network   A network that consists of a series of interconnected circuits that route individual packets of data over one of several routes, offering flexibility and high reliability.

A packet-switched network may also be called connectionless because it contains many different possible connections and routes that a packet might take to reach its destination.

The term often refers to networks using the international standard X.25.

See also packet switching.

packet switching   A data-transmission method that simultaneously routes and transmits data packets from many customers over a communications channel or telephone line, thus optimizing use of the line.

An addressed packet is routed from node to node until it reaches its destination, although related packets may not all follow the same route to that destination. Because long messages may be divided into several packets, packet sequence numbers are used to reassemble the original message at the destination node.

The standard for packet-switching networks is defined in CCITT recommendation X.25. The Internet is an example of a packet-switching network.

See also Consultative Committee for International Telephony and Telegraphy; packet-switched network.

PAD   *See* packet assembler/disassembler.

page   A single document available on the World Wide Web or on a corporate intranet. A page can contain any combination of text, graphics, animated graphics, audio, and video and can be static or dynamic.

See also HyperText Markup Language.

page-mode RAM   A memory-management technique used to speed up the performance of dynamic RAM (DRAM).

In a page-mode memory system, the memory is divided into pages by specialized DRAM chips. Consecutive accesses to memory addresses in the same page result in a page-mode cycle that takes about half the time of a regular DRAM cycle.

paged memory management unit
Abbreviated PMMU. A specialized chip designed to manage virtual memory. High-end processors, such as the Motorola 68040 and the Intel Pentium, have all the functions of a PMMU built into the chip itself.

See also virtual memory.

PalmPilot   The hand-held computer from 3Com Corporation, which has proved to be extremely popular, with more than 1 million units sold to date.

See also 3Com Corporation.

PAP   *See* Packet-level Procedure; Password Authentication Protocol; Printer Access Protocol.

parallel communications   The transmission of information from computer to computer or from computer to peripheral device, in which all the bits that make up the character are transmitted at the same time over a multiline cable.

See also serial communications.

parallel port   An input/output (I/O) port that manages information eight bits at a time; often used to connect a parallel printer.

See also parallel communications; RS-232-C; serial communications; serial port.

parallel processing   A computing method that can be performed by systems containing two or more processors operating simultaneously. In parallel processing, all processors work on different aspects of the same program at the same time, in order to share the computational load.

Parallel-processing computers can achieve incredible speeds. The Cray X-MP48 peaks at 1000 million floating-point operations per second (1000 MFLOP) using four extremely powerful processors, and parallel-hypercube systems, first marketed by Intel, can exceed 65,536 processors with speeds of up to 262 billion floating-point operations per second (262 GFLOP).

In all but the most trivial parallel-processing applications, the programmer or the operating system must assign approximate processor loads; otherwise, it is possible for non-optimized systems to fail to take advantage of the power available and, in the worst case, run more slowly than on single-processor systems.

All this speed is used for applications such as weather forecasting, in which the predictive programs can take as long to run as the weather actually takes to arrive, 3-D seismic modeling, groundwater and toxic flow studies, and the modeling of full-motion dinosaur images used in movies.

See also asymmetrical multiprocessing; symmetrical multiprocessing.

parent directory   In a hierarchical directory system, such as that used by MS-DOS,

P

283

OS/2, Windows, and Unix, the directory immediately above the current directory. The special symbol .. is shorthand for the name of the parent directory.

See also period and double-period directories.

parent object   In Novell Directory Services (NDS), an object that contains another object. This term is relative, because any particular parent object also has parent objects of its own and can be considered a child object from a certain perspective.

parity   In communications, a simple form of error checking that uses an extra or redundant bit after the data bits but before the stop bit or bits. Parity may be set as follows:

- **Odd**   Indicates that the sum of all the 1 bits in the byte plus the parity bit must be odd. If the total is already odd, the parity bit is set to zero; if it is even, the parity bit is set to one.

- **Even**   If the sum of all the 1 bits is even, the parity bit must be set to zero; if it is odd, the parity bit must be set to one.

- **Mark**   The parity bit is always set to one and is used as the eighth bit.

- **Space**   The parity bit is set to zero and is used as the eighth bit.

- **None**   If parity is set to none, there is no parity bit, and no parity checking is performed.

The parity settings used by both communicating computers must match. Most online services, such as CompuServe or America Online, use no parity and an 8-bit data word.

See also asynchronous transmission; parity checking; parity error.

parity bit   An extra or redundant bit used to detect data transmission errors.

See also parity.

parity checking   A check mechanism applied to a character or a series of characters that uses the addition of extra or redundant parity bits.

Parity checking is useful for a variety of purposes, including asynchronous communications and computer memory coordination.

See also parity.

parity error   A mismatch in parity bits that indicates an error in transmitted data.

See also parity.

partition   1. A portion of a hard disk that the operating system treats as if it were a separate drive. In Windows, a hard disk can be divided into several partitions. A primary partition, generally assigned the drive letter C, might contain files that start the computer. You could also create a non-Windows partition and use it for a different operating system. In Novell NetWare, a server must have a NetWare partition defined in order to function as a part of the NetWare file system. Other partitions can manage file systems used by other operating systems.

2. In Novell NetWare, a grouping or collection of objects in the Novell Directory Services (NDS) database. Each partition consists of a container object, all the objects in it, and data about all those objects. Partitions do not include any information about the file system or the directories or files contained there. The data in a partition is also known as a replica.

See also disk mirroring; leaf object; replica; replication; Root object; volume.

partition table   **1.** An area of storage on a hard disk that contains information about the partitions the disk contains. This information is usually recorded during the initial preparation of the hard disk before it is formatted.

2. In Novell Directory Services (NDS), a list on each server containing the NDS replicas. For each replica on the server, the partition table contains the partition name, type, time stamp, and partition state.

passive hub   A device used in some networks to split a transmission signal, allowing additional hubs to be added to the network, sometimes at the expense of distance.

See also active hub.

passive termination   A method used to terminate a Small Computer System Interface (SCSI) chain of devices. Passive termination is a simple termination method that works best with four or fewer devices on a SCSI daisy chain.

See also active termination; forced perfect termination; Small Computer System Interface.

pass-through authentication   In Microsoft Windows NT, an authentication method used when the user account must be authenticated, but the computer used for the logon is neither the domain controller for the account nor the computer on which the user account is defined. In such a case, the computer used for the logon passes the logon information through to the domain controller where the user account is defined.

See also domain; domain controller; user account.

password   A security method that identifies a specific, authorized user of a computer system, a network, or a resource by a unique string of characters.

In general, passwords should be a mixture of upper- and lowercase letters and numbers and should be more than six characters. Here are some general guidelines:

- Passwords should be kept secret and changed frequently. The worst passwords are the obvious ones: people's names or initials, place names, phone numbers, birth dates, and anything to do with computers or Star Trek. There are a limited number of words in the English language, and it is easy for a computer to try them all relatively quickly.

- Change all passwords every 90 days, and change those associated with high-security privileges every month. Some network operating systems require that passwords expire even more frequently. For example, in NetWare 5, passwords expire after 40 days by default.

- Some systems provide default passwords, such as MANAGER, SERVICE, or GUEST, as part of the installation process. These default passwords should be changed immediately.

- Limit concurrent sessions to one per system.

- Do not allow more than two or three invalid password attempts before disconnecting.

- Do not allow generic accounts.

- Promptly remove the accounts of transferred or terminated people, as well as all unused accounts.

- Review the security log files periodically.

See also authentication; Challenge-Handshake Authentication Protocol; Password Authentication Protocol.

Password Authentication Protocol Abbreviated PAP. A security protocol that requires a user to enter a user name and password before gaining access to a secure server.

See also Challenge-Handshake Authentication Protocol.

password encryption In certain operating systems, the password you enter to gain access to the system is not stored as ordinary text, but is encrypted, and this encrypted form is compared against the encrypted password stored on the server. If the two match, the logon continues; if not, the logon attempt is rejected.

See also Challenge-Handshake Authentication Protocol; Password Authentication Protocol.

password protection The use of one or more passwords to prevent unauthorized access to computer systems.

patch panel A panel, usually located in a wiring closet, that contains rows of telephone-type modular jacks. A patch panel allows the network administrator to connect, disconnect, move, and test network devices by changing these connections.

path The complete location of a directory or a file in the file system. Also called pathname or directory path.

See also Universal Naming Convention.

pathname *See* path.

Payload Type Identifier Abbreviated PTI. In an Asynchronous Transfer Mode (ATM) cell, a field contained in the 5-byte cell header that defines the type of information in the payload area, including user, network, and management information.

See also Cell Loss Priority; Header Error Control; Virtual Channel Identifier; Virtual Path Identifier.

PB *See* petabyte.

PBP *See* Packet Burst Protocol.

PBX *See* private branch exchange.

PC98 A personal computer design guide for 1998–99 from Intel, Microsoft, and others, covering the PC system, bus, and devices, including guidelines for various types of mobile PCs.

PC98 also describes requirements for manageability, remote boot support, and specifications for 1394. The basic PC98 should have no ISA (Industry Standard Architecture) devices; PC99 is expected to do away with ISA slots as well.

See also Advanced Configuration and Power Interface; Web-Based Enterprise Management; Wired for Management; Zero Administration for Windows.

PC-based router   A router, such as the NetWare Multiprotocol Router or Multiprotocol Router Plus, that operates on a standard Intel-based personal computer.

PC Card   A term that describes plug-in cards that conform to the PCMCIA (Personal Computer Memory Card International Association) standard. A PC Card is about the size of a credit card and uses a 68-pin connector with longer power and ground pins that will always engage before the signal pins engage.

Several versions of the standard have been approved by PCMCIA:

• **Type I**   The thinnest PC Card, only 3.3 millimeters (0.13 inch) thick, used for memory enhancements, including dynamic RAM, static RAM, and flash memory.

• **Type II**   A card used for modems or network interface cards, 5 millimeters (0.2 inch) thick; may also hold a Type I card.

• **Type III**   A 10.5 millimeter (0.4 inch) card, used for mini-hard disks and other devices that need more space, including wireless network interface cards; may also hold two Type I or Type II cards.

In theory, each PC Card adapter can support 16 PC Card sockets (if there is enough space), and as many as 255 adapters can be installed in a PC that follows the PCMCIA standard; in other words, PCMCIA allows a maximum of 4080 PC Cards on one computer.

Most PC Card devices are modems, Ethernet and token-ring network adapters, dynamic RAM, and flash memory cards, although mini-hard disks, wireless LAN adapters, and SCSI adapters are also available.

See also PC Memory Card International Association.

PC Card slot   An opening in the case of a portable computer, intended to receive a PC Card; also known as a PCMCIA slot.

PC Connection, Inc.   A direct marketer of PCs, peripherals, accessories, and networking products to the home, government, business, and educational markets. PC Connection was one of the first companies to provide overnight delivery of products and toll-free technical support.

For more information on PC Connection, see www.pcconnection.com.

PC-DOS   *See* Personal Computer Disk Operating System.

PCI local bus   *See* Peripheral Component Interconnect local bus.

PCI-X   A revision to the PCI standard proposed by IBM, Hewlett-Packard, and Compaq that increases the bus width to 64 bits, the bus speed to 133MHz, and the maximum throughput to 1GB per second. This revision is aimed at future workstation and server design.

Several vendors also offer hot-plug PCI slots that allow you to replace a failed component without a system reboot.

See also 1394; local bus; Peripheral Component Interconnect local bus; Plug and Play; Universal Serial Bus.

P

PCMCIA *See* PC Memory Card International Association.

PCMCIA slot *See* PC Card slot.

PC Memory Card International Association Abbreviated PCMCIA. A nonprofit association, formed in 1989, with more than 320 members in the computer and electronics industries, that developed a standard for credit-card-sized, plug-in adapters designed for portable computers.

PCONSOLE A Novell NetWare workstation utility used to set up and manage print queues and print servers on the network.

See also NetWare Administrator.

PCS *See* Personal Communications Services.

PC Service and Support Certified Professional A certification from Learning Tree designed for the technician. Courses and exams cover basic PC assembly and troubleshooting, installation and configuration of operating systems and peripherals, and optimization of networks.

PDA *See* personal digital assistant.

PDF *See* Portable Document Format.

PDN *See* private data network; public data network.

peer-to-peer architecture A network architecture in which two or more nodes can communicate with each other directly, without the need for any intermediary devices. In a peer-to-peer system, a node can be both a client and a server.

See also peer-to-peer network.

peer-to-peer network A LAN in which drives, files, and printers on each PC can be available to every other PC on the network, eliminating the need for a dedicated file server. Each PC can still run local applications.

Peer-to-peer networks introduce their own system management problems, including administration and responsibility for system backup, reliability, and security. Peer-to-peer systems are often used in relatively small networks, with two to ten users, and can be based on MS-DOS, Windows, or Unix. Performance is not usually as good on a peer-to-peer network as under the client/server model, especially under heavy traffic loads.

See also client/server architecture.

PEM *See* Privacy Enhanced Mail.

Pentium A family of microprocessors introduced by Intel in 1993. The Pentium represents the continuing evolution of the 80486 family of microprocessors and adds several notable features, including instruction code and data caches and a built-in floating-point processor and memory management unit. It also has a superscalar design and dual pipelining, which allow the Pentium to execute more than one instruction per clock cycle, a 32-bit address bus, and a 64-bit data bus.

Available in a range of clock speeds, from 60MHz all the way up to 233MHz, the Pentium is equivalent to 3.1 million transistors, more than twice that of the 80486.

See also Intel Corporation; Pentium II; Pentium III; Pentium Pro.

Pentium II   A family of microprocessors from Intel. The Pentium II represents the continuing evolution of the Pentium family of microprocessors and adds several notable features, including integrated L1/L2 caches of up to 2MB that can be accessed at the full clock speed and a built-in floating-point processor and memory management unit. It also has a superscalar design and dual pipelining, which allow the Pentium II to execute more than one instruction per clock cycle.

Available in a range of clock speeds, from 233MHz all the way up to 450MHz, the Pentium II can use a 100MHz system bus and is equivalent to 7.5 million transistors, more than twice that of the Pentium.

See also Intel Corporation; Pentium; Pentium Pro.

Pentium III   A family of microprocessors from Intel. The Pentium III represents the continuing evolution of the Pentium family of microprocessors and adds several notable features, including 50 new floating-point instructions and 8 new registers to speed up floating-point calculations in scientific and engineering calculations, along with 12 new multimedia instructions to increase MPEG-2 performance and speech recognition. The most controversial new feature is the processor serial number, designed to increase network and online shopping security, but feared by many as a threat to privacy.

Available in a whole range of clock speeds, initially from 450MHz to 500MHz versions, the Pentium III can use the Pentium II

100MHz system bus and is equivalent to 9.5 million transistors.

See also Intel Corporation; Pentium; Pentium II; Streaming SIMD Extensions.

Pentium Pro   A family of microprocessors introduced by Intel in 1995. The Pentium Pro is optimized for the execution of 32-bit software and is available with clock speeds from 150 to 200MHz. With a 32-bit data bus running at 60 or 66MHz, it supports superscalar architecture and pipelines and contains the equivalent of 5.5 million transistors.

Dynamic execution (a combination of branch prediction and speculative execution) allows the processor to anticipate and schedule the next instructions for execution. Pentium Pro offers up to 1MB of Level 2 cache that runs at the same speed as the processor.

See also Intel Corporation; Pentium; Pentium II.

PeopleSoft, Inc.   A major developer of large enterprise resource planning (ERP) applications for finance, materials and inventory management, distribution, human resources, and manufacturing, all within a single computing environment.

For more information on PeopleSoft, see `www.peoplesoft.com`.

Performance Monitor   In Microsoft Windows NT, a network and server monitoring tool that displays resource use for selected system-level components; you can also use Performance Monitor to troubleshoot performance problems and assess

P

hardware upgrade requirements. Information can be logged to a file for later analysis.

period   The . character; pronounced "dot." Used to indicate the name of the current directory in a pathname and to separate the elements in a domain name, as in www.sybex.com.

period and double-period directories

In a hierarchical directory system, a shorthand way of referring to directories. The period (.) represents the current directory, and the double period (..) represents the directory immediately above the current directory.

See also parent directory; root directory.

Peripheral Component Interconnect local bus

Abbreviated PCI local bus. A specification introduced by Intel in 1992 for a local bus that allows up to 10 PCI-compliant expansion cards to be plugged into the computer. One of these expansion cards must be the PCI controller card, but the others can include a video card, network interface card, SCSI interface, or any other basic function.

The PCI controller exchanges information with the computer's processor, either 32 or 64 bits at a time, and allows intelligent PCI adapters to perform certain tasks concurrently with the main processor by using bus-mastering techniques.

PCI is compatible with ISA (Industry Standard Architecture), EISA (Extended Industry Standard Architecture), and MCA (Microchannel Architecture) expansion buses for backward compatibility with older technologies. PCI can operate at a bus speed of 32MHz and can manage a maximum throughput of 132MBps with a 32-bit data path or a rate of 264MBps with a 64-bit data path.

See also 1394; local bus; PCI-X; Plug and Play; Universal Serial Bus.

Perl   Acronym formed from Practical Extraction and Report Language. Perl is an interpreted programming language developed by Larry Wall, used to manipulate text, files, and processes and to print reports on the extracted information.

Perl is rapidly becoming the system administrator's answer to all those problems that a C program does not seem to fit. It does not have the arbitrary limitations of other languages, so lines can be of any length, arrays can be of any size, variable names can be as long as you care to make them, and binary data does not cause problems.

permanent swap file   A swap file that, once created, is used over and over again. This file is used in virtual memory operations, in which hard-disk space is used in place of RAM.

See also temporary swap file.

permanent virtual circuit   Abbreviated PVC. A permanent communications circuit, created and maintained even when no data is being transmitted.

A PVC has no setup overhead and gives improved performance for periodic transmissions that require an immediate connection. Packets are transferred in order over a specific path and arrive at their destination in the same order.

See also switched virtual circuit.

permissions   In a network or multiuser environment, the ability of a user to access certain system resources, including files and directories. Permissions are based on the rights given to user accounts by the system administrator.

See also rights.

permuted index   A special kind of index used in several of the Unix system manuals. Many of the Unix manuals treat each command on a separate page, and these pages are not numbered continuously; they are numbered only within each command. This makes it easy to add or remove pages as requirements change, but it can make it difficult to find specific information. The permuted index is the solution.

The permuted index has three columns. The central column, where you start your search, is in alphabetical order. The column to the right lists the command that performs the function and the section number in the man pages where you will find a detailed description, and the column on the left contains additional keywords to help confirm that you have found the correct entry.

See also man pages.

Personal Communications Services
Abbreviated PCS. A digital wireless communications technology that includes voice, data, and video.

PCS competes with the traditional analog cellular phone system, but PCS's digital technology can provide clearer voice quality, better security through encryption, and lower costs, as well as additional services such as messaging, voice mail, and caller ID.

Personal Computer Disk Operating System   Abbreviated PC-DOS. The version of the DOS operating system supplied with PCs made by IBM.

PC-DOS and MS-DOS began as virtually identical operating systems, with only a few minor differences in device driver names and file sizes, but after the release of DOS 6 (MS-DOS 6.2 and PC-DOS 6.1), the two grew much further apart.

See also Microsoft Disk Operating System.

personal digital assistant   Abbreviated PDA. A tiny, pen-based, battery-powered computer that combines personal organization software with fax and e-mail facilities into a unit that fits into your pocket. PDAs are available from several manufacturers, including Apple's Newton, and others from 3Com, Casio, Tandy, Toshiba, Motorola, Sharp, Sony, GRiD, and AT&T.

Personal Information Manager   Abbreviated PIM. A multipurpose software package that combines a word processor, database, and other accessory modules to allow the user to manipulate data in a less structured way than required by conventional programs. A PIM can store notes, memos, names and addresses, appointments, and to-do lists, and it may be part of the software used in a PDA (personal digital assistant).

Personal NetWare   Novell's peer-to-peer network replacement for NetWare Lite, released in 1994, that provides MS-DOS and Microsoft Windows users with the ability to share files, printers, CD-ROMs, and other resources, as well as run standard network applications. Other features include simplified network administration, increased security, and a single login so that users can view or access all network resources at once.

Personal NetWare can manage a maximum of 50 workstations per server and a maximum of 50 servers on each network, giving a maximum of 2500 nodes per network.

peta-   Abbreviated P. A metric system prefix for one quadrillion, or 10^{15}. In computing, based on the binary system, peta has the value of 1,125,899,906,842,624, or the power of 2 (2^{50}) closest to 1 quadrillion.

petabyte   Abbreviated PB. Usually 1,125,899,906,842,624 bytes (2^{50}), but may also refer to 1 quadrillion bytes (10^{15}).

PGP   See Pretty Good Privacy.

physical address   See hardware address.

physical device   An item of hardware, such as a disk drive or a tape drive, that is physically separate from other devices.

physical drive   A real drive in the computer that you can see or touch, as opposed to a conceptual or logical drive. One physical drive may be divided into several logical drives, which are parts of the hard disk that function as if they were separate disk drives.

See also partition; volume.

physical layer   The first and lowest of the seven layers in the OSI Reference Model for computer-to-computer communications. The physical layer defines the

physical, electrical, mechanical, and functional procedures used to connect the equipment.

See also OSI Reference Model.

physical unit   Abbreviated PU. The name used in IBM's Systems Network Architecture (SNA) to indicate a physical device and its associated resources within the network.

See also logical unit.

PIM   See Personal Information Manager.

pin-compatible   A description of a chip or other electronic component with connecting pins exactly equivalent to the connecting pins used by a different device. With a pin-compatible chip, you can easily upgrade a system by replacing the older chip with the newer version.

See also plug-compatible.

Ping   Acronym formed from packet internet groper. A TCP/IP command used to test for network connectivity by transmitting a special ICMP (Internet Control Message Protocol) diagnostic packet to a specific node on the network, forcing the node to acknowledge that the packet reached the correct destination. If the node responds, the link is operational; if not, something is wrong. The word *ping* is often used as a verb, as in "ping that workstation to see if it's alive."

Ping is designed for network testing, troubleshooting, and measurement, and because of the large load it can impose on a busy, working network, it should not be used during normal operations, unless the system administrator is tracing a specific problem on the network.

ping of death A very large, specially constructed ICMP packet that violates the rules for packet size and content, designed to crash the receiving computer.

See also brute-force attack; denial of service attack; dictionary attack.

pinouts The configuration and purpose of each pin in a multipin connector.

pipe A section of memory that can be used by a program or a command to pass information to a second command for processing. The information is stored in a first-in first-out basis and is not altered during transmission. A pipe is opened like a file and is read from or written to in the same way; pipes are also unidirectional in that one pipe is used to read data and another is used to write data.

A special form of pipe, known as a named pipe, originated in the Unix operating system. A named pipe allows two processes to exchange information. This concept has been extended in several network operating systems as a method of interprocess communication, allowing data to be exchanged between applications running on networked computers.

See also mailslots; named pipe; semaphore; shared memory; socket.

pipeline A mechanism used in microprocessors that speeds up the processing of instructions.

The Intel Pentium processor features two pipelines, one for data and one for instructions, and can process two instructions per clock cycle. A processor with two or more pipelines is said to be superscalar.

See also superscalar.

pipeline burst cache A secondary or L2 cache associated with a microprocessor that allows fast data-transfer rates. Pipeline burst cache requires RAM chips that can synchronize with the microprocessor's clock.

pipeline stall A microprocessor design error that leads to delays in the processing of an instruction.

pipelining **1.** In processor architecture, a method of fetching and decoding instructions that ensures that the processor never needs to wait; as soon as one instruction is executed, the next one is ready.

2. In parallel processing, the method used to pass instructions from one processing unit to another.

See also parallel processing.

PKI *See* Public Key Infrastructure.

PKUNZIP A very popular file decompression utility available as shareware. PKUNZIP uncompresses files or archives created by PKZIP; both programs are usually available together.

See also PKZIP; WinZip.

PKZIP A very popular file compression utility available as shareware. PKZIP not only compresses files to save disk space or cut modem transmission times, but also

P

combines compressed files to create compressed archives.

See also PKUNZIP; WinZip.

plaintext Text that has not been encrypted in any way and that can be intercepted and read easily while in transit; usually applied to an unencrypted password.

See also cleartext.

platform **1.** An operating system environment, such as a NetWare platform or a Unix platform.

2. A computer system based on a specific microprocessor, such as an Intel-based platform or a PowerPC-based platform.

platform-specific routers Routers based on a specific and proprietary hardware architecture, which is usually vendor-specific.

player A small program launched or used by a Web browser to process a specific type of file that the browser cannot handle. A player is a program that deals with sound files.

See also helper; plug-in; viewer.

plenum cable Cable with a special Teflon coating designed for use in suspended ceilings, in inside walls, or between floors.

The Teflon coating provides low flame-spread and low, nontoxic smoke in the case of an accident. Plenum cables should meet the CMR (Communications Riser Cable) or CMP (Communications Plenum Cable) specifications of the National Electric Code and are often used for cable runs in air-return areas.

See also riser cable.

Plug and Play Abbreviated PnP. A standard from Compaq, Microsoft, Intel, and Phoenix that defines techniques designed to make PC configuration simple and automatic. A user can plug in a new device, and the operating system will recognize it and configure it automatically when the system is next started.

PnP adapters contain configuration information stored in nonvolatile memory, which includes vendor information, serial number, and checksum information. The PnP chipset allows each adapter to be isolated, one at a time, until all cards have been properly identified by the operating system.

The PnP-compatible BIOS isolates and identifies PnP cards at boot time, and when you insert a new card, the BIOS performs an auto-configuration sequence enabling the new card with appropriate settings.

New PCs with flash BIOS will be easy to upgrade so that they can take advantage of PnP; older systems with ROM-based BIOS will need a hardware change before they can take full advantage of PnP.

See also Peripheral Component Interconnect local bus; Plug and Pray.

Plug and Pray What most of us do when our Plug-and-Play systems do not work automatically.

plug-compatible Any hardware device designed to work in exactly the same way as a device manufactured by a different company. For example, all external serial devices are plug-compatible, because you can replace one with another without changing the cabling or connector.

See also pin-compatible.

plug-in   A small program you can link in to your Web browser to add a special capability not originally present or to recognize new file types or content. Plug-ins are available from a huge number of companies and are usually free.

See also helper.

PMMU   *See* paged memory management unit.

PNNI   See Private Network-to-Network Interface.

PnP   *See* Plug and Play.

POH   *See* power-on hours.

PointCast, Inc.   The largest privately held media company on the Internet, providing online news to corporations. The PointCast broadcast receives more than 120 million hits a day and offers access to a collection of more than 600 leading business sources.

Unlike the World Wide Web and other Internet applications, PointCast uses server push technology, in which the server automatically sends new data to a client without a specific request from that client.

For more information on PointCast, see www.pointcast.com.

point-to-point link   A direct connection between two, and only two, locations or nodes.

Point-to-Point Protocol   Abbreviated PPP. A TCP/IP protocol used to transmit IP datagrams over serial lines and dial-up telephone point-to-point connections.

PPP allows a PC to establish a temporary direct connection to the Internet via modem and appear to the host system as if it were an Ethernet port on the host's network.

PPP provides router-to-router, host-to-router, and host-to-host connections and also provides an automatic method of assigning an IP address so that mobile users can connect to the network at any point.

See also PPP Multilink; Point-to-Point Tunneling Protocol; Serial Line Internet Protocol.

Point-to-Point Tunneling Protocol   Abbreviated PPTP. A proprietary networking protocol proposed by Microsoft that supports virtual private networks, allowing remote users to access Windows NT Server systems across the Internet without compromising security. PPTP allows corporations to use public networks rather than leasing its own lines for wide area communications.

See also encapsulation; Layer 2 Tunneling Protocol; PPP Multilink; tunneling.

point of presence   Abbreviated POP. A connection to the telephone company or to long-distance carrier services.

polling   A method of controlling the transmission sequence of devices on a shared circuit or multi-drop line by sending an inquiry to each device asking if it wants to transmit. If a device has data to send, it sends back an acknowledgment, and the

P

transmission begins. Three methods are in common use:

- **Roll-call**   A master station uses a polling list to locate the next node to poll.

- **Hub**   A node polls the next node in sequence.

- **Token-passing**   A token is passed to the next node in sequence. This node can transmit or pass the token to the next device.

polymorphic virus   A form of virus that can change its appearance to avoid detection. The virus encrypts itself using a special formula each time an infection occurs. Virus-detecting software uses special scanning techniques to find and remove polymorphic viruses.

See also boot sector virus; file-infecting virus; macro virus; multipart virus; stealth virus, vaccine; virus.

POP   *See* point of presence; Post Office Protocol.

port   **1.** To move a program or an operating system from one hardware platform to another. For example, Windows NT portability refers to the fact that the same operating system can run on both Intel and reduced instruction set computing (RISC) architectures.

2. The point at which a communications circuit terminates at a network, serial, or parallel interface card, usually identified by a specific port number or name.

3. A number used to identify a connection point to a specific Internet protocol.

See also portable; port number.

portability   The ability to transfer an application or operating system from one vendor's hardware to another, quickly and easily, without rewriting the software and without affecting its performance.

This can be achieved in several ways:

- Write the program in a portable language, such as C, C++, or Java.

- Use only standard programming language features.

- Use only standard libraries.

- Don't make assumptions about word size or byte ordering.

- Use layers of software to distance the application from operating system or hardware dependencies.

portable   Describes the degree to which a program can be moved easily to different computing environments with a minimum number of changes. Applications written for the Unix operating system are often described as portable applications, as are Java applets.

See also Java.

portable computer   Any computer light and small enough to be carried easily. There are two types:

- **Laptop computers,** which are small enough to be used in an airplane seat and powerful enough to run major operating systems and popular business applications. Extended battery life is making the laptop a serious alternative to the desktop system.

- **Notebook computers,** which are smaller than laptops and about the size of a textbook or student notebook, but still capable of running major applications. A notebook computer will easily fit into a briefcase.

Major advances in battery life and the use of flash memory are part of the continuing development of portable computers.

See also docking station; port replicator.

Portable Document Format   Abbreviated PDF. A file format standard developed by Adobe Systems and others for use in electronic documents. A file in this format usually has the filename extension of .PDF.

Portable Operating System Interface Abbreviated POSIX. A collection of IEEE standards that defines a complete set of portable operating system services. POSIX is based on Unix services, but it can be implemented by many other operating systems.

Each of the standards defines a specific aspect of an operating system, including such areas as system administration, system security, networking, and the user interface.

When program or operating system service meets the appropriate POSIX standard, it is said to be POSIX-compliant.

See also IEEE standards.

port multiplier   A concentrator that provides multiple connections to the network.

port number   The default identifier for a TCP/IP (Transmission Control Protocol/Internet Protocol) or Internet process.

For example, ftp (File Transport Protocol), HTML (HyperText Markup Language), and Telnet are all available at preassigned unique port numbers so that the computer

knows how to respond when it is contacted on a specific port; Web servers use port 80, and SMTP (Simple Mail Transfer Protocol) e-mail is always delivered to port 25. You can override these defaults by specifying different values in a URL, but whether they will work depends on the configuration on the target system.

A total of 65,535 port numbers are available for use with TCP, and the same number are available for UDP (User Datagram Protocol).

See also port.

port replicator   A device containing standard computer ports used to avoid constantly connecting and disconnecting peripherals from a portable computer.

A port replicator duplicates all your computer's ports and may even add a Small Computer System Interface (SCSI) port or a second Universal Serial Bus port. The external monitor, full-sized keyboard, and mouse you use in the office are connected to the port replicator; when it is time to take the portable computer on the road, you simply unplug the port replicator, leaving everything attached to the replicator for your return.

See also docking station.

portal   A large Web site that acts as a gateway to the Internet and may also offer search facilities, free e-mail, online chat, instant messaging, as well as other services, including hard news, sports, and personal finance. Portals make money by selling advertising space.

POSIX *See* Portable Operating System Interface.

POST *See* power-on self test.

post An individual article or e-mail message sent to a Usenet newsgroup or mailing list, rather than a message sent to an individual.

See also posting; Usenet.

Postal Telephone and Telegraph Abbreviated PTT. The official government body that administers and manages the telecommunications systems in many European countries.

posting Sending an article or an e-mail message to a Usenet newsgroup.

See also post; Usenet.

Post Office Protocol Abbreviated POP. An Internet mail server protocol that also provides an incoming mail storage mechanism.

POP works with Simple Mail Transfer Protocol (SMTP), which actually moves the e-mail from one system to another, and the latest version of the standard is POP3.

When a client connects to a POP3 server, all the messages addressed to that client are downloaded; there is no ability to download messages selectively. Once the messages are downloaded, the user can delete or modify messages without further interaction with the server.

In some locations, POP3 is being replaced by another standard, Internet Mail Access Protocol (IMAP) version 4.

See also Internet Mail Access Protocol; Simple Mail Transfer Protocol.

power conditioning The use of protective and conditioning devices to filter out power surges and spikes and ensure clean power. There are three main types of power-conditioning devices:

- **Suppression,** which protects against sudden destructive transient voltages.

- **Regulation,** which modifies the power waveform back to a clean sine wave. A UPS (uninterruptible power supply) is a common form of voltage regulator. It may be online, actively modifying the power, or offline and available only after the line voltage drops below a certain level.

- **Isolation,** which protects against noise. These types of devices are often expensive.

Because power conditioning is expensive, usually only the servers or hosts in a network are protected. Surge suppressors may be used with workstations or other important network nodes, such as bridges or routers.

See also blackout; brownout; power surge; spike; surge.

Power Mac A series of computers from Apple Computer, Inc., based on the PowerPC chip. Although Power Macs run on the PowerPC chip rather than on the traditional Motorola chips, they run a version of the Macintosh operating system and look and feel just like 680x0-based computers. They can also run MS-DOS and Windows software under emulation.

power-on hours   Abbreviated POH. A cumulative count of the hours since the last time the system was started.
See also mean time between failures.

power-on self test   Abbreviated POST. A set of diagnostic programs loaded from ROM before any attempt is made to load the operating system; designed to ensure that the major system components are present and operating. If a problem is found, the POST firmware displays an error message on the screen, sometimes with a diagnostic code number indicating the type of fault.

PowerPC   A family of RISC-based, superscalar microprocessors jointly developed by Apple, Motorola, and IBM, with a 32-bit address bus and a 64-bit data bus.

- The 601 houses 2.8 million transistors, runs at 110MHz, and is designed for use in high-performance, low-cost PCs.

- The 66MHz 602 is targeted at the consumer electronics and entry-level computer markets.

- The low-wattage 603e is aimed at battery-powered computers.

- The 604 is for high-end PCs and workstations.

- The 64-bit 620 is available in a 133MHz version capable of executing four instruction per clock cycle and is designed for servers and high-performance applications.

- The 750 (also known as the G3) is available in a range of processors running from 333 to 400MHz with an integrated L2

cache of 1MB and is equivalent to 6.35 million transistors.

power supply   A part of the computer that converts the power from a wall outlet into the lower voltages, typically 5 to 12 volts DC (direct current), required internally in the computer. PC power supplies are usually rated in watts, ranging from 90 to 300 watts. If the power supply in a computer fails, nothing works—not even the fan.

power surge   A sudden, brief, and often destructive increase in line voltage. A power surge may be caused by an electrical appliance, such as a photocopier or elevator, or by power being reapplied after an outage.
See also power conditioning; surge; surge suppressor.

PPP   *See* Point-to-Point Protocol.

PPP Multilink   An extension to the Point-to-Point Protocol that can provide bandwidth on demand by combining multiple links between two systems; a process also known as *bonding*. PPP Multilink provides the negotiation features and protocols that allow systems to indicate that they can bond. The links can be of different types and different speeds.
See also inverse multiplexing; Point-to-Point Protocol.

PPTP   *See* Point-to-Point Tunneling Protocol.

preemptive multitasking   A form of multitasking in which the operating system executes an application for a specific period of time, according to its assigned priority. At that time, it is preempted, and another

299

task is given access to the CPU for its allocated time. Although an application can give up control before its time is up, such as during input/output waits, no task is ever allowed to execute for longer than its allotted time period.

See also cooperative multitasking; timeslice multitasking.

presentation layer The sixth of seven layers of the OSI Reference Model for computer-to-computer communications. The presentation layer defines the way in which data is formatted, presented, converted, and encoded.

See also OSI Reference Model.

Pretty Good Privacy Abbreviated PGP. A popular public-key encryption and digital certificate program, originally written by Phil Zimmermann, available at no charge from certain Internet sites.

PGP uses Diffie-Hellman public-key algorithms, is available for Microsoft Windows and Macintosh platforms, and works with most popular messaging applications such as Microsoft Exchange, Eudora, and Claris Emailer for the Macintosh.

See also Privacy Enhanced Mail; RSA Data Security.

PRI *See* Primary Rate ISDN.

primary domain controller In a Microsoft Windows NT domain, a computer running Windows NT Server that authenticates domain logons and manages the directory database for the domain. All changes to all accounts in the domain are automatically tracked and sent to the primary do-

main controller. There can be only one primary domain controller in any domain.

See also backup domain controller; domain; domain controller.

primary key *See* key.

primary member One of two members of a mirror set. The primary member contains the original data; the shadow member contains the copy.

See also disk mirroring; shadow member.

Primary Rate ISDN Abbreviated PRI. An ISDN (Integrated Services Digital Network) service that provides 23 B (bearer) channels, capable of speeds of 64Kbps, and one D (data) channel, also capable of 64Kbps. The combined capacity of 1.544Mbps is equivalent to one T1 channel.

See also Basic Rate ISDN.

primary time server In Novell NetWare, a server that provides time information to secondary time servers and to workstations.

A primary time server must synchronize time information with at least one other primary or reference time server.

See also reference time server; secondary time server; single reference time server.

PRINTCON A Novell NetWare workstation utility used to create, view, or modify print-job configurations on the network. Configuration options include the printer to be used, the print queue to process the job through, the print-device mode, the printer form number, and the number of copies.

PRINTDEF   A Novell NetWare workstation utility used to create, view, and modify printer definitions on the network.

Printer Access Protocol   Abbreviated PAP. The protocol used in AppleTalk networks to manage communications between computers and printers.

See also AppleTalk.

Printer Agent   In Novell Distributed Print Services, a printer object that replaces the Print Queue, Printer, and Printer Server objects used in other Novell printing environments.

printer emulation   The ability of a printer to change modes so that it behaves like a printer from another manufacturer. For example, many dot-matrix printers offer an Epson printer emulation in addition to their own native mode. Most laser printers offer a Hewlett-Packard LaserJet emulation.

See also emulator; terminal emulation.

print queue   A collection of documents waiting to be printed on a particular network printer.

See also Novell Distributed Print Services.

print server   A server that handles printing for all users on the network. A print server collects print jobs sent by applications running on other networked PCs, places them in a print queue on the hard disk, and routes them to one or more printers attached to the print server.

See also local printer; Novell Distributed Print Services.

print spooler   In an operating system or network operating system, the software that coordinates print jobs sent to a shared printer when that printer is busy. Each print job is stored in a separate file and is printed in turn when the printer becomes free.

Priority Access Control Enabled   Abbreviated PACE. A technology from 3Com Corporation designed to deliver on-time multimedia over switched Ethernet networks with insufficient bandwidth and without the ability to prioritize traffic. This is accomplished by the use of the PACE-enabled switches that allow the switch port and end stations to take turns when transmitting.

Privacy Enhanced Mail   Abbreviated PEM. An e-mail standard that uses a patented RSA encryption scheme to provide a confidential method of authentication. PEM is little used due to the proprietary nature of the encryption scheme.

See also Secure MIME; RSA.

private automatic branch exchange   Abbreviated PABX. An automatic telephone system that serves a particular location, such as an office, providing connections from one extension to another, as well as a set of connections to the external telephone network. Many PABXs handle computer data and may include X.25 connections to a packet-switched network.

See also private branch exchange.

private branch exchange   Abbreviated PBX. A telephone system, usually owned by the customer, that serves a particular location, such as an office, providing connections from one extension to another, as well

P

as a set of connections to the external telephone network.

See also private automatic branch exchange.

private data network   Abbreviated PDN. A highly secure and very expensive network of leased lines built for a single user, usually a corporation.

PDNs are used to transmit highly sensitive data such as banking and other financial information. The service provider guarantees a certain bandwidth will always be available, although some of that bandwidth may go unused during periods of light traffic.

See also Virtual Private Network.

private key   One of two keys used in public key encryption. The user keeps the private key secret and uses it to encrypt digital signatures on outgoing messages and to decrypt incoming messages.

See also public key encryption.

private leased circuit   A leased communications circuit, available 24 hours a day, 7 days a week, that connects a company's premises with a remote site.

Private Network-to-Network Interface   Abbreviated PNNI. A dynamic link-state routing protocol for Asynchronous Transfer Mode (ATM)-based networks. Any given ATM network may include ATM switches from several vendors; PNNI provides a routing protocol to communicate configuration information about the network to these groups of switches.

See also Integrated-Private Network-to-Network Interface.

privileged mode   An operating mode supported in protected mode in Intel processors that allows the operating system and certain classes of device drivers to manipulate parts of the system, including memory and input/output ports. Applications cannot be executed in privileged mode.

See also protected mode; privilege level; real mode.

privilege level   **1.** Those rights granted to a user or a group of users by the network administrator that determine the functions the user can execute. Rights form an important component of network security and can include supervisor rights and read, write, erase, and modify rights, along with several others.

2. A form of protection built into Intel microprocessors. The Intel microprocessor architecture provides two broad classes of protection. One is the ability to separate tasks by giving each task a separate address space. The other mechanism operates within a task to protect the operating system and special processor registers from access by applications. Within a task, four privilege levels are defined. The innermost ring is assigned privilege level 0 (the highest, or most trusted, level), and the outermost ring is privilege level 3 (the lowest, or least privileged, level). Rings 1 and 2 are reserved for the operating system and operating system extensions; level 3 is available to applications. This protection is maintained by complex circuitry in the processor's memory management unit.

PRN   In MS-DOS, Windows, and OS/2, the logical device name for a printer, usually the first parallel port, which is also known as LPT1.

See also parallel port.

process   In a multitasking operating system, a program or a part of a program. All EXE and COM files execute as processes, and one process can run one or more other processes.

See also session; thread.

Professional Server Expert   Abbreviated PSE. A certification from IBM that offers specialization in a specific network operating system, including Novell NetWare, OS/2 Warp Server, or Windows NT Server.

See also Professional Server Specialist.

Professional Server Specialist   Abbreviated PSS. An introductory hardware certification from IBM designed to assess knowledge of IBM Netfinity and PC server architecture, installation, configuration, and management.

See also Professional Server Expert.

Profile object   In Novell NetWare, a special Novell Directory Services (NDS) object used to assign the same login script to a group of users. A Profile login script is executed after the container login script has executed, but before the user login script.

programming language   A language used to write a program that the computer can execute. Almost 200 programming languages exist. An example is the popular C language, which is well suited to a variety of computing tasks. With C, programmers can write anything from a device driver, to an application, to an operating system.

Certain kinds of tasks, particularly those involving artificial intelligence (LISP or Prolog), process control (Forth), or highly mathematical applications (Fortran and APL), can benefit from a more specific language.

Programming languages are also divided into low-level languages, such as assembly language, and high-level languages, such as C, C++, and Java.

See also assembly language; compiler; interpreter; machine language.

Project Athena   A Massachusetts Institute of Technology project that ran from 1983 to 1991, sponsored by MIT, DEC, and IBM, and developed the X Window system and Kerberos authentication, as well as several other important relational database and network-related systems.

See also Kerberos; X Window.

promiscuous mode   A mode in which a network device or interface card captures all the packets on the network, not just those addressed to it specifically.

Network analyzers work in promiscuous mode to monitor network traffic and to perform statistical analyses of the traffic.

See also network analyzer; sniffer.

propagation delay   In communications, any delay between the time a signal enters the transmission channel and the time it is received.

P

303

This delay is relatively small across a LAN, but can become considerable in satellite communications, in which the signal must travel from one earth station to the satellite and back to earth again. Unusually long delays may require the use of specialized hardware to ensure that the link is not broken prematurely.

property **1.** In Novell NetWare, a characteristic of an object in Novell Directory Services (NDS); also known as an attribute. User object properties include name, login name, password restrictions, e-mail address, and other related information.

2. In Microsoft Windows, a characteristic of an object or device, accessed via that object's Properties dialog box.

property rights In Novell NetWare, characteristics of an object in Novell Directory Services (NDS). Property rights are Add or Delete Self, Compare, Read, Supervisor, and Write.

proprietary software Software developed in-house by a particular business or government agency and never made available commercially to the outside world.

The operating systems used in certain portable computers and PDAs (personal digital assistants) may also be considered proprietary, because they are specific to one system and are not generally available anywhere else.

protected mode In Intel processors, an operating state that supports advanced features. Protected mode in these processors provides hardware support for multitasking and virtual memory management,

and it prevents programs from accessing blocks of memory that belong to other executing programs.

In 16-bit protected mode, supported on 80286 and higher processors, the CPU can address a total of 16MB of memory directly; in 32-bit protected mode, supported on 80386 and higher processors, the CPU can address up to 4GB of memory.

Microsoft Windows NT, OS/2, and most versions on Unix running on Intel processors run in protected mode.

See also real mode.

protocol In networking and communications, the formal specification that defines the procedures to follow when transmitting and receiving data. Protocols define the format, timing, sequence, and error checking used on the network.

See also communications protocol; OSI Reference Model; protocol stack.

protocol analyzer A hardware or combined hardware and software product used to analyze the performance data of the network and to find and troubleshoot network problems.

Protocol analyzers vary greatly in complexity. Some use dedicated hardware and can decode as many as 150 protocols; others convert an existing networked PC into a network-specific analyzer.

See also network analyzer; sniffer.

protocol converter A combined hardware and software product that converts from one network protocol to another;

used when two dissimilar networks are connected.

See also gateway.

protocol stack   The several layers of software that define the computer-to-computer or computer-to-network protocol.

Several companies have developed important proprietary protocol stacks, including Novell NetWare's IPX/SPX, but the trend these days is moving toward more open systems such as TCP/IP (Transmission Control Protocol/Internet Protocol).

See also OSI Reference Model.

protocol suite   *See* protocol stack.

protocol tunneling   *See* tunneling.

proxy server   A software package running on a server positioned between an internal network and the Internet.

The proxy server filters all outgoing connections so that they appear to be coming from the same machine, in an attempt to conceal the underlying internal network structure from any intruders. By disguising the real structure of the network, the proxy server makes it much more difficult for an intruder to mount a successful attack.

A proxy server will also forward your requests to the Internet, intercept the response, and then forward the response to you at your network node. A system administrator can also regulate the external sites to which users can connect.

See also dual-homed host; firewall.

PSE   *See* Professional Server Expert.

PSS   *See* Professional Server Specialist.

PSTN   *See* Public Switched Telephone Network.

PTI   *See* Payload Type Identifier.

PTT   *See* Postal Telephone and Telegraph.

PU   *See* physical unit.

public data network   Abbreviated PDN. Any government-owned or government-controlled commercial packet-switched network, offering wide-area services to data-processing users.

public key encryption   An encryption scheme that uses two keys. In an e-mail transaction, the public key encrypts the data, and a corresponding private key decrypts the data. Because the private key is never transmitted or publicized, the encryption scheme is extremely secure.

For digital signatures, the process is reversed; the sender uses the private key to create the digital signature, which can then be read by anyone who has access to the corresponding public key. This confirms that the message really is from the apparent sender.

See also digital signature; private key.

Public Key Infrastructure   A proposal to provide a structure for verifying and authenticating users involved in transactions on the Internet or on corporate intranets and extranets.

The proposal involves a set of trusted certificate authorities (CAs) who would publish a person's public key and vouch for the

P

authenticity of the data using a digital signature or certificate. Other CAs would then vouch for those CAs, and they in turn would be vouched for by other CAs.

See also certificate authority; digital signature.

public network   Normal voice telephone systems; also called the direct distance dial (DDD) network.

Public Switched Telephone Network
A designation used by the ITU to describe the local telephone company.

Public trustee   In Novell NetWare, a special trustee, used only for trustee assignments.

The Public trustee allows objects in Novell Directory Services (NDS) that do not have any other rights to have the rights granted to the Public trustee. This is similar to the way the user GUEST or the group EVERYONE worked in earlier versions of Novell NetWare.

punch-down block   A connecting device used for telephone lines; also known as a quick-connect block. The wires are pushed into metal teeth that strip the insulation away and make a good connection.

push   *See* server push.

PVC   *See* permanent virtual circuit.

QIC   *See* quarter-inch cartridge.

QoS   *See* quality of service.

quadrature amplitude modulation   In communications, a data-encoding technique used by modems. Quadrature amplitude modulation is a combination of phase and amplitude change that can encode multiple bits on a single carrier signal. For example, the CCITT V.42bis standard uses 4 phase changes and 2 amplitudes to create 16 different signal changes.

See also trellis-coded modulation.

quality of service   Abbreviated QoS. The network requirements to support a specific application. Different types of networks and network traffic have a different QoS.

QoS includes the ability to guarantee the delivery of time-sensitive data, control bandwidth, set priorities for specific network traffic, and provide an appropriate level of security.

QoS is often associated with the delivery of data such as live video, while at the same time maintaining sufficient bandwidth for the delivery of normal network traffic, perhaps at a lower data rate.

See also bandwidth on demand; Fast IP; IP Multicast; IP over ATM; IP switching; multicast.

Quantum Corporation   A major manufacturer of disk storage systems. Quantum now makes a wide variety of disk types, including IDE, SCSI, solid-state, and Fibre Channel.

For more information on Quantum Corporation, see `www.quantum.com`.

quarter-inch cartridge   Abbreviated QIC. A set of tape standards defined by the Quarter-Inch Cartridge Drive Standards Association, a trade association established in 1987. Several standards are in use today as Table Q.1 shows.

TABLE Q.1 QIC CAPACITIES

QIC Standard	Capacity	Tape Type
QIC-24	60MB	full-sized cartridge
QIC-40	40MB	mini cartridge
QIC-80	80MB	mini cartridge
QIC-100	40MB	mini cartridge

TABLE Q.1 QIC CAPACITIES *(CONTINUED)*

QIC Standard	Capacity	Tape Type
QIC-120	125MB	full-sized cartridge
QIC-128	128MB	mini cartridge
QIC-150	250MB	full-sized cartridge
QIC-380	380MB	mini cartridge
QIC-525	525MB	full-sized cartridge
QIC-1000	1GB	full-sized cartridge
QIC-1350	1.35GB	full-sized cartridge
QIC-3010	340MB	mini cartridge
QIC-3020	680MB	full-sized cartridge
QIC-4GB	4GB	full-sized cartridge
QIC-5GB	5GB	full-sized cartridge

query language In a database management system, a programming language that allows a user to extract and display specific information from a database.

Structured Query Language (SQL) is an international database query language that allows the user to issue high-level commands or statements, such as SELECT or INSERT, to create or modify data or the database structure.

See also Structured Query Language.

question mark A wildcard character used in many operating systems to represent a single character in a filename or filename extension.

See also asterisk.

queue A temporary list of items waiting for a particular service, stored on disk in a special directory. For example, a print queue is a list of documents waiting to be printed on a network printer.

See also print queue.

quick-connect block *See* punch-down block.

QuickTime   A cross-platform data format from Apple Computer, Inc., used to display movies. QuickTime synchronizes as many as 32 tracks containing time-based digital data such as sound, video, MIDI, or other control information. A QuickTime movie created on one platform can be played back on another without modification; versions are available for Macintosh and Microsoft Windows.

Q

R

RAD   *See* Rapid Application Development.

radio frequency interference   Abbreviated RFI. Many electronic devices, including radios, televisions, computers, and peripherals, can interfere with other signals in the radio-frequency range by producing electromagnetic radiation. The use of radio frequencies is generally regulated by government agencies.

See also Class A certification; Class B certification; extremely low-frequency emission; Federal Communications Commission.

RADIUS   *See* Remote Authentication Dial In User Service.

RADSL   *See* Rate-Adaptive Digital Subscriber Line.

RAID   *See* redundant array of inexpensive disks.

RAM   *See* random-access memory.

RAM chip   A semiconductor storage device, either dynamic RAM or static RAM.

RAM disk   An area of memory managed by a special device driver and used as a simulated disk; also called virtual drive. Because the RAM disk operates in memory, it works much faster than a regular hard disk. However, anything stored on a RAM disk will be erased when the computer is turned off, so contents must be copied onto a real disk to be saved.

See also disk cache.

random access   Describes the ability of a storage device to go directly to the required memory address without needing to read from the beginning every time data is requested.

In a random-access device, the information can be read directly by accessing the appropriate memory address. There is nothing random or haphazard about random access; a more precise term is *direct access*.

See also sequential access.

random-access memory   Abbreviated RAM. The main system memory in a computer, used for the operating system, applications, and data.

See also dynamic RAM; static RAM.

Rapid Application Development   Abbreviated RAD. A set of client/server application-development tools designed to speed up the development of robust applications for SQL databases.

See also Structured Query Language.

RARP   *See* Reverse Address Resolution Protocol.

RAS   *See* Remote Access Server.

Rate-Adaptive Digital Subscriber Line   Abbreviated RADSL. An Asymmetric Digital Subscriber Line (ADSL) service with a provision for testing the line length and quality before starting the service and adjusting the line speed accordingly.

See also Asymmetric Digital Subscriber Line; High-Bit-Rate Digital Subscriber Line; Single-Line Digital Subscriber Line; Very-High-Bit-Rate Digital Subscriber Line.

RBOC   *See* Regional Bell Operating Companies.

RCDD   *See* Registered Communications Distribution Designer.

RCONSOLE   A Novell NetWare workstation utility that allows network administrators to manage routers and servers from a remote PC using a modem or from a workstation on the network. RCONSOLE establishes the connection to the server and converts the PC into a virtual server console. This function is also available in NetWare Administrator from the Tools menu.

In NetWare 3, use ACONSOLE to perform this function.

See also NetWare Administrator; REMOTE.

RDP   *See* Remote Desktop Protocol.

read-after-write verification   A method of checking that data is written to a hard disk correctly. Data is written to the disk and then read back and compared with the original data still held in memory. If the data read from the disk matches, the data in memory is released. If the data does not match, that block on the disk is marked as bad, and another attempt is made to write the data elsewhere on the disk.

README file   A plain text file that contains information about the software, placed on the distribution disks by the manufacturer.

The filename may vary slightly; it might be READ.ME, README.1ST, README .TXT, or README.DOC, for example. README files may contain last-minute, important information that is not in the program manuals or online help system.

You should always look for a README file when installing a new program on your system; it may contain information pertinent to your specific configuration. You can open a README file in any word processor or text editor because the file does not contain embedded formatting commands or program-specific characters.

read-only   Describes a file or other collection of information that can only be read; it cannot be updated in any way or deleted.

Certain important operating system files are designated as read-only to prevent their accidental deletion. Also, certain types of ROM and some devices such as archive backup tapes and CD-ROMs can be read from but not changed.

read-only memory   Abbreviated ROM. A semiconductor-based memory system that stores information permanently, retaining its contents when power is switched off. ROMs are used for firmware, such as the BIOS in the PC. In some portable computers, applications and even the operating system are stored in ROM.

See also flash memory.

RealAudio   Technology developed by RealNetworks (previously known as Progressive Networks, Inc.) that lets you play audio files as they are in the process of being downloaded, rather than waiting until the complete file has arrived, which gives a much faster response time. RealAudio uses UDP (User Datagram Protocol) as the delivery mechanism.

See also IP Multicast; multicasting; streaming; User Datagram Protocol.

real mode   **1.** An operating state supported by all processors in the Intel 80*x*86 family, and the only operating mode supported by MS-DOS. In real mode, the processor can directly address 1MB of memory. Unlike protected mode, real mode does not offer any advanced hardware features for memory management or multitasking.

2. In Microsoft Windows, an operating mode that runs Windows using less than 1MB of extended memory. Real mode is not used in Windows 3.1 or later.

See also protected mode.

RealNetworks, Inc.   Developer of streaming audio and video technology for use over the Internet; previously known as Progressive Networks.

For more information on RealNetworks, Inc., see www.real.com.

See also RealAudio; streaming.

Realtime Streaming Protocol   Abbreviated RTSP. A proposed protocol from Netscape and RealNetworks for streaming live and prerecorded audio and video across the Internet and corporate intranets. RTSP also includes features for bidirectional control, support for IP Multicast, and system security.

See also IP Multicast; RealAudio; Real-time Transport Protocol; Resource Reservation Protocol.

Real-time Transport Protocol   Abbreviated RTP. A protocol designed for use in online videoconferencing applications involving multiple participants.

RTP can be used with any continuous data stream and so is suitable for use in interactive simulators and with control and measurement applications. RTP uses UDP (User Datagram Protocol) as the delivery mechanism.

See also Realtime Streaming Protocol; Resource Reservation Protocol; User Datagram Protocol.

reboot   To restart the computer and reload the operating system, usually after a crash.

In some cases, you may be able to restart the computer from the keyboard; in more severe crashes, you may have to turn the computer off and then back on again.

See also boot.

Receive Data   Abbreviated RXD. A hardware signal defined by the RS-232-C standard and used to carry serial data from one device to another.

See also Transmit Data.

record locking   A method used to control access to individual records in a database.

In a multiuser environment, there is always the possibility that two users will attempt to update the same record at the same time but with different information. The initial attempt to solve this problem was to use file locking in which the first user to access the file locks out all other users and prevents them from opening the file. After the file is updated and closed again, the next user can gain access.

File locking can seriously degrade overall system performance as many users attempt to access the same files time after time. To avoid this slowdown, many database management systems use record locking, which limits access to individual records within the database files.

See also file and record locking.

recursion   In programming, the ability of a subroutine to call itself.

Recursion is often used when solving problems that repeat the same processing steps. However, some limiting factor must be present; otherwise, the program will never stop.

Red Hat Software   A major distributor of Linux. Red Hat Linux is a three-CD package, containing a stable version of the Linux kernel, a large set of operating system utilities, source code, Apache HTTP Server, sendmail, and Perl, as well as trial versions of commercial software.

SAP, IBM, Compaq, Oracle, Intel, and Novell have all made equity investments in Red Hat Software.

For more information on Red Hat Software, see www.redhat.com.

See also Apache HTTP Server; Linux; Perl.

Red Horde   A nickname for Novell, Inc., the leading network operating system software company, as well as the NetWare resellers worldwide. Red is Novell's corporate color.

redirection   1. In Unix and many other operating systems, a shell mechanism that causes the standard input from a program to come from a file rather than from the terminal; it also causes standard output and standard error to go to a file rather than to the terminal. Because Unix is a file-based operating system, and terminals and other devices are treated as though they are files, a program doesn't care or even know if its output is going to a terminal or to a file.

2. A mechanism used by most of the popular Web server software packages that reroutes clients attempting to access a specific URL to a different URL, either on the same or on a different server. Redirection is a convenient way to avoid dead links.

See also link rot; pipe; Uniform Resource Locator.

redirector   A software module loaded onto all the workstations on a network that intercepts application requests for file- and printer-sharing services and diverts them to the file server for action.

See also NetWare shell; NETx.COM; requester.

R

reduced instruction set computing

Abbreviated RISC, pronounced "risk." A processor that recognizes only a limited number of assembly-language instructions.

RISC chips are relatively cheap to produce and debug because they usually contain fewer than 128 instructions. RISC processors are commonly used in workstations, and they can be designed to run up to 70 percent faster than processors that use complex instruction set computing (CISC).

See also complex instruction set computing; IBM RS/6000; instruction set.

redundant array of inexpensive

disks Abbreviated RAID. In networking and mission-critical applications, a method of using several hard disk drives (often SCSI or Integrated Drive Electronics [IDE] drives) in an array to provide fault tolerance in the event that one or more than one drive fails.

Each level of RAID is designed for a specific use:

- **RAID 0** Data is striped over one or more drives, but there is no redundant drive. RAID 0 provides no fault tolerance because the loss of a hard disk means a complete loss of data. Some classification schemes omit RAID 0 for this reason.

- **RAID 1** Two hard disks of equal capacity duplicate or mirror each other's contents. One disk continuously and automatically backs up the other disk. This method is also known as disk mirroring or disk duplexing, depending on whether one or two independent hard-disk controllers are used.

- **RAID 2** Bit-interleaved data is written across several drives, and then parity and error-correction information is written to additional separate drives. The specific number of error-correction drives depends on the allocation algorithm in use.

- **RAID 3** Bit-interleaved data is written across several drives, but only one parity drive is used. If an error is detected, the data is reread to resolve the problem. The fact that data is reread in the event of an error may add a small performance penalty.

- **RAID 4** Data is written across drives by sectors rather than at the bit level, and a separate drive is used as a parity drive for error detection. Reads and writes occur independently.

- **RAID 5** Data is written across drives in sectors, and parity information is added as another sector, just as if it were ordinary data. This level of RAID can provide faster performance as the parity information is written across all the drives, rather than to a single parity drive.

There is not much difference in speed or quality among these levels. The appropriate level of RAID for any particular installation depends on network usage. RAID levels 1, 3, and 5 are available commercially, and levels 3 and 5 are proving popular for networks.

Several vendors have created their own RAID levels, including 6, 7,10, 11, and 35. Some of these are actually combinations of existing RAID levels, such as Compaq's Level 0+1, which combines RAID levels 0 and 1.

See also backup; disk striping; disk striping with parity; parity; single large expensive disk.

reentrant Describes a programming technique that allows one copy of a program to be loaded into memory and shared. When one program is executing reentrant code, a different program can interrupt and then start or continue execution of that same code.

Many operating system service routines use reentrant code so that only one copy of the code is needed. The technique is also used in multithreaded applications, in which different events are taking place concurrently in the computer.

reference time server In Novell NetWare, a server that provides externally derived time data to secondary time servers and to workstations. Reference time servers take part in time synchronization, but they do not change their time except in response to the external time source.

See also primary time server; secondary time server; single reference time server.

regedit In Microsoft Windows, an application that knowledgeable users can access to edit the contents of the Registry database. In Windows NT, this application is called regedit32.

See also Registry.

Regional Bell Operating Companies

Abbreviated RBOC. The telephone companies formed as a result of the breakup of AT&T, finalized in 1984.

Each of the RBOCs was assigned a specific geographical area, and each of these areas was divided into service areas known as local access and transport areas (LATA).

See also Local Exchange Carrier.

Registered Communications Distribution Designer Abbreviated RCDD. A certification from BICSI (a telecommunications association) for those involved in the design and installation of low-voltage wiring infrastructures in new construction or in existing buildings. An additional specialization, RCDD: Local Area Network, is available for those involved with designing and installing LAN cabling.

R

Registry In the Microsoft Windows family of operating systems, a system database containing configuration information.

The operating system continually references the Registry database for information on users and groups, the applications installed on the system and the type of document each can create, what hardware is available and which ports are in use, and property sheets for folders and application icons.

Changes to the Registry are usually made automatically as configuration information is changed using Control Panel applications or the Administrative Tools; however, knowledgeable users can make changes directly using the application regedit or regedit32.

The Registry database replaces the text-based .INI configuration files used in earlier versions of Windows and replaces the MS-DOS configuration files AUTOEXEC.BAT and CONFIG.SYS.

See also regedit.

Registry Editor   *See* regedit.

regular expression   In Unix, a sequence of characters that can match a set of fixed-text strings used in searching for and replacing text.

Many Unix programs, including vi, ed, emacs, grep, and awk, use regular expressions.

relational database   A database model in which the data always appears from the point of view of the user to be a set of two-dimensional tables, with the data presented in rows and columns.

The rows in a table represent records, which are collections of information about a specific topic, such as the entries in a doctor's patient list. The columns represent fields, which are the items that make up a record, such as the name, address, city, state, and zip code in an address list database.

See also database model.

Relative Distinguished Name   In Novell Directory Services (NDS), a shortened Distinguished Name that identifies an object by its relationship within the current context.

Relative Distinguished Names do not begin with a period, but you can use a period at the end of the name to move up the NDS tree.

See also Common name; Context; Distinguished Name; NDS tree.

REMOTE   A Novell NetWare server utility used to access the server console from a PC or a workstation or by using a modem.

See also RCONSOLE.

remote access   A workstation-to-network connection, made using a modem and a telephone line, that allows data to be sent and received over large distances. Remote access and authentication and security for such access is managed differently in different network operating systems.

See also private data network; public data network; Virtual Private Network.

Remote Access Server   Abbreviated RAS. In Microsoft Windows NT Server, a software package that allows remote users to connect to the server via modem and access network resources. Users can connect to the server using a telephone line and an analog modem, an ISDN connection, or an X.25 network.

Remote Authentication Dial In User Service   Abbreviated RADIUS. A third-party authentication server attached to a network.

Remote users dial in to the server, and the access server requests authentication services from the RADIUS server. The RADIUS server authenticates users and gives them access to network resources. The access server is acting as a client to the RADIUS server.

See also access server; authentication; challenge-response authentication.

remote boot   A technique used to boot a workstation from an image file on the file server rather than from a local drive attached directly to the workstation.

remote connection   *See* remote access.

remote-control program   A program that allows the user to link two PCs together so that one of the computers controls the operation of the other. The connection may be over a dedicated serial line, a local-area network, or a modem-to-modem communications link. Each computer runs a copy of the remote-control program.

Remote-control programs are particularly useful for troubleshooting problems at computers located far from the technical support center, for installing or removing demonstration software without needing to visit the customer site, for training remote users, and for telecommuting.

Popular remote control programs include Symantec's pcAnywhere, Microcom's Carbon Copy, and Traveling Software's LapLink for Windows.

See also mobile computing; wireless communications.

Remote Desktop Protocol   Abbreviated RDP. An extension to the International Telecommunications Union (ITU) T.120 protocol that provides the connection between a thin client and the terminal server. RDP works with Microsoft Windows workstations using TCP/IP (Transmission Control Protocol/Internet Protocol).

See also Independent Computing Architecture; thin client.

remote digital loopback test   A capability of certain modems that allows the whole circuit to be tested.

See also loopback.

Remote File System   Abbreviated RFS. A distributed file system network protocol that allows programs running on a computer to use network resources as though they were local. Originally developed by AT&T, RFS has been incorporated as a part of Unix System V Interface Definition.

Remote Procedure Call   Abbreviated RPC. A set of procedures used to implement client/server architecture in distributed programming.

RPC describes how an application initiates a process on another network node and how it retrieves the appropriate result.

RPCs were first implemented by Sun Microsystems and Hewlett-Packard systems running the Unix operating system.

See also Common Object Request Broker Architecture; Distributed Component Object Model; Object Request Broker.

remote resource   Any device not attached to the local node, but available through the network.

remote user   A user who logs in to the network using a modem and telephone line from a site located some distance from the main network.

A remote user may always dial in from the same location, as in the case of a telecommuter working from home, or may dial in from a different location every time, as in the case of mobile sales people.

See also mobile computing; remote access; wireless communications.

repeater   A simple hardware device that moves all packets from one local-area

R

network segment to another by regenerating, retiming, and amplifying the electrical signals.

The main purpose of a repeater is to extend the length of the network transmission medium beyond the normal maximum cable lengths.

See also active hub; bridge; brouter; router.

replica In Novell Directory Services (NDS), a copy of a directory partition.

Replicas are designed to eliminate a single point of failure and to provide faster access to users across a wide-area network.

NetWare contains three major types of replicas:

- **Master** The original replica, created during system installation. A Master replica of the Root partition is stored in a hidden directory on the first file server installed.

- **Read-Write** Used to read or update Novell Directory Database (NDD) information. There will be at least two Read-Write replicas for each partition to ensure that the NDD will continue to function even if some of the servers with replicas are unavailable.

- **Read-Only** Used to display but not modify NDD information.

A fourth replica type, Subordinate Reference, is important to NDS communications. This is a link between a parent partition and a child partition, containing a list of the servers in which replicas of the child partition are stored, their addresses, and replica types, as well as other NDS

partition information. Subordinate Reference replicas are maintained by the operating system and cannot be changed by users or the system administrator.

See also Novell Directory Services; NetWare Directory Database; partition; replica synchronization.

replica synchronization In Novell Directory Services (NDS), the process used to exchange information between a partition's replicas to ensure that all information is up-to-date.

When a change is made to a replica, synchronization ensures that the change is made available to all other replicas as soon as possible.

See also Novell Directory Services; partition; replica.

replication The process of synchronizing data stored on two or more computers either for backup purposes or to make the information more accessible to users at different locations.

In Microsoft Windows NT Server, replication is used to duplicate data to another server; the server holding the master copy of the data is called the export server, and the server receiving the data is known as the import server.

In Novell Directory Services (NDS), replication is used to distribute all or part of the Novell Directory Database to other servers.

requester Special software loaded onto a networked workstation to manage communications between the network and the workstation. This software may also be referred to as a shell, redirector, or client, depending on the networking system in use.

See also NetWare shell; NetWare DOS Requester; NET*x*.COM.

Request for Comment Abbreviated RFC. A document or a set of documents in which proposed Internet standards are described or defined.

Well over a thousand RFCs are in existence, and they represent a major method of online publication for Internet technical standards.

See also Internet Engineering Task Force.

Request to Send Abbreviated RTS. A hardware signal defined by the RS-232-C standard to request permission to transmit.

See also Clear to Send.

reserved memory In MS-DOS, a term used to describe that area of memory between 640Kb and 1MB, also known as upper memory. Reserved memory is used by MS-DOS to store system and video information.

See also memory management.

reserved word *See* keyword.

resource **1.** Any part of a computer system that can be used by a program as it runs. Resources include memory, hard and floppy disks, networking components, the operating system, printers, and other output devices, as well as queues, security features, and other less well defined data structures.

2. In HTML, any URL, directory, or application that the server can access and send to a requesting client.

See also HyperText Markup Language; Uniform Resource Locator.

Resource Reservation Protocol Abbreviated RSVP. An Internet protocol designed to deliver data on time and in the right order over TCP/IP (Transmission Control Protocol/Internet Protocol) networks.

RSVP is a control and signaling protocol, not a routing protocol, and it works by reserving bandwidth from one end system to another; this reduces the bandwidth available to other users.

See also IP switching; Real-time Transport Protocol.

response time The time lag between sending a request and receiving the data.

Response time can be applied to a complete computer system, as in the time taken to look up a certain customer record, or to a system component, as in the time taken to access a specific cluster on disk or for a memory circuit to return data requested by the processor.

restore To copy files from a backup or archival storage to their normal location, especially when the files are being copied to replace files lost by accident.

See also backup.

retensioning A maintenance operation required by certain tape drives to ensure correct tape tension; retensioning fast forwards and then rewinds the entire tape or tape cartridge.

Return key *See* Enter key.

R

Reverse Address Resolution Protocol
Abbreviated RARP. A part of the TCP/IP
(Transmission Control Protocol/Internet
Protocol) protocol suite that allows a computer, more specifically a diskless workstation, to obtain an IP address from a server
when only the hardware address is known.

See also Address Resolution Protocol;
hardware address; IP address.

REXX Acronym formed from Restruc-
tured Extended Executor Language. A
scripting language from IBM, originally
written by Mike Cowlishaw of IBM UK in
1979 for the VM mainframe environment
and now available on many operating systems, including OS/2, Unix, and VMS.

REXX is a general-purpose interpreted language and uses English-like words, rather
than the sometimes terse syntax of C or C++.

RFC *See* Request for Comment.

RFI *See* radio frequency interference.

RFS *See* Remote File System.

RG-58 A 50-ohm coaxial cable, used in
Ethernet networks, that conforms to the
IEEE 802.3 10Base2 standard.

RG-59 A 75-ohm coaxial cable used in
ARCnet and in television.

RG-62 A 93-ohm coaxial cable used in
ARCnet LANs or in IBM 3270 applications.

right angle bracket The > symbol that
is used in Unix and other operating systems
to direct the output from a command to a
file or to a device.

Also commonly used in e-mail messages to
indicate the text has been cut from another
e-mail message.

rights In a network or multiuser environment, the ability of a user to access certain system resources, including files and
directories. Permissions are based on the
rights given to user accounts by the system
administrator.

See also inherited rights.

rightsizing The process of matching a
corporation's goals to the computing and
network solutions available to maximize
business effectiveness in reaching that goal.

See also downsizing; outsourcing; service
bureau.

ring network A network topology in the
form of a closed loop or circle, with each
node in the network connected to the next.

Messages move in one direction around the
system. When a message arrives at a node,
the node examines the address information
in the message. If the address matches the
node's address, the message is accepted;
otherwise, the node regenerates the signal
and places the message back on the network
for the next node in the system. It is this re-
generation that allows a ring network to
cover greater distances than star networks
or bus networks. Ring networks normally
use some form of token-passing protocol to
regulate network traffic.

The failure of a single node can disrupt network operations; however, fault tolerant
techniques have been developed to allow
the network to continue to function in the
event one or more nodes fail.

See also token-ring network.

RING NETWORK

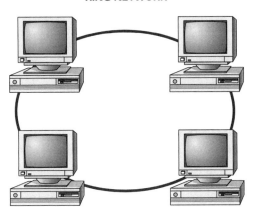

R

RIP   *See* Routing Information Protocol.

RISC   *See* reduced instruction set computing.

riser cable   Any cable that runs vertically between floors in a building. Riser cable may be run through special conduits or inside the elevator shaft.

See also plenum cable.

RJ-11   A commonly used modular telephone connector. RJ-11 is a four-wire (two-pair) connector most often used for voice communications.

RJ-12   A commonly used modular telephone connector. RJ-12 is a six-wire (three-pair) connector most often used for voice communications.

RJ-11

RJ-45   A commonly used modular telephone connector. RJ-45 is an eight-wire (four-pair) connector used for data transmission over unshielded twisted-pair (UTP) cable and leased telephone line connections.

RLL encoding   An efficient method of storing information on a hard disk. Compared with older, less-efficient methods, such as modified frequency modulation encoding (MFM), RLL encoding effectively doubles the storage capacity of a disk.

See also advanced run-length limited encoding.

rlogin   A Unix utility that establishes a terminal to remote host connection on a TCP/IP (Transmission Control Protocol/Internet Protocol) network. Once the connection is established, any commands you enter will run on the remote system.

roaming user profile   In Microsoft Windows NT Server, a user profile stored on the server and downloaded to a workstation that follows a user from one computer to another, allowing users to access their profile from any location on the network.

See also local user profile; mandatory user profile.

robot   Sometimes abbreviated bot. A World Wide Web application that automatically locates and collects information about new Web sites. Robots are most often used to create large databases of Web sites.

See also spider.

Rockwell Semiconductor Systems   A major manufacturer of chip sets for modems, cellular and cordless telephones, fax machines, PC-based videoconferencing systems, and high-speed communications systems.

For more information on Rockwell Semiconductor Systems, see www.rockwell.com.

roll back   The ability of a database management system to abort a transaction against the database before the transaction is complete and return to a previous stable condition.

See also roll forward; transaction processing.

RJ-45

roll forward The ability of a database management system to re-create the data in the database by rerunning all the transactions listed in the transaction log.

See also roll back; transaction processing.

ROM *See* read-only memory.

ROM BIOS *See* BIOS.

root **1.** In many operating systems, the name of the directory at the top of the directory tree from which all other directories are descended.

2. In Unix, the name of the superuser, user number 0. The system administrator uses this account for certain administrative tasks. One of the main objectives of an intruder on a Unix system is to gain root user status. Once achieved, the intruder has unlimited access to the system.

See also avatar; root directory.

root directory In a hierarchical directory structure, such as that used in Unix and many other operating systems, the directory from which all other directories must branch. You cannot delete the root directory.

See also parent directory; period and double-period directories.

Root object In Novell Directory Services (NDS), the original container object, created when NDS is first installed.

The Root object contains all other NDS objects and cannot be deleted, renamed, or moved. Sometimes written [Root].

ROT-13 Pronounced "rote-13." A simple encoding scheme often used to scramble posts to Usenet newsgroups.

ROT-13 works by swapping each alphabetic character with another 13 characters removed from its location in the alphabet, so that a becomes n, and so on; numbers and punctuation are unaffected.

ROT-13 makes the article unreadable until the text is decoded and is often used when the subject matter might be considered offensive. Many newsreaders have a built-in command to unscramble ROT-13 text, and if you use it, don't be surprised by what you read. If you think you might be offended, don't decrypt the post.

You will also find other, inoffensive material encoded by ROT-13, including spoilers that give away the ending of a book or film and answers to puzzles or riddles.

router An intelligent connecting device that can send packets to the correct LAN segment to take them to their destination.

Routers link LAN segments at the network layer of the OSI Reference Model for computer-to-computer communications. The networks connected by routers can use similar or different networking protocols.

A router may be one or more of the following types:

- **Central** Acts as a network backbone, connecting many LANs.

- **Peripheral** Connects individual LANs to either a central router or to another peripheral router.

- **Local** Operates within its LAN driver's cable-length limitations.

R

• **Remote**   Connects beyond its device driver limitations, perhaps through a modem or remote connection.

• **Internal**   Part of a network file server.

• **External**   Located in a workstation on the network.

See also bridge; brouter; gateway.

routing   The process of directing packets from a network source node to the destination node.

Routing Information Protocol   Abbreviated RIP. A routing protocol used on TCP/IP (Transmission Control Protocol/Internet Protocol) networks that maintains a list of reachable networks and calculates the degree of difficulty involved in reaching a specific network from a particular location by determining the lowest hop count.

The Internet standard routing protocol Open Shortest Path First (OSPF) is the successor to RIP.

See also Open Shortest Path First.

routing protocol   The protocol that enables routing by the use of a specific routing algorithm that determines the most appropriate path between the source and destination nodes.

Routing protocols provide dynamic routing configuration; without routing protocols, system administrators would have to manually configure routing tables.

See also Open Shortest Path First; Routing Information Protocol; routing table.

routing table   A table stored in a router; used to keep track of routes to specific network destinations.

See also routing protocol.

RPC   *See* Remote Procedure Call.

RPL   A Novell NetWare server utility that allows users to boot diskless workstations from files on the server.

See also remote boot.

ROUTER

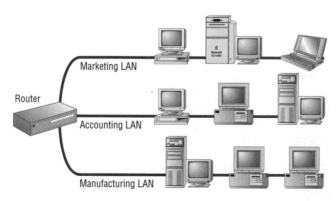

RS-232-C A recommended standard (RS) interface established by the Electronic Industries Association (EIA). Also known as EIA/TIA-232.

The standard defines the specific electrical, functional, and mechanical characteristics used in asynchronous transmissions between a computer (data terminal equipment, or DTE) and a peripheral device (data communications equipment, or DCE). RS is the abbreviation for recommended standard, and the C denotes the third revision of that standard. RS-232-C is compatible with the CCITT V.24 and V.28 standards, as well as ISO IS2110.

RS-232-C uses a 25-pin or 9-pin DB connector. The accompanying illustration shows the pinouts used in a DB-25 male connector. It is used for serial communications between a computer and a peripheral device, such as a printer, modem, or mouse. The maximum cable limit of 15.25 meters (50 feet) can be extended by using high-quality cable, line drivers to boost the signal, or short-haul modems.

See also 1394; High Speed Serial Interface; Universal Serial Bus.

R

RS-232-C INTERFACE

Signal	Pin number		Pin number	Signal
secondary transmitted data	14		1	protective ground
DCE transmitter signal element timing	15		2	transmitted data
secondary received data	16		3	received data
receiver signal element timing	17		4	request to send
no defined signal designation	18		5	clear to send
secondary request to send	19		6	data set ready
data terminal ready	20		7	signal ground/common return
signal quality detector	21		8	received line signal detector
ring indicator	22		9	+ voltage
data signal rate selector	23		10	- voltage
DTE transmitter signal element timing	24		11	no defined signal designation
no defined signal designation	25		12	secondary received line signal detector
			13	secondary clear to send

RS-422   A recommended standard (RS) interface established by the Electronic Industries Association (EIA). Also known as EIA/TIA-422.

The standard defines the electrical and functional characteristics used in a balanced serial interface, but does not specify a connector. Manufacturers who use this standard use many different types of connectors with nonstandard pin configurations. Serial ports on some Macintosh computers are RS-422 ports.

RS-423   A recommended standard (RS) interface established by the Electronic Industries Association (EIA). Also known as EIA/TIA-423.

The standard defines the electrical and functional characteristics used in an unbalanced serial interface, but does not specify a connector. Manufacturers who use this standard use many different types of connectors with nonstandard pin configurations.

RS-449   A recommended standard (RS) interface established by the Electronic Industries Association (EIA). Also known as EIA/TIA-449.

The standard defines the specific electrical, functional, and mechanical characteristics used in serial binary data interchange, and it is often used with synchronous transmissions.

RS-449 may be implemented using a 37-pin or 9-pin DB connector; the accompanying illustration shows a DB-37 male connector.

RS-485   A recommended standard (RS) interface established by the Electronic Industries Association (EIA). Also known as EIA/TIA-485.

RS-485 is similar to RS-422, except that the associated drivers are tri-state rather than dual-state. RS-485 can be used in multipoint applications, in which one computer controls as many as 64 devices.

RS-530   A recommended standard (RS) interface established by the Electronic Industries Association (EIA). Also known as EIA/TIA-530.

The standard defines the specific electrical, functional, and mechanical characteristics used in transmitting serial binary data, either synchronously or asynchronously, using a 25-pin DB connector.

RS-530 works in conjunction with RS-422 (balanced electrical circuits) or RS-423 (unbalanced electrical circuits) and allows data rates from 20Kbps to 2Mbps. The maximum distance depends on the electrical interface in use. RS-530 is compatible with CCITT V.10, V.11, X26; MIL-188/114, and RS-449.

RS/6000   *See* IBM RS/6000.

RS-449 INTERFACE

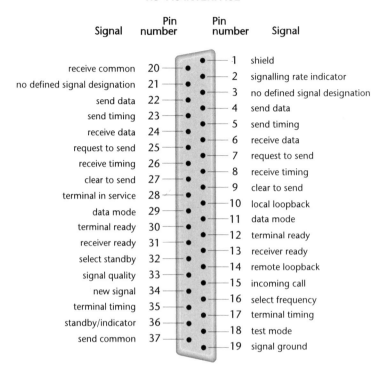

Signal	Pin number	Pin number	Signal
		1	shield
receive common	20	2	signalling rate indicator
no defined signal designation	21	3	no defined signal designation
send data	22	4	send data
send timing	23	5	send timing
receive data	24	6	receive data
request to send	25	7	request to send
receive timing	26	8	receive timing
clear to send	27	9	clear to send
terminal in service	28	10	local loopback
data mode	29	11	data mode
terminal ready	30	12	terminal ready
receiver ready	31	13	receiver ready
select standby	32	14	remote loopback
signal quality	33	15	incoming call
new signal	34	16	select frequency
terminal timing	35	17	terminal timing
standby/indicator	36	18	test mode
send common	37	19	signal ground

R

RSA A public key, or asymmetric, encryption scheme invented by and named for three mathematicians—Ron Rivest, Adi Shamir, and Len Adleman.

The theoretical background to RSA is that it is very difficult to find the factors of a very large number that is the product of two prime numbers. RSA has been analyzed closely and is considered very secure provided a sufficiently long key is used.

RSA Data Security A leading publisher of encryption software, founded by mathematicians Ron Rivest, Adi Shamir, and Len Adleman.

The company holds patents on several important encryption schemes and provides encryption and security consulting services.

For more information on RSA Data Security, see www.rsa.com.

RS-530 INTERFACE

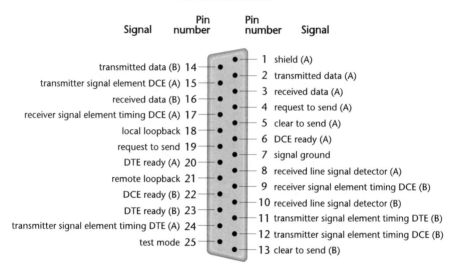

	Signal	Pin number	Pin number	Signal
transmitted data (B)	14	1	shield (A)
transmitter signal element DCE (A)	15	2	transmitted data (A)
received data (B)	16	3	received data (A)
receiver signal element timing DCE (A)	17	4	request to send (A)
local loopback	18	5	clear to send (A)
request to send	19	6	DCE ready (A)
DTE ready (A)	20	7	signal ground
remote loopback	21	8	received line signal detector (A)
DCE ready (B)	22	9	receiver signal element timing DCE (B)
DTE ready (B)	23	10	received line signal detector (B)
transmitter signal element timing DTE (A)	24	11	transmitter signal element timing DTE (B)
test mode	25	12	transmitter signal element timing DCE (B)
		13	clear to send (B)

RSVP   *See* Resource Reservation Protocol.

RTP   *See* Real-time Transport Protocol.

RTS   *See* Request to Send.

RTSP   *See* Realtime Streaming Protocol.

run-time version   A special, limited-capability release of software bundled with a single product that allows that product to run, but does not support any of the other applications capable of running in that same environment. The run-time version provides some but not all the features of the full product.

RXD   *See* Receive Data.

S

S3 Inc. A leader in the field of multimedia and graphics accelerator chips, S3 Inc. sells to companies such as Compaq, Dell, and Diamond Multimedia, who use the chips in their systems and on add-in cards.

For more information on S3 Inc., see www.s3.com.

SAA *See* Systems Application Architecture.

sag A short-term drop in line voltage to between 70 and 90 percent of the nominal voltage.

See also power conditioning; spike; surge.

salvageable files In Novell NetWare, files that have been deleted by users, but that are recoverable.

The FILER utility can display a list of deleted files and can recover the files providing they have not been overwritten in whole or in part.

If the directory containing the deleted file is also deleted, the file is saved in a system directory called DELETED.SAV in the volume's root directory.

SAM *See* Security Accounts Manager.

SAM database In Microsoft Windows NT, the Security Accounts Manager database that holds all the user accounts, groups, policies, and other information relating to the domain.

The SAM database is maintained by the User Manager for Domains utility and is accessed internally by the Security Accounts Manager.

See also domain; Security Accounts Manager.

same-server migration In Novell NetWare, one of the methods used to upgrade from NetWare 2 to NetWare 4.

The process involves upgrading the file system to the NetWare 3 format first and then upgrading to NetWare 4. The server hardware must be capable of running NetWare 4.

See also across-the-wire migration.

Samsung/AST Research The more than 30 companies in the Samsung Group manufacture everything from consumer electronics to notebook PCs and monitors to ATM switches, and Samsung Electronics is one of the largest producers of DRAM and other semiconductors in the world.

For more information on Samsung, see www.samsung.com, and for more information on AST Research, see www.ast.com.

SAN *See* storage area network.

sandbox In the Java programming system, an area within which the Java applet may execute. The sandbox is created by the Java Virtual Machine.

The applet can do anything it likes within the sandbox, but it cannot read or alter any data outside the sandbox. This security measure allows users (at least in theory) to run untrusted code without compromising the security of their own environment.

See also Java; Java applet; Java Virtual Machine.

Santa Cruz Operation, Inc. Abbreviated SCO. Developers of several important strains of Unix, including XENIX, SCO UNIX, and the SCO OpenServer series of products.

SCO began shipping Unix products based on Intel processors in 1982, and now SCO accounts for approximately 40 percent of the Unix market, with more than 8,000 applications available from various vendors.

In 1995, SCO bought the rights to Unix from Novell, and recently the company combined UnixWare and OpenServer into a single integrated operating system.

For more information on SCO, see www.sco.com.

See also OpenServer; UnixWare.

Santa Cruz Operation Advanced Certified Engineer Abbreviated SCO ACE. A certification from Santa Cruz Operation based on its SCO Unix products. Three specializations are available: Server Track, Open Server Track, and UnixWare Track.

SAP *See* Service Advertising Protocol.

SAP AG One of the world's largest independent software suppliers, based in Walldorf, Germany.

SAP's flagship product goes under the unassuming name of R/3, but the product

serves a large part of the corporate client/server world and encompasses accounting and controlling, production and materials management, human resources management, plant maintenance, workflow software, quality management, sales and distribution, and project management.

For more information on SAP, see www.sap.com.

SAS *See* single-attached station.

SATAN *See* Security Administrator Tool for Analyzing Networks.

Scalable Performance Architecture Abbreviated SPARC. A 32-bit reduced instruction set computing (RISC) processor from Sun Microsystems.

See also SPARCstation; Sun Microsystems, Inc.

scalablility The ability of an operating system to add system resources to provide faster processing or to handle increased loads in anticipation of future needs.

In practice, this usually means that an operating system is available on a range of increasingly capable hardware, with only modest increases in price at each level.

Schedule service In Microsoft Windows NT, a system service that performs an automated task at a specific time using the AT command.

Schema In Microsoft Active Directory, the definition of the objects and their properties that can be stored in the Active Directory database.

The Active Directory Schema is flexible and allows programmers to add new objects and to add new properties to existing objects.

See also Active Directory; Global Catalog; Multimaster Replication; Object

SCO *See* Santa Cruz Operation, Inc.

SCO ACE *See* Santa Cruz Operation Advanced Certified Engineer.

SCOadmin A set of graphical system administrator tools provided with Santa Cruz Operation (SCO) OpenServer.

SCOadmin lets you add or remove users, manage printers and filesystems, and check your network configuration quickly and easily.

SCO OpenServer A set of Unix products from Santa Cruz Operation (SCO). OpenServer includes a journaling filesystem, integrated symmetrical multiprocessing, a set of graphical administration tools, and a Web server. You can also run MS-DOS and Windows applications under software emulation.

See also Santa Cruz Operation, Inc.; SCO Unix.

SCO Unix A popular version of Unix from Santa Cruz Operation (SCO), based on System V, Release 3.2, with many System V, Release 4 enhancements.

SCO Unix includes the Korn shell, X Window, Level C2 security, multiprocessor support, and the ability to run MS-DOS and Windows applications under software emulation.

See also Santa Cruz Operation, Inc.

script A small program or macro invoked at a particular time.

For example, a login script may execute the same specific set of instructions every time a user logs in to a network. A communications script may send user-identification information to an Internet Service Provider (ISP) each time a subscriber dials up the service.

scripting The process of invoking a script, written in a scripting language, from an HTML document on a Web site.

Scripts can be written in a range of languages, including Perl, Tcl, REXX, JavaScript, JScript, or even Microsoft Visual Basic.

See also Common Gateway Interface; JavaScript; Perl; REXX; Tcl.

S

SCSI *See* Small Computer System Interface.

SCSI-1 A commonly used name for the first Small Computer System Interface (SCSI) definition, published in 1986; has an 8-bit parallel interface and a maximum data transfer rate of 5MBps.

See also Fast SCSI; Fast/Wide SCSI; SCSI-2; SCSI-3; Small Computer System Interface; Ultra SCSI; Ultra2 SCSI; Wide Ultra SCSI; Wide Ultra2 SCSI.

SCSI-2 A 1994 extension to the Small Computer System Interface (SCSI) definition.

This standard broadened the 8-bit data bus to 16 or 32 bits (also known as Wide SCSI), doubling the data transfer rate to 10 or 20Mbps (also known as Fast SCSI). Wide SCSI and Fast SCSI can be combined to give Fast/Wide SCSI, with a 16-bit data bus and a maximum data-transfer rate of 20Mbps. SCSI-2 is backward compatible with SCSI-1, but for maximum benefit, you should use SCSI-2 devices with a SCSI-2 controller.

SCSI-2 also adds new commands, and although the connector is physically smaller, it uses 68 pins rather than the 50 in SCSI-1. Higher data-transfer rates are achieved by using synchronous rather than asynchronous transfers.

See also Fast SCSI; Fast/Wide SCSI; SCSI; SCSI-1; SCSI-3; Small Computer System Interface; Ultra SCSI; Ultra2 SCSI; Wide Ultra SCSI; Wide Ultra2 SCSI.

SCSI-3   An extension to the Small Computer System Interface (SCSI) standard.

This definition increased the number of connected peripherals from 7 to 16, increased cable lengths, added support for a variety of interfaces including a serial interface, a Fibre Channel interface, a 1394 interface, and support for Serial Storage Architecture and several packet interfaces.

Data-transfer rates depend on the hardware implementation, but data rates in excess of 160Mbps are possible.

See also 1394; Fast SCSI; Fast/Wide SCSI; Fibre Channel; Small Computer System Interface; SCSI-1; SCSI-2; Serial Storage Architecture; Ultra SCSI; Ultra2 SCSI; Wide Ultra SCSI; Wide Ultra2 SCSI.

SCSI bus   Another name for the Small Computer System Interface (SCSI) interface and communications protocol.

SCSI terminator   The Small Computer System Interface (SCSI) interface must be correctly terminated to prevent signals echoing on the bus.

Many SCSI devices have built-in terminators that engage when they are needed. With some older SCSI devices, you must add an external SCSI terminator that plugs into the device's SCSI connector.

See also active termination; forced perfect termination; passive termination.

scuzzy   *See* Small Computer System Interface.

SDH   *See* Synchronous Digital Hierarchy.

SDK   *See* software development kit.

SDLC   *See* Synchronous Data Link Control.

SDRAM   *See* synchronous DRAM.

SDSL   *See* Single-Line Digital Subscriber Line.

Seagate Desktop Management Suite   A package of network management utilities from Seagate Software, Inc., that includes hardware and software inventory, server monitoring, client monitoring and control, network traffic monitoring, virus protection, remote access, remote control, and print-queue management.

The Desktop Management Suite also uses Seagate's Crystal Reports and includes more than 80 standard reports as well as facilities to create custom reports.

See also Desktop Management Interface.

Seagate Technology, Inc. A major manufacturer of storage technology solutions, including tape drives, hard disks, as well as network information management software and the reporting package, Crystal Reports.

For more information on Seagate Technology, Inc., see `www.seagate.com`.

search drive A drive that the operating system searches when the requested file is not located in the current directory.

See also current drive.

search engine A special Web site that lets you perform keyword searches to locate Web pages; see Appendix A for a list of popular search engines.

To use a search engine, you enter one or more keywords or, in some cases, a more complex search string such as a Boolean expression. The search engine returns a list of matching Web pages, newsgroups, and FTP archives taken from its database, usually ranked in some way, that contain the expression you are looking for, along with a brief text description of the material.

Searching this database is much faster than actually searching the Internet, but the accuracy and relevance of the information it contains depend on how often the data is updated and on the proportion of the Web that is actually searched for new content.

See also portal.

secondary cache Cache memory located on the motherboard rather than on the microprocessor; also known as L2 cache.

Secondary cache can significantly improve system performance.

second source In computer hardware, an alternative supplier of an identical product. Second sources are a safety net for the buyer, because there are at least two suppliers for one product.

secondary time server In Novell NetWare, a server that does not determine the network time, but receives that information from a primary or single reference time server.

See also primary time server; reference time server; single reference time server.

Secure HTTP Abbreviated S-HTTP, S/HTTP, or HTTP-S. An extension to the Hypertext Transfer Protocol (HTTP), from Enterprise Integration Technology, that allows Web browsers and servers to sign, authenticate, and encrypt an HTTP packet at the application layer.

S-HTTP is not widely used and is being replaced by Secure Sockets Layer (SSL).

See also Secure Sockets Layer.

Secure MIME Abbreviated S/MIME. An extension to the Multipurpose Internet Mail Extension (MIME) e-mail standard that adds security in the form of the RSA public-key algorithm.

See also Multipurpose Internet Mail Extension; Pretty Good Privacy; Privacy Enhanced Mail.

Secure Sockets Layer Abbreviated SSL. An interface originally developed by Netscape that provides encrypted data

S

transfer between client and server applications over the Internet.

SSL works at the network level and so can be used by any SSL-compliant application. Applications that use SSL use RSA public key encryption and digital signatures to establish the identity of the two parties in the transaction.

See also RSA; Secure HTTP; SOCKS.

Secure WAN　Abbreviated S/WAN. An initiative from RSA Data Security designed to create secure firewall-to-firewall connections over the Internet.

S/WAN creates a Virtual Private Network (VPN) over the Internet, and all data transmitted on this VPN is encrypted to keep it secure.

See also IPSec; SOCKS; Virtual Private Network.

security　Operating system controls used by the network administrator to limit users' access to approved areas.

The National Security Agency document called "Trusted Computer System Evaluation Criteria" (TCSEC) specifies security levels that vendors must follow to comply with Department of Defense security standards.

This publication details standards for security levels used to control access to computer systems from Class A1, the highest verifiable security level, to Class D, the lowest, which has no security.

Class C2 is the security level most appropriate to the business world; higher levels of security tend to intrude too much into normal commercial working patterns. C2 security requires that the operating system provide individual logins with separate accounts and a verifiable audit trail, that resources have owners, and that files and other system resources be protected from other processes that might corrupt them.

An operating system that lets anyone have unfettered access, such as MS-DOS or the MacOS, falls into the D category. C1 and C2 levels can be implemented in a commercial environment. After the B1 level, the computing environment changes radically, and many of the mandatory access-control mechanisms become impractical for normal commercial operations.

See also intruder.

Security Accounts Manager　Abbreviated SAM. In Microsoft Windows NT, the security system that manages and provides access to the account or SAM database.

SAM authenticates a user name and password against information contained in the database and creates an access token that includes the user's permissions.

See also SAM database; security identifier.

Security Administrator Tool for Analyzing Networks　Abbreviated SATAN. A software package, available free over the Internet, that allows network administrators to identify gaps in their security systems.

Critics of the program argue that SATAN lets hackers exploit the information contained in the program on how to infiltrate these security systems, but so far, the program seems to have acted as a wake-up call for network administrators.

See also intruder; security.

security equivalence   In Novell Directory Services (NDS), when an object or trustee receives the same rights given to another object.

See also implied security equivalence; explicit security equivalence.

security ID   *See* security identifier.

security identifier   Abbreviated security ID or SID. In Microsoft Windows NT, a unique name that identifies a logged-on user to the internal security system.

A SID contains a complete set of permissions and can apply to a single user or to a group.

See also Security Accounts Manager.

semaphore   An interprocess communication signal that indicates the status of a shared system resource, such as shared memory, in a multitasking operating system.

There are several types of semaphores:

Event   Allows a thread to tell other threads that an event has occurred and that it is safe for them to resume execution.

Mutual exclusion (mutex)   Protects system resources, such as files, data, and peripheral devices, from simultaneous access by several processes.

Multiple wait (muxwait)   Allows threads to wait for multiple events to take place or for multiple resources to become free.

See also mailslots; named pipe; pipe; shared memory; socket.

sendmail   A Unix system utility program or daemon that acts as a mail transport agent in an e-mail system, receiving messages from a user's e-mail program and then routing the mail to the correct destination. Normal users rarely come into direct contact with sendmail; it is difficult to administer and is a known security problem.

See also Post Office Protocol; Simple Mail Transfer Protocol.

sequel   *See* Structured Query Language.

Sequenced Packet eXchange   Abbreviated SPX. A set of Novell NetWare protocols implemented on top of IPX (Internetwork Packet eXchange) to form a transport-layer interface.

S

SPX provides additional capabilities over IPX. For example, it guarantees packet delivery by having the destination node verify that the data were received correctly. If no response is received within a specified time, SPX retransmits the packet. If several retransmissions fail to return an acknowledgment, SPX assumes that the connection has failed and informs the operator. All packets in the transmission are sent in sequence, and they all take the same path to their destination node.

See also Internetwork Packet eXchange.

sequential access   An access method used by some storage devices, such as tapes, that requires them to start at the beginning to find a specific storage location. If the information is toward the end of the tape, access can take a long time.

See also random access.

serial communications The transmission of information from computer to computer or from computer to peripheral device one bit at a time.

Serial communications can be synchronous and controlled by a clock, or they can be asynchronous and coordinated by start and stop bits embedded in the data stream. The sending and receiving devices must both use the same baud rate, parity setting, and other communication parameters.

See also 1394; asynchronous transmission; High Speed Serial Interface; RS-232-C; RS-422; RS-423; RS-449; RS-485; RS-530; Serial Storage Architecture; synchronous transmission; Universal Serial Bus.

Serial Line Internet Protocol Abbreviated SLIP. A protocol used to run Internet Protocol over serial lines or telephone connections using modems.

SLIP allows a computer to establish a temporary direct connection to the Internet via modem and to appear to the host system as if it were a port on the host's network.

SLIP is slowly being replaced by PPP (Point-to-Point Protocol).

See also Internet Protocol; Point-to-Point Protocol.

serial port A computer input/output port that supports serial communications, in which information is processed one bit at a time.

RS-232-C is a common protocol used on serial ports when communicating with modems, printers, mice, and other peripherals.

See also parallel port.

Serial Storage Architecture Abbreviated SSA. A high-performance serial interface, originally developed by IBM, used to connect peripherals, such as scanners, disk drives, optical disks, and printers, to workstations or servers.

A typical SSA interface has two ports with a total bandwidth of 80Mbps and can manage two 20Mbps transmissions simultaneously, one in each direction. The shielded four-wire cable is configured as two pairs, and the maximum cable length is 25 meters (82 feet).

SSA is also specified as a physical layer serial interface in SCSI-3.

See also 1394; Fibre Channel; SCSI-3; serial communications.

server Any computer that makes access to files, printing, communications, and other services available to users of the network.

In large networks, a dedicated server runs a special network operating system; in smaller installations, a nondedicated server may run a personal computer operating system with peer-to-peer networking software running on top.

A server typically has a more advanced processor, more memory, a larger cache, and more disk storage than a single-user workstation. A server may also have several processors rather than just one and may be dedicated to a specific support function such as printing, e-mail, or communications. Many servers also have large power supplies, UPS (uninterruptible power supply) support, and fault-tolerant features, such as RAID technology.

On the Internet, a server responds to requests from a client, usually a Web browser.

See also access server; communications/ modem server; file server; print server; Web server.

server application   In Object Linking and Embedding (OLE), an application that creates OLE objects.

See also Object Linking and Embedding.

server-based application   An application run from the server rather than from a local hard disk.

See also client application; thin client.

Server Manager   A Microsoft Windows NT Server utility used to manage domains, workgroups, and computers.

Server Message Block   Abbreviated SMB. A distributed file-system network protocol, developed by Microsoft and adopted by many other vendors, that allows a computer to use the files and other resources of another computer as though they were local. For network transfers, SMBs are encapsulated within the NetBIOS network control block packet.

server push   A mechanism used on the Internet whereby a client application, usually a Web browser, maintains an open connection to a Web site, and the Web server provides new content to the client automatically, as soon as the new content becomes available. This process continues until the server decides to close the connection.

See also client pull.

server root   A directory on a Web server that contains the server program as well as configuration and information files.

Server service   In Microsoft Windows NT Server, a service that manages access to and sharing of local resources attached to the network.

server side include   Abbreviated SSI. A method used to create dynamic Web pages.

The INCLUDE statement is used to embed commands within an HTML document and tells the Web server to perform specific tasks. A common way of using INCLUDE is to tell the server to load the contents of another external file at a specific point in the original HTML document.

SSIs can degrade server performance due to the number of repeated disk accesses they make, and they can also prove to be a security problem.

See also Extensible Markup Language; HyperText Markup Language.

service   In Microsoft Windows NT, a process that performs a particular system function and often provides an API (application programming interface) so that other processes can take advantage of its abilities.

See also Alerter service; Messenger service; Server service.

Service Advertising Protocol   Abbreviated SAP. A protocol that provides a method for servers, printers, and other devices to advertise their services on a Novell NetWare network and allows routers to create

S

and maintain a database of current internetwork server information.

SAP packets are normally broadcast every 60 seconds and include the name, network address, and type of service offered by a server.

SAP traffic can be excessive on large networks, and SAP filtering is often used to reduce the traffic; SAP traffic can be severely reduced or even eliminated from rarely used servers.

service bureau   A company that provides data processing or business software development services to its customers.

A service bureau might provide typesetting, prepress production, optical document scanning, or other services.

By using a service bureau, a company can avoid the high hardware and personnel costs associated with running its own in-house services.

See also outsourcing.

Service Level Agreement   Abbreviated SLA. An agreement between a user and a service provider that defines the terms and conditions of the service, as well as being a means for evaluating the service provided against the service specified.

See also Internet Service Provider; service provider.

service pack   A periodic update to the Microsoft Windows family of operating systems.

A service pack includes fixes to bugs and problems reported by both customers and

by Microsoft and may also contain additional new features or applications.

Service Profile Identifier   Abbreviated SPID. An 8- to 14-character identifier associated with an ISDN connection that defines the services available on that connection.

The SPID is actually stored at the telephone company central office and is accessed by and used to identify your ISDN service. Don't lose it; your ISDN system will not run without it.

See also Integrated Services Digital Network.

service provider   A general term used to describe those companies providing a connection to the Internet or to other communications services. Access methods vary from high-speed dedicated access to dialup using SLIP or PPP.

See also Internet Service Provider.

servlet   A small application that is written in the Java programming language and runs on a Web server.

SERVMAN   A Novell NetWare utility used to manage the server and view network information, including operating system performance parameters and IPX/SPX (Internetwork Packet eXchange/Sequenced Packet eXchange) settings.

It also provides a convenient front end to the SET command, as well as information about the number of running processes, NetWare Loadable Modules (NLMs) installed, volumes mounted, users logged in, and name spaces loaded.

In NetWare 5, SERVMAN has been merged into MONITOR.
See also MONITOR; SET.

session   1. The time during which a program is running on either a local or a remote computer.

2. An MS-DOS or a Microsoft Windows program run as a separate protected task under certain multitasking operating systems, such as OS/2.

3. In communications, the name for the active connection between a mainframe terminal (or a personal computer emulating a terminal) and the computer itself. Many different transactions or message exchanges may take place during a single session.
See also process; thread.

session layer   The fifth of seven layers of the OSI Reference Model for computer-to-computer communications.

The session layer coordinates communications and maintains the session for as long as it is needed, performing security, logging, and administrative functions.
See also OSI Reference Model.

SET   A Novell NetWare server command used to establish operating system parameters, including parameters for communications, the memory pool, file and directory caching, the disk and file system, locking, transaction tracking, the NetWare Core Protocol (NCP), and error handling.

The SET command is also used by many other operating systems, including MS-DOS, OS/2, and Unix, to establish environment values.

setup string   *See* control code.

SFT   *See* System Fault Tolerance.

sgi   *See* Silicon Graphics, Inc.

SGML   *See* Standard Generalized Markup Language.

SGRAM   *See* synchronous graphics RAM.

shadow member   One of two members of a mirror set. The primary member contains the original data; the shadow member contains the copy. The shadow member is read only if the primary member cannot be read.
See also disk mirroring; primary member.

shadow memory   The technique of copying the contents of the BIOS ROM into faster RAM when the computer first boots up.

Because RAM is usually two to three times faster than ROM, and the speedier access reduces the time required to execute a BIOS routine, the processor spends more time working and less time waiting.

share   In Microsoft Windows NT, a resource such as a printer or a directory, shared by a server or a peer on the network.

shared folder   In a networked Macintosh, a folder that is available to other users, either without restriction or through a password. A shared folder in the Macintosh is comparable to a network directory on a PC.

shared memory   An interprocess communications technique in which the same memory is accessed by more than one program

S

running in a multitasking operating system. Semaphores or other management elements prevent the applications from colliding or trying to update the same information at the same time.

See also mailslots; named pipe; pipe; semaphore; socket.

shell   In Unix, the command processor. The shell accepts commands from the user, interprets them, and passes them to the operating system for execution.

The three major shells are the Bourne shell (the original Unix shell from AT&T), the C shell (developed as a part of the BSD Unix efforts), and the Korn shell (also developed by AT&T).

In recent years several public-domain shells have become popular, including Bash (the Bourne-again shell), which is often used on Linux, Tcsh, and Zsh.

See also Bash shell; Bourne shell; C shell; Korn shell.

shielded cable   Cable protected against electromagnetic and radio frequency interference (RFI) by metal-backed mylar foil and plastic or PVC.

See also unshielded cable.

shielded twisted-pair cable   Abbreviated STP. Cable with a foil shield and copper braid surrounding the pairs of wires.

The wires have a minimum number of twists per foot of cable length; the greater the number of twists, the lower the crosstalk. STP offers high-speed transmission for useful distances, and it is often associated with Token Ring networks, but its bulk quickly fills up wiring conduits.

See also crosstalk; shielded cable; unshielded twisted-pair cable.

SHIELDED TWISTED-PAIR CABLE

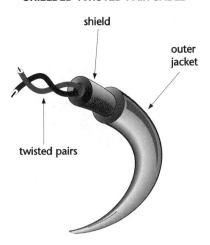

shield

outer jacket

twisted pairs

short   *See* short circuit.

short circuit   Often abbreviated to short. A circuit that is accidentally completed at a point too close to its origin to allow normal or complete operation. In cabling, a short circuit often occurs when two stripped wires touch.

shortcut keystroke   *See* key combination.

shortest-path routing   A routing algorithm in which paths to all network destinations are calculated. The shortest path is then determined by a cost assigned to each link.

short-haul modem   A simple, low-cost modem that can transmit information only over short distances, such as from one side of a building to the other side.

See also line driver; long-haul modem.

S-HTTP   *See* Secure HTTP.

S/HTTP   *See* Secure HTTP.

SID   *See* security identifier.

SIG   *See* special interest group.

signal-to-noise ratio   Abbreviated SNR. The ratio between the desired signal and the unwanted noise at a specific point in a cable; a measure of signal quality.

SNR is particularly important in networks using unshielded twisted-pair cable (UTP). SNR specifications for token-ring networks are much more stringent than those for 10BaseT or ARCnet.

signature   A short text file that is automatically added to the end of your e-mail or Usenet posts.

A signature file usually contains your name (or alias) and e-mail address, and some people like to add pithy quotes; whatever your signature file contains, remember to keep it short.

Silicon Graphics Certified IRIX Network Administrator   An advanced certification from Silicon Graphics designed to demonstrate proficiency in administering Silicon Graphics IRIX-based networks.

Silicon Graphics Certified IRIX System Administrator   A basic certification from Silicon Graphics designed to demonstrate proficiency in administering Silicon Graphics IRIX systems.

Silicon Graphics, Inc.   Sometimes abbreviated sgi. A major manufacturer of Unix and RISC-based graphics workstations and supercomputers.

The company's workstations are used in product engineering, computer simulation, data warehousing, and in Hollywood post-production facilities to add special effects.

For more information on Silicon Graphics Inc, see www.sgi.com.

Simple Mail Transfer Protocol   Abbreviated SMTP. The TCP/IP (Transmission Control Protocol/Internet Protocol) protocol that provides a simple e-mail service and is responsible for moving e-mail messages from one e-mail server to another. SMTP provides a direct end-to-end mail delivery, which is rather unusual; most mail systems use store-and-forward protocols.

S

341

The e-mail servers run either Post Office Protocol (POP) or Internet Mail Access Protocol (IMAP) to distribute e-mail messages to users.

Many third-party vendors sell host software capable of exchanging SMTP e-mail with proprietary e-mail systems, such as IBM's PROFS.

See also Internet Mail Access Protocol; Post Office Protocol; store-and-forward.

Simple Network Management Protocol   Abbreviated SNMP. A standard protocol, part of the TCP/IP (Transmission Control Protocol/Internet Protocol) suite, used to manage and monitor nodes on a network. The accompanying illustration shows how the SNMP manager and agent are organized.

SNMP is a communications protocol for collecting information about devices on the network, including hubs, routers, and bridges. Each piece of information to be collected about a device is defined in a Management Information Base (MIB). SNMP uses UDP (User Datagram Protocol) to send and receive messages on the network.

SIMPLE NETWORK MANAGEMENT PROTOCOL

SNMP manager

| management application |
| SNMP manager |
| UDP |
| IP |
| network protocol |

SNMP agent

| SNMP managed resources |
| SNMP agent |
| UDP |
| IP |
| network protocol |

network

single-attached station   Abbreviated SAS. In the Fiber Distributed Data Interface (FDDI), a device attached to only one of the dual, counter-rotating rings.

Noncritical devices, such as workstations, are often connected using SASs, because they are less expensive than dual-attached stations (DASs).

See also dual-attached station; Fiber Distributed Data Interface.

single-ended SCSI   A Small Computer System Interface (SCSI) bus-wiring scheme that uses a single wire for each signal transmitted on the bus. Used more often than differential SCSI.

See also differential SCSI; Small Computer System Interface.

single large expensive disk   Abbreviated SLED. The traditional alternative to RAID (redundant array of inexpensive disks), used by most networks.

Single-Line Digital Subscriber Line   Abbreviated SDSL; sometimes called Symmetrical Digital Subscriber Line. A symmetrical, bidirectional Digital Subscriber Line service that operates on one twisted-pair wire.

SDSL can provide data rates of up to the T1 rate of 1.544Mbps over a cable length of up to 1,000 feet, and because it operates above the voice frequency, voice and data can be carried on the same connection at the same time.

See also Asymmetric Digital Subscriber Line; Digital Subscriber Line; High-Bit-Rate Digital Subscriber Line; Rate-Adaptive Digital Subscriber Line; Very-High-Bit-Rate Digital Subscriber Line.

single login   An authentication process that allows users to log in to a complex network only once rather than requiring them to log in to each separate network element.

Additional connections and drive mappings are managed in the background as a part of the authentication process. Also known as single sign-on.

single-mode fiber   Narrow diameter fiber-optic cable in which lasers rather than LEDs are used to transmit signals through the cable.

Single-mode fiber allows only one route for a light wave to pass through, and it can transmit signals over considerable distances. For this reason, it is often used in telephone networks rather than in local-area networks.

See also multimode fiber.

single reference time server   In Novell NetWare, the server that determines the network time and provides that information to workstations and to secondary time servers on the network.

Single reference time servers are not compatible with reference or primary time servers.

See also primary time server; reference time server; secondary time server.

single sign-on   *See* single login.

single-user logon   In Microsoft Windows NT, a mechanism that allows a user to connect to multiple servers, domains, and applications with a single logon.

See also single login.

S

single-user system   A computer system designed for use by one person at a time, often on a personal computer.

Windows 95 and 98, MS-DOS, the MacOS, OS/2 Warp, and Windows NT Workstation are all examples of single-user operating systems. Unix and most network operating systems are multiuser systems.

Site   In Microsoft Active Directory, one or more TCP/IP (Transmission Control Protocol/Internet Protocol) subnets linked by reliable network connections.

site license   A software license that covers all the installed copies of a software package at a specific location or locations.

Some large corporations and government institutions prefer to negotiate a site license rather than try to pay for and keep track of all the individual copies they use. A site license may allow unlimited copies for internal use, or it may limit the number of copies of a program the corporation can use concurrently.

See also application metering; concurrent license.

SLA   *See* Service Level Agreement.

slash   The / character. In many operating systems, used to separate command-line switches that alter the default settings for an operating system command.

Used in Unix as the name of the root filesystem and also to separate elements (files and directories) in a directory pathname.

SLED   *See* single large expensive disk.

SLIP   *See* Serial Line Internet Protocol.

Small Computer System Interface   Abbreviated SCSI, which is pronounced "scuzzy."

A high-speed parallel interface defined by the ANSI X3T9.2 committee. SCSI is used to connect a computer to peripheral devices using only one port. Devices connected in this way are said to be "daisy-chained," and each device must have a unique identifier or priority number.

SCSI has been standard on the Macintosh since the Mac Plus was introduced, and it is available on personal computers as a single host adapter, using a special connector.

SCSI is often used to connect hard disks, tape drives, CD-ROM drives, and other mass storage media, as well as scanners and printers.

Features of the SCSI definition include:

- The bus can manage simultaneous reads and writes.

- The original standard supports as many as 7 devices on a single host adapter; new standards support as many as 16 devices and a bus length of up to 25 meters (80 feet).

- SCSI devices have their own control circuitry and can disconnect from the host adapter to process tasks on their own, freeing the bus for other purposes.

Table S.1 lists the various SCSI standards, along with the bus speed in Mbps, the bus width in bits, and the maximum number of devices supported.

See also Fast SCSI; Fast/Wide SCSI; SCSI-1; SCSI-2; SCSI-3; Ultra SCSI; Ultra2 SCSI; Wide Ultra SCSI; Wide Ultra2 SCSI.

TABLE S.1 SCSI STANDARDS

SCSI Standard	Maximum Bus Speed	Bus Width	Maximum Devices
SCSI-1	5	8	8
Fast SCSI	10	8	8
Fast/Wide SCSI	20	16	16
Ultra SCSI	20	8	8
Wide Ultra SCSI	40	16	16
Ultra2 SCSI	40	8	8
Wide Ultra2 SCSI	80	16	16

S

small office/home office   Abbreviated SOHO. That portion of the market for computer services occupied by small offices and home-based businesses rather than by large corporate buyers. SOHO is a small but growing market sector characterized by very well informed buyers.

The large number of home offices is the result of many factors in the economy, including corporate downsizing and cheaper, more capable computers and office equipment, and is a trend that is likely to continue.

See also telecommuting.

smart hub   A concentrator, used in Ethernet or ARCnet networks, with certain network-management facilities built in to firmware that allow the network administrator to control and plan network configurations; also known as an intelligent hub.

In token-ring networks, a smart hub is known as a Controlled Access Unit (CAU). A CAU can determine if nodes are operating, connect and disconnect nodes, and monitor node activity.

See also Controlled Access Unit.

smart terminal   *See* intelligent terminal.

SMB   *See* Server Message Block.

SMDS   *See* Switched Multimegabit Data Services.

smiley   A group of text characters used in e-mail and in Usenet posts to indicate humor or some other emotion. You must turn a smiley on its side for it to make sense.

Hundreds of smileys are in common use, and new ones are invented all the time. Two popular favorites are :-), to indicate smiling, and ;-), to indicate winking.

See also emoticon.

S/MIME   *See* Secure MIME.

SMM   *See* system management mode.

SMS   *See* Storage Management Services.

SMTP   *See* Simple Mail Transfer Protocol.

SNA   *See* Systems Network Architecture.

SNA gateway   A hardware and software device that connects an SNA (Systems Network Architecture) mainframe to a local-area network.

SNA gateway products are available from Microsoft and from Novell.

See also Microsoft SNA Server; NetWare for SNA.

snail mail   A rude reference to the relatively slow speed of the conventional postal service when compared with the speed of online e-mail systems.

sneakernet   An informal method of file sharing in which a user copies files on to a floppy disk and then carries the disk to the office of a co-worker.

sniffer   A small program loaded onto a system by an intruder, designed to monitor specific traffic on the network.

The sniffer program watches for the first part of any remote login session that includes the user name, password, and host name of a person logging in to another machine.

Once this information is in the hands of the intruder, he or she can log on to that system at will. One weakly secured network can therefore expose not only the local systems, but also any remote systems to which the local users connect.

Sniffer is also the name of a network analyzer product from Network General.

See also intruder; network analyzer; spoofing; Trojan Horse.

SNMP   *See* Simple Network Management Protocol.

SNR   *See* signal-to-noise ratio.

social engineering   A method used by intruders to collect password information from genuine users by false pretenses.

Social engineering can take many forms. For example, a potential intruder telephones a busy technical support department, claiming to be a new service engineer who has just lost his password. Rather than go through the appropriate procedures, the technical support person assigns a new password over the phone and implements it on the system so that the new engineer can use it immediately.

See also brute-force attack; dictionary attack; sniffer.

socket   **1.** A general-purpose interprocess communication mechanism, originally developed in the Unix world. Sockets allow processes that are not running at the same time or on the same system to exchange information; pairs of cooperating sockets manage communications between the processes on your computer and those on a remote computer in a networked environment. You can read data from or write data to a socket just as you can to a file. Sockets are now used in many other environments.

2. That part of an IPX (Internetwork Packet eXchange) internetwork node address that represents the destination of an IPX packet. Certain sockets are reserved by NetWare for particular applications. For example, IPX delivers all NetWare Core Protocol (NCP) request packets to socket 451h.

See also mailslots; named pipe; pipe; semaphore; shared memory; WinSock.

socket services Part of the software support needed for PCMCIA (PC Memory Card International Association) hardware devices in a portable computer, controlling the interface to the hardware.

Socket services is the lowest layer in the software that manages PCMCIA cards. It provides a BIOS-level software interface to the hardware, effectively hiding the specific details from higher levels of software. Socket services also detect when you insert or remove a PCMCIA card and identify the type of card.

See also card services.

SOCKS A proxy protocol that provides a secure channel between two TCP/IP (Transmission Control Protocol/Internet Protocol) systems, usually a Web browser running on an internal corporate intranet and a Web server on the Internet.

SOCKS provides firewall services, as well as fault tolerant features, auditing, and management.

See also firewall; proxy server; Secure Sockets Layer; Secure WAN.

soft modem *See* controllerless modem.

software An application program or operating system that a computer can execute. *Software* is a broad term that can imply one or many programs, and it can also refer to applications that may consist of more than one program.

software development kit Abbreviated SDK. A package that contains useful software development tools, such as editors, compilers, debuggers, libraries, and technical information.

software interrupt An interrupt generated by an instruction in a program, often called a trap.

See also hardware interrupt.

software license A license to use a software package subject to certain conditions. These conditions usually define the rights of the purchaser and limit the liability of the program's publisher.

See also application metering; site license.

software piracy The illegal copying and distribution of copyrighted software. Copying software, like duplicating any copyrighted material, is illegal.

In an attempt to discourage software piracy, the Software Publishers Association (SPA) has run several advertising campaigns, including a billboard showing a pair of handcuffs and the message "Copy software illegally and you could get this hardware absolutely free." The SPA has been successful in persuading companies to inventory their software so that corporations know which software copies they have purchased legally.

Software Publishers Association   Abbreviated SPA. An association of software developers and distributors most notable for their tactics in fighting software piracy, including extremely blunt advertising campaigns and unannounced visits to companies suspected of acts of piracy.

software suite   A selection of business applications sold as a single integrated package.

The standard version of a software suite usually includes a word processor, a spreadsheet, presentation graphics, and an e-mail program, and the professional version will often add a database program. The cost of the suite is significantly less than the cost of purchasing each application separately. Additional benefits include inter-application communications, easy installation of the whole package, and reduced training time.

Microsoft Office and Lotus SmartSuite are examples of popular software suites.

SOHO   *See* small office/home office.

Solaris   A version of Unix from SunSoft that runs on Intel-based PCs and Sun workstations; SunSoft is a subsidiary of Sun Microsystems.

Solaris is based on Unix System V Release 4 and includes networking support, the OpenWindows graphical user interface, and DeskSet, an integrated desktop that includes some 50 productivity tools. Solaris

supports a Java Virtual Machine as well as the Common Desktop Environment and WebNFS. Multiprocessor systems are supported, and Solaris uses symmetrical multiprocessing techniques to take advantage of the additional processing power.

See also Common Desktop Environment; Java Virtual Machine; SunOS; WebNFS.

SOM   *See* System Object Model.

SONET   *See* Synchronous Optical Network

source address   The address portion of a packet or datagram that identifies the sender.

See also destination address.

source license   A software license that gives the user the right to possess and modify the original source code from which an application or operating system is created.

In the past, source licenses have either been simply impossible to obtain or have been prohibitively expensive. With the spread of open source software, things are changing.

See also binary license; open source software

source routing   IBM's Token Ring method of routing data frames through a network consisting of multiple LANs by specifying the route to be traveled in each frame. The route is actually determined by the end stations through a discovery process supported by source-bridge routers.

IBM bridges can be of two types:

- Single-route broadcasting allows certain bridges to pass the packet so that only a single copy arrives on each ring in the network.

- All-routes broadcasting sends the packet across all the possible routes in the network, so as many copies of the packet arrive at the destination as there are bridges in the network.

SPA   *See* Software Publishers Association.

space parity   *See* parity.

spanning tree   A network segment that is free of logical loops; a network structure that has a root node and one path, usually the shortest distance, that connects all the other nodes.

This tree structure is used in bridged networks to make routing decisions, especially if multiple paths connect nodes, because these loops could lead to packets looping on their way to their destination.

spanning tree algorithm   A technique based on the IEEE 802.1 standard that finds the most desirable path between segments of a multilooped, bridged network.

If multiple paths exist in the network, the spanning tree algorithm finds the most efficient path and limits the link between the two networks to this single active path. If this path fails because of a cable failure or other problem, the algorithm reconfigures the network to activate another path, thus keeping the network running.

SPARC   *See* Scalable Performance Architecture.

SPARCstation   A Sun Microsystems family of Unix workstations based on the SPARC processor.

SPARCstations range from small, diskless desktop systems to high-performance, tower servers in multiprocessor configurations.

See also Scalable Performance Architecture; Sun Microsystems, Inc.

SPEC benchmarks   *See* Systems Performance Evaluation Cooperative benchmarks.

special group   In Microsoft Windows NT Server, a group whose membership is predefined and automatically updated.

Special groups provide an easy way to describe sets of users. For example, the Everyone group always includes all domain users and is updated automatically as user accounts are added and deleted.

special interest group   Abbreviated SIG. A group that meets to share information about a specific topic, such as particular hardware, software, programming languages, or operating systems. A SIG is often part of a user group or other organization.

SPID   *See* Service Profile Identifier.

spider   A World Wide Web application that automatically locates and collects information about new Web sites. Spiders are most often used to create large databases of Web sites that in turn are accessed by search engines responding to user requests for information.

See also robot; search engine.

S

spike   A short, transient electrical signal, often of very high amplitude.

See also power conditioning; power surge; surge suppressor.

splat   A slang expression for the asterisk character (*) that you can yell across a crowded room without fear of being misunderstood.

See also bang.

splitter server   In Internet video, a server that receives a video signal and then re-broadcasts that signal across a network.

See also IP multicast; multicast; stream thinning.

spoofing   A security breach in which an intruder logs on to the system by pretending to be a genuine user.

The intruder may obtain another person's user name and password in casual conversation or, in a more concerted attack, may use a network analyzer to monitor and capture network traffic.

See also brute-force attack; dictionary attack; sniffer; social engineering; Trojan Horse.

spooler   *See* print spooler.

SPX   *See* Sequenced Packet eXchange.

SQE   Abbreviation for signal quality error. *See* heartbeat.

SQL   *See* Structured Query Language.

SRAM   *See* static RAM.

SSA   *See* Serial Storage Architecture.

SSE   *See* Streaming SIMD Extensions.

SSI   *See* server side include.

SSL   *See* Secure Sockets Layer.

ST506 Interface   A popular hard-disk interface standard developed by Seagate Technologies, first used in IBM's PC/XT computer.

The interface is still used in systems with disk capacities smaller than about 40MB. ST506 has a relatively slow data-transfer rate of 5Mbps.

A later variation of ST506, called ST412, adds several improvements. Because these two interfaces are so closely related, they are often referred to as ST506/412.

See also Enhanced Small Device Interface; Integrated Drive Electronics; Small Computer System Interface.

ST   *See* straight-tip connector.

Standard Generalized Markup Language   Abbreviated SGML. A 1986 standard (ISO 8879) for defining the structure and managing the contents of any digital document.

The standard specifies a definition for formatting a digital document so that it can be modified, viewed, or output on any computer system. Each SGML document consists of two parts:

- The DTD (Document Type Definition) defines the structure of the document.

- The DI (Document Instance) describes the data or text of the document.

HTML, used in World Wide Web documents on the Internet, is a part of SGML.

See also Extensible Markup Language; HyperText Markup Language; Virtual Reality Modeling Language.

Standby Monitor   In a Token Ring network, a network node that serves as a backup to the Active Monitor and can take over in the event that the Active Monitor fails.

See also Active Monitor.

star network   A network topology in the form of a star.

At the center of the star is a wiring hub or concentrator, and the nodes or workstations are arranged around the central point representing the points of the star. Wiring costs tend to be higher for star networks than for other configurations, because each node requires its own individual cable. Star

networks do not follow any of the IEEE standards.

See also bus network; ring network; topology.

star-dot-star   A commonly available file specification (*.*) that uses the asterisk wildcard character. It is equivalent to specifying any combination of filename and filename extension.

StarLAN   A network operating system from AT&T that implements CSMA/CD (Carrier Sense Multiple Access/Collision Detection) protocols on twisted-pair cable transmitting at 1Mbps; a subset of 802.3.

In 1988, StarLAN was renamed StarLAN 1, and StarLAN 10 was launched. StarLAN 10 is a 10Mbps Ethernet version that uses twisted-pair cable or fiber-optic cable.

S

STAR NETWORK

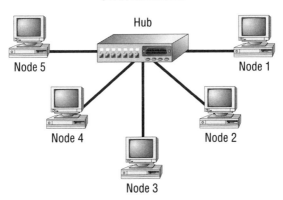

Hub

Node 5

Node 1

Node 4

Node 2

Node 3

start bit   In asynchronous transmissions, a start bit is transmitted to indicate the beginning of a new data word.

See also data bits; parity; stop bit.

STARTUP.NCF   A Novell NetWare server configuration boot file that loads the NetWare server's disk driver, along with name spaces and certain SET parameters.

See also SET.

stateless filter   *See* packet-level filter.

static RAM   Abbreviated SRAM, pronounced "ess-ram." A type of computer memory that retains its contents as long as power is applied; it does not need constant refreshment, as required by dynamic RAM (DRAM) chips.

An SRAM chip can store only about one-fourth of the information that a DRAM chip of the same complexity can hold. However, SRAM, with access times of 10 to 25 nanoseconds, is much faster than DRAM, at 80 nanoseconds or more, and is often used in caches. SRAM is four to five times as expensive as DRAM.

static routing   A method used to preprogram connecting paths between networks into a router by a network administrator.

If a connection fails, the administrator must reprogram the router to use a new path. In most large networks, the delay that this causes is unacceptable, and dynamic routing is used instead. Dynamic routing automatically locates and uses the best available path and recalculates paths if a connection fails.

See also dynamic routing.

statistical multiplexing   Abbreviated stat mux. In communications, a method of sharing a transmission channel by using statistical techniques to allocate resources.

A statistical multiplexer can analyze traffic density and dynamically switch to a different channel pattern to speed up the transmission. At the receiving end, the different signals are merged back into individual streams.

See also frequency-division multiplexing; inverse multiplexing; time-division multiplexing.

stat mux   *See* statistical multiplexing.

stealth virus   A form of virus that attempts to hide from antivirus software and from the operating system by remaining in memory.

See also boot sector virus; file-infecting virus; macro virus; multipart virus; polymorphic virus; Trojan Horse; vaccine.

stop bit   In asynchronous transmissions, a stop bit is transmitted to indicate the end of the current data word. Depending on the convention in use, one or two stop bits are used.

See also data bits; parity; start bit.

storage area network   Abbreviated SAN. A method used to physically separate the storage function of the network from the data-processing function.

SAN provides a separate network devoted to storage and so helps to reduce network traffic by isolating large data transfers such as backups. Most of the SAN vendors, including StorageTek and Compaq, use a Fibre

Channel–based SAN system, although IBM has proposed a proprietary architecture.

See also network attached storage.

Storage Management Services   Abbreviated SMS. A set of Novell NetWare Loadable Modules and other software that allows data to be backed up and retrieved from the server and from workstations attached to the network. SMS is independent of both the hardware used to create the backup and also the file systems actually being backed up or restored.

store-and-forward   A method that temporarily stores messages at intermediate nodes before forwarding them to the next destination. This technique allows routing over networks that are not available at all times and lets users take advantage of off-peak rates when traffic and costs might be lower.

See also message switching.

STP   *See* shielded twisted-pair cable.

straight-tip connector   Abbreviated ST. A fiber-optic cable connector that maintains the perfect alignment of the ends of the connected fibers, required for efficient light transmission.

stream   In Internet video, an end-to-end connection between a client and a server that lets a user start to look at a video clip before the whole file has finished downloading.

streaming   A method used to deliver audio and video content in real time so that the person using the system can interact with the data stream.

A client downloads a portion of the audio/video file, decompresses it, and starts to view the video clip before the rest of the file arrives. Data is built up in a buffer before the playback begins, and the next part of the file is downloaded as the first part plays.

See also IP Multicast multicasting.

S

STRAIGHT-TIP CONNECTOR

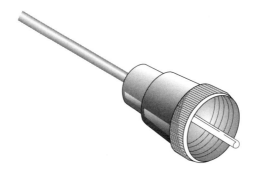

Streaming SIMD Extensions Abbreviated SSE. A set of multimedia instructions introduced with Intel's Pentium III.

SSE provides four main improvements over the Pentium II instruction set:

- Eight new directly addressable 128-bit floating-point registers.

- Eight new instructions for streaming data to and from memory.

- Twelve new Single Instruction, Multiple Data (SIMD) integer instructions.

- Fifty new SMID floating-point instructions.

SSE can benefit 3-D graphics, 2-D images, speech recognition, and MPEG-2 encoding, as well as scientific and engineering applications. Most standard office and business applications will see little or no improvement.

See also Pentium III.

Streaming Single Instruction, Multiple Data Extensions *See* Streaming SIMD Extensions.

streaming tape A high-speed tape backup system designed to optimize throughput; the tape is not stopped during a backup. To use streaming tape, the computer and backup software must be fast enough to keep up with the tape drive.

See also DC-2000; tape cartridge.

STREAMS A Novell NetWare Loadable Module (NLM) that provides a common interface between NetWare and transport protocols such as IPX/SPX, TCP/IP, and SNA.

STREAMS allows services to be provided across the network regardless of the transport protocol in use, because the protocol is transparent to the operating system.

streams A function within Unix that provides flexible communications paths between processes and device drivers.

stream thinning In Internet video, the process of removing video frames to protect the audio feed.

Stream thinning is used to preserve the connection in times of network congestion and to avoid a forced reconnection and its associated disruptive effect on the transmission. Stream thinning restores the full video signal once additional bandwidth becomes available.

StreetTalk The distributed global naming and directory service for Banyan VINES network operating system. The StreetTalk database contains all the necessary information about all nodes and devices on the network, and this database is updated constantly.

Under StreetTalk, all users, printers, and servers have a three-part StreetTalk address in the form of device or user name, domain name, and organization name. StreetTalk also allows nicknames for nodes and devices.

SteetTalk is designed to manage a large number of different environments, including Banyan networks, Windows NT, Unix, and Novell NetWare.

See also domain directory services; Enterprise Network Services; global directory services; NetWare Directory Services; X.500.

string   *See* character string.

stripe set   A single volume created across multiple hard disk drives and accessed in parallel to optimize disk-access time.
See also disk striping; disk striping with parity.

strong password   A password that is specifically designed to be difficult to guess. Strong passwords are always more than 10 characters and always include punctuation characters and numbers.
See also password; weak password.

structured graphics   *See* object-oriented graphics.

Structured Query Language   Abbreviated SQL, pronounced "sequel." In relational database management systems, a query language developed by IBM for use in mainframe applications.

SQL was adopted by Oracle Corporation for use in its database management systems running on all platforms, not just mainframes, and subsequently emerged as a de facto standard for all database management packages.

SQL contains about 60 commands and is used to create, modify, query, and access data organized in tables. It can be used either as an interactive interface or as embedded commands in an application:

• Dynamic SQL statements are interactive, and they can be changed as needed. If you normally access SQL from a command-line environment, you are using dynamic SQL, which is slower than static SQL but much more flexible.

• Static SQL statements are coded into application programs, and as a result, they do not change. These statements are usually processed by a precompiler before being bound into the application.

Many databases implement SQL queries behind the scenes, enabling communication with database servers in systems with client/server architecture.

SQL is an ANSI standard in the United States, as well as a worldwide International Organization for Standardization (ISO) standard.
See also Open Database Connectivity.

structured wiring   A planned cabling system for enterprise-wide network communications, including both voice and data. AT&T's Premises Distribution Systems and IBM's Cabling System are both structured wiring designs.

subdirectory   A directory contained within another directory. The root directory is the top-level directory, from which all other directories must branch. In common use, subdirectory is synonymous with directory or folder.
See also current directory; parent directory; period and double-period directories.

sub-hive   An organizational element in the Microsoft Windows Registry, similar to a subdirectory on a hard disk.

A sub-hive may contain other sub-hives or may contain keys. Microsoft documentation sometimes refers to sub-hives as sub-keys.
See also hive; key; Registry.

sub-key   *See* sub-hive.

S

subnet   A logical network created from a single IP address. A mask is used to identify bits from the host portion of the address to be used for subnet addresses.

See also address classes; Classless Inter-Domain Routing; IP address; subnet address; subnet mask.

subnet address   The subnet portion of an IP address. In a subnetted network, the host part of the IP address is divided into a subnet portion and a host portion by a subnet mask.

See also address classes; Classless Inter-Domain Routing; IP address; subnet; subnet mask.

subnet mask   A number or, more correctly, a bit pattern that identifies which parts of an IP address correspond to the network, subnet, and host portions of the address. Also referred to as an address mask.

See also address classes; Classless Inter-Domain Routing; IP address; subnet; subnet address.

subscribe   To post to a Usenet newsgroup or to join a mailing list. This is not a subscription in the sense of a magazine subscription; no money ever changes hands.

Sun Certified Solaris Administrator

A basic certification from Sun Microsystems designed to recognize technical expertise in installing and administering Solaris-based systems.

See also Sun Microsystems, Inc.

Sun Certified Solaris Network Administrator   An advanced certification from Sun Microsystems designed to recognize technical expertise in networking and administering Solaris-based systems and in the security aspects of Solaris.

See also Sun Microsystems, Inc.

Sun Microsystems, Inc.   A manufacturer of high-powered workstations and one of the major technical forces in the Unix world.

Sun workstations run Solaris, a version of Unix based on Unix System V Release 4, and range from small, diskless desktop systems to high-performance, tower servers in multiprocessor configurations.

For more information on Sun Microsystems, Inc., see www.sun.com.

See also Java; Jini; Network File System; Solaris.

SunOS   A Unix operating system from Sun Microsystems. SunOS is based on BSD Unix; Solaris is based on System V Release 4.

See also Solaris; Sun Microsystems, Inc.

superpipelining   A preprocessing technique used by some microprocessors in which two or more execution stages (such as fetch, decode, execute, or write back) are divided into two or more pipelined stages, giving considerably higher performance.

superscalar   A microprocessor architecture that contains more than one execution unit, or pipeline, allowing the processor to execute more than one instruction per clock cycle.

For example, the Pentium processor is superscalar, with two side-by-side pipelines for integer instructions. The processor determines whether an instruction can be executed in parallel with the next instruction in line. If it does not detect any dependencies, the two instructions are executed.

See also complex instruction set computing; reduced instruction set computing.

superserver   A computer specifically designed for use as a network server.

A superserver is a very high performance system, often characterized by scalable input/output channels, complex multiprocessing features, and a large price tag. It may have several processors, large amounts of error-correcting memory, cache memory, and hard-disk space, as well as fault-tolerant features, such as redundant power supplies.

superuser   A special Unix privilege level, with unlimited access to all files, directories, and commands.

The system administrator must become the superuser to perform certain functions, such as creating new accounts, changing passwords, and other administrative tasks that ordinary users are not allowed to perform for security reasons. The superuser's login name is usually root, with a user ID of 0.

See also avatar.

surfing   To browse your way through various Internet resources, exploring tangents whenever you feel like it.

surge   A short, sudden, and often destructive increase in line voltage. A voltage-regulating device, known as a surge

suppressor, can protect computer equipment against surges.

See also power conditioning; spike; surge suppressor.

surge protector   *See* surge suppressor.

surge suppressor   A voltage-regulating device placed between the computer and the AC line connection that protects the computer system from power surges; also known as a surge protector.

See also power conditioning.

SVC   *See* switched virtual circuit.

SVID   *See* System V Interface Definition.

S/WAN   *See* Secure WAN.

swap   To temporarily move a process from memory to disk, so that another process can use that memory space. When space becomes available again, the process is swapped back into memory. This allows more processes to be loaded than there is physical memory space to run them simultaneously.

swapping   The process of exchanging one item for another. In a virtual memory system, swapping occurs when a program requests a virtual memory location that is not currently in memory. Swapping may also refer to changing floppy or compact disks as needed when using a single disk drive.

swap space   On a hard disk, a file used to store parts of running programs that have

S

been swapped out of memory temporarily to make room for other running programs.

A swap file may be permanent, always occupying the same amount of hard-disk space, even though the application that created it may not be running, or temporary, created as and when needed.

See also permanent swap file; temporary swap file; virtual memory.

Switched 56   A switched four-wire digital data service available from a local exchange carrier that operates at 56Kbps.

See also Virtual Private Network.

Switched Multimegabit Data Services   Abbreviated SMDS. A high-speed metropolitan-area network service based on the 802.6 standard for use over T1 and T3 circuits. SMDS supports Ethernet, Token Ring, and FDDI (Fiber Distributed Data Interface) gateways.

See also Asynchronous Transfer Mode.

switched virtual circuit   Abbreviated SVC. A communications circuit that is established for the duration of the session and then disconnected, much like a normal voice telephone call. SVCs are used extensively in X.25 networks

See also permanent virtual circuit.

Sybase, Inc.   A leading supplier of database management and applications development software, including PowerBuilder, a rapid application development environment, and PowerJEnterprise, a Java development package.

For more information on Sybase, Inc., see www.sybase.com.

Symantec Corporation   A leading developer of utility programs for the PC and the Macintosh whose products include application and system software, security and antivirus packages, remote productivity, and Internet access.

For more information on Symantec Corporation, see www.symantec.com.

Symmetrical Digital Subscriber Line
See Single-Line Digital Subscriber Line

symmetrical multiprocessing   A multiprocessing design that assigns a task to a processor in response to system load as the application starts running. This design makes for a much more flexible system than asymmetrical multiprocessing, in which the programmer matches a specific task to a certain processor while writing the program.

In symmetrical multiprocessing, the overall workload is shared by all processors in the system; system performance increases as more processors are added into the system. The drawback is that symmetrical multiprocessing operating systems are much harder to design than asymmetrical multiprocessing operating systems.

See also asymmetrical multiprocessing.

synchronization   The timing of separate elements or events to occur simultaneously. In computer-to-computer communications, the hardware and software must be synchronized so that file transfers can take place.

See also asynchronous transmission; synchronous transmission.

Synchronous Data Link Control   Abbreviated SDLC. The data-link protocol most widely used in networks that conform to IBM's SNA (Systems Network Architecture).

SDLC is a bit-oriented synchronous protocol that organizes information into well-defined units known as frames. SDLC is similar to the HDLC (High-level Data Link Control) protocol defined by the International Organization for Standardization (ISO).

See also data-link layer; High-level Data Link Control; Systems Network Architecture.

Synchronous Digital Hierarchy   Abbreviated SDH. A set of fiber-optic–based standards from the ITU for use with SONET and ATM in Europe

synchronous DRAM   Abbreviated SDRAM. A high-speed memory technolo-

gy, faster than EDO RAM; used in workstations and servers.

synchronous graphics RAM   Abbreviated SGRAM. A type of high-speed dynamic RAM used in video adapters.

Synchronous Optical Network   Abbreviated SONET. A set of fiber-optic–based communications standards with transmission rates from 51.84Mbps to 13.22Gbps.

First proposed by Bellcore in the mid-1980s, SONET was standardized by ANSI, and the ITU adapted SONET in creating the worldwide Synchronous Digital Hierarchy (SDH) standard.

SONET uses synchronous transmissions in which individual channels (called tributaries) are merged into higher-level channels using time-division multiplexing techniques. Data is carried in frames of 810 bytes, which also includes control information known as the overhead.

See also Optical Carrier; Synchronous Digital Hierarchy.

S

SYNCHRONOUS DATA LINK CONTROL

data start field	address field	control field	information field	cyclic redundancy check	data redundancy check	end flag

synchronous transmission A transmission method that uses a clock signal to regulate data flow.

In synchronous transmissions, frames are separated by equal-sized time intervals. Timing must be controlled precisely on the sending and the receiving computers. Special characters are embedded in the data stream to begin synchronization and to maintain synchronization during the transmission, allowing both computers to check for and correct any variations in timing.

See also asynchronous transmission.

syntax The formal rules of grammar as they apply to a specific programming language or operating system command; in particular, the exact sequence and spelling of command elements required for the command to be interpreted correctly.

syntax error An error in the use of a programming language or operating system command syntax, such as misspelling a keyword or omitting a required space.

SyQuest Technology, Inc. A leading manufacturer of removable storage media, particularly the SCSI-based removable hard disk available for the PC and the Macintosh.

For more information on SyQuest Technology, Inc., see www.syquest.com.

System III The release of Unix from AT&T prior to the release of System V.

System III was the first version of Unix to be ported to the Intel family of processors and formed the basis for SCO's release of XENIX.

System IV A version of Unix from AT&T that was never released outside the company, mostly to avoid confusion with the 4.*x*BSD series of products.

System V The last version of Unix from AT&T, pronounced "System Five." The latest release is known as System V Release 4.2, often abbreviated SVR4 or SVR4.2.

System V Interface Definition Abbreviated SVID. A set of documents released by AT&T that defined the Unix System V interfaces and operating system calls.

system administration The day-to-day administrative and management tasks performed by the system administrator, including:

- Starting up and shutting down the system
- Setting the system time and date
- Assigning and changing passwords
- Adding and removing users and groups
- Installing, upgrading, and removing application packages and installing operating system upgrades
- Backing up the system, storing archives off location, and restoring backups as needed
- Installing and configuring new hardware such as printers, storage devices, and communications systems
- Monitoring system performance and making tuning adjustments as necessary

See also system administrator.

System Administration: Informix Dynamic Server A certification from Informix designed for individuals who configure, maintain, and tune Informix Dynamic Server databases.

See also Database Specialist: Informix-4GL Certified Professional.

system administrator   The person charged with the responsibility of managing the system.

In a very large system, the system administrator may in fact be several people or even a department; if you are running Linux on your system at home, you have to be your own system administrator.

See also system administration.

SYSTEM directory   In Novell NetWare, the SYS:SYSTEM directory created during installation. This directory contains NetWare operating system files and directories, as well as NetWare Loadable Modules (NLMs) and network administrator utilities.

System Fault Tolerance   Abbreviated SFT. In Novell NetWare, a method of duplicating data on several hard disks so that if one disk fails, the data is still available from another disk.

Several levels of hardware and software SFT are available in NetWare, with each level of redundancy decreasing the possibility of catastrophic data loss. For example, SFT I includes HotFix redirection, and SFT II adds disk duplexing and disk mirroring. SFT III uses duplicate servers so that all transactions are recorded on both; if one fails, the other can take over.

See also disk striping; redundant array of inexpensive disks; Transaction Tracking System.

system management mode   Abbreviated SMM. In the Intel family of microprocessors, a low power consumption mode used to conserve battery power. All recent Intel processors have SMM and so are suitable for use in portable, battery-powered computers.

System Object Model   Abbreviated SOM. A specification from IBM that allows objects created in different environments to communicate.

See also Distributed System Object Model.

Systems Application Architecture
Abbreviated SAA. A set of IBM standards, first introduced in 1987, that defines a consistent set of interfaces for future IBM software. Three standards are defined:

• **Common User Access (CUA)**   A graphical user interface definition for products designed for use in an object-oriented operating environment. The OS/2 desktop follows CUA guidelines in its design, and Microsoft Windows implements certain CUA features.

• **Common Programming Interface (CPI)**   A set of application programming interfaces (APIs) designed to encourage independence from the underlying operating system. The standard database query language is Structured Query Language (SQL).

• **Common Communications Support (CCS)**   A common set of communications protocols that interconnect SAA systems and devices.

S

Systems Network Architecture Abbreviated SNA. IBM's proprietary terminal-to-mainframe protocol, introduced in 1974.

SNA describes a seven-layer system, with each layer building on the services provided by the previous layer. Devices on an SNA system are usually connected using the SDLC protocol, running over serial lines. SNA is not compatible with the seven-layer OSI Reference Model.

Systems Performance Evaluation Cooperative benchmarks Abbreviated SPEC benchmarks. A set of ten standardized tests designed to measure workstation performance.

Six of the tests evaluate floating-point performance, and four tests concentrate on integer performance.

Results are reported as SPECmarks, a geometric mean of all ten scores.

SYSTEMS NETWORK ARCHITECTURE

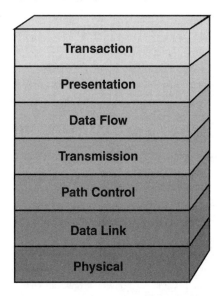

Transaction
Presentation
Data Flow
Transmission
Path Control
Data Link
Physical

T

T *See* tera-.

T1 A long-distance, point-to-point circuit, providing 24 channels of 64Kbps, giving a total bandwidth of 1.544Mbps.

The standard T1 frame is 193 bits long, made up of twenty-four 8-bit voice samples and one synchronization bit. It transmits 8000 frames per second. When a T1 service is made available in single 64Kbps increments, it is known as fractional T1.

In Europe, the comparable circuit is known as E-1, and it has a speed of 2.054Mbps. T1 has been superseded by the CCITT DS-1 designation.

See also fractional T1; T-carrier.

T1 multiplexer A statistical multiplexer that divides the 1.544MbpsT1 bandwidth into 24 separate 64Kbps channels of digitized data or voice.

See also fractional T1; T1.

T1 small aperture terminal Abbreviated TSAT. A small satellite terminal used for digital communications that can handle T1 data rates of up to 1.544Mbps.

See also fractional T1; T1.

T.120 A group of communications and applications protocols that support real-time, multipoint data communications over local area networks and ISDN, dial-up, and Internet connections. T.120 became well known after Microsoft incorporated it into the NetMeeting package.

See also H.323; Microsoft NetMeeting.

T2 A long-distance, point-to-point communications service, providing up to 4 T1 channels.

T2 offers 96 channels of 64Kbps, for a total bandwidth of 6.3Mbps. T2 is not available commercially, although it is used within telephone company networks.

See also T1; T-carrier.

T3 A long-distance, point-to-point communications service, providing up to 28 T1 channels.

T3 can carry 672 channels of 64Kbps, for a total bandwidth of 44.736Mbps, and is usually available over fiber-optic cable. T3 is used almost exclusively by AT&T and the regional telephone operating companies, although certain large private corporations are using T3 with digital microwave or fiber-optic networks.

In Europe, T3 has been superseded by the CCITT DS-3 designation.

See also T1; T-carrier.

T

T4 A long-distance, point-to-point communications service, providing up to 168 T1 channels.

T4 can carry 4032 channels of 64Kbps, for a total bandwidth of 274.176Mbps. T4 can be used for both digitized voice and data transmission.

See also T1; T-carrier.

table In a relational database system, a table is comparable to a database file, but is more highly structured.

The organization of a table is logical, not physical. Each row (or record) in a table contains a unique key, or primary key, so that any item of data in the table can be retrieved by referring only to that key. Through the process known as normalization, all data items in a row are made to depend only on this primary key. View and data dictionaries in a relational database take the form of two-dimensional tables.

tag An element in HTML used to annotate a document. A tag is text enclosed by angle brackets that tells the client Web browser how to display each part of the document. For example, the tag <H1> indicates the start of a level one heading, and the tag </H1> indicates the end of a level one heading.

See also element; HyperText Markup Language.

tag switching A technology from Cisco Systems, Inc., that integrates data-link layer switching with network layer routing for large-scale networks, allowing the integration of ATM switches into the Internet and implementing routing on top of those switches.

See also Asynchronous Transfer Mode; IP over ATM; IP switching.

tap A connector that attaches to a cable without blocking the passage of information along that cable; a connection onto the main transmission medium of the network.

tape cartridge A self-contained tape storage module, containing tape much like that in a video cassette. Tape cartridges are primarily used to back up hard-disk systems.

See also DC-2000; quarter-inch cartridge; Zip drive.

tape drive A computer peripheral device that reads from and writes to magnetic tape.

The drive may use tape on an open reel or from an enclosed tape cartridge. Because tape-management software must search from the beginning of the tape every time it wants to find a file (a process called sequential access), tape is too slow to use as a primary storage system; however, tapes are frequently used to back up hard disks.

See also streaming tape.

TAPI *See* Telephony API.

tar In Unix, a utility program that can create, list, add to, and retrieve from an archive file, which is usually stored on tape. The archive file has the filename extension .tar.

The archive created by tar is not compressed and can be further processed by the Unix compress (extension .Z) or gzip (extension .gz) utilities to give compound extensions such as filename.tar.Z or filename.tar.gz.

task   Any independent running program and the set of system resources that it uses. A task may be an operating system process or part of an application.

See also context switching; multitasking; task switching.

Task Manager   In Microsoft Windows NT, an application that allows a user to manually inspect the tasks running on the computer and select individual tasks for shutdown. Task Manager is opened by pressing Ctrl+Alt+Del.

task switching   To change from one running program to another quickly, either at the direction of the operating system or at the request of the user.

TB   *See* terabyte.

T-carrier   A digital communications service from a common carrier for voice or data transmission.

The four-level, time-division multiplexing specification for the U.S. telephone system allows the bit stream of the smaller carriers to be multiplexed into the larger ones.

The following are the four service levels:

- **T1**   Provides 24 channels of 64Kbps, giving a total bandwidth of 1.544Mbps. When a T1 service is made available in single 64Kbps increments, it is known as fractional T1.

- **T2**   The equivalent of 4 T1 services, T2 offers 96 channels of 64Kbps, for a total bandwidth of 6.3Mbps.

- **T3**   The equivalent of 28 T1 circuits, T3 offers 672 channels of 64Kbps, for a total bandwidth of 44.736Mbps. T3 is available commercially, but is not often used for LANs.

- **T4**   The equivalent of 168 T1 circuits, T4 provides 4,032 channels of 64Kbps, for a total bandwidth of 274.176Mbps.

See also T1; T2; T3; T4.

T

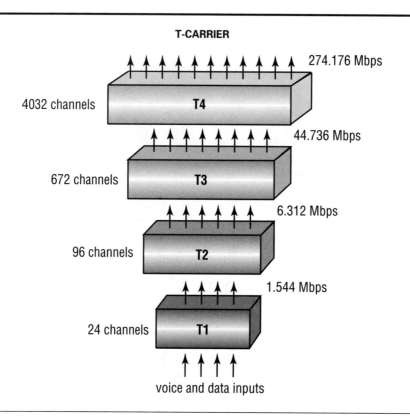

T-CARRIER

274.176 Mbps

4032 channels — T4

44.736 Mbps

672 channels — T3

6.312 Mbps

96 channels — T2

1.544 Mbps

24 channels — T1

voice and data inputs

Tcl   *See* Tool Command Language.

TCM   *See* trellis-coded modulation.

TCO   *See* total cost of ownership.

T-connector   A T-shaped device, used with coaxial cable, that connects two thin Ethernet cables and also provides a third connector for the network interface card.

T-CONNECTOR

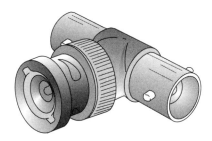

TCP   *See* Transmission Control Protocol.

TCP/IP   *See* Transmission Control Protocol/Internet Protocol.

TCP ports   In a TCP/IP network when a computer connects with another computer to access a specific service, and end-to-end connection is established and a socket is set up at each end of the connection. This socket is created at a particular port number, depending on the application in use. Table T.1 lists the port numbers used for some of the common protocols.

T

TABLE T.1 PORT NUMBERS FOR COMMON PROTOCOLS

Port Number	Protocol
21	File Transfer Protocol
23	Telnet
25	Simple Mail Transfer Protocol
70	Gopher
79	Finger
80	Hypertext Transfer Protocol
119	Network News Transfer Protocol

TDM *See* time-division multiplexing.

TDMA *See* Time Division Multiple Access.

TDR *See* time-domain reflectometer.

Technical and Office Protocol Abbreviated TOP. An Ethernet implementation for use in an engineering environment, developed by Boeing Corporation.
See also Manufacturing Automation Protocol.

telecommunications A general term for the electronic transmission of all forms of information, including digital data, voice, fax, sound, and video, from one location to another over some form of communications link.

Telecommunications Industry Association Abbreviated TIA. An important trade group, active in the areas of standards development, trade shows, international marketing, and legislative efforts.

The TIA often works in close association with the Electronic Industries Association (EIA).

For more information on TIA, see www.tiaonline.org.

See also Electronic Industries Association.

telecommuting Working at home on a computer connected to the office by modems and telephone lines instead of commuting to the office.

Telecommuting saves time, cuts down on automobile use and pollution, and decreases stress. Some local and state governments actively encourage telecommuting to keep the number of commuters as low as possible. Most studies indicate that home workers are happier and more productive. However, some jobs do not lend themselves to telecommuting; welding and brain surgery are very difficult to do over the phone.
See also small office/home office.

teleconferencing The use of audio, video, animation, and application sharing, linked by a communications channel, to allow widely separated individuals to take part in a discussion or meeting.

Desktop video and chalkboard programs such as Microsoft NetMeeting are becoming more and more common, and groupware applications such as Lotus Notes are helping people work together.

Telephony API Abbreviated TAPI. A standard telephone interface for Microsoft Windows, developed by Intel and Microsoft, designed to allow applications to set up and control calls.

TAPI does not define the method of data transmission used once a call is in progress. It is completely independent of the telephone network itself and can be used on public-switched telephone networks, ISDN, and IP networks.
See also Telephony Services API.

Telephony Services API Abbreviated TSAPI. A standard telephone interface developed by AT&T and Novell, designed to allow applications to set up and control calls. TSAPI is available as a NetWare

Loadable Module for NetWare 4.01 and later.

TSAPI requires that the PBX (private branch exchange) be linked to a server and so has greater control over the call than does Telephony API.

See also Telephony API.

Telnet A terminal emulation protocol, part of the TCP/IP suite of protocols and common in the Unix world, that provides remote terminal-connection services.

The most common terminal emulations are for Digital Equipment Corporation (DEC) VT-52, VT-100, and VT-220 terminals, although many companies offer additional add-in emulations.

See also tn3270.

temporary swap file A swap space that is created every time it is needed. A temporary swap file can consist of several discontinuous pieces of hard-disk space. A temporary swap file does not occupy hard-disk space if the application that created it is not running.

See also swap space; permanent swap file; virtual memory.

ter A term describing a tertiary CCITT recommendation, an alternative or extension to the primary or secondary recommendation.

See also bis.

tera- Abbreviated T. A prefix that means 10^{12} in the metric system, 1,000,000,000,000; commonly referred to as one trillion in the American numbering system, and one million million in the British numbering system.

terabyte Abbreviated TB. In computing, usually 2^{40}, or 1,099,511,627,776 bytes. Terabytes are used to represent extremely large hard-disk capacities.

terminal emulation A method of operation or software that makes a personal computer or a workstation act like a terminal attached to a mainframe, usually for the purpose of telecommunications. Communications programs often include popular emulations, such as ANSI, VT-52, VT-100, VT-200, and TTY.

See also Telnet; tn3270.

terminate-and-stay-resident program Abbreviated TSR. A small accessory or utility program that stays loaded in memory, even when it is not actually running. A TSR can be invoked quickly to perform a specific task.

TSR's are often used with single-tasking operating systems such as MS-DOS.

terminator A device attached to the last peripheral device in a series or the last node on a network.

For example, the last device on a SCSI bus must terminate the bus; otherwise, the bus will not perform properly. A 50-ohm resistor is placed at both ends of an Ethernet cable to prevent signals reflecting and interfering with the transmission.

See also active termination; forced perfect termination; passive termination.

T$_E$X A typesetting language developed by Donald E. Knuth of Stanford University,

T

capable of professional-quality typeset text, particularly of mathematical equations and scientific, Japanese, Chinese, Cyrillic, and Arabic text.

T_EX is not easy for the casual user to master, but several packages are available containing macros designed to solve specific typesetting problems.

text file   See ASCII file.

text mode   A mode in which the computer displays characters on the screen using the built-in character set, but does not show any graphics characters or a mouse pointer. Also known as character mode.

TFTP   See Trivial File Transfer Protocol.

thick Ethernet   Connecting coaxial cable used on an Ethernet network; also known as thicknet.

The cable is 1 centimeter (0.4 inch) thick, almost as thick as your thumb, and can be used to connect network nodes up to a distance of approximately 1006 meters (3300 feet). Thick Ethernet is primarily used for facility-wide installations.

See also thin Ethernet.

thicknet   See thick Ethernet.

thin client   In a client/server network, a client that requires relatively small amounts of local memory and hard-disk space and leaves most of the processing to the server. Sometimes called a Windows terminal.

In some cases, the client operating system, as well as the applications the client runs

and the data it manipulates, all reside on the server.

See also NetPC; network computer; total cost of ownership; Zero Administration for Windows.

thin Ethernet   Connecting coaxial cable used on an Ethernet network; also known as thinnet.

The cable is 5 millimeters (0.2 inch) thick, about as thick as your little finger, and can be used to connect network nodes up to a distance of approximately 165 meters (500 feet). Thin Ethernet is primarily used for office installations.

See also thick Ethernet.

thinnet   See thin Ethernet.

thrashing   An excessive amount of disk activity that causes a virtual memory system to spend all its time swapping pages in and out of memory, and no time executing the application.

Thrashing can be caused when poor system configuration creates a swap file that is too small or when insufficient memory is installed in the computer. Increasing the size of the swap file or adding memory are often the best ways to reduce thrashing.

thread   **1.** A concurrent process that is part of a larger process or program. In a multitasking operating system, a single program may contain several threads, all running at the same time. For example, one part of a program can be making a calculation while another part is drawing a graph or a chart.

2. A connected set of postings to a Usenet newsgroup. Many newsreaders present postings as threads rather than in strict chronological order.

See also multiprocessing; newsgroup; newsreader; Usenet.

threaded newsreader   An application used to read the articles posted to Usenet newsgroups.

A threaded newsreader groups the newsgroup posts into threads of related articles, whereas unthreaded newsreaders present them in their original order of posting. Of the two types, threaded newsreaders are much more convenient to use.

See also newsgroup; newsreader; Usenet.

throughput   A measure of the data-transfer rate through a complex communications or networking scheme.

Throughput is considered an indication of the overall performance of the system. For example, the throughput of a server depends on the processor type, operating system in use, hard disk capacity, network interface card in use, and the size of the data transfer buffer.

In communications, throughput is usually measured as the number of bits or packets processed each second.

See also bandwidth.

TIA   *See* Telecommunications Industry Association.

TIA/EIA structured cabling standards   Standards specified by the Electronics Industry Association/

Telecommunications Industries Association (EIA/TIA), including:

- ANSI/EIA/TIA-568-1991 Commercial Building Telecommunications Wiring.

- EIA/TIA TSB-36 Additional Cable Specifications for UTP Cables. 1991.

- EIA/TIA TSB-40 Telecommunications Systems Bulletin—Additional Transmission Specifications for UTP Connecting Hardware. 1992.

- ANSI/EIA/TIA-568A 1995 revises the original 568 document and adds material from TSB-36 and TSB-40.

- ANSI/EIA/TIA-569-1990 Commercial Building Standard for Telecommunications Pathways and Spaces.

- ANSI/EIA/TIA-570-1991 Residential and Light Commercial Telecommunications Wiring Standard.

- ANSI/EIA/TIA-606-1993 Administration Standard for the Telecommunications Infrastructure of Commercial Buildings.

- ANSI/EIA/TIA-607-1994 Commercial Building Grounding and Bonding Requirements for Telecommunications.

Local codes and standards may impose additional requirements.

See also cabling standards.

ticket   A token within the Kerberos authentication system that contains the user's name and address, as well as the service the user requested, security information, a time deadline, and other authentication information.

See also authentication; Kerberos.

371

tie line   A private circuit, leased from a communications carrier, connecting two or more points in a single organization.

Time Division Multiple Access   Abbreviated TDMA. A technique used to allocate multiple channels on the same frequency on a cellular phone or satellite communications system.

See also Code Division Multiple Access.

time-division multiplexing   Abbreviated TDM. A method of sharing a transmission channel by dividing the available time equally between competing stations. At the receiving end, the different signals are merged back into their individual streams.

See also frequency-division multiplexing; inverse multiplexing; statistical multiplexing.

time-domain reflectometer   Abbreviated TDR. A diagnostic tool used to detect cabling faults.

A TDR calculates the length of a cable by measuring the time it takes for a reflected pulse to return to the TDR and then multiplying that by the nominal velocity of propagation.

time to live   Abbreviated TTL. A mechanism used to ensure that misdirected information doesn't end up traveling a TCP/IP network or the Internet for all eternity.

Each IP datagram contains a TTL value; once this value reaches zero, the datagram is simply assumed to be undeliverable and is discarded.

timeout   Many procedures require a device to respond or reply to an inquiry within a certain period of time; if the device does not respond, a timeout condition occurs, thus preventing the procedure from hanging up the computer.

Timeouts are also used in communications to detect transmission failures. Some timeouts are fixed, such as the amount of time during which an operating system will attempt to access a modem or printer; others can be specified by the user.

time-slice multitasking   A form of multitasking in which the operating system assigns the same small time period to each process in turn.

See also cooperative multitasking; preemptive multitasking.

time stamp   An identification code that includes the time that an event took place.

Most operating systems add a time stamp to indicate a file's create time. Automatic error logging or security auditing processes often add a time stamp to critical events such as changes to passwords or accounts.

time synchronization   A method of synchronizing time across all servers on the network so that all servers report the same time.

tn3270   A special version of the Telnet program specifically designed for use with large IBM computers using 3270 and 327*x* series terminals. Most of the computers on the Internet use Unix, but if you ever encounter an IBM mainframe, you will definitely need tn3270.

So how do you know when to use tn3270 rather than Telnet? It's time to load up tn3270 if you try to connect to an Internet host with Telnet and one of the following happens:

- The on-screen messages are all in uppercase letters rather than the usual Unix mix of uppercase and lowercase letters.
- You see VM or MVS anywhere in the login message. These are both names of IBM operating systems.
- Your session is aborted before it really gets started.

See also Telnet.

token passing   A network access method that uses a circulating electronic token to prevent multiple nodes from transmitting on the network simultaneously.

Before a node can transmit, it must be in possession of the token. Fiber Distributed Data Interface (FDDI), Token Ring, and Token Bus networks all use token passing to avoid packet collisions.

See also Carrier Sense Multiple Access/Collision Detection; token-ring network.

Token Ring network   IBM's implementation of the token-ring network architecture, which uses a token-passing protocol transmitting at 4 or 16Mbps.

Using standard telephone wiring, a Token Ring network can connect a maximum of 72 devices; with shielded twisted-pair (STP) wiring, each ring can support a maximum of 256 nodes. Although it is based on a closed-loop ring structure, a Token Ring network uses a star-shaped cluster of as many as eight nodes, all attached to the same wiring concentrator or Multistation Access Unit (MAU). The MAUs are then connected to the main ring circuit.

A Token Ring network can include personal computers, minicomputers, and mainframes. The IEEE 802.5 standard defines token-ring networks.

token-ring network   A LAN with a ring structure that uses token passing to regulate traffic on the network and avoid collisions.

On a token-ring network, the controlling network interface card generates a token that controls the right to transmit. This token is continuously passed from one node to the next around the network. When a node has information to transmit, it captures the token, sets its status to busy, and adds the message and the destination address. All other nodes continuously read the token to determine if they are the recipient of a message. If they are, they collect the token, extract the message, and return the token to the sender. The sender then removes the message and sets the token status to free, indicating that it can be used by the next node in sequence.

See also 802.5; Carrier Sense Multiple Access/Collision Detection; Token Ring network.

T

TOKEN RING NETWORK

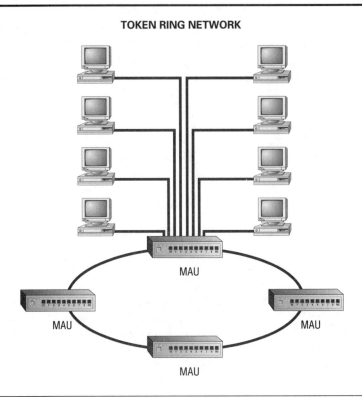

Tool Command Language Abbreviated Tcl, pronounced "tickle." Developed by John Ousterhout while at the University of California at Berkeley, Tcl is a general-purpose extensible scripting language supplied as a C library on Unix systems.

Tcl is also available in versions for MS-DOS, Windows, and the Macintosh.

See also Perl; REXX; scripting.

TOP *See* Technical and Office Protocol.

top-level domains On the Internet, the highest category of host name, which either signifies the type of institution or the country of its origin.

In the United States, the most common top-level domains include:

- **com** A commercial organization. Most companies end up in this category.

- **edu** An educational establishment such as a university.

- **gov** A branch of the U.S. government.

- **int** An international organization such as NATO or the United Nations.

- **mil** A branch of the U.S. military.

· net   A network organization.

· org   A nonprofit organization.

Most countries also have unique domains named after their international abbreviations; for example, ca represents Canada, uk represents Great Britain, and jp represents Japan.

See also domain; domain name: Domain Name Service.

topology   The map of a network. Physical topology describes where the cables are run and where the workstations, nodes, routers, and gateways are located. Networks are usually configured in bus, ring, star, or mesh topologies. Logical topology refers to the paths that messages take to get from one user on the network to another.

TOPS   A local-area network (LAN) from TOPS Corporation that uses the LocalTalk protocol to connect Apple computers, PCs, and Sun workstations.

Toshiba Corporation   One of the largest manufacturers of electrical equipment in the world, a major supplier of notebook computers, and a co-developer of the digital video disc.

For more information on Toshiba Corporation, see www.toshiba.com.

total cost of ownership   Abbreviated TCO. A term first used by the Gardener Group in an attempt to quantify the real cost of a particular computer solution.

TCO encompasses the direct costs of the hardware and the software required and then adds in costs for maintenance and support, costs for the users performing their own technical support rather than their official job, and system productivity costs.

See also NetPC; network computer; thin client; Zero Administration for Windows.

TP   *See* twisted-pair cable.

tracert   A utility used on TCP/IP networks to trace the route that datagrams take between the server and another system. As tracert also tells you how long each hop takes, it can be a useful tool in identifying system trouble spots.

trackball   A device used for pointing, designed as a space-saving alternative to the mouse.

A trackball contains a movable ball that you rotate with your fingers to move the cursor on the screen. Because it does not need the area of flat space that a mouse needs, trackballs are popular with users of portable computers. The Apple PowerBook includes a trackball as part of the keyboard case, Microsoft has released a small trackball that clips onto the side of a laptop computer, and IBM has developed a dual-button, touch-sensitive pointing stick called the TrackPoint.

traffic   The flow of messages and data carried by a communications channel or link. Traffic on a data network is normally measured in bits transferred in a given time period.

transaction   A single activity within a computer system, such as an entry into an airline reservation database, that is executed in real time rather than as a batch process.

T

transaction processing A processing method in which transactions are executed immediately when they are received by the system, rather than at some later time as in batch-processing systems. Airline reservation databases and automatic teller machines are examples of transaction-processing systems.

See also on-line transaction processing; roll back; roll forward; two-phase commit.

Transaction Tracking System Abbreviated TTS. A fault-tolerant feature of Novell NetWare that maintains the integrity of databases by backing out or rolling back incomplete transactions that result from a failure in a network component.

transceiver A contraction of transmitter/receiver. A device capable of both transmitting and receiving data.

The data may be located on the network interface card that connects a workstation to a network, or it may be on a separate device. A transceiver can convert between an AUI (Attachment Unit Interface) Ethernet connection and another type of cabling, such as fiber-optic, coaxial, or unshielded twisted pair (UTP).

transfer rate *See* data-transfer rate.

transient *See* surge.

Transmission Control Protocol Abbreviated TCP. The transport-level protocol used in the TCP/IP suite of protocols. It works above IP in the protocol stack and provides reliable data delivery over connection-oriented links.

TCP adds a header to the datagram that contains the information needed to get the datagram to its destination. The source port number and the destination port number allow data to be sent back and forth to the correct processes running on each computer. A sequence number allows the datagrams to be rebuilt in the correct order in the receiving computer, and a checksum verifies that the data received is the same as the data sent. In addition to these fields, the TCP header contains the following information:

- **Acknowledgment number** Indicates that the data was received successfully. If the datagram is damaged in transit, the receiver discards the data and does not send an acknowledgment to the sender. After a specified timeout expires, the sender retransmits data for which no acknowledgment has been received.

- **Offset** Specifies the length of the header.

- **Reserved** Variables set aside for future use.

- **Flags** Indicate that this packet is the end of the data or that the data is urgent.

- **Window size** Provides a way to increase packet size, which can improve efficiency in data transfers.

- **Urgent pointer** Gives the location of urgent data.

- **Options** Reserved for future use or for special options as defined by the protocol.

- **Padding** Ensures that the header ends on a 32-bit boundary.

The data immediately follow this header information.

See also Internet Protocol; Transmission Control Protocol/Internet Protocol; User Datagram Protocol.

Transmission Control Protocol/ Internet Protocol   Abbreviated TCP/IP. A set of communications protocols first developed by the Defense Advanced Research Projects Agency (DARPA) in the late 1970s. The set of TCP/IP protocols encompasses media access, packet transport, session communications, file transfer, e-mail, and terminal emulation.

TCP/IP is a widely published open standard, and while completely independent of any specific hardware or software company, it is supported by a huge number of vendors and is available on many different computers, from PCs to mainframes, running many different operating systems. Many corporations, universities, and government agencies use TCP/IP, and it is also the basis of the Internet.

TCP/IP is separated from the network hardware and will run over Ethernet, token-ring, X.25 networks, and dial-up connections. It is a routable protocol, so datagrams can be sent over specific routes, and it has reliable and efficient data-delivery mechanisms. TCP/IP uses a common expandable addressing scheme, so any system can address any other system, even in a network as large as the Internet, and new networks can be added without service disruptions.

The popularity that the TCP/IP family of protocols enjoys today did not arise just because the protocols were available or even because the U.S. government mandated their use. They are popular because they are robust, solid protocols that solve many of the most difficult networking problems and do so in an elegant and efficient way.

See also Address Resolution Protocol; File Transfer Protocol; Hypertext Transfer Protocol; Internet Control Message Protocol; Internet Mail Access Protocol; Internet Protocol; Post Office Protocol; Simple Mail Transfer Protocol; Simple Network Management Protocol; Telnet; tn3270; User Datagram Protocol.

T

TCP HEADER

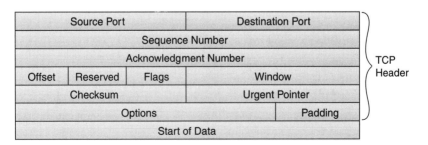

Source Port	Destination Port	
Sequence Number		
Acknowledgment Number		
Offset	Reserved	Flags	Window	
Checksum	Urgent Pointer	
Options	Padding	
Start of Data		

TCP Header

TRANSMISSION CONTROL PROTOCOL/INTERNET PROTOCOL

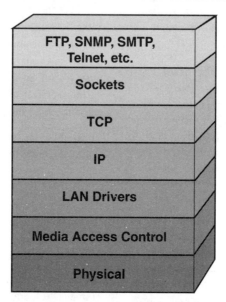

transmission medium The physical cabling used to carry network information, such as fiber-optic, coaxial, shielded twisted-pair (STP), and unshielded twisted-pair (UTP) cabling.

transmission mode The manner in which communications can take place between a sender and a receiver.

Several modes are defined, as follows:

- **Simplex** Communications can go in only one direction, so the sender can use the whole of the available bandwidth.

- **Half-duplex** Communications can go in two directions, but only in one direction at a time.

- **Full-duplex** Communications can go in two directions simultaneously.

- **Echo-plex** A rare mode in which characters are retransmitted to the sender for error-checking purposes.

Transmit Data Abbreviated TXD. A hardware signal defined by the RS-232-C standard that carries information from one device to another.

See also Receive Data.

transport layer The fourth of seven layers of the OSI Reference Model for computer-to-computer communications. The transport layer defines protocols for message structure and supervises the validity of the transmission by performing some error checking.

See also OSI Reference Model.

trap *See* software interrupt.

trap door An entry point in a computer network, through which an intruder can gain access without authentication.

tree In Microsoft Active Directory, a hierarchy of domains linked via trust relationships that share the same namespace, Directory Schema, and Global Catalog.

See also Active Directory; Directory Schema; Global Catalog.

Tree object In Novell Directory Services (NDS), the hierarchical organization of all the objects on the network into a single structure.

See also container object; Novell Directory Services; Organization object.

trellis-coded modulation Abbreviated TCM. A form of quadrature amplitude modulation used in modems that operate at 9600 bits per second or higher. TCM encodes data as a set of bits associated with both phase and amplitude changes.

Trivial File Transfer Protocol Abbreviated TFTP. A little-used and simplified version of the TCP/IP file transfer protocol that does not include password protection.

Because it has no security associated with it, most system administrators do not support its use and recommend File Transfer Protocol instead.

See also File Transfer Protocol.

Trojan Horse A type of computer virus that pretends to be a useful program, such as a game or a utility, to entice you to use it, when in reality it contains special code that will intentionally damage any system onto which it is loaded.

See also logic bomb.

trusted domain In Microsoft Windows NT Server, a domain that a trusting domain will allow to authenticate logons.

See also trusting domain; trust relationship.

trustee In Novell NetWare, a user or group object that has been granted rights to work with a directory, an object, or a file.

See also Public trustee; trustee assignment.

trustee assignment In Novell NetWare, a mechanism that determines how a user can access an object, a directory, or a file. Also known as trustee rights.

For example, trustee rights regulate whether a user can read a file, change it, change its name, delete it, or control other users' trustee rights to it. Trustee rights are assigned to individual users, and one user's rights can be different from another user's rights to the same directory

See also Public trustee; trustee.

trustee rights *See* trustee assignment.

trusting domain In Microsoft Windows NT Server, a domain that lets users and groups in the trusted domain use its resources.

See also trusted domain; trust relationship.

T

379

trust relationship In Microsoft Windows NT Server, a link between domains that allows pass-through authentication, in which a trusting domain allows the logon authentication of a trusted domain.

With the right trust relationships, a user with one user account in one domain has the potential to access the whole network. Global groups and user accounts defined in the trusted domain can be assigned rights and permissions in a trusting domain, even though those accounts do not exist in the trusting domain's directory database.

See also authentication; pass-through authentication; trusted domain; trusting domain; user account.

TSAPI *See* Telephony Services API.

TSAT *See* T1 small aperture terminal.

TSR *See* terminate-and-stay-resident program.

TTL *See* time to live.

TTS *See* Transaction Tracking System.

tunneling The encapsulation of one protocol within another, often used to transport a local-area network protocol across a backbone that does not support that particular protocol.

Tunneling is also used to create pseudo-connections across connectionless networks such as the Internet and may be referred to as protocol encapsulation or synchronous pass-through.

See also encapsulation; Point-to-Point Tunneling Protocol.

twinaxial cable A cable with two coaxial cables inside a single insulating shield. Twinaxial cable is used with IBM AS/400 minicomputers.

TWINAXIAL CABLE

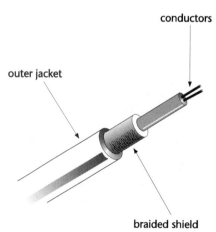

conductors

outer jacket

braided shield

twisted-pair cable   Abbreviated TP. Cable that comprises two or more pairs of insulated wires twisted together, at six twists per inch.

In twisted-pair cable, one wire carries the signal and the other is grounded. The cable may be shielded or unshielded. Telephone wire installed in modern buildings is often twisted-pair wiring.

two-phase commit   A method used in transaction processing to ensure data is posted to shared databases correctly by dividing the writing of data into two steps.

Each of the steps must receive a verification of completeness from the shared databases; otherwise, the transaction-processing system rolls back the transaction and tries again.

See also on-line transaction processing; roll back; roll forward; transaction processing.

TXD   *See* Transmit Data.

Type 1–9 cable   IBM Cabling System specifications, as follows:

- **Type 1**   Shielded, twisted, dual-pair cable with 22-gauge solid conductors and a braided shield. Used with Token Ring networks.

- **Type 2**   Two-pair, shielded cable with solid conductors and a braided shield. Type 2 also includes four pairs of unshielded voice-grade lines, giving a total of six pairs in the same sheath.

- **Type 3**   Four unshielded, solid, twisted pairs, used for voice or data. IBM's variant of twisted-pair telephone wire.

- **Type 4**   No published specification.

- **Type 5**   Dual 100/140 micron fiber-optic cable; IBM now recommends 125-micron fiber-optic cable, which is the current industry standard for fiber-optic cable.

- **Type 6**   Shielded, two-pair, braided cable used for patch cables. Type 6 is more flexible than Type 1 cable.

- **Type 7**   No published specification.

- **Type 8**   Shielded, dual-pair cable with no twists, housed in a flat jacket; commonly used under carpets.

- **Type 9**   Shielded, dual-pair, plenum cable with solid or braided conductors and a fire-resistant outer coating, for use between floors in a building.

See also American Wire Gauge; cabling standards; plenum cable; riser cable; structured wiring.

T

type-ahead buffer   *See* keyboard buffer.

typefull naming   In Novell Directory Services (NDS), a formal method used to name objects that includes name types for each part of the name. For example, `.CN=Gary.OU=Marketing.O=Sybex`.

See also typeless naming.

typeless naming   In Novell Directory Services (NDS), a common method used to name objects that does not include name types for each part of the name. For example, `.Gary.Marketing.Sybex`.

See also typefull naming.

U

UART   *See* universal asynchronous receiver/transmitter.

UBR   *See* Unspecified Bit Rate.

UDP   *See* User Datagram Protocol.

Ultra SCSI   An extension of the SCSI-2 standard that increases the data-transfer rate to 20Mbps independent of the bus width. Ultra SCSI supports four to eight devices depending on cable type and length.

See also SCSI-2; Small Computer System Interface.

Ultra2 SCSI   An extension of the SCSI-2 standard that increases the data transfer rate to 40Mbps over an 8-bit bus. Ultra2 SCSI supports a maximum of 8 devices.

See also SCSI-2; Small Computer System Interface.

Ultra Wide SCSI   An extension of the SCSI-2 standard that increases the data-transfer rate to 80Mbps over a 16-bit bus. Ultra2 SCSI supports a maximum of 16 devices.

See also SCSI-2; Small Computer System Interface.

Ultrix   A version of Unix from Digital Equipment Corporation that looks and works like BSD Unix.

See also BSD Unix.

UMB   *See* upper memory block.

unauthorized access   To gain entry to a computer system using a stolen or guessed password.

See also hacker; intruder.

unbundled software   **1.** Software sold with a computer system that is priced separately, rather than included as part of a package.

2. A feature in an application repackaged and sold by itself at a lower price.

See also bundled software.

UNC   *See* Universal Naming Convention.

uncompress   The process of restoring a compressed file to its original form.

See also unzip.

undelete   To recover an accidentally deleted file. Many operating systems include commands you can use to recover a deleted file; however, once the file has been overwritten on your hard disk by a new file, the original is lost, and the only way to get it back is to reload it from a recent backup.

See also file recovery.

unicast   The broadcast of individual audio or video signals from a server to individual clients to provide an on-demand video service.

See also IP multicast; multicast.

Unicode A 16-bit character code, defined by the Unicode Consortium and by ISO 10646, that supports a maximum of 65,536 unique characters rather than the 256 characters available in the current ASCII character set.

By using two bytes to represent each character, Unicode allows almost all the world's written languages to be represented in a single character set; for example, the Chinese language defines almost 10,000 basic ideographs. When universally adopted, Unicode will make multilingual software much easier to write and maintain.

Products such as Novell NetWare and Microsoft Windows NT provide Unicode support.

See also American Standard Code for Information Interchange; double-byte character set; Extended Binary Coded Decimal Interchange Code.

Uniform Resource Characteristic Abbreviated URC. A mechanism designed to provide additional information about an Internet site or a Web page.

A URC lists pairs of attributes and their values and might contain author information,

keywords, prices, a copyright statement, or even a digital certificate, along with their associated Uniform Resource Identifiers.

See also Uniform Resource Identifier; Uniform Resource Locator.

Uniform Resource Identifier Abbreviated URI. In the HTTP message header, a set of characters that identifies a resource such as a file from anywhere on the Internet.

The URI includes Uniform Resource Names and Uniform Resource Locators to identify the file by type and location.

See also Uniform Resource Name; Uniform Resource Locator.

Uniform Resource Locator Abbreviated URL. An address for a resource on the Internet.

URLs are used as a linking mechanism between Web pages and as a method for Web browsers to access Web pages.

A URL specifies the protocol to be used to access the resource (such as HTTP or FTP), the name of the server where the resource is located (as in `www.sybex.com`), the path to that resource (as in `/catalog`), and the name of the document to open (`/index.html`).

U

UNIFORM RESOURCE LOCATOR

Protocol   Server Hostname   Path   Document Name

http://www.sybex.com/catalog/index.html

Uniform Resource Name Abbreviated URN. A proposal from the IETF (Internet Engineering Task Force) for a naming scheme that will identify Internet resources by name, irrespective of where they are located.

See also Uniform Resource Locator.

UniForum A nonprofit organization founded in 1980 dedicated to improve Unix through the open exchange of ideas and information between users and developers.

Previously known as /usr/group, UniForum has several hundred thousand members in many countries throughout the world.

uninterruptible power supply Abbreviated UPS; pronounced "you-pea-ess." An alternative power source, usually consisting of a set of batteries, used to power a computer system if the normal power service is interrupted or falls below acceptable levels.

A UPS system is usually applied only to the most critical devices on the network, such as servers, routers, gateways, and independent hard disks. They are of two main types:

• An online UPS continuously monitors and modifies the power flowing through the unit. If an outage occurs, the UPS continues to provide regulated power.

• A standby UPS monitors the AC level, but only switches in when the power drops below a preset level; it contains circuitry capable of switching to backup power in 5 milliseconds or less.

See also power conditioning; UPS monitoring.

universal asynchronous receiver/ transmitter Abbreviated UART; pronounced "you-art." An electronic module that combines the transmitting and receiving circuitry needed for asynchronous communications over a serial line.

See also asynchronous transmission.

Universal Coordinated Time In Novell NetWare, the standard system time based on Greenwich Mean Time (GMT).

Local time on a NetWare server is defined in terms of the difference from GMT; for example, Pacific Standard Time is GMT minus eight hours.

Universal Naming Convention Abbreviated UNC. In Microsoft Windows NT Server, a scheme used to gain access to a shared resource.

The general form of a UNC is:

\\servername\sharename\path\filename

The servername portion identifies the name of the server where the resource is located, and sharename identifies the name of the shared file resource under which the information has been shared. This is followed by the path and filename of the resource.

Universal Serial Bus Abbreviated USB. A standard from Intel and Microsoft for a high-speed peripheral bus designed to remove the need for almost all the connectors on the back of a personal computer.

USB defines the ports and bus characteristics with data transfer rates of up to 12Mbps over a single cable of up to 5 meters (16 feet). USB is capable of supporting a maximum of

63 devices such as external CD-ROM drives, printers, external modems, mice, and the keyboard and also supplies power to some devices so there is no need for separate power cords or batteries. Most personal computers will have two USB ports.

See also 1394.

universal synchronous receiver/ transmitter Abbreviated USRT. An electronic module that combines the transmitting and receiving circuitry needed for synchronous communications over a serial line.

See also synchronous transmission.

Unix Pronounced "yoo-nix." A multiuser, multitasking operating system, originally conceived in 1969 at AT&T's Bell Labs by Ken Thompson and Dennis Ritchie. Since then, Unix has gone on to become the most widely used general purpose operating system in the world.

Over the last 25 years, there have been three major strands in Unix development:

- Original AT&T Unix from Versions 1 to 7, and Systems III to V.

- Microsoft/SCO XENIX.

- Berkeley releases from 1BSD to 4.4BSD.

In addition, a large number of commercial Unix-related systems have been released by developers such as Apple, Digital Equipment Corporation, Hewlett-Packard, IBM, SCO, Silicon Graphics, and Sun Microsystems. Unix is available on a huge range of hardware, from a PC to a supercomputer.

Several free (or almost free) versions of Unix are available in the Intel world, including Linux, FreeBSD, and NetBSD; since they contain no proprietary code, they are not affected by licensing agreements other than the GNU General Public License.

Unix today is a very different animal from the Unix of the 1980s. A typical system then consisted of a minicomputer serving a collection of dumb terminals. Unix today is more likely to be a graphical workstation on a network or a Web server on the Internet and is a large and complicated commercial offering, serving a wide range of applications.

See also Advanced Interactive Executive; A/UX; Berkeley Unix; BSD Unix; FreeBSD; Interactive Unix; Linux; NetBSD; SCO Unix; Solaris; System V Interface Definition; UnixWare.

Unix client Any computer running Unix that connects to the network.

Unix shell In Unix, a program that acts as a user interface, interpreting commands typed at the keyboard and passing them on to the operating system.

The shell sets up standard input, standard output, and standard error, lets you customize your Unix session environment, and gives access to a shell programming language for creating shell scripts.

Some versions of Unix provide only one shell, while others provide a selection from which you can choose to use the one you like best.

Common shells include the following:

- **Bourne** Very compact and simple to use; the original Unix shell.

- **Korn** Perhaps the most popular shell; an upward compatible extension to the

U

385

Bourne shell with a history file, command-line editing, aliases, and job control.

- **C**   The first BSD shell, the C shell uses C-like syntax and offers a history mechanism, aliasing, and job control.

- **Bash**   The Bourne-again shell from the Free Software Foundation extends the capabilities of the Bourne shell in a similar way to the Korn shell.

- **Rc**   A small, compact, and elegant shell with a strong C flavor but without command-line editing and job control.

- **Tcsh**   An enhanced version of the C shell.

- **Zsh**   A large shell that seems to offer all the features available in all the other shells.

See also Bash shell; Bourne shell; C shell; Korn shell.

UnixWare   A release of the Unix operating system, originally from Novell, now available from SCO.

UnixWare is a 64-bit operating system that combines SCO's OpenServer system with previous versions of UnixWare and includes Netscape's FastTrack Server for Web site creation. A separate software development kit, which includes a C/C++ compiler, a debugger, and other development tools, is also available.

See also Santa Cruz Operation, Inc.

unmoderated newsgroup   A Usenet newsgroup or mailing list in which posts are not subject to review before distribution. You will find the discussions in unmoder-ated newsgroups to be wildly spontaneous, but they may also contain more than their share of flames and flame wars.

See also alt newsgroups; moderated newsgroup.

unshielded cable   Any cable not protected from electromagnetic interference or radio frequency interference (RFI) by an outer foil shield.

unshielded twisted-pair cable   Abbreviated UTP. Cable that contains two or more pairs of twisted copper wires.

The greater the number of twists, the lower the crosstalk. UTP is offered in both voice grade and data grade. The advantages of UTP include ease of installation and low cost of materials. Its drawbacks are limited signaling speeds and shorter maximum cable-segment lengths.

See also crosstalk; shielded twisted-pair cable.

Unspecified Bit Rate   Abbreviated UBR. A type of Asynchronous Transfer Mode (ATM) service that provides spare bandwidth to noncritical services such as file transfers.

See also Asynchronous Transfer Mode; Available Bit Rate; Constant Bit Rate; Variable Bit Rate.

unsubscribe   To remove the name of a Usenet newsgroup from the list of newsgroups maintained by your newsreader. If you change your mind, you can always subscribe to the newsgroup again in the future.

See also newsgroup; subscribe.

UNSHIELDED TWISTED-PAIR CABLE

outer jacket

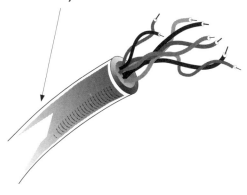

unzip   The process of uncompressing an archive created by PKZIP, WinZip, compress, or gzip.

See also uncompress.

upgradable computer   A computer system specifically designed to be upgraded as technology advances.

The amount of circuitry that must be changed when you make the upgrade and the method of upgrading differ from one upgradable computer to another. At a minimum, you must replace the processor; at most, you need to change nearly all the circuitry installed in the computer. In some systems, the use of a ZIF socket to hold the main processor makes an upgrade easy; in other systems, replacing the main processor can be extremely difficult.

upgrade   **1.** The process of installing a newer and more powerful version of a software or hardware product. For example, you may upgrade to a newer and more capable version of a software package, such as Microsoft Word, or to a larger hard disk. In the case of hardware, an upgrade is often called an upgrade kit.

2. A new and more powerful version of software (a noun referring to the improved software itself).

uplink   The transmission of information from an earth station to a communications satellite.

See also downlink.

upload   In communications, sending a file or files from one computer to another over a network or via a modem. For example, you might upload a file to a network server.

See also download.

upper memory   *See* reserved memory.

U

upper memory block Abbreviated UMB. The memory between 640KB and 1MB in a personal computer running MS-DOS. This area was originally reserved for system and video use; however, not all the space is used. The unused portions are the UMBs.

With an Intel 80386 (or later) processor, as much as 120KB of additional memory can be gained by accessing UMBs. This space can be used to load device drivers and terminate-and-stay-resident programs.

UPS *See* uninterruptible power supply.

UPS monitoring The process that a server uses to make sure that an attached UPS (uninterruptible power supply) system is functioning properly.

See also power conditioning.

uptime The length or percentage of time during which a computer system is functioning and available for use.

See also downtime; power-on hours.

upward compatibility The design of software that incorporates the capability to function with other, more powerful products likely to become available in the near future. Adherence to design standards makes upward compatibility possible.

URC *See* Uniform Resource Characteristic.

URI *See* Uniform Resource Identifier.

URL *See* Uniform Resource Locator.

URN *See* Uniform Resource Name.

USB *See* Universal Serial Bus.

Usenet Contraction of user network; sometimes written as UseNet or USENET, pronounced "yooz-net." An international, noncommercial network, linking many thousands of Unix sites.

Although there is a very close relationship between the Internet and Usenet, they are not the same thing by any means. Usenet predates the Internet; in the early days, information was distributed by dial-up connections and UUCP software. Not every Internet computer is part of Usenet, and not every Usenet system can be reached from the Internet.

Like the Internet, Usenet has no central governing body; it is run by the people who use it. With tens of thousands of newsgroups, Usenet is accessed by millions of people every day, in more than 100 countries.

See also Usenet newsgroups.

Usenet articles An individual e-mail message sent to a Usenet newsgroup.

Usenet newsgroups The individual discussion groups within Usenet.

Usenet newsgroups contain articles posted by Internet and Usenet subscribers; very few of them actually contain hard news.

Most newsgroups are concerned with a single subject, and the range of subjects throughout Usenet is simply phenomenal; if people are interested in a topic, you will find a newsgroup for that topic.

user Any person allowed to access a computer system or network.

user account A security mechanism used to control access to a network or to a multiuser computer system, established and maintained by the network administrator. Elements of a user account include password information, rights and permissions, and information about the groups to which the user belongs.

User Datagram Protocol   Abbreviated UDP. The connectionless, transport-level protocol used in the TCP/IP suite of protocols, usually bundled with IP-layer software. Because UDP does not add overhead, as does connection-oriented TCP, UDP is often used with SNMP (Simple Network Management Protocol) applications.

Multicast applications, such as Mbone and the Real-time Transport Protocol, that deliver audio and video streams use UDP as their delivery mechanism because the acknowledgment and retransmission services offered by TCP are not needed and add too much overhead. If a packet of audio data is lost, retransmission is neither practical nor desirable.

See also multicast backbone; Real-time Transport Protocol; Transmission Control Protocol.

user group   A group of users of a specific computer or software package who meet to share tips and listen to industry experts.

Some PC user groups hold large, well-attended monthly meetings, run their own Web sites, and publish newsletters of exceptional quality.

See also special interest group.

User Manager for Domains   In Microsoft Windows NT Server, an administrative tool used to manage accounts,

groups, and security policies throughout the domain.

See also user rights policies.

User object   In Novell Directory Services (NDS), an object that represents a user with access to the network.

See also Leaf object; Organization object; Root object; user template.

user rights policies   In Microsoft Windows NT Server, a mechanism used to determine the rights that users and groups possess when trying to perform network tasks. User rights policies are administered by the User Manager for Domains tool.

See also User Manager for Domains.

user template   In Novell Directory Services (NDS), a special User object that assigns default property values and rights when a new user is created.

A user template speeds up the process of creating a large number of new users at the same time, especially if these users share details such as locations, account restrictions, and so on.

See also User object.

U.S. Robotics Corporation   A major manufacturer of modems and creator of the PalmPilot personal digital assistant; merged with 3Com Corporation in 1998 in one of the largest deals in telecommunications-industry history.

For more information on U.S. Robotics Corporation, see `www.usr.com`.

USRT   *See* universal synchronous receiver/transmitter.

U

UTP *See* unshielded twisted-pair cable.

uucp Pronounced "you-you-cee-pee." A standard set of Unix utilities used to manage the transmission of information between Unix systems and to Usenet newsgroups, using serial connections and regular telephone lines. The name is derived from "Unix-to-Unix copy."

These utilities were originally developed by Mike Lesk at Bell Labs in the 1970s, and a version known as HoneyDanBer uucp was developed in the 1980s by P. Honeyman, D. A. Nowitz, and B. E. Redman. An even newer version, known as Taylor uucp, is available on many systems, particularly Linux.

See also Network News Transport Protocol.

uudecode Pronounced "you-you-de-code."

1. To convert a text file created by the Unix uuencode utility back into its original binary form. Graphical images and other binary files are often sent to Usenet newsgroups in this form, because the newsgroups can only handle text and don't know how to manage binary files.

2. The name of the utility program that performs a text-to-binary file conversion. Originally a Unix utility, uudecode is now available for most operating systems.

See also uucp; uuencode.

uuencode Pronounced "you-you-en-code."

1. To convert a binary file such as a graphical image into a text file so that the file can be sent over the Internet or to a Usenet newsgroup as a part of an e-mail message. When you receive a uuencoded text file, you must process it through the Unix uudecode utility to turn it back into a graphical image that you can view.

2. The name of the utility that performs a binary-to-text file conversion. Originally a Unix utility, uuencode is now available for most operating systems.

See also uucp; uudecode.

V

V.17   A CCITT (ITU) Group 3 fax modulation standard for transmitting fax data at up to 14,400bps, with a fallback to 12,000bps as line conditions deteriorate.

V.21   A CCITT (ITU) standard for 300bps modems using full-duplex transmission over dial-up lines. This standard is not compatible with the Bell 103 standard widely used in the United States.

V.22   A CCITT (ITU) standard for 600bps and 1200bps full-duplex modems over two-wire, dial-up, or leased lines. V.22 uses phase-shift keying modulation.

V.22 bis   A CCITT (ITU) standard for 2400bps full-duplex modems over dial-up and two-wire leased lines, with fallback to 1200bps and then 600bps operation. V.22 bis uses quadrature amplitude modulation.

V.23   A CCITT (ITU) standard for 600bps or 1200bps synchronous or asynchronous half-duplex modems used on dial-up lines.

V.24   A CCITT (ITU) definition of the interface between a modem and a computer system. V.24 is functionally equivalent to the RS-232-C standard, but does not specify connectors or pin assignments; those are defined in ISO 2110.

V.25   A CCITT (ITU) standard for automatic calling and answering circuits over dial-up lines using a parallel interface. V.25

includes the disabling of echo suppression on manually dialed calls.

V.25 bis   A CCITT (ITU) standard for automatic calling and answering circuits over dial-up lines with three modes: asynchronous, character-oriented synchronous, and bit-oriented synchronous (HDLC/SDLC). V.25 bis does not include modem configuration commands.

V.26   A CCITT (ITU) standard for 1200bps, full-duplex modems used over four-wire leased lines.

V.26 bis   A CCITT (ITU) standard for 1200bps and 2400bps full-duplex modems used on dial-up lines.

V.27   A CCITT (ITU) standard for 4800bps, full-duplex modems used with four-wire leased lines, with a manual equalizer.

V.27 bis   A CCITT (ITU) standard for 2400bps or 4800bps, full-duplex modems used with four-wire leased lines. The main advance over V.27 is the addition of an automatic adaptive equalizer for use on leased circuits.

V.27 ter   A CCITT (ITU) standard for 2400bps or 4800bps, full-duplex modems used with dial-up lines. Used in some CCITT Group 3 fax transmissions.

See also CCITT Groups 1–4.

V

V.29 A CCITT (ITU) standard for 9600bps modems used with point-to-point, four-wire leased lines. This standard has been adopted for CCITT Group 3 fax transmissions over dial-up lines at 9600bps and 7200bps.

See also CCITT Groups 1–4.

V.32 A CCITT (ITU) standard for 9600bps modems, with fallback to 4800bps, used over two-wire, dial-up lines or two-wire or four-wire leased lines, with echo canceling to remove any telephone-line echo, and quadrature amplitude modulation.

V.32 encodes four data bits for each baud to give an effective throughput of 9600bps and includes trellis-coded modulation error-correcting techniques. V.32 is the first standard for 9600bps modems using standard lines anywhere in the world.

V.32 bis A CCITT (ITU) standard extending V.32 to 7200, 12,000, and 14,400 bits per second. V.32 bis uses trellis-coded modulation.

V.32 terbo A pseudo-standard proposed by AT&T and others that supports transmission at up to 19, 200bps.

The name is a pun and does not represent an ITU standard; the next revision of the V.32 standard after V.32 bis will be V.32 ter, and V.32 terbo has been replaced by the ITU standard V.34.

See also V.fast.

V.33 A CCITT (ITU) standard for 12,000bps and 14,400bps modems used over four-wire, leased circuits, with time-division multiplexing available for line sharing.

V.34 A CCITT (ITU) standard for 28.8Kbps modems using trellis-coded modulation techniques and advanced data compression.

See also V.fast.

V.42 A CCITT (ITU) standard for error correction rather than for a modem. V.42 uses LAP-M (Link Access Procedure-Modem) as the primary error-correcting protocol, with MNP (Microcom Networking Protocol) classes 2 through 4 as an alternative.

V.42 can be used with V.22, V.22 bis, V.26 ter, V.32, and V.32 bis.

V.42 bis A CCITT (ITU) standard that adds a British Telecom Lempel-Ziv data-compression technique to V.42 error correction, usually capable of achieving a compression ratio of 3.5 to 1.

V.54 A CCITT (ITU) standard that specifies the loopback tests incorporated into modems for testing the telephone circuit and isolating any transmission problems.

V.56 bis A CCITT (ITU) standard that defines a network transmission model used to evaluate modem performance over two-wire voice-grade circuits.

V.90 A CCITT (ITU) standard for modems; also known as the 56K modem standard. V.90 describes an asymmetric connection, with theoretical speeds of up to 56Kbps downstream and an upstream connection rate of up to 33.6Kbps.

V.90 modems attain their high speed by assuming the circuit is a digital circuit and reducing the number of analog-to-digital conversions they perform, except for the conversion that takes place for outbound traffic at the user's modem.

Whether you actually achieve these rates depends on the quality of the phone line and the distance to the local telephone company central office. If the other end of the connection is not digital, the modem switches into full analog mode at 28.8 or 33.6Kbps.

In order to reduce crosstalk between adjacent lines, the FCC has placed restrictions on maximum signal strength levels, and so 54Kbps is the theoretical maximum data rate.

See also K56Flex; X2.

V.110 A CCITT (ITU) standard that specifies how DTE (data terminal equipment) using synchronous or asynchronous serial interfaces is supported on an ISDN (Integrated Services Digital Network).

V.120 A CCITT (ITU) standard that specifies how DTE (data terminal equipment) using synchronous or asynchronous serial interfaces is supported on an ISDN (Integrated Services Digital Network) using a protocol to encapsulate the transmitted data.

vaccine A utility program designed to protect files from viruses. By adding a small amount of code to an existing file, the vaccine program causes an alert to be generated if a virus does attack.

See also antivirus program; boot sector virus; file-infecting virus; infection; macro virus; multipart virus; polymorphic virus; stealth virus; Trojan Horse; virus.

Value Added Network Abbreviated VAN. Commercially available turn-key data networks from companies such as CompuServe, GE Information Services, and Infonet Services Corporation.

VANs are available on a leased-line or a dial-up rate and save an organization the trouble of setting up the equipment and contracting for the lines and service. VANs can also provide additional services such as message routing, resource management, and protocol-conversion services.

value-added process Abbreviated VAP. In Novell NetWare 2.*x*, an application that adds functions to the network operating system, such as print server or communications server software.

NetWare Loadable Modules (NLMs) provide a similar function in later versions of NetWare.

See also Virtual Loadable Module.

value-added reseller Abbreviated VAR. A company that adds value to a system, repackages it, and then resells it to the public.

This added value can take the form of better documentation, user support, service support, system integration, or sometimes just a

V

new nameplate on the box. For example, Canon makes the print engine used in many laser printers, including those from Hewlett-Packard (HP); in this case, Canon is an OEM (original equipment manufacturer) and HP is the VAR.

value entry   In Microsoft Windows, the actual data in the Registry, stored in the keys. Each value entry has a name, a data type (which determines the length and the format of the value), and the value itself.

See also hive; key; Registry; sub-hive; sub-key; volatile key.

values   In Novell Directory Services (NDS), the actual data stored in the properties of an NDS object. Properties can have more than one value; some are required, and others are optional.

vampire tap   A connector used to connect one cable segment to another. A needle on the connector pierces the cable insulation to make a connection to the wire within.

VAN   *See* Value Added Network.

VAP   *See* value-added process.

vaporware   A slang term for a product that has been announced but has missed its release date, often by a large margin, and so is not actually available.

VAR   *See* value-added reseller.

Variable Bit Rate   Abbreviated VBR. A connection-oriented Asynchronous Transfer Mode service for real-time applications for which minor data loss is acceptable, and

for non-real-time VBR applications such as transaction processing.

See also Asynchronous Transfer Mode; Available Bit Rate; Constant Bit Rate; Unspecified Bit Rate.

VAX   Digital Equipment Corporation's (DEC's) popular line of minicomputers and workstations, first introduced in 1977.

See also DECnet; VMS.

VBA   *See* Visual Basic for Applications.

VBR   *See* Variable Bit Rate.

VBScript   A version of Microsoft Visual Basic used as a scripting language in Microsoft Internet Explorer Web browser and in Microsoft Internet Information Server.

See also scripting.

VCC   *See* Virtual Channel Connection.

VCI   *See* Virtual Channel Identifier.

VDSL   *See* Very-High-Bit-Rate Digital Subscriber Line.

vector graphics   *See* object-oriented graphics.

vendor   The person or company that manufactures, supplies, or sells computer hardware, software, or related services.

Vendor Independent Messaging   Abbreviated VIM. An e-mail API originally developed by Lotus, and supported by Apple, IBM, MCI, Novell, and Oracle and other e-mail vendors. Developers use VIM to add e-mail capabilities to their applications.

Microsoft supports its own e-mail API, Messaging API (MAPI), and a VIM-to-MAPI dynamic link library makes it possible to exchange messages between the two interfaces.

See also Messaging API.

version number   A method of identifying a particular software or hardware release, assigned by the developer, that often includes numbers before and after a decimal point; the higher the number, the more recent the release.

The number before the decimal point indicates the major revision levels (as in Microsoft Windows NT 3 and Windows NT 4), and the part after the decimal indicates a minor revision level (as in Windows NT 3.5 and Windows NT 3.51). In some cases, a minor revision can produce a significant difference in performance.

Many people steer clear of any release labeled 1.0, because this number implies the first release of a product that may not have had extensive real-world use. Microsoft has avoided this issue with the release of Windows systems tied to the year, as in Windows 98 and Office 2000.

vertical application   An application specifically created for a narrow and specialized market or profession. Software designed for veterinary hospital management is an example of a vertical application.

vertical bar   The | symbol. Used in Unix and in other operating systems to pipe the output of one command into the input of another.

Very-High-Bit-Rate Digital Subscriber Line   Abbreviated VDSL. A higher-speed version of Asymmetric Digital Subscriber Line (ADSL).

VDSL is asymmetrical with a higher downstream data-transfer rate than its upstream rate. Upstream rates can be from 1.6Mbps to 2.3Mbps, and downstream rates range from 12.96Mbps to 51.84Mbps, depending on the distance involved.

See also Asymmetric Digital Subscriber Line; Digital Subscriber Line; High-Bit-Rate Digital Subscriber Line; Rate-Adaptive Digital Subscriber Line; Single-Line Digital Subscriber Line.

very low-frequency emission   Abbreviated VLF. Radiation emitted by a computer monitor and other common household electrical appliances, such as televisions, hair dryers, electric blankets, and food processors.

VLF emissions range from 2 to 400kHz and decline with the square of the distance from the source. Emissions are not constant around a computer monitor; they are higher from the sides and rear, and weakest from the front of the screen.

Sweden is the only country to have defined a set of standards for monitor emissions. In 1990, Mat Oct Provadet (MPR), the Swedish National Board for Meteorology and Testing, revised its guidelines for acceptable VLF emissions as less than or equal to 25 nanoTesla (nT). A nanoTesla is a unit of measurement for small magnetic fields.

See also extremely low-frequency emission; radio frequency interference.

V

very small aperture terminal Abbreviated VSAT. A small satellite terminal used for digital communications, from 1 to 3 meters (3.3 to 10 feet) in diameter, capable of managing digital transmissions of up to 56Kbps. Satellites that can handle T1 data rates of up to 1.544Mbps are known as TSATs.

VESA *See* Video Electronics Standards Association.

VESA local bus Abbreviated VL bus; also known as VL local bus. A local bus architecture introduced by VESA (Video Electronics Standards Association), in which as many as three VL bus adapter slots are built into the motherboard. The VL bus allows for bus mastering. The most common VL bus adapters are video adapters, hard-disk controllers, and network interface cards.

See also Peripheral Component Interconnect local bus; PC Card.

V.everything A marketing term used by some modem manufacturers to describe modems that comply with both the K56Flex and X2 proposed standards as well as with the adopted CCITT (ITU) V.90 standard.

A V.everything modem should be compatible with any other modem capable of operating at the same speed.

V.Fast An interim modem standard for uncompressed data-transfer rates of up to 28.8Kbps over dial-up voice-grade phone lines. Made obsolete by the publication of the CCITT (ITU) V.34 standard.

See also V.34.

vi A popular Unix screen editor, originally written by Bill Joy as part of the BSD Unix systems. Pronounced "vee-eye."

video adapter An adapter that provides the text and graphics output to the monitor. Some later video adapters, such as the SVGA, are included in the circuitry on the motherboard rather than as separate plug-in boards.

video conferencing A method used to allow people at remote locations to join in a conference and share information. Originally done with analog video and expensive satellite links, video conferencing is now performed with compressed digital video transmitted over a local-area network or the Internet.

From an application standpoint, video conferencing has gone way beyond looking at a picture of a person; users can look at and update charts, make drawings or sketches on a chalkboard, update spreadsheets, and so on, all online.

A video camera and a speakerphone are linked to a PC at each site, and the PC in turn is linked to the network.

See also CU-SeeMe; desktop video; H.323; Microsoft NetMeeting; T.120.

Video Electronics Standards Association Abbreviated VESA. An association of video graphics adapter and monitor manufacturers that sets standards for personal computer video. VESA is most notable for its role in standardizing Super VGA (SVGA) hardware and the development of the VESA local bus.

See also VESA local bus.

video RAM   Abbreviated VRAM, pronounced "vee-ram." Special-purpose RAM with two data paths for access (conventional RAM has just one). These two paths let a VRAM board manage two functions at once: refreshing the display and communicating with the processor. VRAM does not require the system to complete one function before starting the other, so it allows faster operation for the whole video system.

viewer   An application launched by a Web browser to view a file that the browser cannot display by itself. Sometimes called a helper application.

A viewer displays video clips and animation files.

See also helper; player; plug-in.

ViewSonic Corp.   A manufacturer of high-performance monitors, flat-panel LCD and LCD projectors, and professional monitors for CAD/CAM and graphic design.

For more information on ViewSonic Corp., see www.viewsonic.com.

VIM   *See* Vendor Independent Messaging.

VINES   *See* Banyan VINES.

Virtual Channel Connection   Abbreviated VCC. In Asynchronous Transfer Mode (ATM), a logical connection between two end stations. A VCC can be either switched or dedicated.

See also Asynchronous Transfer Mode; Virtual Path Connection.

Virtual Channel Identifier   Abbreviated VCI. In an Asynchronous Transfer Mode (ATM) cell header, a 16-bit field used to identify virtual channels between users or between users and networks.

See also Asynchronous Transfer Mode.

virtual circuit   A temporary shared communications path that appears to the user as a dedicated connection. A virtual circuit is maintained only for as long as the customer requires a connection; the next time a call is placed, a different virtual circuit may be used.

See also bandwidth on demand; permanent virtual circuit; switched virtual circuit.

virtual console   A feature found in Linux, UnixWare, and other operating systems that allows you to log on to the same terminal as though you were different users. Also known as a virtual terminal.

To open a new virtual console, hold the Alt key as you press one of the F1 to F8 function keys; as you press each function key, you see a new screen complete with its own login prompt. Each virtual console displays its output on its own virtual screen.

virtual data network   A method used to provide full interconnection of all LAN segments without using dedicated circuits so that customers pay only for the services they actually use. Also known as a virtual LAN.

See also bandwidth on demand; virtual circuit.

V

virtual directory   A directory that appears to a user to be located on the service they are accessing, but which is actually located on a linked server. Virtual directories are often used on Web servers where they are used to balance the overall load, but still present a single, simple view of the information present.

virtual drive   *See* RAM disk.

virtual LAN   *See* virtual data network.

Virtual Loadable Module   Abbreviated VLM. A Novell NetWare modular program that runs on each MS-DOS client and allows that workstation to communicate with the server.

The NetWare DOS Requester consists of several VLMs that replace and provide backward compatibility with the NetWare shells used in earlier versions of NetWare.

See also NetWare DOS Requester; NetWare Loadable Module.

virtual machine   An environment created by the operating system that gives each executing application the illusion that it has complete control of an independent computer and can access all the system resources that it needs.

For example, the Intel 80386 (and higher) processor can run multiple MS-DOS applications in completely separate and protected address spaces using virtual 8086 mode.

In the Java environment, a Java applet executes inside the Java Virtual Machine.

See also Java Virtual Machine.

virtual memory   A memory-management technique that allows information in physical memory to be swapped out to a hard disk if necessary.

This technique provides applications with more memory space than is actually available in the computer. True virtual-memory management requires specialized hardware in the processor for the operating system to use; it is not just a matter of writing information out to a swap area on the hard disk at the application level.

In a virtual memory system, programs and their data are divided into smaller pieces called *pages*. When more memory is needed, the operating system decides which pages are least likely to be needed soon (using an algorithm based on frequency of use, most recent use, and program priority), and it writes these pages out to disk. The memory space that they used is now available to the rest of the system for other applications. When these pages are needed again, they are loaded back into real memory, displacing other pages.

See also permanent swap file; swapping; swap space.

Virtual Path Connection   Abbreviated VPC. In Asynchronous Transfer Mode (ATM), a set of logical Virtual Channel Connections (VCCs) between two end stations. All channels in a specific VPC connect the same two end stations.

See also Asynchronous Transfer Mode; Virtual Channel Connection.

Virtual Path Identifier   Abbreviated VPI. In an Asynchronous Transfer Mode

(ATM) cell header, an 8-bit field used to identify virtual paths between users or between users and networks.

See also Asynchronous Transfer Mode.

Virtual Private Network Abbreviated VPN. Originally, a private network for voice and data built from traditional carrier services. More recently, a VPN is an encrypted private tunnel across the Internet.

Virtual Reality Modeling Language Abbreviated VRML. A specification and file format for three-dimensional rendering used in conjunction with Web browsers and that uses existing Web protocols and works within the Internet framework.

VRML is a subset of Silicon Graphics' Inventor File Format, created by Mark Pesce and Tony Parisi in 1994.

virtual root The root directory that a user sees when connected to a Web server.

The virtual root is an alias to an actual location on a hard disk, either on the Web server or on a different server. This technique allows one URL to represent the Web site, while, at the same time, allowing the Webmaster to change the root directory without affecting the URL.

See also Uniform Resource Locator.

Virtual Telecommunications Access Method Abbreviated VTAM. IBM software that runs on a mainframe computer running the MVS or VM operating system.

VTAM controls communications in an SNA (Systems Network Architecture) environment. VTAM supports a range of network protocols, including SDLC (Synchronous Data Link Control) and Token Ring.

virtual terminal *See* virtual console.

virus A program intended to damage a computer system without the user's knowledge or permission.

A virus clones itself from disk to disk or from system to system over a network. Numbers are hard to come by, but certain authorities claim that there are approximately 30,000 known viruses, with 400 new ones appearing each month.

A virus may attach itself to a program or to the partition table or boot track on a hard disk. When a certain event occurs, a date passes, or a specific program executes, the virus is triggered into action.

See also boot sector virus; file-infecting virus; macro virus; multipart virus; polymorphic virus; stealth virus; Trojan Horse; vaccine.

Visual Basic for Applications Abbreviated VBA. A version of Microsoft Visual Basic included with Microsoft Windows 98 applications such as Excel; it is used to write everything from simple macros to complex custom applications.

VL bus *See* VESA local bus.

VLF *See* very low-frequency emission.

VL local bus *See* VESA local bus.

VLM *See* Virtual Loadable Module.

VM *See* virtual machine.

V

VMS   A 32-bit, multiuser, multitasking, virtual memory operating system from Digital Equipment Corporation (DEC) for the VAX line of computers.

See also DECnet; VAX.

voice mail   A computerized store-and-forward system for voice messages.

A voice-mail system uses prerecorded messages to route the caller to the correct person, department, or mailbox and then digitizes the incoming messages and stores them on disk for review by the recipient. Users can often forward voice-mail messages to another department or person after attaching their own comments.

See also electronic mail.

volatile key   In Microsoft Windows, a Registry key whose contents are constructed at the time the system boots, rather than being permanently stored in a hive file.

See also hive; key; Registry; sub-hive; sub-key; value entry.

volume   In the Novell networking world, a volume is the highest level of the file server directory and file structure.

Large hard disks can be divided into several volumes when the network operating system is first installed, and with volume spanning, volumes can include multiple physical drives.

volume label   In many operating systems, the name assigned to a disk by the user, displayed on the first line of a directory listing. The Macintosh, on which disks are often referred to by name, uses the term *volume name* instead.

volume name   *See* volume label.

volume reference number   *See* volume serial number.

volume serial number   In several operating systems, a unique number assigned to a disk during the formatting process. This number is displayed at the beginning of a directory listing. The MacOS assigns a similar number, known as a volume reference number, that programs can use when referring to disks.

volume spanning   In Novell NetWare, a mechanism that allows a volume to include several physical hard disks.

See also volume.

VPC   *See* Virtual Path Connection.

VPI   *See* Virtual Path Identifier.

VP/ix   An MS-DOS emulation package from Sun Microsystems that allows you to access programs and data files under the MS-DOS partition and use them in the Unix environment as a task under Unix. To the user, the sessions look exactly as they would if you changed partitions and booted MS-DOS.

VPN   *See* Virtual Private Network.

VRAM   *See* video RAM.

VRML   *See* Virtual Reality Modeling Language.

VSAT   *See* very small aperture terminal.

VT-52, VT-100, VT-200 A series of asynchronous terminals manufactured by Digital Equipment Corporation (DEC) that uses a specific set of control codes for display management. Many communications and terminal-emulation packages include emulations of these terminals.

VTAM *See* Virtual Telecommunications Access Method.

V

W

W3   *See* World Wide Web.

W3C   *See* World Wide Web Consortium.

WABI   *See* Windows Application Binary Interface.

WAIS   *See* Wide Area Information Service.

wait state   A clock cycle during which no instructions are executed, because the processor is waiting for data from memory. Static RAM chips and paged-mode RAM chips are becoming popular because they can store information without being constantly refreshed by the processor, thus eliminating the wait state. A computer that can process information without wait states is known as a zero-wait-state computer.

WAN   *See* wide-area network.

warm boot   A reboot performed after the operating system has been running for some period of time, by pressing Ctrl+Alt+Del rather than cycling the power to the computer.

Warp   *See* OS/2.

WATS   *See* Wide Area Telephone Service.

wavelength division multiple access
Abbreviated WDMA. A technique that manages multiple transmissions on a fiber-optic cable system using wavelength division multiplexing (WDM).

WDMA divides each channel into a set of time slots using time-division multiplexing, and data from different sources is assigned to a repeating set of time slots.

See also time-division multiplexing; wavelength division multiplexing.

wavelength division multiplexing
Abbreviated WDM. A frequency-division multiplexing (FDM) technique that allows a single fiber-optic cable to carry multiple light signals rather than a single light signal. WDM places each signal on a different frequency.

See also frequency-division multiplexing; inverse multiplexing; time-division multiplexing; statistical multiplexing.

WBEM   *See* Web-Based Enterprise Management.

WDM   *See* wavelength division multiplexing.

WDMA   *See* wavelength division multiple access.

weak password   A password that is easy to guess, such as an English word, any reference to Star Trek or Star Wars, or a word or number that relates to the user, such as the name of a family member or a birth date.

See also password; strong password.

Web *See* World Wide Web.

Web-Based Enterprise Management

Abbreviated WBEM. A platform-independent management standard, originally proposed by BMC Software, Cisco Systems, Compaq, Intel, and Microsoft and now supported by more than 70 companies, to allow network, systems, and applications software data from a variety of sources to be accessed and reported by management applications regardless of the original source of that data.

See also Desktop Management Interface; Simple Network Management Protocol; total cost of ownership; Wired for Management.

Web browser A client application that lets you look at hypertext documents, follow links to other HTML documents, and download files on the Internet or on a corporate intranet.

When you find something that interests you as you browse through a hypertext document, you can click on that object, and the system automatically takes care of accessing the Internet host that holds the document you requested; you don't need to know the IP address, the name of the host system, or any other details.

A Web browser will also display the graphics in a Web page, play audio and video clips, and execute small Java or ActiveX programs called applets, although certain older Web browsers may need helper, or plug-in, applications to perform some of these tasks.

Netscape Navigator and Microsoft Internet Explorer are examples of popular Web browsers.

See also ActiveX; helper; HyperText Markup Language; player; plug-in; Uniform Resource Locator; viewer; World Wide Web.

Webmaster The person responsible for maintaining and administering a Web site.

WebNFS A technology from Sun Microsystems that extends the Network File System (NFS) to the Internet.

WebNFS makes file access across the Internet as easy as local file access, provides enhanced download performance, and can automatically resume a file transfer after a broken connection is restored.

Web page Information placed on a Web server for viewing with a Web browser. A Web page can contain text, graphics, audio or video clips, and links to other Web pages.

See also Web browser.

Web portal *See* portal.

Web server A hardware and software package that provides services to client computers running Web browsers.

Clients make requests in the form of HTTP messages; the server responds to these messages, returning Web pages or other requested documents to the client. Most Web servers run a version of Unix or Microsoft Windows NT Server.

See also Hypertext Transfer Protocol; Web browser; Web page; World Wide Web.

W

Web site   A group of HTML documents and associated scripts supported by a Web server on the World Wide Web.

Most Web sites have a home page used as a starting point or index into the site, with other Web pages or even other Web sites connected by links. To connect to a Web site, you need an Internet connection and a Web browser.

See also HyperText Markup Language; Web browser; Web page; World Wide Web.

wedged   A slang expression for a frozen or hung terminal.

Western Digital Corp   A major manufacturer of storage systems, including 3.5-inch Enhanced IDE drives for PCs, high-capacity SCSI drives for workstations and servers, and RAID systems.

For more information on Western Digital Corp, see www.wdc.com.

WfM   *See* Wired for Management.

whiteboard   An application that lets several network users look at and share images, data, and text simultaneously, as they all participate in a common conference call.

Each person's comments and suggestions are labeled and separated from the comments made by others participating in the call.

White Pine Software   Distributors of the popular Cu-SeeMe application, a video conferencing and videophone product that works over the Internet.

For more information on White Pine Software, see www.wpine.com.

whitespace   A collective name used for groups of spaces, tabs, and newlines, those printable characters that only produce blank spaces.

Wide Area Information Service   Abbreviated WAIS, pronounced "ways." A service used to access text databases or libraries on the Internet.

WAIS uses simple natural-language queries and takes advantage of index searches for fast retrieval. Unlike Gopher, which searches only the names of Gopher resources, WAIS can search the content of all documents retrievable from WAIS databases. WAIS is particularly adept at searching through collections of Usenet newsgroups, electronic texts, and newspaper archives. WAIS has largely been replaced by the search engines now available on the World Wide Web.

See also search engine.

wide-area network   Abbreviated WAN. A network that connects users across large distances, often crossing the geographical boundaries of cities or states.

See also local-area network; metropolitan-area network.

Wide Area Telephone Service   Abbreviated WATS. A discounted toll service available from all long-distance and local telephone companies that provides unlimited use of a telephone circuit for a fixed charge.

wideband   In communications, a channel capable of handling more frequencies than a standard 3kHz voice channel.

wideband transmission   *See* broadband network.

Wide SCSI   A version of the SCSI-2 standard that provides data transfer rates of up to 20MBps over a 16-bit data bus.

See also Fast SCSI; Fast/Wide SCSI; SCSI-1; SCSI-2; SCSI-3; Small Computer System Interface; Ultra SCSI; Ultra2 SCSI; Wide Ultra SCSI; Wide Ultra2 SCSI.

Wide Ultra SCSI   A version of the SCSI-2 standard that provides data transfer rates of up to 40MBps over a 16-bit data bus.

See also Fast SCSI; Fast/Wide SCSI; SCSI-1; SCSI-2; SCSI-3; Small Computer System Interface; Ultra SCSI; Ultra2 SCSI; Wide SCSI.

Wide Ultra2 SCSI   A version of the SCSI-2 standard that provides data transfer rates of up to 80MBps over a 16-bit data bus.

See also Fast SCSI; Fast/Wide SCSI; SCSI-1; SCSI-2; SCSI-3; Small Computer System Interface; Ultra SCSI; Ultra2 SCSI; Wide SCSI; Wide Ultra SCSI.

wildcard character   A character that represents one or more unknown characters. In many operating systems, a question mark (?) represents a single unknown character in a filename or filename extension, and an asterisk (*) represents any number of unknown characters.

See also star-dot-star.

WinCGI   A Common Gateway Interface (CGI) that allows HTTP applications to be written in Visual Basic. WinCGI has largely been replaced by other types of Web server extensions.

See also Common Gateway Interface; Hypertext Transfer Protocol.

window   In a graphical user interface, a rectangular portion of the screen that acts as a viewing area for applications.

Windows can be tiled so that they are displayed side by side, or they can be cascaded so that their individual title bars are always visible. They then can be individually moved and sized on the screen. Some programs can open multiple document windows inside their application window to display several word-processing or spreadsheet data files at the same time.

See also X Window.

Windows   *See* Microsoft Windows.

Windows 3.1   *See* Microsoft Windows 3.1.

Windows 95   *See* Microsoft Windows 95.

Windows 98   *See* Microsoft Windows 98.

Windows Application Binary Interface   Abbreviated WABI. A specification developed by Sun Microsystems that defines how Microsoft Windows applications run on Unix workstations. The WABI interface translates the system calls made by the application into system calls that the underlying Unix system can provide.

Windows CE   *See* Microsoft Windows CE.

W

Windows client Any computer running Windows that connects to the network.

Windows Internet Naming Service Abbreviated WINS. A Microsoft Windows NT Server service that maps NetBIOS computer names used in Windows networks to IP addresses used in TCP/IP-based networks. WINS is almost completely automated; it builds its own database and manages updates to the database.

See also network basic input/output system; IP address.

Windows Network Transit Protocol *See* WinSock.

Windows NT Diagnostics A utility program from Microsoft that is used to look at and troubleshoot a Windows NT Server system; also known as winmsd.

Windows NT Diagnostics details transport information and network statistics, as well as service, resource, environment, and device driver information.

Windows NT Server *See* Microsoft Windows NT Server.

Windows NT Workstation *See* Microsoft Windows NT Workstation.

Windows Sockets *See* WinSock.

Windows terminal *See* thin client.

winmsd *See* Windows NT Diagnostics.

WINS *See* Windows Internet Naming Service.

WinSock An API for writers of TCP/IP-related software. Also known as Windows Sockets or Windows Network Transit Protocol.

WinSock is designed to provide the same kinds of services that Berkeley sockets provide in the Unix world. In Windows, WinSock is implemented as a dynamic link library (DLL) that sits below the application but above the TCP/IP stack. Developers write programs that communicate with the DLL, which converts the commands and messages and passes them to the TCP/IP protocol stack below.

The latest version, WinSock 2, supports multiple communications protocols, including IPX (Internetwork Packet eXchange), DECnet, and XNS (Xerox Network Services), as well as real-time multimedia communications across a wide range of communications circuits.

Wintel A contraction of Windows and Intel. Pertaining to an Intel-based computer that runs Microsoft Windows.

WinZip A popular Windows file compression and decompression program from Nico Mak Computing, Inc.

Wired for Management Abbreviated WfM. A specification from Intel to make Intel-based systems more manageable.

WfM supports the Desktop Management Interface (DMI) and includes asset management, remote wake-up, power management, and system configuration and reconfiguration.

See also Advanced Configuration and Power Interface; Web-Based Enterprise Management.

wireless communications   A method of connecting a node or a group of nodes into the main network using a technology other than conventional cabling.

The following methods are in use:

- **Infrared line of sight**   High-frequency light waves are used to transmit data between nodes up to 24.4 meters (80 feet) apart using an unobstructed path; infrared beams cannot pass through masonry walls. Data rates are relatively high, in the tens of megabits per second range.

- **High-frequency radio**   High-frequency radio signals transmit data to nodes from 12.2 to 39.6 meters (40 to 130 feet) apart, depending on the nature of obstructions separating them; the signal can penetrate thin walls but not supporting masonry. Data rates are usually less than 1Mbps.

- **Spread-spectrum radio**   A small set of frequencies are available for wireless LANs without FCC approval. The 902 to 928Mhz band is known as the Industrial, Scientific, Medical (ISM) band and is not regulated. The 2.4 to 2.483Ghz band is regulated and requires an FCC license for use. Spread-spectrum nodes can be up to 243.8 meters (800 feet) apart in an open environment, and these radio waves can pass through masonry walls. However, in an environment with fully enclosed offices, distances are limited to 33.5 meters (110 feet). Data rates are usually less than 1Mbps.

Wireless LANs are not always completely wireless and may be used to replace the cabling on certain network segments or to connect groups of networks that use conventional cabling.

See also mobile computing.

wiring closet   A location where cables are gathered together to connect to the central wiring in an office or building.

word length   **1.** The standard data unit in a particular computer. The most common words are 8, 16, 32, or 64 bits in length.

2. In communications, the number of data bits in a data word.

workflow software   Software that allows users to move and manage information among themselves, combining the functions of e-mail, imaging, and document management.

A document moves through various stages of processing as it is edited, signed, or validated by the various members of the workgroup. Each stage is orchestrated and validated by the workflow software.

See also workgroup.

workgroup   A group of individuals who work together and share the same files and databases over a local-area network. Special software coordinates the workgroup and allows users to edit and exchange files and update databases as a group.

See also workflow software.

working directory   Jargon for the current working directory; also known as the current directory.

W

workstation   **1**. In networking, any personal computer attached to the network.

2. A high-performance computer optimized for graphics applications, such as computer-aided design (CAD), computer-aided engineering (CAE), or scientific applications.

World Wide Web   Abbreviated WWW, W3, or simply the Web. A huge collection of hypertext pages on the Internet.

World Wide Web concepts were developed in Switzerland by the European Laboratory for Particle Physics (known as CERN), but the Web is not just a tool for scientists; it is one of the most flexible and exciting tools in existence.

Hypertext links connect pieces of information (text, graphics, animation, audio, and video) in separate HTML pages located at the same or at different Internet sites, and you explore these pages and links using a Web browser such as Netscape Navigator or Microsoft Internet Explorer.

You can also access a Web resource directly if you specify the appropriate URL (Uniform Resource Locator).

World Wide Web traffic is growing faster than most other Internet services, and the reason for this becomes obvious once you try a capable Web browser; it is very easy and a lot of fun to access World Wide Web information.

See also HyperText Markup Language; Internet; portal; search engine; Web browser.

World Wide Web Consortium   Abbreviated W3C. An international consortium founded in 1994 to develop protocols for the continuing evolution of the World Wide Web.

For more information on the World Wide Web Consortium, see www.w3.org.

WORM   Acronym for Write Once Read Many. A high-capacity optical storage device that can only be written to once, but that can be read a number of times.

WORM devices can store huge amounts of data, as much as 1 terabyte, are highly reliable, and are well suited to archival and other nonchanging storage.

write-back cache   A technique used in cache design for writing information back into main memory.

In a write-back cache, the cache stores the changed block of data, but only updates main memory under certain conditions, such as when the whole block must be overwritten because a newer block must be loaded into the cache or when the controlling algorithm determines that too much time has elapsed since the last update. This method is rather complex to implement, but is much faster than other designs.

See also cache; write-through cache.

Write Once Read Many   *See* WORM.

write-through cache   A technique used in cache design for writing information back into main memory.

In a write-through cache, each time the processor returns a changed bit of data to the cache, the cache updates that information in both the cache and in main memory. This method is simple to implement, but is not as fast as other designs; delays can be introduced when the processor must wait to complete write operations to slower main memory.

See also cache; write-back cache.

WWW *See* World Wide Web.

W

X *See* X Window.

X2 A modem technology from U.S. Robotics (now part of 3COM) that provides a data rate of up to 56Kbps downstream and up to 40Kbps upstream. Replaced by the V.90 standard.

See also K56Flex; V.90.

X.21 A CCITT (ITU) standard that defines a protocol used in a circuit-switching network.

X.25 A CCITT (ITU) standard, developed in 1976, that defines the connection between a terminal and a public packet-switched network.

X.25 describes the electrical connections, the transmission protocol, error detection and correction, and other aspects of the link. X.25 standards parallel the lowest three levels of the OSI Reference Model for computer-to-computer communications: the physical layer, data-link layer, and network layer.

X.25 gateway *See* X.75.

X.28 A CCITT (ITU) standard, developed in 1977, that defines a DTE/DCE (data terminal equipment/data communications equipment) interface for accessing a PAD (packet assembler/disassembler) in a public data network that does not cross an international boundary but is confined within one country.

X.29 A CCITT (ITU) standard, developed in 1977, for user data and the exchange of control information between a PAD (packet assembler/disassembler) and packet-mode DTE (data terminal equipment) or another PAD.

X.75 A CCITT (ITU) standard that defines the procedures used to connect two separate packet-switched networks, such as those located in separate countries; often referred to as an X.25 gateway.

X.200 A CCITT (ITU) standard that documents the seven-layer OSI Reference Model for computer-to-computer communications.

X.400 A CCITT (ITU) recommended standard, released in 1984 and revised several times since then, for public or private international e-mail distribution systems, defining how messages will be transferred across the network or between two or more connected heterogeneous networks.

X.400 defines the components of an electronic address as well as the details of the envelope surrounding the message and the rules to follow when converting between message types, such as text or fax.

See also X.500; X.509.

X.500 A CCITT (ITU) recommended standard, first released in 1988 and revised several times since then, for a global directory system for locating e-mail users, to be used with the X.400 e-mail services. X.500

is similar to a hierarchical worldwide telephone book.

The Lightweight Directory Access Protocol (LDAP), now widely accepted in the Internet community, is a subset of X.500, and products such as Novell Directory Services (NDS) are based on X.500.

See also Lightweight Directory Access Protocol; Novell Directory Services; X.400; X.509.

X.509   A CCITT (ITU) suggested standard for authentication services, including digital signatures, based on X.500.

X Consortium   A group of vendors that develops products based on the X Window specifications.

Originally formed in 1988 at MIT by Apple, AT&T, Digital Equipment Corporation, Hewlett-Packard, and Sun Microsystems, in 1993 the X Consortium became an independent, nonprofit organization.

XCSE   *See* Xylan Certified Switching Expert.

XCSS   *See* Xylan Certified Switching Specialist.

XENIX   A version of Unix developed from AT&T Version 7 as a joint venture between Microsoft and Santa Cruz Operation (SCO) and released in 1980.

XENIX was intended to support commercial applications on the IBM PC—versions were also developed for the Motorola 68000 and Zilog Z8000 processors—and for a while XENIX was the most successful Unix in terms of sheer numbers sold. Microsoft sold its interest in XENIX to SCO in 1987.

Xerox Network Services   Abbreviated XNS. A multilayer communications protocol, first developed by Xerox, and later used by Novell and other network software suppliers. XNS also supports a distributed file system that lets users access other computers' files and printers as if they were local.

XFree86   A version of the X11R6 X Window system freely available for Intel-based Unix systems such as Linux and FreeBSD.

XML   *See* Extensible Markup Language.

Xmodem   A popular file transfer protocol available in many off-the-shelf and shareware communications packages.

Xmodem was originally developed by Ward Christiansen for early PCs using the CP/M operating system. Xmodem divides the data for a transmission into blocks. Each block consists of the start-of-header character, a block number, 128 bytes of data, and a checksum. An acknowledgment byte is returned to the sender if the checksum calculation is identical to the sender's checksum; however, this requirement to acknowledge every transmitted block can lead to poor performance.

An extension to Xmodem, called Xmodem-CRC, adds a more stringent error-checking method by using a cyclical redundancy check (CRC) to detect transmission errors rather than Xmodem's simple additive checksum.

Another variation is Xmodem-1K, which transfers data in 1024-byte blocks.

See also Kermit; Ymodem; Zmodem.

X

XMS *See* Extended Memory Specification.

XNS *See* Xerox Network Services.

XON/XOFF In asynchronous transmissions between two PCs, a simple method of flow control.

The receiving PC sends an XOFF control character (ASCII 19, Ctrl+S) to pause the transmission of data when the receive buffer is full and then sends an XON character (ASCII 17, Ctrl+Q) when it is ready to continue the transmission.

See also flow control; handshaking.

X/Open *See* Open Group.

XT *See* crosstalk.

X terminal A high-quality graphics terminal with a large amount of memory; designed for use with the X Window system. X terminals usually contain X server software in read-only memory.

See also X Window.

X Window A windowing environment developed at MIT for Unix workstations. Often referred to simply as X.

X Window is an open and nonproprietary bit-mapped graphics system, designed to be independent of both the display hardware and the underlying operating system. It is supported by all the major workstation vendors.

X Window implements a client/server environment, but with the sense of the terms reversed from today's common usage.

See also X terminal.

Xylan Certified Switching Expert Abbreviated XCSE. An advanced certification from Xylan for system professionals who design, maintain, and troubleshoot switched networks.

See also Xylan Certified Switching Specialist.

Xylan Certified Switching Specialist Abbreviated XCSS. A basic certification from Xylan for system professionals who develop solutions for switched networks that covers basic concepts of frame and cells switching.

See also Xylan Certified Switching Expert.

Y

Y2K problem The inability of some older computer programs to process dates correctly after midnight on December 31, 1999.

Computer programmers in the 1960s and '70s abbreviated the date field to two digits, partly to save space and partly because they were convinced that the software would be rewritten before the abbreviated date ever became a problem. So Y2K isn't really a bug; the programmers and designers did it on purpose.

This means that older software reads 99 as 1999, and as the year 2000 begins, it will interpret 00 as the first day of 1900.

Dates and calculations based on dates are used in almost all business, sales, accounting, and commercial software, much of which was written in computer languages no longer in common use. Without expensive and time-consuming modifications and testing, these systems will at best provide unpredictable results after January 1, 2000; at worst, they will simply fail to operate.

Year 2000 bug *See* Y2K problem.

Yellow Pages A name for the security and file-access databases on Unix systems. These databases are now known as the Network Information Service (NIS).

See also Network Information Service.

Ymodem A popular file transfer protocol available in many off-the-shelf and shareware communications packages.

Ymodem, a variation of the Xmodem protocol, divides the data to be transmitted into blocks; each block consists of the start-of-header character, a block number, 1KB of data, and a checksum. Ymodem's larger data block means less overhead for error control when compared with Xmodem, but if the block has to be retransmitted because the protocol detects an error, there is more data to resend. Ymodem also incorporates the capabilities to send multiple files in the same session and to abort file transfer during the transmission.

See also Kermit; Zmodem.

Z

.Z Filename extension that identifies a Unix file compressed by the gzip or the compact utility.

.z Filename extension that identifies a Unix file compressed by the compress utility.

ZAK *See* Zero Administration Kit.

ZAW *See* Zero Administration for Windows.

Z.E.N.works *See* Novell Z.E.N.works.

Zero Administration Kit Abbreviated ZAK. A collection of tools, scripts, and methodologies used by system administrators to simplify the implementation of secure management on the Windows family of operating systems.

ZAK allows system administrators to perform three main functions quickly and easily:

- To centralize configuration

- To eliminate local access to the desktop computer

- To allow storage of data and applications on the server rather than on the client

See also Advanced Configuration and Power Interface; Desktop Management Interface; NetPC; network computer; thin client; total cost of ownership; Wired for Management; Zero Administration for Windows.

Zero Administration for Windows Abbreviated ZAWS. A Microsoft-led initiative designed to lower the total cost of ownership of Windows-based network clients in the corporate world.

ZAW has evolved over time and now focuses on three main areas:

- Installing an operating system on a new computer or on a new hard disk in an existing computer

- Deploying applications from central servers to the desktop

- Distributing modifications or upgrades to applications

See also NetPC; network computer; thin client; total cost of ownership.

Zero Insertion Force socket A specially designed chip socket that makes replacing a chip easier and safer.

To change a chip in a ZIF socket, you raise a lever beside the socket to free the original chip's pins from the socket. You then slide the old chip out and slide in the replacement chip, taking care to align the pins and holes. Finally, you lower the lever again. A ZIF socket minimizes damage to the delicate pins that connect the chip to the rest of the system.

zero-slot LAN A local-area network that uses one of the existing serial or parallel ports on the computer rather than a special network interface card plugged in to the computer's expansion bus.

Because zero-slot LANs can only transmit as fast as the computer's output port, they are considerably slower than networks that use network-specific hardware and software. The maximum length of each cable segment is also severely limited, so zero-slot LANs can network only two or three computers. The advantage of a zero-slot LAN is its low cost compared with dedicated network systems.

See also peer-to-peer network.

zero-wait-state computer   A computer that can process information without processor wait states, which are clock cycles during which no instructions are executed because the processor is waiting for data from a device or from memory.

Static RAM chips and paged-mode RAM chips are becoming popular because they can store information without being constantly refreshed by the processor, thus eliminating the wait state.

See also wait state.

ZIF socket   *See* Zero Insertion Force socket.

.ZIP   Filename extension that identifies a file compressed by the PKZIP or WinZip utilities.

See also PKZIP; WinZip; ZIP file.

Zip Drive   A popular removable storage device from Iomega Corporation, capable of storing 100MB on relatively cheap, portable, 3.5-inch disks.

Zip Drives have emerged as the de facto standard personal computer backup device.

See also Iomega Corporation.

ZIP file   A file whose contents have been compressed by one of the popular file-compression utilities, such as PKZIP, WinZip, or other comparable program; the filename extension is .ZIP.

A ZIP file can contain a single compressed file or a whole collection of archives. A file compressed in this way is said to have been zipped.

To uncompress a ZIP file, use the same utility that compressed it originally. Some ZIP files are self-extracting and can uncompress themselves when you click their icon.

See also file compression; PKZIP; WinZip; .ZIP.

zipped   *See* ZIP file.

Zmodem   A popular file transfer protocol available in many off-the-shelf and shareware communications packages.

Zmodem is similar to Xmodem and Ymodem but is designed to handle larger data transfers with fewer errors. Zmodem also includes a feature called checkpoint restart, which allows an interrupted transmission to resume at the point of interruption, rather than starting again at the beginning of the transmission.

See also Kermit; Xmodem; Ymodem.

zombie   In Unix and other operating systems, a dead process that has not yet been deleted from the process table.

Most zombies disappear almost immediately, although from time to time, you may find one that is impossible to delete without rebooting the system. Zombies do not

Z

consume any system resources, other than their slot in the process table.

zone   On a local-area network such as AppleTalk, a logical subgroup of users within a larger group of interconnected networks.

Appendix A: Information on the Internet

This appendix contains a selection of the networking resources available on the World Wide Web, broken out by category to help you find the information you are looking for quickly and easily. To be consistent with the rest of this book, I have not specified the protocol used to access each Web site; unless a different protocol is specified, you can simply assume that HTTP will work in all cases. Just add `http://` to the beginning of each Web address in your browser when you access a site.

The Web is in a constant state of flux as URLs change and Web sites disappear. The better-organized sites will simply post a link to the new location if they make substantive changes, and you can use that new link to go right to the new or reorganized site. Other sites reorganize themselves periodically as a part of their housekeeping; the information you want is still available, but you have to look in another place to find it or use the site's built-in search engine to find it.

When all else fails, use one of the Web sites listed in the "Portals and Search Engines" section of this appendix. In it you will find a list of the sites you can use to search the Web for documents using keywords, phrases, or even Boolean expressions. See each individual search engine site for details.

Hardware Companies

This section lists the major manufacturers and suppliers of networking and computer hardware.

Acer Group	`www.acer.com.tw`
Adaptec, Inc.	`www.adaptec.com`
Advanced Micro Devices, Inc.	`www.amd.com`
Apple Computer, Inc.	`www.apple.com`
Ascend Communications, Inc.	`www.ascend.com`

Appendix A: Information on the Internet

AST Research	www.ast.com
Bay Networks, Inc.	www.baynetworks.com
Cabletron Systems	www.cabletron.com
Canon, Inc.	www.canon.com
Cirrus Logic, Inc.	www.cirrus.com
Cisco Systems, Inc.	www.cisco.com
Compaq Computer Corporation	www.compaq.com
Cyrix	www.cyrix.com
Dell Computer Corporation	www.dell.com
Dialogic Corporation	www.dialogic.com
Digital Equipment Corporation	www.digital.com
Gateway, Inc.	www.gateway.com
Hewlett-Packard Company	www.hp.com
Integrated Device Technology	www.idt.com
Intel Corporation	www.intel.com
IBM	www.ibm.com
Iomega Corporation	www.iomega.com
Lexmark International, Inc.	www.lexmark.com
Lucent Technologies, Inc.	www.lucent.com

Microcom, Inc.	www.microcom.com
Micron Technology	www.micronpc.com
Motorola, Inc.	www.motorola.com
National Semiconductor Corporation	www.national.com
NEC Corporation	www.nec.com
Packard-Bell	www.packardbell.com
Quantum Corporation	www.quantum.com
Rockwell Semiconductor Systems	www.rockwell.com.
S3, Inc.	www.s3.com
Samsung Electronics	www.samsung.com
Seagate Technology, Inc.	www.seagate.com
Silicon Graphics, Inc.	www.sgi.com
Sun Microsystems, Inc.	www.sun.com
SyQuest Technology, Inc.	www.syquest.com
Toshiba Corporation	www.toshiba.com
U.S. Robotics Corporation	www.usr.com
ViewSonic Corp.	www.viewsonic.com
Western Digital Corp.	www.wdc.com

Software and Service Companies

This section lists the major providers of networking operating systems, applications software, and online and other services.

America Online	www.aol.com
Baan Company	www2.baan.com
Banyan Systems, Inc.	www.banyan.com
Caldera, Inc.	www.caldera.com
CompuServe, Inc.	www.compuserve.com
Computer Associates International	www.cai.com
Gartner Group, Inc.	www.gartner.com
Informix Software, Inc.	www.informix.com
Inprise Corporation	www.inprise.com
Learning Tree International	www.learningtree.com
Marimba, Inc.	www.marimba.com
Microsoft, Inc.	www.microsoft.com
Netscape Communications Corporation	www.netscape.com
Network Associates, Inc.	www.networkassociates.com
Novell, Inc.	www.novell.com
Oracle Corporation	www.oracle.com
PC Connection	www.pcconnection.com

PeopleSoft, Inc.	www.peoplesoft.com
PointCast, Inc.	www.pointcast.com
RealNetworks, Inc.	www.real.com
Red Hat Software	www.redhat.com
RSA Data Security	www.rsa.com
SCO	www.sco.com
SAP	www.sap.com
Sybase, Inc.	www.sybase.com
Symantec Corporation	www.symantec.com
White Pine Software	www.wpine.com

Internet Organizations

Here you will find URLs relating to the main Internet organizations.

Internet Society	www.isoc.org
Internet Architecture Board	www.iab.org/iab
Internet Engineering Steering Group	www.ietf.org/iesg.htm
Internet Engineeirng Task Force	www.ietf.org
Internet Research Task Force	www.irtf.org
International Ad Hoc Committee	www.iahc.org
Internet Assigned Numbers Authority	www.isi.edu/iana

World Wide Web Consotium	www.w3.org
Federal Networking Council	www.fnc.gov

Standards Groups and Trade Organizations

This section provides URLs for the major network-related standards groups and trade associations.

Active Group	www.activex.org
ANSI	www.ansi.org
ATM Forum	www.atmforum.com
CERN	www.cern.ch
CERT	www.cert.org
EIA	www.eia.org
FCC	www.fcc.gov
IEEE	www.ieee.org
IrDA	www.irda.org
ISO	www.iso.ch
ITU	www.itu.ch
NCSC	www.ncsc.com
Object Management Group	www.omg.org

Open Group	www.opengroup.org
TIA	www.tiaonline.org

Portals and Search Engines

The distinction between a Web portal and a search engine continues to blur, so they are grouped together in this section.

Alta Vista	www.altavista.digital.com
America Online	www.aol.com
Chickclick	www.chickclick.com
ESPN	www.espn.com
Excite	www.excite.com
GoTo.com	www.goto.com
Hotbot	www.hotbot.com
Infoseek	www.infoseek.com
Ivillage	www.ivillage.com
Lycos	www.lycos.com
Netcenter	www.netcenter.com
Northern Light	www.nlsearch.com
Snap!	www.snap.com
Yahoo!	www.yahoo.com

Open Source Software

This section contains details on where to find open-source software, as well as URLs for some of the organizations supporting open source and free software.

Open Source Initiative	www.opensource.org
Free Software Foundation	www.fsf.org
Slashdot	www.slashdot.org
O'Reilly Open Source Center	opensource.oreilly.com
The Apache Project	www.apache.org
GNU	www.gnu.org
Linux Online	www.linux.org
The Linux Kernel Archives	www.kernel.org
The Linux Documentation Project	metalab.unc.edu/LDP
Linux Web pages	www.linux-center.org
The Perl Institute	www.perl.org
Netscape's Mozilla Project	www.mozilla.org
XFree86	www.xfree86.org
FreeBSD Project	ftp.freebsd.org
Open BSD	www.openbsd.org

Local Exchange Carriers

This section lists the companies providing local carrier services throughout the United States.

Ameritech, Inc.	www.ameritech.com
Bell Atlantic Corp	www.bell-atl.com
Bell South	www.bellsouth.com
GTE Service Corp	www.gte.com
NYNEX Corp	www.nynex.com
Pacific Bell	www.pacbell.com
SBC Communications, Inc.	www.sbc.com
U.S. West Communications Group	www.uswest.com

Interexchange Carriers

This section lists the carriers that provide long-distance service in the United States.

AT&T Corp	www.att.com
LDDS WorldCom, Inc.	www.wcom.com
GTE Service Corp.	www.gte.com
MCI Telecommunications Corp.	www.mci.com
Sprint Communications Company	www.sprintbiz.com
MFS Communications Company	www.mfsdatanet.com
Norlight Telecommunications, Inc.	www.norlight.com

Appendix B: Certification Programs

This appendix presents information on the many and varied computer and networking certification programs available in the industry. Table B.1 lists the abbreviations and complete names for the most common certification programs, and Table B.2 lists all the network-related certification programs offered by each company or computer-industry organization.

TABLE B.1 CERTIFICATION PROGRAM ABBREVIATIONS

Abbreviation	Certification Program
A+	A+ Certification
AASE	Associated Accredited Systems Engineer
ABCP	Associate Business Continuity Professional
ACE	Advanced Certified Engineer
ACTE	Ascend Certified Technical Expert
ASE	Accredited Systems Engineer
BAC	Baan Advanced Certification
BBC	Baan Basic Certification
BNCE	Bay Networks Certified Expert
BNCS	Bay Networks Certified Specialist
CATE	Certified Advanced Technical Expert
CBCP	Certified Business Continuity Professional
CBE	Certified Banyan Engineer
CBS	Certified Banyan Specialist

TABLE B.1 CERTIFICATION PROGRAM ABBREVIATIONS *(CONTINUED)*

Abbreviation	Certification Program
CC	Certified Consultant
CCIE	Cisco Certified Internetworking Expert
CCP	Certified Computing Professional
CDA	Certified Database Administrator
CDIA	Certified Document Image Architect
CE	Certified Expert
CINA	Certified IRIX Network Administrator
CISA	Certified Information System Auditor
CISA	Certified IRIX System Administrator
CISSP	Certified Information Systems Security Professional
CJD	Certified Java Developer
CJP	Certified Java Programmer
CLP	Certified Lotus Professional
CLS	Certified Lotus Specialist
CNA	Certified Novell Administrator
CNE	Certified Novell Engineer
CNI	Certified Novell Instructor
CNP	Certified Network Professional

App B

Appendix B: Certification Programs

TABLE B.1 CERTIFICATION PROGRAM ABBREVIATIONS *(CONTINUED)*

Abbreviation	Certification Program
CNX	Certified Network Expert
CPDA	Certified Powerbuilder Developer Associate
CPDP	Certified Powerbuilder Developer Professional
CPTS	Certified Performance and Tuning Specialist
CS	Certified Specialist
CSA	Certified Solaris Administrator
CSE	Certified Solutions Expert
CSE	Certified Systems Expert
CSE	Certified Switching Expert
CSNA	Certified Solaris Network Administrator
CSS	Certified Switching Specialist
CU	Certified User
CUE	Certified Unicenter Engineer
MBCP	Master Business Continuity Professional
MCNE	Master Certified Novell Engineer
MCP	Microsoft Certified Professional
MCSD	Microsoft Certified Solutions Developer
MCSE	Microsoft Certified Systems Engineer

TABLE B.1 CERTIFICATION PROGRAM ABBREVIATIONS *(CONTINUED)*

Abbreviation	Certification Program
MOE	Microsoft Office Expert
MOES	Microsoft Office Expert Specialist
MOPS	Microsoft Office Proficient Specialist
N+	Network+ Certification
NCIP	Novell Certified Internet Professional
PSE	Professional Server Expert
PSS	Professional Server Specialist
RCDD	Registered Communications Distribution Designer

TABLE B.2 COMPUTER AND NETWORKING CERTIFICATION PROGRAMS

Company	Certification Program Name
Ascend	Ascend Certified Technical Expert
Baan	Baan Basic Certification
	Baan Advanced Certification in Enterprise Logistics
	Baan Advanced Certification in Enterprise Finance
	Baan Advanced Certification in Enterprise Tools
	Baan Advanced Certification in Enterprise Modeler
Banyan	Certified Banyan Specialist
	Certified Banyan Specialist: Windows NT
	Certified Banyan Engineer

429

TABLE B.2 COMPUTER AND NETWORKING CERTIFICATION PROGRAMS *(CONTINUED)*

Company	Certification Program Name
Bay Networks	Bay Networks Certified Specialist: Hub Technology
	Bay Networks Certified Expert: Hub Technology
	Bay Networks Certified Specialist: Router Technology
	Bay Networks Certified Expert: Router Technology
	Bay Networks Certified Specialist: Network Management Technology
	Bay Networks Certified Expert: Network Management Technology
	Bay Networks Certified Specialist: Switching Technology
	Bay Networks Certified Expert: Remote Access Technology
BICSI	Registered Communications Distribution Designer
	Registered Communications Distribution Designer: LAN Specialty
Cisco	Cicso Certified Internetworking Expert: WAN Switching Expert
	Cicso Certified Internetworking Expert: ISP Dial Expert
	Cicso Certified Internetworking Expert: Routing and Switching Expert
Compaq	Associate Accredited Systems Engineer Specializing in Novell IntranetWare
	Associate Accredited Systems Engineer Specializing in Microsoft Windows NT
	Accredited Systems Engineer Specializing in Novell IntranetWare
	Accredited Systems Engineer Specializing in Microsoft Windows NT
Computer Associates	Certified Unicenter Engineer
CompTIA	A+ Certification
	Certified Document Image Architect
	Network+ Certification
CNX Consortium	Certified Network Expert

TABLE B.2 COMPUTER AND NETWORKING CERTIFICATION PROGRAMS *(CONTINUED)*

Company	Certification Program Name
Disaster Recovery Institute International	Associate Business Continuity Professional Certified Business Continuity Professional Master Business Continuity Professional
Hewlett-Packard	HP OpenView Certified Consultant: Unix HP OpenView Certified Consultant: Windows NT HP OpenView Certified Consultant: Unix and Windows NT
IBM	Certified Solutions Expert: Net Commerce Certified Solutions Expert: Firewall Resources IBM Certified AIX User IBM Certified Specialist: AIX System Administration IBM Certified Specialist: AIX Support IBM Certified Specialist: AS/400 Associate System Operator IBM Certified Specialist: AS/400 Professional System Operator IBM Certified Specialist: AS/400 Associate System Administrator IBM Certified Specialist: AS/400 Professional System Administrator IBM Certified Specialist: OS/2 Warp Server Administration IBM Certified Expert: OS/2 Warp Server IBM Certified Specialist: OS/2 LAN Server Administration IBM Certified Expert: OS/2 LAN Server IBM Certified Systems Expert: OS/2 Warp IBM Certified Advanced Technical Expert: RS/6000 AIX Professional Server Expert Professional Server Expert: Novell NetWare Professional Server Expert: OS/2 Warp Server Professional Server Expert: Windows NT Server

App B

Appendix B: Certification Programs

TABLE B.2 COMPUTER AND NETWORKING CERTIFICATION PROGRAMS *(CONTINUED)*

Company	Certification Program Name
Informix	Database Specialist: Informix Dynamic Server
	System Administration: Informix Dynamic Server
	Informix-4GL Certified Professional
Institute for Certification of Computing Professionals	Certified Computing Professional
International Information Systems Security Certification Consortium	Certified Information Systems Security Professional
Information Systems Audit and Control Association	Certified Information Systems Auditor
Learning Tree International	Internet/Intranet Certified Professional
	Internetwork Certified Professional
	Local Area Networks Certified Professional
	PC Service and Support Certified Professional
	Unix Systems Certified Professional
	Wide Area Networks Certified Professional
Lotus	Certified Lotus Specialist
	Certified Lotus Professional: Application Developer
	Certified Lotus Professional: Principal Application Developer
	Certified Lotus Professional: System Administrator
	Certified Lotus Professional: Principal System Administrator
	Certified Lotus Professional: cc Mail System Administrator

TABLE B.2 COMPUTER AND NETWORKING CERTIFICATION PROGRAMS *(CONTINUED)*

Company	Certification Program Name
Microsoft	Microsoft Certified Professional +Internet
	Microsoft Certified Systems Engineer +Internet
	Microsoft Certified Systems Engineer
	Microsoft Certified Solutions Developer
	Microsoft Office Proficient Specialist
	Microsoft Office Expert Specialist
	Microsoft Office Expert
Network Professional Association	Certified Network Professional
Novell	Certified Novell Administrator
	Certified Novell Engineer
	Certified Novell Instructor
	Novell Certified Internet Professional
	Novell Internet Architect
	Novell Internet Business Strategist
	Novell Intranet Manager
	Master Certified Novell Engineer
	Novell Web Designer
Oracle	Certified Database Administrator
	Certified Application Developer
SCO	Advanced Certified Engineer: Server Track
	Advanced Certified Engineer: OpenServer Track
	Advanced Certified Engineer: UnixWare Track

App B

Appendix B: Certification Programs

TABLE B.2 COMPUTER AND NETWORKING CERTIFICATION PROGRAMS *(CONTINUED)*

Company	Certification Program Name
Silicon Graphics	Certified IRIX System Administrator
	Certified IRIX Network Administrator
Sun Microsystems	Certified Java Programmer
	Certified Java Developer
	Certified Solaris Administrator
	Certified Solaris Network Administrator
Sybase	Certified PowerBuilder Developer Associate
	Certified PowerBuilder Developer Professional
	Certified Database Administrator
	Certified Performing and Tuning Specialist
Xylan	Xylan Certified Switch Specialist
	Xylan Certified Switch Expert

Appendix C: ASCII Character Set

Table C.1 shows the first 32 characters (0–31) from the American Standard Code for Information Interchange (ASCII), also known as the control characters.

Table C.2 shows the 7-bit standard ASCII character set (comprising characters 32–127), which is implemented on all computers that use ASCII.

Table C.3 shows characters 128–255 of the 8-bit IBM extended ASCII character set.

App C

TABLE C.1 ASCII CONTROL CHARACTERS

DECIMAL	CHARACTER	CONTROL COMBINATION
0	NUL (Null)	Ctrl+@
1	SOH (Start of heading)	Ctrl+A
2	STX (Start of text)	Ctrl+B
3	ETX (End of text)	Ctrl+C
4	EOT (End of transmission)	Ctrl+D
5	ENQ (Enquire)	Ctrl+E
6	ACK (Acknowledge)	Ctrl+F
7	BEL (Bell)	Ctrl+G
8	BS (Backspace)	Ctrl+H
9	HT (Horizontal tab)	Ctrl+I
10	LF (Line feed)	Ctrl+J
11	VT (Vertical tab)	Ctrl+K
12	FF (Form feed)	Ctrl+L
13	CR (Carriage return)	Ctrl+M

TABLE C.1 ASCII CONTROL CHARACTERS *(CONTINUED)*

DECIMAL	CHARACTER	CONTROL COMBINATION
14	SO (Shift out)	Ctrl+N
15	SI (Shift in)	Ctrl+O
16	DLE (Data link escape)	Ctrl+P
17	DC1 (Device control 1)	Ctrl+Q
18	DC2 (Device control 2)	Ctrl+R
19	DC3 (Device control 3)	Ctrl+S
20	DC4 (Device control 4)	Ctrl+T
21	NAK (Negative acknowledgement)	Ctrl+U
22	SYN (Synchronous idle)	Ctrl+V
23	ETB (End transmission block)	Ctrl+W
24	CAN (Cancel)	Ctrl+X
25	EM (End of medium)	Ctrl+Y
26	SUB (Substitute)	Ctrl+Z
27	ESC (Escape)	Ctrl+[
28	FS (File separator)	Ctrl+/
29	GS (Group separator)	Ctrl+]
30	RS (Record separator)	Ctrl+^
31	US (Unit separator)	Ctrl+_

TABLE C.2 STANDARD 7-BIT ASCII CHARACTER SET

DECIMAL	CHARACTER	DECIMAL	CHARACTER
32	space	51	3
33	!	52	4
34	"	53	5
35	#	54	6
36	$	55	7
37	%	56	8
38	&	57	9
39	'	58	:
40	(	59	;
41	)	60	<
42	*	61	=
43	+	62	>
44	,	63	?
45	-	64	@
46	.	65	A
47	/	66	B
48	0	67	C
49	1	68	D
50	2	69	E

TABLE C.2 STANDARD 7-BIT ASCII CHARACTER SET *(CONTINUED)*

DECIMAL	CHARACTER	DECIMAL	CHARACTER
70	F	89	Y
71	G	90	Z
72	H	91	[
73	I	92	\
74	J	93	]
75	K	94	^
76	L	95	_
77	M	96	`
78	N	97	a
79	O	98	b
80	P	99	c
81	Q	100	d
82	R	101	e
83	S	102	f
84	T	103	g
85	U	104	h
86	V	105	i
87	W	106	j
88	X	107	k

TABLE C.2 STANDARD 7-BIT ASCII CHARACTER SET *(CONTINUED)*

DECIMAL	CHARACTER	DECIMAL	CHARACTER
108	l	118	v
109	m	119	w
110	n	120	x
111	o	121	y
112	p	122	z
113	q	123	{
114	r	124		
115	s	125	}
116	t	126	~
117	u	127	DEL

TABLE C.3 IBM EXTENDED ASCII CHARACTER SET

DECIMAL	CHARACTER	DECIMAL	CHARACTER
128	Ç	135	ç
129	ü	136	ê
130	é	137	ë
131	â	138	è
132	ä	139	ï
133	à	140	î
134	å	141	ì

App C

TABLE C.3 IBM EXTENDED ASCII CHARACTER SET *(CONTINUED)*

DECIMAL	CHARACTER	DECIMAL	CHARACTER
142	Ä	161	í
143	Å	162	ó
144	É	163	ú
145	æ	164	ñ
146	Æ	165	Ñ
147	ô	166	ª
148	ö	167	º
149	ò	168	¿
150	û	169	^{2}
151	ù	170	^{3}
152	ÿ	171	½
153	Ö	172	¼
154	Ü	173	¡
155	¢	174	«
156	£	175	»
157	¥	176	
158	₧	177	
159	ƒ	178	
160	á	179	│

TABLE C.3 IBM EXTENDED ASCII CHARACTER SET *(CONTINUED)*

DECIMAL	CHARACTER	DECIMAL	CHARACTER
180	⊣	199	╟
181	╡	200	╚
182	╢	201	╔
183	╖	202	╩
184	╕	203	╦
185	╣	204	╠
186	║	205	═
187	╗	206	╬
188	╝	207	╧
189	╜	208	╨
190	╛	209	╤
191	┐	210	╥
192	└	211	╙
193	?	212	╘
194	>	213	╒
195	£	214	╓
196	–	215	╫
197	1	216	╪
198	╞	217	┘

TABLE C.3 IBM EXTENDED ASCII CHARACTER SET *(CONTINUED)*

DECIMAL	CHARACTER	DECIMAL	CHARACTER
218	⌐	237	f
219	∎	238	´
220	▬	239	\
221	▮	240	[
222	∎	241	6
223	∎	242	∫
224	~	243	π
225	1	244	(
226	G	245	)
227	p	246	4
228	Σ	247	<
229	s	248	8
230	m	249	8
231	t	250	-
232	F	251	=
233	Q	252	n
234	V	253	2
235	W	254	∎
236	1	255	

Appendix D: EBCDIC Character Set

Table D.1 shows all 256 characters that make up the Extended Binary Coded Decimal Interchange Code (EBCDIC) character set.

TABLE D.1 EBCDIC CHARACTER SET

Decimal	Character	Decimal	Character
0	NUL (null)	14	SO (shift out)
1	SOH (start of heading)	15	SI (shift in)
2	STX (start of text)	16	DLE (data length escape)
3	ETX (end of text)	17	DC1 (device control 1)
4	SEL (select)	18	DC2 (device control 2)
5	HT (horizontal tab)	19	DC3 (device control 3)
6	RNL (required new line)	20	RES/ENP (restore/enable presentation)
7	DEL (delete)	21	NL (new line)
8	GE (graphic escape)	22	BS (backspace)
9	SPS (superscript)	23	POC (program-operator communication)
10	RPT (repeat)	24	CAN (cancel)
11	VT (vertical tab)	25	EM (end of medium)
12	FF (form feed)	26	UBS (unit backspace)
13	CR (carriage return)	27	CU1 (customer use 1)

App D

TABLE D.1 EBCDIC CHARACTER SET *(CONTINUED)*

Decimal	Character	Decimal	Character
28	IFS (interchange file separator)	42	SM/SW (set mode/switch)
29	IGS (interchange group separator)	43	CSP (control sequence prefix)
30	IRS (interchange record separator)	44	MFA (modify field attribute)
31	IUS/ITB (interchange unit separator/intermediate transmission block)	45	ENQ (enquiry)
32	DS (digit select)	46	ACK (acknowledge)
33	SOS (start of significance)	47	BEL (bell)
34	FS (field separator)	48-49	not assigned
35	WUS (word underscore)	50	STN (synchronous idle)
36	BYP/INP (bypass/inhibit presentation)	51	IR (index return)
37	LF (line feed)	52	PP (presentation position)
38	ETB (end of transmission block)	53	TRN (transport)
39	ESC (escape)	54	NBS (numeric backspace)
40	SA (set attribute)	55	EOT (end of transmission)
41	SFE (start field extended)	56	SBS (subscript)
		57	IT (indent tab)

TABLE D.1 EBCDIC CHARACTER SET *(CONTINUED)*

Decimal	Character	Decimal	Character
58	RFF (required form feed)	90	!
59	CU3 (customer use 3)	91	$
60	DC4 (device control 4)	92	*
61	NAK (negative acknowledge)	93	)
62	not assigned	94	;
63	SUB (substitute)	95	¬ (Logical NOT)
64	SP (space)	96	-
65	RSP (required space)	97	/
66-73	not assigned	98-105	not assigned
74	¢	106	¦ (broken pipe)
75	.	107	,
76	<	108	%
77	(	109	-
78	+	110	>
79	| (Logical OR)	111	?
80-89	not assigned	112-120	not assigned

TABLE D.1 EBCDIC CHARACTER SET *(CONTINUED)*

Decimal	Character	Decimal	Character
121	`	138-144	not assigned
122	:	145	j
123	#	146	k
124	@	147	l
125	'	148	m
126	=	149	n
127	"	150	o
128	not assigned	151	p
129	a	152	q
130	b	153	r
131	c	154-160	not assigned
132	d	161	~
133	e	162	s
134	f	163	t
135	g	164	u
136	h	165	v
137	I	166	w

TABLE D.1 EBCDIC CHARACTER SET *(CONTINUED)*

Decimal	Character	Decimal	Character
167	x	210	K
168	y	211	L
169	z	212	M
170-191	not assigned	213	N
192	{	214	O
193	A	215	P
194	B	216	Q
195	C	217	R
196	D	218-223	not assigned
197	E	224	\
198	F	225	NSP (numeric space)
199	G		
200	H	226	S
201	I	227	T
202	SHY (syllable hyphen)	228	U
203-207	not assigned	229	V
208	}	230	W
209	J	231	X

TABLE D.1 EBCDIC CHARACTER SET *(CONTINUED)*

Decimal	Character	Decimal	Character
232	Y	245	5
233	Z	246	6
234-239	not assigned	247	7
240	0	248	8
241	1	249	9
242	2	250-254	not assigned
243	3	255	EO (eight ones)
244	4		

The Dictionary of Networking—Now on CD!

On the accompanying CD, we've included an electronic version of the Dictionary of Networking, complete with hyperlinked cross-references and URLs. With clear definitions of over 3,000 networking terms, you'll never get stumped by industry jargon again.

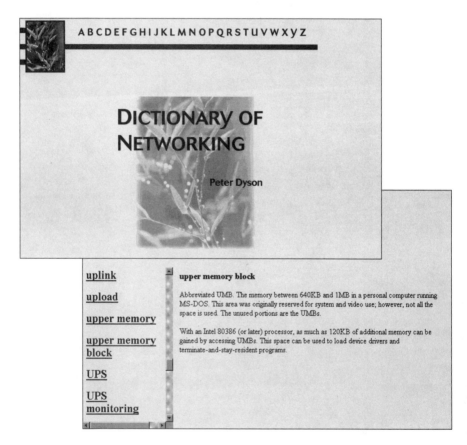

NOTE For further details, see the readme.txt file located in the root directory of the CD.